'I WAS IN THE SPIRIT ON THE LORD'S DAY'
A PENTECOSTAL ENGAGEMENT WITH WORSHIP
IN THE APOCALYPSE

'I Was in the Spirit on the Lord's Day'

A Pentecostal Engagement with Worship in the Apocalypse

Melissa L. Archer

CPT

CPT Press
Cleveland, Tennessee

'I Was in the Spirit on the Lord's Day'
A Pentecostal Engagement with Worship in the Apocalypse

Published by CPT Press
900 Walker ST NE
Cleveland, TN 37311
USA
email: cptpress@pentecostaltheology.org
website: www.cptpress.com

Library of Congress Control Number: 2014956062

ISBN-10: 1935931466
ISBN-13: 9781935931461

CONTENTS

ACKNOWLEDGEMENTS

This monograph is a slightly altered version of my PhD thesis completed at Bangor University under the supervision of Dr. John Christopher Thomas. I am truly humbled by its appearance in publication, and I hope that it will in some small way make a contribution to Pentecostalism as well as to Revelation studies. I wish to express my profound gratitude to my family, my parents, and Ken's family for their never-ending encouragement and support during the years that it has taken me to complete this study. A word of thanks must also go to my church family at Woodward Church of God in Athens, TN for the role they have played in providing spiritual nurturing and nourishment for me and my family. To my PhD supervisor, Dr. John Christopher Thomas, I owe a tremendous debt of gratitude for seeing in me things I could not see, for providing gracious and patient guidance through every step of the study, and for sharing his considerable wisdom and expertise. My fellow Bangor University PhD students – especially, Larry McQueen, Chris Green, Jeff and Karen Holley, Randall Ackland, O'Dell Bryant, and Steffen Schumacher – have provided great feedback, support, and friendship during this journey. My colleagues at Lee University, Pentecostal Theological Seminary, and, now, Southeastern University have all been a source of personal encouragement and support.

This work would never have come to fruition without the love and encouragement of my husband, Ken. Thank you for always believing in and encouraging me. You are my inspiration. To our sons, Trent and Tyler, who have never known a time in their lives when one or the other of their parents were not in school, thank you for your unwavering love and understanding. It is to my children, Trent and Tyler, and Tyler's wife, Christina, that I lovingly dedicate this study. It is my prayer that you will continue to follow the Lamb wherever he goes.

ABBREVIATIONS

Early Pentecostal Periodicals

AF	*The Apostolic Faith*
CE	*The Christian Evangel*
COGE	*The Church of God Evangel*
LRE	*The Latter Rain Evangel*
TBM	*The Bridegroom's Messenger*
TP	*The Pentecost*
WE	*Weekly Evangel*
WW	*Word and Witness*

Other

ABD	Freedman, D.N. (ed.), *Anchor Bible Dictionary* (6 vols; Garden City: Doubleday, 1992)
ACNT	Augsburg Commentary on the New Testament
AJPS	*Asian Journal of Pentecostal Studies*
BECNT	Baker Exegetical Commentary on the New Testament
BNTC	Black's New Testament Commentaries
BTCB	Brazos Theological Commentary on the Bible
BZNW	Beihefte zur Zeitschrift für die neutestamentliche Wissenschaft
CBQ	*Catholic Biblical Quarterly*
CBR	*Currents in Biblical Research*
DPCM	Burgess, S.M., *et al.* (eds.), *Dictionary of Pentecostal and Charismatic Movements* (Grand Rapids: Zondervan, 1988)
EPPET	Explorations in Practical, Pastoral and Empirical Theology
IVP	InterVarsity Press
IVPNTC	IVP New Testament Commentary Series

JBL	*Journal of Biblical Literature*
JEPTA	*Journal of the European Pentecostal Theological Association*
JETS	*Journal of the Evangelical Theological Society*
JPT	*Journal of Pentecostal Theology*
JPTSup	Journal of Pentecostal Theology Supplement Series
JSNT	*Journal for the Study of the New Testament*
JSNTS	Journal for the Study of the New Testament Supplement Series
LXX	Septuagint
NCCS	New Covenant Commentary Series
Neot	*Neotestamentica*
NIBC	New International Biblical Commentary
NIGTC	New International Greek New Testament Commentary
NIDPCM	Burgess, S.M., and E.M. van der Maas (eds.), *The New International Dictionary of Pentecostal and Charismatic Movements* (Grand Rapids: Zondervan, 2003).
NovT	*Novum Testamentum*
NTS	*New Testament Studies*
PTMS	Princeton Theological Monograph Series
SBLSP	*Society of Biblical Literature Seminar Papers*
SNTSMS	Society for New Testament Studies Monograph Series
TDNT	Kittel, G., and G. Friedrich (eds.), *Theological Dictionary of the New Testament* (trans. Geoffrey W. Bromiley; 10 vols; Grand Rapids: Eerdmans, 1964-1976)
WBC	Word Biblical Commentary Series
ZNW	*Zeitschrift für die neutestamentliche Wissenschaft*

INTRODUCTION

I. The Task

As a fourth-generation Pentecostal born and raised in a pastor's home, I have two very distinct childhood memories that center on the Apocalypse. The first is that my initial experience of Spirit-baptism came during a time of prayer that closed a small group Bible study led by my father on the topic of the four horses in the Apocalypse (Rev. 6.1-8). The second is the distinct experience of terror I felt when our church watched a movie titled *A Thief in the Night* about the idea of missing the rapture.[1] I can still hear the haunting lyrics to the movie's theme song, 'I Wish We'd All Been Ready', by Larry Norman, as well as see myself as a young child hiding behind the couch whenever I happened to come home from school to an empty house. I was sure I had missed the rapture and been 'left behind'. This second experience, coupled with the Dispensational understanding of Revelation with which I, like many North American Pentecostals, grew up, made me afraid even to read the Apocalypse! It was actually not until I took a graduate course on the Apocalypse that I began to discover the worship embedded in the book. It is that course that began my journey that has led me to this study. This study is a Pentecostal narrative reading of the Apocalypse that examines its theme of worship. The results of the narrative reading will then be put into conversation with Pente-

---

[1] The movie was produced in 1972 (I was six years old) as the first in a series of movies written by Russell S. Doughten. I later saw its sequel, *A Distant Thunder*, produced in 1978. The third and fourth installments of this series (which I did not see) were *Image of the Beast* (1981) and *The Prodigal Planet* (1983). The more recent *Left Behind* series of books and movies has introduced a new generation to the distinct Dispensational reading of the Apocalypse.

costalism to offer proposals for a Pentecostal theology of worship based on the Apocalypse.

II. Structure and Flow of the Argument

This study begins in chapter one with a survey of modern scholarly literature related to the theme of worship in the Apocalypse. The review is divided into four sections: 1) The theme of worship as a whole; B) The hymns in the Apocalypse; C) Revelation 4–5; and D) Additional worship scenes. Because no monograph has yet to appear on the theme of worship in the entire Apocalypse, this survey focuses on periodicals, book chapters, and monographs written on individual texts related to worship.

Chapter two lays out the methodology for the study. In this study I will engage Pentecostalism through a brief overview of North American Pentecostalism as well as Pentecostal hermeneutics. Further, I will employ *Wirkungsgeschichte* as a way to discover how the worship in the Apocalypse influenced early Pentecostals as attested in the early Pentecostal periodical literature. Narrative criticism is briefly introduced as a method conducive to Pentecostals, given the orality of Pentecostalism as well as their conditioning to view Scripture as story. Finally, this study makes overtures for the construction of a Pentecostal theology of worship based on the findings of the reading.

Chapter three is a careful reading of the early Pentecostal periodical materials, following the model established by Kimberly E. Alexander and built upon by Larry R. McQueen and Chris E.W. Green.[2] A variety of periodicals from both the Wesleyan-Holiness and Finished Work streams of the tradition covering the time span of 1906–1916, a decade traditionally viewed as the heart of the Pentecostal tradition, are mined for their effective history as to how the worship practices of early Pentecostals were influenced by the worship found in the Apocalypse.

---

[2] K.E. Alexander, *Pentecostal Healing: Models in Theology and Practice* (JPTS 29; Blandford Forum: Deo Publishing, 2006); L.R. McQueen, *Towards as Pentecostal Eschatology: Discerning the Way Forward* (JPTS 39; Blandford Forum: Deo Publishing, 2012); C.E.W. Green, *Toward a Pentecostal Theology of the Lord's Supper: Foretasting the Kingdom* (Cleveland: CPT Press, 2012).

Chapter four consists of a sustained narrative reading of the Apocalypse with a focus on the theme of worship. In addition to the prologue and epilogue, the text of the Apocalypse is divided according to the four ἐν πνεύματι ('In the Spirit') phrases. Emphasis is placed upon how the text might have been experienced by John's implied hearers without any assumptions about what they would or would not have known pertaining to his perceived sources.[3] In each section of the text, the presence of liturgical elements and their role in interpreting the narrative will be explicated.

Chapter five is devoted to offering overtures for the construction of a Pentecostal theology of worship based on the central tenants concerning worship derived from the narrative reading of the Apocalypse. It is hoped that this chapter will encourage Pentecostals and others to re-discover the Apocalypse as a rich resource for liturgy.

The study concludes with contributions made by this study as well as suggestions for further research.

---

[3] In this study, I am operating with the following presuppositions: The implied author of the Apocalypse is someone named John, who is likely a prophetic figure familiar to the Johannine community and known to the implied audience, the seven churches of Asia identified in Rev. 1.11. It was written sometime in the late first century, possibly under the reign of the emperor Domitian. It shares affinities with other apocalyptic literature and contains numerous allusions to and echoes of Old Testament scripture. Because narrative criticism focuses on the story being told rather than the reconstruction of historical events, the sources behind John's work are at best only theoretical.

1

THE ROLE OF WORSHIP IN THE APOCALYPSE:
A SURVEY OF MODERN LITERATURE

I. Introduction

All interpreters of the Apocalypse recognize the scenes of worship scattered throughout the narrative as being one of its most distinctive features. Despite this acknowledgement, the overall theme of worship in the Apocalypse has received relatively little scholarly attention. The primary texts that receive the most consideration are Revelation 4–5 due to their heavy concentration of hymnic material. However, the hymns of the Apocalypse as a whole have been the subject of a limited amount of attention. To date, there are no published monographs devoted exclusively to the overall theme of worship in the Apocalypse. The intention of this chapter is to provide a survey of modern literature related to the theme of worship in the Apocalypse. This review will not survey commentaries unless they contain excurses or specific discussion on the theme of worship as the commentaries will be engaged in my reading of Revelation. The first section will survey the scholarly literature which discusses the role of worship within the whole of the Apocalypse. The second section will review the literature dedicated to the hymns of the Apocalypse. The third section will survey the literature pertaining to Revelation 4–5, and the final section will survey the literature pertaining to the remainder of the worship scenes.

II. Worship in the Apocalypse

Leonard Thompson

In his 1990 commentary on Revelation, Leonard Thompson devotes a chapter to the worship found in the Apocalypse which he titles 'Unity through the Language of Worship'.[1] Thompson views the liturgical language in the Apocalypse as one of its primary unifying forces. His chapter is divided into four sections. In the first section, Thompson briefly explores the presence of liturgical language in the prologue and epilogue[2] of the Apocalypse. He suggests that while the epistolary elements ground the Apocalypse in a specific space and time, the liturgical elements create a visionary world that is beyond time and space.[3]

In the second section, Thompson discusses the distribution of liturgical language in Revelation 4.1–22.5, with most of his attention focused on the initial worship scene found in Revelation 4–5. In his description of the heavenly throne room, the Seer shows dependence upon both Old Testament and apocalyptic traditions, while at the same time adapting and modifying the traditions for his own purpose. Thompson further argues that John employs current images from the political realm and the Roman imperial cult in subversive ways to demonstrate that the God of heaven is the only God worthy of praise. By means of 'unambiguously Christian' symbolism, Jesus, in Revelation 5, is introduced as a Lion/Lamb who alone is able to open God's sealed scroll/book. Thompson suggests that this scroll/book might be viewed as a 'Christian book of liturgy' which is 'disclosed only in the worship of the Christian community (whether in heaven or on earth)'.[4] After this initial exploration of Revelation 4–5, Thompson briefly identifies and

---

[1] L.L. Thompson, *The Book of Revelation: Apocalypse and Empire* (Oxford: Oxford University Press, 1990), pp. 53-73.

[2] Thompson, *The Book of Revelation*, p. 55, views the prologue's combination of epistolary elements and liturgical language as a way to 'establish the divine authority of what is being said' whereas in the epilogue, the combination of epistolary and liturgical language is used to encourage the audience to maintain faithful in light of the expectancy of Jesus' return.

[3] Thompson, *The Book of Revelation*, p. 56.

[4] Thompson, *The Book of Revelation*, p. 59.

describes the rest of the worship scenes in the Apocalypse with limited commentary.

In the third section of the chapter, Thompson examines the relationship between heavenly worship and eschatology. For Thompson, the significance of the worship scenes derives from the nature of the apocalyptic genre.[5] The worship scenes are John's way of expressing the 'spatial dimension of transcendent reality', whereas the dramatic narratives express the 'temporal dimension of transcendent reality'.[6] The worship scenes are a vivid portrayal of 'eschatological realities in the present',[7] and they offer a liturgical reflection on eschatological themes. Thompson notes that John connects worship to eschatology by setting the eschatological drama in heavenly worship and by demonstrating that heavenly worship celebrates in the present eschatological events yet to come. Thus, the narrative events of the seals and trumpets, for example, are purposefully punctuated with scenes of celebratory worship as are the scenes depicting the casting down of Satan and the destruction of Babylon. In addition, the worship scenes and dramatic narrations are often presented in homologous fashion; that is, they share similar 'motifs and attributes'.[8]

In the final section Thompson discusses the worshipping community of the Apocalypse, suggesting that the Apocalypse is

---

[5] Thompson, *The Book of Revelation,* p. 63, relies on the definition of Apocalyptic crafted by John Collins and others in the Apocalypse Group of the Society of Biblical Literature: 'A genre of revelatory literature with a narrative framework, in which a revelation is mediated by an otherworldly being to a human recipient, disclosing a transcendent reality which is both temporal, insofar as it envisages eschatological salvation, and spatial insofar as it involves another, supernatural world'.

[6] Thompson, *The Book of Revelation,* p. 63.

[7] Thompson, *The Book of Revelation,* p. 64.

[8] Thompson, *The Book of Revelation,* p. 68, mentions the following examples of this linkage: Precious stones are used in describing the heavenly throne room (Rev. 4.3) and eschatological New Jerusalem (Rev. 21.11, 18-21); the throne is 'fixed' or 'situated' in heaven (Rev. 4.2) and New Jerusalem is 'foursquare' or 'cubed' (Rev. 21.16). Several links occur between the worship scene in Rev. 7.13-17 and the description of New Jerusalem: the reference to 'washed stoles' (Rev. 7.14 and 22.14); the statement that God will dwell with his people (Rev. 7.15 and 21.3), the reference to God giving water to the thirsty (Rev. 7.16 and 21.6); and, people worshipping God and the Lamb (Rev. 7.17 and 21.4).

addressed to *Christian* communities in Asia.[9] For the Seer, worship functions as a 'radical equalizer' as all people, from the mighty to the small, join together in worship of God.[10] The worship in the Apocalypse serves to create an egalitarian community of worshippers of the Lamb who are to be clearly distinguished from non-Christian communities. The Apocalypse functions as liturgical material for the Asian churches. In John's communities, the worship service becomes the context for celebrating the reign of God and the Lamb, the present reality of future eschatological events, and the link between heaven and earth.[11]

Marianne Meye Thompson

In 1992, Marianne Thompson's article 'Worship in the Book of Revelation' was published.[12] Thompson views the Apocalypse as the New Testament's most important book related to worship.[13] The worship of heaven portrayed in its visions is paradigmatic for earthly worship.[14] After examining the historical setting of the Apocalypse, Thompson discusses the imagery of worship found within the book.[15] Third, Thompson discusses the Apocalypse's revelation of God as the Supreme Being worthy of worship. God is to be worshipped because God is the sovereign Creator.[16] God's purposes for creation and for humanity are being worked out, most decidedly in

---

[9] The worshipping community must be Christian for 'no other community would worship the slain Lamb'. Thompson, *The Book of Revelation*, p. 70.

[10] Thompson, *The Book of Revelation*, p. 69.

[11] Thompson, *The Book of Revelation*, pp. 72-73.

[12] M.M. Thompson, 'Worship in the Book of Revelation', *Ex Auditu* 8 (1992), pp. 45-54.

[13] Thompson, 'Worship in the Book of Revelation', p. 45, has as her first sentence: 'There is no book of the New Testament in which worship figures so prominently, provides so much of the language and imagery, and is so fundamental to its purpose and message as the book of Revelation'.

[14] Thompson, 'Worship in the Book of Revelation', p. 49. The worship scenes are intended to encourage the faithful 'not by being given instructions on how to worship, but by being granted an image of the God whom they worship'.

[15] Thompson, 'Worship in the Book of Revelation', pp. 48-49. In this section she notes the vocabulary of worship (*latreuein, leitourgein* [*sic*], and *proskynein*) and the use of cultic imagery (priests, temple, altar, bowls). She indicates that the significance of portraying the people of God by means of cultic imagery is to underscore that 'they are known by their activity of worship, and not just by what they do but by whom they worship as well' (p. 48).

[16] Thompson, 'Worship in the Book of Revelation', p. 50.

the person and work of Jesus, the Lamb; therefore, worship of God and the Lamb 'belong together'.[17] Thompson concludes her article with some reflections on worship in the Apocalypse. God is to be worshipped because God is worthy; thus, worship is 'the human response to one infinitely greater … or Wholly Other'. God is to be worshipped because God is sovereign; God's intentions for the created order will be brought to pass. Worship 'is the natural and expected response to the vision of God' and should never be viewed as an 'irrelevant or escapist solution to the problems of life'. Worship 'lifts us out of the world to God, and so necessarily drives us out into the same world of which God is creator, sustainer, and redeemer'. [18] Worship is for those who live 'in the middle' – between 'creation and the eschaton, between earth and heaven'. In worship, one focuses not on some 'future or otherworldly reward, but on God'. Worship orders the life of the worshipper, enabling him or her to attend to God.[19]

Richard Bauckham

In 1993, Richard Bauckham published two works on the Apocalypse, both of which give attention to worship.[20] For Bauckham, the significance of the worship scenes in the Apocalypse is that they provide evidence for the development of Christology in the primitive Christian communities.[21] In *The Climax of Prophecy*, Bauckham devotes his fourth chapter to an exploration of the worship of Jesus in the Apocalypse. He compares the Apocalypse with the *Ascension of Isaiah* and contends that both writings reflect the thought-world of apocalyptic Christianity.[22] Key for Bauckham is the fact that both

---

[17] Thompson, 'Worship in the Book of Revelation', p. 50.

[18] Thompson, 'Worship in the Book of Revelation', p. 51.

[19] Thompson, 'Worship in the Book of Revelation', p. 52.

[20] R.J. Bauckham, *The Climax of Prophecy: Studies on the Book of Revelation* (Edinburgh: T&T Clark, 1993); *idem*, *The Theology of the Book of Revelation* (Cambridge: Cambridge University Press, 1993).

[21] See also R. Bauckham, 'The Worship of Jesus in Apocalyptic Christianity', *NTS* 27 (1981), pp. 322-41; *idem*. 'Jesus, Worship of,' in David N. Freedman (ed.), *ABD* (Garden City, NY: Doubleday, 1992), III, pp. 812-19.

[22] Bauckham, *The Climax of Prophecy*, pp. 140-48. Bauckham denotes both the similarities of the *Ascension of Isaiah* to Merkabah mysticism (pp. 141-42) and their differences (pp. 142-43). The differences center on angelology. Bauckham sees the *Ascension of Isaiah* to be 'deliberately rejecting a form of Merkabah mysticism (whether Jewish or Christian is not clear) in which angels were reverenced and

writings, which are roughly contemporaneous, contain a vision of the worship of Jesus in heaven and a prohibition against the worship of angels.

Bauckham demonstrates how John utilizes the prohibition against the worship of angels as a way to direct attention to the worship of God, who is 'the true transcendent source of revelation'.[23] Jesus, rather than being an intermediary like the angels, is also the source of revelation. Bauckham indicates that for John, 'Jesus belongs with God as giver, while the angel belongs with John as instrument … the monotheistic prohibition of the worship of angels does not prohibit the worship of Jesus'.[24] John's adaptation of this tradition enables him to delineate for his readers the differences between true and false worship. In portraying the worship of Jesus in the inaugural throne-room scene of Revelation 4–5, John clearly establishes the unique worthiness of Jesus as distinct from all other creatures as the 'divine agent of salvation and judgment'.[25] Bauckham is careful to point out that while Jesus as the Lamb is worshipped along with God in the climactic hymn in Rev. 5.13, John's sensitivity to monotheism is expressed in the fact that Jesus is not an alternative object of worship; rather, Jesus shares in the worship of God.

In *The Theology of the Book of Revelation*, Bauckham underscores the theme of worship in the Apocalypse. He connects the theme to the theological concern for the monotheistic worship of God. In the throne-room scene, John focuses less on the physical description of God and more on the throne and the continuous worship going on around the throne. By this, the reader is reminded that 'true knowledge of who God is is inseparable from worship of God', and

---

invoked both as obstacles and as aids in the mystical ascent to heaven' (p. 143). Bauckham also treats the subject of the worship of Christ, the worship of the Holy Spirit (called 'the Beloved'), and the worship of God in the *Ascension of Isaiah* (pp. 145-46).

[23] Bauckham, *The Climax of Prophecy*, p. 134.

[24] Bauckham, *The Climax of Prophecy*, p. 135.

[25] Bauckham, *The Climax of Prophecy*, p. 136. Bauckham further notes that in the apocalyptic and Merkabah traditions God is portrayed in the heavenly throne-room as receiving ceaseless angelic worship.

indeed cannot be 'truly experienced except as worship'.[26] Jesus is clearly connected with God in the Apocalypse,[27] and Bauckham re-states much of what he writes in *The Climax of Prophecy* concerning the worship ascribed to Jesus. He suggests that the worship of Jesus as God was a development of Jewish monotheism in which Jewish Christians understood Jesus to be included 'in the reality of the one God'.[28] As the doxology of Rev. 1.5-6 and the hymn of Rev. 5.9-10 indicate, the worship of Jesus in the earliest Christian communities arises because of his work of redemption.[29] John wishes, however, to express more than a functional divinity for Jesus; that is, John is concerned to show Jesus as a divine being somehow belonging to the 'reality of the one God'.[30] Therefore, in Revelation, 'what Christ does, God does' and it is precisely because of this that Jesus is wor-shipped.[31]

Wes Howard-Brook and Anthony Gwyther

Wes Howard-Brook and Anthony Gwyther's 1999 commentary de-votes a chapter ('The Empire of the World Has Become the Empire

---

[26] Bauckham, *The Theology of the Book of Revelation*, pp. 32-33.

[27] Bauckham focuses on John's use of the titles, 'the Alpha and the Omega', 'the beginning and the end,' and 'the first and the last' for both God and Jesus (see Rev. 1.8, 17-18; 21.6; 22.13). Additionally, Bauckham shows how these titles appear in connection with the announcement of the Parousia (Rev. 1.7 with God as the Alpha and Omega; Rev. 22.12 with Christ as the Alpha and Omega) and the announcement of new life (Rev. 1.18 with Christ as the first and the last; Rev. 21.5-6 with God as the beginning and the end). Bauckham thus sees an ABB'A' chiastic structure. Bauckham, *The Theology of the Book of Revelation*, pp. 54-58.

[28] Bauckham, *The Theology of the Book of Revelation*, p. 62.

[29] Bauckham, *The Theology of the Book of Revelation*, p. 62: 'The salvation was too closely connected with Jesus himself for Jesus to be bypassed in worship offered to God for it, but at the same time it was salvation from God that Jesus gave and so Jesus was not treated as an alternative object of worship alongside God. He was included in worship of God'.

[30] Bauckham, *The Theology of the Book of Revelation*, p. 62,

> The reason why John does not use the word 'God' of Jesus will be the same reason that accounts for the general slowness of this usage in becoming estab-lished Christian practice. He wants neither to say that Jesus simply is, without any distinction, the God Jesus called God and Father (a usage John reflects in 1:6; 2:28; 3:5, 12, 21), nor to seem to speak of two gods. But it is also notable that many times when he is talking most deliberately about God he does not call God 'God' either. *He says far more about the deity of God by calling him 'the Al-pha and Omega' than he does by calling him 'God', and he also calls Jesus 'the Alpha and the Omega'* (emphasis mine).

[31] Bauckham, *The Theology of the Book of Revelation*, p. 63.

of Our Lord and of His Messiah: Liturgy and Worship in Revelation') to the worship scenes in the Apocalypse.[32] After suggesting a number of functions which the worship scenes serve,[33] they proceed to examine each of the seven worship scenes.[34] In their summarization of the content of the first scene (Rev. 4.2-11), the authors point to John's utilization of both Jewish and Greco-Roman sources in the description of the heavenly throne room and the events taking place therein. They argue that worship is shown to be largely a 'political act;' that is, God is worshipped because God possesses all power and authority.[35] In the second scene (Rev. 5.8-14), the Lamb is deemed worthy of worship by all of creation because of his sacrificial death. The third scene (Rev. 7.9-17) celebrates those who have washed their robes in the blood of the Lamb. Key to the liturgy of this section is Rev. 7.10 ('Salvation belongs to our God who is seated on the throne, and to the Lamb'). The authors tie the concept of salvation to the *Pax Romana* and suggest that 'those who have been washed clean in the Lamb's blood are precisely those who have refused to abide by this imperial propaganda'.[36] The fourth scene (Rev. 11.15-18) is introduced by the sounding of the seventh trumpet and proclamation of the kingdom of God (Rev. 11.15). For the authors, this liturgical section echoes 'the transition from the first biblical era to the second' and serves as a warning that all empires will come to end.[37] The fifth worship scene (Rev. 14.1-5)

---

[32] W. Howard-Brook and Anthony Gwyther, *Unveiling Empire: Reading Revelation Then & Now* (Maryknoll: Orbis Books, 1999), pp. 197-221.

[33] The authors list the following functions: 1) to remind the hearers that *God is listening and will respond* to their prayers; 2) to generate solidarity in the churches 'through shared song and other forms of communal prayer'; 3) to 'drown out and parody the liturgies' of the imperial and mystery cults; 4) to contrast with 'the silencing of song' in Babylon; and 5) to remind the hearers of what they should celebrate, namely, 'the enthronement of God and the Lamb with royal power over all creation' (p. 197).

[34] The authors also provide a helpful chart in which they identify the worshippers, the titles used for those who receive worship, the forms of worship, and the content of worship for each of the worship scenes (pp. 198-202).

[35] Howard-Brook and Gwyther, *Unveiling Empire*, p. 206.

[36] Howard-Brook and Gwyther, *Unveiling Empire*, p. 211.

[37] Howard-Brook and Gwyther, *Unveiling Empire*, pp. 212-13.

reveals those who have become the beast's prisoners of war[38] appearing with the Lamb on Mount Zion. They are also identified with the 144,000 (Rev. 7.4), but here they are further described as having the mark of the Lamb on their foreheads and having been bought from the land. This scene is a stark contrast between those who can buy and participate in commerce (followers of the beast) and those who have been bought and participate in the liturgy of heaven (followers of the Lamb). The sixth worship scene (Rev. 15.2-4) follows the harvesting of the earth, of which the 144,000 are the first fruits. The song sung in this scene is identified as the Song of Moses and the Lamb. This reinforces the Apocalypse's theme of a singular people of God formed out of people from every nation, tribe and tongue. God is celebrated as a just and powerful king who is worthy of worship.[39] The final worship scene (Rev. 19.1-8) celebrates God's destruction of Babylon and anticipates the Marriage Supper of the Lamb. In this song, 'no longer is there need to plead with God for justice, for justice has been done'.[40]

The authors conclude that the scenes are 'powerful tools' for creating a community united in solidarity and commitment to God. Worship is a political statement – a stand against empire – both in John's day and in the present day as the community is called upon to celebrate joyously the reign of God and of the Lamb.[41]

Steven Friesen

Steven Friesen devotes a chapter in his 2001 commentary to the issues of worship and authority.[42] Friesen explores the concept of

---

[38] The authors translate αἰχμαλωσίαν in 13.10 as 'prisoner of war' and see these as the ones celebrating in 14.1-5. Howard-Brook and Gwyther, *Unveiling Empire*, p. 217.

[39] Howard-Brook and Gwyther, *Unveiling Empire*, p. 220, 'The song blends the proclamation of God as powerful and benevolent king, but also as just judge, a capacity desired in any good monarch, and, of course, notoriously lacking in emperors'.

[40] Howard-Brook and Gwyther, *Unveiling Empire*, p. 221.

[41] Howard-Brook and Gwyther, *Unveiling Empire*, p. 221, aptly concludes that when the Christian community gathers for worship, 'we are making a public statement of political allegiance. We are taking a stand against empire, and in celebration of the reign of our just and true God and of the Lamb.'

[42] S.J. Friesen, *Imperial Cults and the Apocalypse of John: Reading Revelation in the Ruins* (Oxford: Oxford University Press, 2001), pp. 194-209. I will only treat his discussion of worship.

worship in its ancient context which included blood sacrifices, libations and/or food offerings. He documents how the concern with meat sacrificed to idols in Revelation reflects a question of proper worship. Revelation also contains activities that reflect modern western ideas of worship, such as temple worship, incense offerings, prostration, and spoken/sung worship to God and the Lamb. Friesen states that worship 'acknowledges beings who have authority' and is 'enfolded in the meaning of sacrifice'. Further, worship requires submission and obedience from the worshippers.[43]

Friesen suggests that Revelation 4–5 asserts that God and the Lamb are the authority figures worthy of worship. He compares this to the Greco-Roman practice of including the imperial family within the pantheon of gods and goddesses. The Lamb is worthy because of his sacrifice. This is reinforced throughout the rest of the text as Jesus is referred to as 'the Lamb that was slaughtered'. The paradox of Jesus' victory through suffering would not have made sense in Greco-Roman society; in fact, Friesen states that 'the matrix within which such a Jesus made sense was in … the kinds of churches John envisioned … in which the bold claims made in worship were not manifest in everyday life'.[44] The Lamb is also the only king and ruler of all and, along with God, is the only one worthy of worship. For Friesen, the worship of God and the Lamb issues a political statement against the authority of Rome.

W. Hulitt Gloer

W. Hulitt Gloer's 2001 article on worship in the Apocalypse seeks to identify the liturgical elements found within the Apocalypse.[45] He identifies the 15 hymns or hymn-like fragments as the most prominent liturgical elements.[46] Gloer offers brief comments on each of

---

[43] Friesen, *Imperial Cults and the Apocalypse of John*, pp. 195-97.

[44] Friesen, *Imperial Cults and the Apocalypse of John*, pp. 200-201.

[45] W. Hulitt Gloer, 'Worship God! Liturgical Elements in the Apocalypse', *Review and Expositor* 93 (Winter 2001), pp. 35-57.

[46] The hymns are as follows: the 'thrice-holy' (Rev. 4.8); three songs ascribing worthiness to God and/or the Lamb (Rev. 4.11; 5.9-10; 5.12); three doxologies (Rev. 5.13; 7.12; 16.5-7); seven songs of victory (Rev. 7.10; 11.15; 11.17-18; 12.10-12; 15.3-4; 19.1-2; 19.6-8); and 'an exhortation to praise God that is itself apparently a hymn' (Rev. 19.5). These hymnic pieces are placed in an 'antiphonal arrangement' resulting in eight 'choral interludes' (Rev. 4.8-11; 5.8-14; 7.9-12; 11.16-19; 16.5-7; 19.1-4, 5-8) (p. 40).

the worship hymns he identifies.[47] This is followed by a short discussion of the possible influences that the liturgical elements reflect; namely, the actual liturgy and worship of the Johannine churches (influenced by the Jewish practices in the temple), or a Eucharistic liturgy. Because the New Testament is 'silent about how and in what order such elements were used', it is impossible to say confidently that the worship of the Apocalypse reflects the worship of the Johannine community.[48] Gloer further suggests parallels between 1) the liturgy of the Apocalypse with that of Merkebah mysticism and the Hekhalot literature, and 2) the liturgy of the Apocalypse and the Roman imperial court (following Aune).[49]

Gloer maintains that John's work contains 'elements that are reflective of Jewish (traditional and non-traditional), Christian, and even pagan traditions'.[50] To conclude his article, Gloer turns to the genre of apocalyptic literature as a way to understand the function of the worship scenes; that is, the worship scenes 'express the spatial dimension of transcendent reality'.[51] As such, in the worship scenes eschatological realities are realized before they are presented in the narrative. The worship of the Apocalypse becomes a real experience of God's kingdom and a means of identifying with God and the Lamb.[52]

Grant Osborne

Among the major commentators on the Apocalypse, only Grant Osborne's 2002 commentary includes worship under the category of 'theological themes' within the book.[53] For Osborne, the worship scenes that are juxtaposed with judgment scenes serve to announce that, even in the midst of present conflict, 'the triumph of God and his people is not only guaranteed but already celebrated'.[54] In this way, the worship scenes repeatedly depict God's sovereign power

---

[47] Gloer, 'Worship God! Liturgical Elements in the Apocalypse', pp. 40-48.

[48] Gloer, 'Worship God! Liturgical Elements in the Apocalypse', p. 49.

[49] Gloer, 'Worship God! Liturgical Elements in the Apocalypse', pp. 50-51.

[50] Gloer, 'Worship God! Liturgical Elements in the Apocalypse, p. 51.

[51] Gloer, 'Worship God! Liturgical Elements in the Apocalypse', p. 52.

[52] Gloer, 'Worship God! Liturgical Elements in the Apocalypse', p. 52, 'The liturgical recital of the Apocalypse becomes a real experience of the kingdom of God'.

[53] G.R. Osborne, *Revelation* (Grand Rapids: Baker Books, 2002), pp. 46-49.

[54] Osborne, *Revelation*, p. 48.

over the evil powers waging war against the people of God. The hymns stress the justice of God's actions and celebrate the destruction of God's enemies. The Apocalypse's final hymns (19.1-10) serve both as a capstone as God's just actions are celebrated and God's people are vindicated and as a prelude to the return of Christ and the imminent wedding supper of the Lamb. Osborne further suggests that there is a final, although unstated, worship scene in Revelation 21.1–22.5 as John depicts life in the New Jerusalem as 'one long experience of worship'.[55]

Olutola Peters

Olutola Peters, in his 2004 monograph, explores the Apocalypse in light of what he identifies as the two main tasks of the church: witness and worship.[56] In a chapter on the theme and mandate of worship, Peters sets out to discover the 'extent to which the mandate to worship is dominant' in Revelation, as well as 'the nature of its connection with the other tasks of the Church, especially the mandate to maintain faithful witness'.[57]

Peters begins by discussing the significance of the worship motif within the Apocalypse by affirming its liturgical context. Peters concludes that John probably had a worship service in mind as he wrote, even if one cannot prove this study. Rather, Peters suggests that the reader can draw implications from the liturgical features to support the mandate of worship in the Church.

Next, Peters turns to an examination of the literary and historical background to the liturgical elements of the Apocalypse. Peters believes that the heavenly worship of the Apocalypse is a reflection of earthly worship in the Asian churches. The 'link between heavenly liturgy and earthly worship provides the churches of Asia Minor with a divine perspective on the object, meaning, nature, and goal of Christian worship'.[58] The primary backdrop against which the worship of the Apocalypse is to be read is, according to Peters, the conflict between Christianity and the imperial cult.

---

[55] Osborne, *Revelation*, p. 49.

[56] O.K. Peters, *The Mandate of the Church in the Apocalypse of John* (New York: Peter Lang, 2004).

[57] Peters, *The Mandate of the Church in the Apocalypse of John*, p. 44.

[58] Peters, *The Mandate of the Church in the Apocalypse of John*, p. 51.

Peters examines the worship scenes and liturgical materials in the Apocalypse by providing brief commentary on Revelation 4–5, 7.9-17, 11.15-19, 14.1-5, 15.2-4, 16.5-7, and 19.1-10. He identifies the object of worship, the subjects of worship, and the character and content of worship in each particular scene. He stresses the point that John carefully weaves together liturgical material as a means of addressing an underlying issue of worship. Because John consistently identifies the object, subjects, and grounds for worship in each of the worship scenes this suggests to Peters that there is a 'comprehensive character' to the worship mandate. Peters observes that worship is expressed through a variety of means in the Apocalypse: prayers, service to God, showing reverence to the name of God, and singing hymns and songs of praise that center on God and the Lamb. Further, worshippers are to be marked by 'purity, humility, victory, allegiance and devotion to the object of worship – an indication that worship involves both the lips and life of the worshiper'. For Peters, the mandate to worship serves the larger mandate to witness.[59]

III. Hymns in the Apocalypse

Reinhard Deichgräber

One of the first scholars to give serious attention to the hymnic material in the Apocalypse was Reinhard Deichgräber. Deichgräber included a chapter on the Apocalypse in his 1967 monograph on hymnic material in early Christianity.[60] In his chapter Deichgräber provides a form-critical analysis of the hymnic pieces in the Apocalypse.[61]

In his commentary on these verses, Deichgräber points out both the relevant Jewish traditional forms that John utilizes as well as the ways in which John modifies and adapts the traditional forms. An example of this from Revelation 4 is the use of the traditional 'Trishagion' in 4.8b that is modified by John with the addition of

---

[59] Peters, *The Mandate of the Church in the Apocalypse of John*, pp. 73-75.

[60] R. Deichgräber, 'Die hymnischen Stücke in der Apokalypse' in *Gotteshymnus und Christushymnus in der frühen Christenheit* (Göttingen: Vanderhoeck & Ruprecht, 1967), pp. 44-59.

[61] He identifies the following texts as hymnic: 4.8, 11; 5.9-10, 12, 13b; 6.10; 7.10, 12; 11.15, 17-18; 12.10-12; 15.3-4; 16.5-7; 19.1-8.

the 'Gottesprädikat' which becomes formulaic for the Seer.[62] The Seer's creative hand in the arrangement and use of the traditional material in the Apocalypse is further seen in Revelation 5. Deichgräber views the content of the hymnic pieces of Revelation 5 as being the composition of the author due to their lack of Jewish source material[63] outside of the designation ᾠδὴν καινὴν ('new song') (Rev. 5.9; see also 14.3) which is taken over from the Psalms (33.3; 96.1; 98.1; 144.9; 149.1).

While Deichgräber gives the most attention to Revelation 4–5, he also makes brief comments on the other worship scenes in the Apocalypse in terms of the way John modifies traditional forms. For example, while he notes that in Rev. 7.12 the form of the doxology is something that has been handed down, he sees the use of the seven-fold ascriptions as characteristic of the author and thus representing his own composition. Similarly, Deichgräber suggests that Rev. 11.17-18, which is based on the 'thanksgiving' Psalms, is also the composition of the author because of the way certain words and phrases are exclusive to the Apocalypse.[64] The 'Gotteshymnus' of Rev. 15.3-4, which he suggests is more carefully crafted than most of the hymnic sections in the Apocalypse, contains traditional hymnic elements such as the rhetorical question, the attributes ascribed to God, the three-fold ὅτι ('that, because') clauses, and the attribute μόνος ('only').[65] Deichgräber identifies Rev. 16.5-6 and 7b as doxologies in praise of God's judgment. The finale, Revelation 19.1-8, is punctuated by the repetition of ἀλληλουϊά ('Hallelujah') and contains a variety of hymnic forms.

Deichgräber indicates that most of the worship songs reflect traditional Jewish usage as evidenced in the Old Testament as well as rabbinic literature and probably represent the early communities' incorporation of the hymns in their worship service. Deichgräber

---

[62] Deichgräber, 'Die hymnischen Stücke in der Apokalypse', p. 49.

[63] Deichgräber, 52, 'Im Gegensatz zu den meisten anderen hymnischen Stücken der Apk finden wir hier keine jüdischen Elemente. Es geht wie das ganze fünfte Kapitel auf den christlichen Seher zurück und nicht auf jüdisches Quellenmaterial' ('In constrast to most other hymnic pieces in the Apocalypse, we find here no Jewish element. The whole fifth chapter goes back to the Christian Seer and not to Jewish source material.')

[64] Deichgräber, 'Die hymnischen Stücke in der Apokalypse', p. 58.

[65] Deichgräber, 'Die hymnischen Stücke in der Apokalypse', p. 56.

concludes it is at least a possibility that the hymnic pieces are a reflection of the author's worshipping community.[66] In particular,
songs of praise appear to have played a great role in the worship of
the community. He further suggests that the placement of the worship scenes in the Apocalypse is significant. By contrasting the worship scenes with scenes of terror or dreadful disasters, the Seer
seeks to comfort and exhort his community in the midst of their
present suffering. The worship of the earthly worshipping community is seen as a proleptic participation in the worship of the heavenly community centered on the Lamb.[67]

John O'Rourke

One year after Deichgräber's publication, John O'Rourke's article
on the hymns of the Apocalypse appeared in publication.[68]
O'Rourke seeks to ascertain whether or not hymnic material is contained in Revelation based on the following criteria: 1) parallelism
similar to that found in the Psalms; 2) 'solemn tone of expression
apt for use in worship' and 3) 'grammatical inconcinnity'. O'Rourke
identifies the most likely examples of hymnic material in the Apocalypse as the doxologies (Rev. 1.6; 5.13; 7.12), acclamations of worthiness (Rev. 4.11; 5.9, 12), and the trisagion (Rev. 4.8).[69] In each of
these, O'Rourke seeks to demonstrate how John made use of pre-
existent materials or, as in the liturgy addressed to the Lamb, utilized the liturgy of the Johannine churches.

The second half of the article is devoted to a discussion of other
places within the Apocalypse where parallelism, rather than literary
form, denotes hymnic material as well as places where expressions
'which seem peculiar in context' (grammatical inconcinnity) point to
hymnic material. O'Rourke concludes that while it is impossible to
prove beyond question that John borrowed 'consciously from
preexisting liturgical sources', he feels 'almost certain' that John did

---

[66] Deichgräber, 'Die hymnischen Stücke in der Apokalypse', p. 59.

[67] Deichgräber, 'Die hymnischen Stücke in der Apokalypse', p. 47.

[68] J.J. O'Rourke, 'The Hymns of the Apocalypse', *CBQ* 30 (1968), pp. 399-
409.

[69] O'Rourke, 'The Hymns of the Apocalypse', p. 400.

borrow from these sources in the composition of 1.4, 5, 8b; 4.8b; 7.12, 15-17; 11.15, 17-18; and 19.5, 6b-8.[70]

Klaus-Peter Jörns

Klaus-Peter Jörns' 1971 monograph examines the form, function, and origin of the hymnic portions of the Apocalypse.[71] His book is divided into two sections. In part one, he examines the hymns of Revelation (4–5; 7.10-12; 11.15b, 17-18; 12.10b-12; 14.3; 15–16; 18.20; 19) and identifies them according to their literary form, much like Deichgräber.

In part two of his work, Jörns discusses the form, function, and origin of the hymnic material as a whole in Revelation. The Seer infuses traditional forms of liturgy with theological and Christological elements that Jörns suggests stems from the practice of the worshipping community.[72] By means of the hymns, the present experience of the worshipping community is both connected to the past (Old Testament liturgy) and to the future (heavenly liturgy). Though the Seer applies a typological interpretation to Israel's beliefs, he also presents Jesus Christ as 1) the Redeemer of the community through his death and resurrection[73] and 2) as the judge of the final events.[74] For Jörns, the theological function of the hymns is tied closely to their position in the Apocalypse.[75] The hymns are connected to 'God's courtroom-events', indicating that God's plan is being enacted and that God's promises are being fulfilled. The hymns function simultaneously as a means of comfort, a call to joy, and as a vehicle for exhortation.[76]

---

[70] O'Rourke, 'The Hymns of the Apocalypse', p. 409. He further states, 'If he did use liturgical hymns, we see how rich is the doctrinal expression used in the singing of early churches, something not without interest today'.

[71] K.-P. Jörns, *Das hymnische Evangelium* (Gütersloh: Gütersloher Verlagshaus Gerd Mohn, 1971).

[72] See specifically pp. 164-66 for his listing of die theologischen Elemente der Hymnen ('the theological elements of the hymns').

[73] Jörns, *Das hymnische Evangelium*, p. 170.

[74] Jörns, *Das hymnische Evangelium*, p. 172.

[75] Jörns, *Das hymnische Evangelium*, p. 173.

[76] Jörns, *Das hymnische Evangelium*, p. 174.

Sophie Laws

Sophie Laws' 1988 commentary on Revelation offers a chapter titled 'Songs of the Lamb'.[77] Laws suggests that worship is the context for John's vision (1.10 and 22.20), and the vision itself is 'punctuated' throughout by 'songs of praise or rejoicing'. She identifies the songs of the Apocalypse as follows: Rev. 4.8, 9-11; 5.8-10, 11-12, 13; 7.10, 11-12; 11.15-18; 14.2-3; 15.2-4; 19.1-4, 6-8.[78] By means of the hymns, Revelation provides a very high Christology – indeed perhaps the highest found in Scripture. After a cursory review of some of the worship scenes and the worshippers in those scenes,[79] Laws identifies the songs in terms of their form and language. The hymn in Rev. 4.8 is the *trisagion* of Isaiah 6, the enthronement Psalms (93, 97, 99) are reflected in Rev. 11.15-18, the 'new songs' of Rev. 5.9 and 14.3 reflect exhortations to 'sing a new song' (Psalms 96, 98), and the 'Hallelujah choruses' of Rev. 19.1, 3, 4, and 6 recall the *Hallel* psalms (Psalms 147–150). Two features of the worship of the Apocalypse are striking because they lack biblical precedent: the ascriptions given to God and the Lamb and the acclamation, 'Worthy art thou …' (Rev. 4.11; 5.9, 12).[80]

Laws sees the antiphonal nature of the singing in the Apocalypse as imitating the role of the chorus in the Hellenistic theater. Like the Greek chorus, the hymns of the Apocalypse have the function of 'commenting on and explaining the action' of the surrounding narrative. Theatre was also a big part of celebrations and festivals in honor of the emperor. A special group of musicians, known as *humnodoi*, had the task of composing songs and choruses for the emperor. These songs often ascribed attributes, such as worthiness, honor, strength, blessing, to the emperor who was variously addressed as Lord and God.[81] Laws suggests that the use of worship material in the Apocalypse, which includes similar ascriptions for God and the Lamb, reflects John's concern for 'conflict between Christian churches and the power of Rome'.[82]

---

[77] S. Laws, *In the Light of the Lamb: Imagery, Parody, and Theology in the Apocalypse of John* (Wilmington: Michael Glazier, Inc., 1988), pp. 69-79.

[78] Laws, *In the Light of the Lamb*, p. 70.

[79] Laws, *In the Light of the Lamb*, pp. 72-74.

[80] Laws, *In the Light of the Lamb*, p. 75.

[81] Laws, *In the Light of the Lamb*, p. 76.

[82] Laws, *In the Light of the Lamb*, p. 77.

Laws concludes with the historical question of whether the Christian worship of the Apocalypse reflects the actual practices of the Christian communities. She briefly points to the New Testament passages where singing is mentioned (Acts 16.25; Jas 5.13; 1 Cor. 14.26; Col. 3.16; Eph. 5.19), and she identifies the Christological hymns and the Lukan Canticles as possible hymns of early Christian communities. Because John's hymns likewise celebrate the kerygma and saving event of Christ, Laws feels it is possible that John is drawing upon the hymns of his community for these songs. Despite this, she cautions against drawing conclusions about John's use of his community's worship as a source for the hymns of the Apocalypse and leaves open the possibility that John may have composed the material himself.

Michael Harris

Michael Harris completed his doctoral study on the hymnic material in the Apocalypse at Southern Baptist Theological Seminary.[83] Harris notes the following passages as being hymnic: Rev. 4.8-11; 5.9-13; 7.10-12; 11.15-18; 12.10-12; 15.3-4; 16.5-7; and 19.1-8. Before dealing with the hymnic material, however, Harris focuses on the role of the narrator as the implied author and his role in leading the implied reader, who Harris identifies as a hermeneutical projection of the narrator, through the events of the Apocalypse. He maintains that throughout Revelation the implied reader is persuaded by the implied author to assume the role of the martyrs. Harris suggests that the hymns of Revelation 4–5 revolve around the concepts of shame and honor.[84] The hymns are instances of 'interpretive commentary' on the events John narrates.[85] The hymns are sung as a

---

[83] M. Harris, *The Literary Function of the Hymns in the Apocalypse of John* (PhD dissertation, The Southern Baptist Theological Seminary, 1988).

[84] Harris sees honor and shame as foundational for an understanding of all the hymns.

[85] Harris, *The Literary Function of the Hymns*, p. 83, notes that interpretive commentary can be about an event or a character. Thus, the hymns of chapter 4 are 'interpretations of the nature and essence of the one upon the throne'. In chapter 5, the hymns provide interpretive commentary on the significance of the Lamb taking the scroll (pp. 103-104). Harris suggests that all of the hymns, with the exception of 15.3-4 and 16.5-6, provide interpretive commentary on the events preceding them. The hymns of 15.3-4 and 16.5-6 offer what Harris terms 'judgmental' commentary on the narrative events.

result of the ability of God and the Lamb to re-establish the injured honor of the believers who are martyred by the beast. The irony of the martyrs' hymns (Rev. 7.10-12; 14.3; 15.3-4) reinforce the implied readers in their identification with the martyrs. The hymnic finale of Rev. 19.1-8 serves as a fitting climax as it repeats all the themes contained in the earlier hymns. In relation to the narrative of Revelation, the hymns have both proleptic and analeptic functions,[86] and they serve to 'maintain contact with the narratee'.[87] Because the hymns function as expressions of praise to God and the Lamb,[88] Harris indicates that they articulate the core values shared by the Christian community.[89] Additionally, Harris explores the hymns in relation to reader response; that is, how the hymns serve to shape the formation of the implied readers. In his conclusion, Harris indicates that the most important discovery from his research into the relationship between the hymns and the implied author is that 'the narratees inscribed in chapters 2–3 become participants in the apocalyptic plot of 4–22'.[90]

David Aune

The first volume of David Aune's three-volume Revelation commentary, published in 1997, contains a short excursus on the hymns of the Apocalypse.[91] Aune identifies 16 hymns in Revelation[92] and suggests that John composed new hymns whose forms are drawn

---

[86] Harris identifies 4.8-11 and 5.9 as the most important analepses in the Apocalypse; the hymns which announce the coming of God's kingdom and the victory of God function proleptically.

[87] Harris, *The Literary Function of the Hymns*, p. 226.

[88] As such, the hymns are examples of epideictic rhetoric.

[89] Harris, *The Literary Function of the Hymns*, p. 301.

[90] Harris, *The Literary Function of the Hymns*, p. 304. Harris understands the hymn in Rev. 7.10-12 as the most explicit statement of this since it is sung by the martyrs who have gone through the great tribulation. 'This hymn', notes Harris, 'is directed to the narratees (implied reader) and informs them of the requirements of entrance in the kingdom'.

[91] D. Aune, *Revelation 1–5* (Waco: Word, 1997), I, pp. 314-17. See also his chapter 'The Influence of Roman Imperial Court Ceremonial on the Apocalypse of John' in D. Aune, *Apocalypticism, Prophecy and Magic in Early Christianity* (Tübingen: Mohr Siebeck, 2006), pp. 99-119.

[92] Aune, *Revelation 1–5*, p. 315 identifies the following as hymns or 'hymnlike compositions': 4.8c, 11; 5.9b-10, 12b, 13b; 7.10b, 12; 11.15b, 17-18; 12.10b-12; 15.3b-4; 16.5b-7b; 19.1b-2, 3, 5b, 6b-8. He suggests these are arranged in seven antiphonal units (4.8-11; 5.9-14; 7.9-12; 11.15-18; 16.5-7; 19.1-4, 5-8).

from a number of different arenas in which hymns were used; namely, the Jewish liturgical traditions of temple worship, Greek hymns, and the pomp of the Roman imperial court. The similarity between the hymns in Revelation and the imperial hymns composed for emperors indicates that titles and ascriptions given to the emperors were the same as those that John ascribed to God. Aune affirms the role of singing or chanting of hymns within the worship of early Christianity (1 Cor. 14.26; Col. 3.16; Jas 5.13; Pliny *Ep.* 10.96; *Odes of Solomon*). For Aune, the hymns in Revelation function as a 'narrative device to interpret the significance of eschatological events'.[93]

Steven Horn

In a 2010 collection of essays entitled *Essays on Revelation: Appropriating Yesterday's Apocalypse in Today's World*, Steven Horn contributes a chapter on the theology of the hymns of Revelation.[94] Horn's premise is that the hymns 'play a pivotal role in understanding the theological themes of Revelation'. He first identifies the hymns, outlines the general theological themes of the hymns, and, finally, provides a summary of the 'theological core of Revelation' as expressed in its hymns.[95]

Rather than only identifying hymns by certain characteristics, Horn maintains that the hymns can better be identified as 'those sayings of praise that appear within the context of worship'; that is, in the worship scenes of Revelation.[96] The worship scenes have specific participants giving praise to God and to Jesus and specific worship imagery. In the worship scenes, the hymns are identified by a form of λέγω ('I say') that precedes them as well as by reference to other aspects of worship. Horn identifies the hymns in the worship scenes as follows: Rev 4.8-11; 5.8-14; 6.10; 7.9-12; 11.15-18; 12.10-12; 15.2-4; 19.1-8.[97]

---

[93] Aune, *Revelation 1–5*, p. 316.

[94] S.N. Horn, 'Hallelujah, the Lord our God, the Almighty Reigns: The Theology of the Hymns of Revelation', in G.L. Stevens (ed.), *Essays on Revelation: Appropriating Yesterday's Apocalypse in Today's World* (Eugene: Pickwick Publications, 2010), pp. 41-54.

[95] Horn, 'Hallelujah, the Lord our God, the Almighty Reigns', p. 42.

[96] Horn, 'Hallelujah, the Lord our God, the Almighty Reigns', p. 42.

[97] Horn, 'Hallelujah, the Lord our God, the Almighty Reigns', p. 43.

Horn next provides a brief summary of the worship scenes with general comments about the hymns found in each scene.[98] This is followed by a brief summary of the theological themes found in the hymns. Here Horn suggests that the theology of the hymns can be described by what they reveal about God's character and works and the unity of God and Jesus. Sovereignty and holiness function as the overarching descriptors of God's character. The work of God, in the hymns, is centered on creation, redemption, judging, and reigning. Horn does not differentiate between God and Jesus because he sees John's vision as so unified that to worship one is to worship the other. Horn lifts up four theological features of the hymns. First, the hymns show God's sovereignty over creation (Rev. 4.8-11), over evil (Rev. 6.10; 11.15-18), over salvation (Rev. 5.8-14; 7.9-12; 12.10-12; 19.1-8), and over the world (Rev. 12.10-12). Further, God's rule is everlasting (Rev. 4.8-11; 12.10-12; 19.1-8).[99] Second, the hymns depict God as a holy and just God who judges the world. Third, the hymns contain Christological elements. The hymns give particular attention to the death of Jesus, by which Jesus is worthy of the same worship as God. Fourth, the hymns declare that the faithful can overcome by remaining faithful to the testimony of Jesus.[100]

Horn concludes his discussion with a brief reflection on the purpose of the hymns in Revelation. First, the hymns encapsulate the theology of the whole book. The dominant theme of sovereignty in the hymns supports the dominant theme of sovereignty throughout Revelation; thus, there is a 'summary relationship that exists between the theology of the hymns and the whole book'. The hymns, says Horn, are an 'easier literary window' through which to study the theology of Revelation. Second, the on-going use of these hymns by the church ensures that such theological themes will continue to be heard by each new generation of worshippers. Third, the hymns provide encouragement for the faithful to persevere.[101]

---

[98] Horn, 'Hallelujah, the Lord our God, the Almighty Reigns', pp. 43-50.

[99] Horn, 'Hallelujah, the Lord our God, the Almighty Reigns', p. 51.

[100] Horn, 'Hallelujah, the Lord our God, the Almighty Reigns', pp. 51-52.

[101] Horn, 'Hallelujah, the Lord our God, the Almighty Reigns', p. 53.

IV. Revelation 4–5

Lucetta Mowry

One of the first scholars to study Revelation 4–5 was Lucetta Mowry.[102] Mowry examines these chapters through the lens of source criticism and suggests that the description of the heavenly throne room recalls the splendor of the royal court. The hymnic pieces found within the chapters have their source in the Psalter as well as in the synagogue services, such as the Kedushah of the Yotzer, of the first century.[103] For Mowry, the most significant aspect of the hymnic material in Revelation 4–5 is that it provides valuable material for the study of the origins of early Christian hymnody.[104]

Mowry suggests that the whole structure of Revelation 4–5 reflects the procedures and order of a Jewish service of worship upon which Christians would have modeled their own services. In affinity with the Jewish worship service, the hymnic pieces of Revelation give worship to God as creator and redeemer. The golden vials represent the prayers of a Jewish worship service, and the two-sided scroll is to be identified as the Torah [based on the tradition from Exod. 32.15 that the Law was engraved on both sides], indicating the reading of Scripture within a Jewish worship service. These, along with the hymns of Revelation 5, lead Mowry to conclude that Revelation 4–5 reflects the setting of 'a Christian service of worship particularly the celebration of the eucharist'.[105]

---

[102] L. Mowry, 'Revelation 4–5 and Early Christian Liturgical Usage', *JBL* 71.2 (1952), pp. 75-84.

[103] In comparing the song of the elders in Rev. 4.11 with the Kedushah of the Yotzer, Mowry notes that while both 'affirm God's creative activity, the form preserved in the book of Revelation compresses and thus tends to subordinate this feature of God's work' (p. 79). Mowry further suggests that Rev. 5.9 is similar to the Geullah benediction of the Shema. Both focus on the redemptive activity of God toward his people; however, Revelation's hymn in celebration of the Lamb is a 'significant departure' because it indicates that a being other than God is worthy to 'assist God and mankind' (p. 80).

[104] Mowry, 'Revelation 4–5 and Early Christian Liturgical Usage', p. 81.

[105] Mowry, 'Revelation 4–5 and Early Christian Liturgical Usage', p. 83:

> That the worship set forth here is used in celebrating the eucharist is suggested by the fact that these Christian lyrics are comparable with the liturgy associated with the Jewish passover, that the stress is on the Agnus Dei and that Rev 4–5 follows an allusion to partaking of the meal with Christ in … Rev 3.20.

Larry Hurtado

Larry Hurtado's 1985 article examines Revelation 4–5 in light of Jewish apocalyptic writings.[106] Hurtado's essay is an attempt to refute the assertions made by Christopher Rowland that Revelation 4 'shows no evidence whatsoever of Christian influence' and that it is 'incidental to the overriding purpose of the work as a whole'.[107] With this in mind, Hurtado sets out to demonstrate that Revelation 4 is influenced by the Christian tradition of the Seer.[108] To do so, Hurtado compares John's heavenly vision with others found in Jewish apocalyptic writings.[109] He maintains that John's relatively simplistic picture of heaven, the throne, and heaven's occupants is a 'deliberate attempt to focus attention on a few important symbols

---

Mowry sees Revelation as providing insight into the earliest Christian worship. To that end, she offers the following reconstruction of a Christian service of worship (likely eucharistic):

> It begins with an invitation to partake of the blessings of the service (Rev 4.1). It continues with the singing of a trisagion, followed by a brief ascription of praise to God as Creator sung by the choir. After the congregation prostrates itself before the altar the major portion of the service is taken up with the reading of the scripture, the prayers which include a psalm of praise to Christ the Slain Lamb. In this psalm the congregation responds with an appropriate versicle. Finally the service closes with the congregational singing of a doxology to God and Christ concluded with a choral Amen. The service in both its main parts dramatically centers around the figure of the Agnus Dei (p. 84).

[106] L.W. Hurtado, 'Revelation 4–5 in the Light of Jewish Apocalyptic Analogies', *JSNT* 25 (1985), pp. 105-24.

[107] Hurtado, 'Revelation 4–5', p. 105.

[108] Hurtado, 'Revelation 4–5', p. 110 states:

> The clear indebtedness of Rev. 4 to the Jewish apocalyptic background of heavenly visions should not stop us from inquiring whether and, if so, how the distinctive features of the passage arise from the Christian faith of the author. Similarly, the more transparently Christian features of Rev. 5 should not blind us to what may be (for us) less easily recognized but important distinctives of Rev. 4.

[109] Hurtado evaluates the following: *1 Enoch* 14 and 71; *2 Enoch* 1-20; *Testament of Levi*; *3 Baruch*, *Apocalypse of Abraham*, *Testament of Abraham*, and *Ascension of Isaiah*. He also draws from the Angel liturgy from Qumran as well as later tradition in the Talmud and *3 Enoch*. All of these texts describe a heavenly ascent, with many also detailing the structure of heaven and the inhabitants of heaven (pp. 107-108). All of the texts depict heaven as wholly 'other' which 'makes the ascent of the visionary to heaven and to the throne of God all the more remarkable' (p. 108). The visions in these primary sources are theocentric and are rarely concerned with a Messiah-figure (p. 109).

of heavenly truth'.[110] One of these important symbols is the 24 elders.[111] Hurtado acknowledges the traditional ways that these elders are identified, but he suggests that John uses them as representative of the Christian elect.[112] Hurtado sees the elders' worship of God as creator (4.11b) as indicative of their understanding that God is the one who brings about eschatological salvation – an idea taken over from Judaism by early Christians. Hurtado briefly touches on Revelation 5 and suggests that the two chapters are 'complementary scenes in one vision' that reflect the Christian worldview of the Seer.[113]

Jean-Pierre Ruiz

In 1995, Ruiz published a brief essay on the hymns found in Revelation 4.8-11 and 5.9-14.[114] In it, he provides a summary of the throne vision as well as his own translation of the passages under consideration. Additionally, he provides brief critical notes on each verse. Ruiz notes the theological and Christological outlook of Revelation 4–5 in the acknowledgement of the worthiness of God as creator and the worthiness of Jesus as redeemer. He concludes that the hymnic materials in Revelation 4–5 invite John's readers to 'recognize the unity of the divine design as it unfolds both in creation and redemption'.[115]

---

[110] Hurtado, 'Revelation 4–5', p. 115.

[111] Hurtado, 'Revelation 4–5', pp. 111-12, sees that the elders are of great significance for John because they appear right after the description of God and God's throne, they are mentioned repeatedly in Revelation 4, and they reappear throughout the rest of Revelation.

[112] Hurtado, 'Revelation 4–5', p. 113, equates the elders with the promises to the overcomers in Revelation 2–3 so that the elders are the 'assurance of the heavenly reality of the promises'.

[113] Hurtado, 'Revelation 4–5', p. 117:

> It should not be forgotten that in Revelation 5 the Lamb is described as already slain and victorious, and hence able to open the sealed book of eschatological triumph. That is, Revelation 5 does not describe the Gospel events but presupposes them as having already happened. The relationship of Revelation 4 to Revelation 5 is not chronological but logical, and the two chapters are not finally contrasts with each other, but complementary scenes in one vision.

[114] J.-P. Ruiz, 'Revelation 4:8-11; 5:9-14: Hymns of the Heavenly Liturgy', *SBLSP* 34 (1995), pp. 216-19.

[115] Ruiz, 'Revelation 4:8-11; 5:9-14', p. 218.

Gottfried Schimanowski

In 2002, Gottfried Schimanowski's work appeared as the first monograph-length published treatment of Revelation 4–5.[116] Schimanowski provides a detailed examination of the heavenly throne-
room scene as well as relevant comments on grammatical aspects in
the texts rather than engaging in formal verse-by-verse commentary.

In the textual analysis of Revelation 4, Schimanowski begins
with a discussion of the open door that John sees and the voice that
John hears. He connects these with parallel materials from the Old
Testament, Qumran, and Jewish apocalyptic literature. Next, he discusses the throne of God, providing a lengthy excursus on throne
descriptions in the Old Testament and other Jewish writings. This is
followed by a discussion of the 24 elders, the seven-fold Spirit, and
the four living creatures. For all of these, Schimanowski explores
possible connections with the Old Testament and other Jewish literature. The remainder of his analysis of Revelation 4 is focused on
the hymnic materials. He provides a lengthy excursus on the *Qadosh*
in Jewish literature, seeing it as foundational for John since it is the
first liturgical text. Schimanowski indicates that the hymnic material
is reflective of the Temple liturgy and the songs of the 24 elders and
four living creatures are sung as part of their duties as priests.[117]

The second half of the monograph examines Revelation 5. According to Schimanowski, the opening καὶ εἶδον ('and I saw') indicates that this is a new vision in which an 'unexpected, new aspect
in the heavenly throne scene moves into the foreground'.[118] He begins his analysis with the scroll and notes its connection to the
scroll of Ezekiel 2. He identifies the places in Revelation where βιβλίον ('book, scroll') occurs (βιβλαρίδιον, 10.2; βιβλίον, 10.8; βιβλίον [βίβλος], 3.5, 17.8) but does not connect any of these with the
scroll in Revelation 5.

Next, Schimanowski spends a great deal of space examining the
image of the Lamb and provides several excurses on the relevant
Jewish background. For him, Revelation 5 reflects the community's
adoration of Christ as the Lamb; further, the acceptance and recog-

---

[116] Gottfried Schimanowski, *Die himmlische Liturgie in der Apokalypse des Johannes: Die frühjüdischen Traditionen in Offenbarung 4–5 unter Einschluss der Hekhalotliteratur*
(Tübingen: Mohr Siebeck, 2002).

[117] Schimanowski, *Die himmlische Liturgie in der Apokalypse des Johannes*, p. 176.

[118] Schimanowski, *Die himmlische Liturgie in der Apokalypse des Johannes*, p. 181.

nition of the authority of the Lamb is celebrated liturgically by the entire cosmos.[119] The chapter concludes with analysis of the hymns to the Lamb, the final hymn to God and the Lamb, and the concluding ἀμήν ('amen'). He suggests that hymnic pieces of chapter 5 point to the joint rule of God and the Lamb and anticipate the unity of God and the Lamb in the final chapter of Revelation.[120]

Schimanowski concludes his monograph by discussing the primary function of Revelation 4–5. For him, the key is the sacrificial death of the Lamb. It is this aspect that garners praise from and connects the heavenly and earthly communities. The five hymns of the throne room scene are specially formed texts of the Christian community and function to break through the borders that separate heaven from earth. The Apocalypse is not just to be read but is to provide a fundamental orientation for the churches.[121] Schimanowski advocates that John likely constructs the hymns of chapter 4 from the liturgy of the synagogue with the hymns of chapter 5 reflecting the remarkable addition of the Lamb to the heavenly liturgy.[122] Schimanowski connects Revelation 4–5 to the end of Revelation where heaven and earth will be transformed into a new unity.[123] For Schimanowski, the heavenly liturgy expressed in Revelation 4–5 is what connects heaven and earth.[124]

Russell Morton

The most recent monograph to appear on the hymns of Revelation 4–5 is by Russell Morton.[125] Morton's stated purpose is to utilize 'the results

---

[119] Schimanowski, *Die himmlische Liturgie in der Apokalypse des Johannes*, p. 234.

[120] Schimanowski, *Die himmlische Liturgie in der Apokalypse des Johannes*, p. 268.

[121] Schimanowski, *Die himmlische Liturgie in der Apokalypse des Johannes*, p. 280. He calls it an audible book (ein hörbares Buch) that is to be read aloud in the churches on the Lord's Day but, more importantly, it is to orient them in their understanding of God and the Lamb.

[122] Schimanowski, *Die himmlische Liturgie in der Apokalypse des Johannes*, p. 282, sees that the death and resurrection of Jesus is a central theological theme of the heavenly liturgy.

[123] Schimanowski, *Die himmlische Liturgie in der Apokalypse des Johannes*, p. 285.

[124] Schimanowski, *Die himmlische Liturgie in der Apokalypse des Johannes*, p. 289.

[125] R. Morton, *One Upon the Throne and the Lamb: A Tradition Historical/Theological Analysis of Revelation 4–5* (New York: Peter Lang, 2007). Morton also published an earlier article that was a precursor to his monograph. See R. Morton, 'Glory to God and to the Lamb: John's Use of Jewish and Hellenistic/Roman Themes in Formatting his Theology in Revelation 4–5', *JSNT* 83 (2001), pp. 89-109.

of tradition analysis as a means of illuminating John's theological purpose in writing the Apocalypse'.[126] After his introductory chapter in which he provides a review of literature, Morton briefly treats the structure of Revelation where he favors the recapitulation structure proposed by both A. Collins and M.E. Boring. This leads to a discussion of the unity of Revelation 4–5, where Morton argues for the unity of these two chapters based on the repetition of similar motifs, the similarity of the hymnic material, and the dependency of Rev. 5.1-2 on what precedes it in Revelation 4.[127] Morton identifies Revelation 4–5 as an 'epiphany vision' which, much like the epiphany visions of Rev. 1.9-20 and 19.11-20.15, introduces a new phase in the vision.[128]

Morton's third and fourth chapters are given to an analysis of the traditions underlying Revelation 4 and 5 respectively. He points to John's adaptation of traditional materials from the (OT) Scriptures, Jewish apocalyptic writings, synagogue ritual, and imperial court rituals. Morton suggests that John's use of traditional sources is intentional and 'serves the purpose of communicating his theological and ethical message'.[129]

Morton's final chapter is a discussion of how John integrates the traditions in Revelation 4–5. John transforms traditional themes in order to 'subordinate' these concepts to his primary concern – the 'victory of God and Christ and their rulership over the cosmos'.[130] Morton proposes four primary areas in which the Seer transforms traditions: the description of the elders, the imperial imagery of the hymns, the apocalyptic traditions used in describing the victorious Christ, and the traditions of the heavenly council scene. First, Morton sees John 'demythologizing' the 24 elders.[131] Second, the imperial

---

[126] Morton, *One Upon the Throne and the Lamb*, p. 28.

[127] Morton, *One Upon the Throne and the Lamb*, p. 70.

[128] Morton also suggests that these epiphany visions are linked by the prominence of a 'written document' (the command to write in Rev. 1.9-20, the scroll in Revelation 4–5, and the opened books in Revelation 19–20), p. 74.

[129] Morton, *One Upon the Throne and the Lamb*, p. 168.

[130] Morton, *One Upon the Throne and the Lamb*, p. 177.

[131] Morton, *One Upon the Throne and the* Lamb, p. 179, argues that the 24 elders are not depicted as gods but are simply 'participants in the heavenly chorus who praise God for what he has done (4.10-11) or act as the interpreters of the heavenly events (5.5; 7.13)'.

language used in the hymnic material in Revelation 4–5 demonstrates the superiority of God and the Lamb. Greco-Roman imperial ceremonies are a 'demonic imitation of the adoration of the true Lord'.[132] Third, Morton maintains that the Seer's depiction of Jesus as the victorious Lamb transforms previous Jewish apocalyptic understandings of eschatology by suggesting that Jesus fulfills those eschatological expectations.[133] Fourthly, the Seer transforms the traditional image of a heavenly council scene to reflect his Christian perspective on the worthiness of Christ. Morton indicates that there are no examples from Hebrew or Jewish apocalyptic literature where a throne scene is used to establish the worthiness of anyone other than God.[134]

Morton concludes that Revelation is to be read as a 'call to ultimate obedience, expressed in the willingness of the followers of the Lamb to emulate his example to victory through martyrdom'.[135] By transforming traditional material, John unveils the 'facade' of the imperial ideology. For Morton, John's theological purpose in Revelation 4–5 is to show that 'Rome cannot be fought with Rome's weapons, but only through confidence in God and God's Lamb, whom John has seen …'[136]

V. Additional Worship Scenes

Balmer Kelly

Balmer Kelly's 2001 expository essay on Revelation 7.9-17 examines the hymnic character of the text by looking at its structure, language, context, and wider relationships.[137] First, Kelly suggests that even though this text was possibly drawn from a variety of sources, such as liturgical sources, martyrological hymns, apocalyptic literature, and the Old Testament, it still has a clear structure of its own.

---

[132] Morton, *One Upon the Throne and the Lamb*, p. 185.

[133] Morton, *One Upon the Throne and the Lamb*, p. 192.

[134] Morton, *One Upon the Throne and the Lamb*, p. 196.

[135] Morton, *One Upon the Throne and the Lamb*, p. 198.

[136] Morton, *One Upon the Throne and the Lamb*, p. 198.

[137] B.H. Kelly, 'Revelation 7:9-17', *Interpretation* 40.03 (2001), pp. 288-95.

It begins with the introductory formula ('After this I looked') and then presents two scenes that contrast one another but are parallel in form.[138] This is followed by a dialogue in typical apocalyptic fashion in which a question is asked by the one who will provide its answer. The answer comes in hymnic form and is the climax of the hymnic material of this scene. Thus, Kelly notes that 'the whole passage ... may properly be understood as a little hymnbook, with each musical entry provided with an appropriate setting'.[139]

Next, Kelly examines the language of the passage. He first discusses the great multitude. Because it is of a size that no one can number, Kelly sees it as a contrast to the multitude of Rev. 7.1-8 which is limited to 144,000. Additionally, the great multitude is from every nation, people, and tongue; by contrast, the multitude of Rev. 7.1-8 is from the tribes of Israel. Kelly sees a deliberate connection between the great multitude of Rev. 7.9-17 and Isa. 49.6.[140] In the hymn (Rev. 7.10) Kelly pauses over the meaning of 'salvation'. He maintains that σωτηρία here has the basic meaning of 'victory' and is to be seen as a kind of vindication rather than as it is traditionally rendered, 'salvation belongs to God'.[141] Those who come through the tribulation and who have washed their robes should not, says Kelly, be identified as the martyrs in the Roman persecution. Rather, these, together with the great multitude, are to be seen as the 'whole body of Christians who through the protective power of God survive the great tribulation which is anticipated in this intermission ...'[142] The final hymn, according to Kelly, has liturgical connections with the worship of the Temple as well as Ps. 23.1-2 and Isa. 25.8. The language of the final hymn borrows much of its phraseology from Isa. 49.10 and functions in a prophetic fashion.[143]

---

[138] Contrast is seen in the cast of characters; parallelism is seen in the use of hymnic material in each scene.

[139] Kelly, 'Revelation 7:9-17', p. 289.

[140] Kelly, 'Revelation 7:9-17', p. 290.

[141] Kelly, 'Revelation 7:9-17', p. 291.

[142] Kelly, 'Revelation 7:9-17', p. 292.

[143] Kelly, 'Revelation 7:9-17', p. 292. He writes,

The prophetic anticipation of a restored and beneficent nature and of a humanity released from the perils and sorrows of present existence gives the author of Revelation, or his source, material to describe the ultimate state of be-

In drawing connections from this text, Kelly suggests that the two visions within Revelation 7 could refer either to the 'final union of Judaism and Christianity in the heavenly realm', or they could be seen as 'the same Christian body as heirs to Judaism and its true remnant ...' He feels that regardless of how the two visions are viewed, the 'flow of apocalyptic thought and calendar' are interrupted; that is, rather than occurring at the conclusion of a series of events, the 'hymnic triumphant vision' occurs as the 'penult' in a series of events.[144] For Kelly, Rev. 7.9-17 is 'an unalloyed "gospel", a seeing and hearing of the final justification of Christian hope'.[145] As such, Kelly believes that the final hymn of Revelation 7, which makes use of future tense verbs, should be translated with the emphatic present (God *does* dwell with his people; they *do not* hunger; God *does* wipe away tears) as a way to state the 'absolute fact' of the declaration of God's victory.[146]

Jan Du Rand

In a 1993 article, Jan Du Rand explores the hymnic material found in Revelation 12–15.[147] Du Rand indicates that the hymns of the Apocalypse provide commentary on their surrounding narratives and invite the reader to participate in the narrative world of the text. Du Rand identifies the following as hymnic material in Revelation: 4.8-11; 5.9-13; 7.10-12; 11.15-18; 12.10-12; 15.3-4; 16.5-7; 19.1-8.[148] Du Rand provides a brief summary of the hymnic passages and the identity of the worshippers before giving focused attention to Revelation 12–15. Revelation 12.1-12 dramatically depicts 'the historical unfolding of salvation and judgment' in the story of the birth of the child (12.5) and the casting down of the Dragon from heaven to

---

lievers. At this point the book stands far more closely to classical Hebrew prophecy than to prior apocalyptic literature.

[144] Kelly, 'Revelation 7:9-17', p. 292.

[145] Kelly, 'Revelation 7:9-17', p. 294.

[146] Kelly, 'Revelation 7:9-17', p. 294.

[147] J. Du Rand, '"Now the Salvation of Our God Has Come ..." A Narrative Perspective on the Hymns in Revelation 12–15', *Neot* 27.2 (1993), pp. 313-30.

[148] Du Rand, 'Now the Salvation of Our God Has Come', p. 316. Du Rand bases his identification on stylistic criteria (such as forms of the verbs, use of particles, rhetorical elements), textual criteria (such as the use of a λέγω ['I say'] formula, petitions to God for help, prayers or songs of praise), and Jörns' classification of verse and anti-verse.

earth (12.9).[149] Du Rand sets out the text of the hymn in Rev. 12.10-12 in three strophes, each consisting of a four-three-four line pattern. Strophe one (v. 10) is identified as the 'acclamatio', strophe two (v. 11) is the 'sacred myth', and strophe three (v. 12) is the 'exhortatio'. Each strophe consists of a 'statement' (vv. 10a; 11a; 12a) and 'cause' (vv. 10b; 11b; 12b). Each cause is indicated grammatically by a ὅτι ('that, because') (strophes one and three) or an epexegetic καί ('and') (strophe two). Additionally, the statement of 12.10a is the proclamation that is further developed in strophes two and three. Strophe two is designated as 'sacred myth' because it recounts both the accuser's downfall as well as the Christ-event. It is an expansion of the cause (10b) of strophe one. Strophe three invites the readers to rejoice because of the announcement of the kingdom of God. Du Rand classifies the hymn as a victory song, which is patterned after Ps. 46.1-8; 48.1-9; 76.1-10; 97.1-5; and 98.1-6.

In summarizing Revelation 12.10-12, Du Rand notes that the hymn serves to interpret the events of 12.1-9. Because of the hymn, the reader is to understand that the defeat of Satan is coupled with the martyrdom of the saints, which is made possible because of the Christ-event. Since the hymn is sung as heavenly worship, the spatial dimension reminds the reader of 'a transcendant [sic] reality in which he or she participates liturgically'.[150]

After providing a narrative overview of Rev. 12.13-14.20, Du Rand next examines the hymn in 15.3-4. Du Rand notes that this hymn serves both as a commentary on the preceding events as well as an introduction to the last series of plagues (Rev. 15.1-16.21) and results in a 'special moment of orientation for the faithful'.[151] He lays out the hymn according to a three-strophe pattern of acclamation (v. 3), exhortation (v. 4a), and cause (v. 4b). Strophes one and three are both doxological in nature. Strophe one makes doxological acclamations about God, and strophe three provides doxological causes in the form of three ὅτι ('that, because') clauses. The exhortation of v. 4a takes the form of a rhetorical question which serves to involve the reader in reacting to the doxology of strophe one. The song is identified in the text as the song of Moses and the

---

[149] Du Rand favors the view that this story is reflective of the combat myth.

[150] Du Rand, 'Now the Salvation of Our God Has Come', p. 323.

[151] Du Rand, 'Now the Salvation of Our God Has Come', p. 326.

Lamb. Du Rand suggests that the song of Moses in Exod. 15.1-18 indicates that the song of Revelation 15 is set within a political context with the beasts represented in the narrative as 'the "new" Pharaoh'. The song in Exodus serves to pre-figure the deliverance brought about by the Christ-event. For Du Rand, this 'intertextual appropriation' plays an important role in the narrative as the faithful live in the light of God's rule on earth through the Christ-event.[152]

Jean-Pierre Ruiz

In this essay, which examines the worship scene contained in Revelation 19.1-10,[153] Ruiz continues his engagement with the Apocalypse that has already resulted in a number of published works.[154] For Ruiz, the primary context of the Apocalypse is political; that is, the Seer seeks to establish a strategy of resistance against the Roman Empire by means of the worship and ritual of the Apocalypse. Ruiz seeks to ascertain the importance of worship (including the angelic directives in Rev. 14.6-7, 19.10, and 22.9) for the seven churches of Asia given the fact that the worship of God takes place in heaven, rather than on earth. The only worship identified as taking place on earth is the false worship given to the Beast and his allies. This raises the question for Ruiz of what the Johannine churches are expected to do as ones living under the rule of Rome.

Ruiz suggests that the climactic worship scene of Rev. 19.1-10 fuses together worship and politics in such a way that the communities are affirmed in their allegiance to God and the Lamb. More than simply a setting, worship represents the 'staging area from which and on the basis of which John mounted his minority counterattack against the convincing claims of the cognitive majority'.[155] Politically, Rev. 19.1-10 celebrates the eschatological victory of God over God's enemies in the destruction of Babylon. Ritually, Rev. 19.1-10 looks forward to the wedding feast of the Lamb. To sing

---

[152] Du Rand, 'Now the Salvation of Our God Has Come', pp. 326-28.

[153] J.-P. Ruiz, 'The Politics of Praise: A Reading of Revelation 19:1-10', *SBLSP* 36 (1997), pp. 374-93.

[154] Jean-Pierre Ruiz, *Ezekiel in the Apocalypse: The Transformation of Prophetic Language in Revelation 16, 17–19,10* (European University Studies 23, 376; Frankfurt am Main: Peter Lang, 1989); *idem*, 'Betwixt and Between on the Lord's Day: Liturgy and the Apocalypse', *SBLSP* 31 (1992), pp. 654-72.

[155] Ruiz, 'The Politics of Praise', p. 381.

the heavenly liturgy and to participate in the heavenly cultic feast, participants must not participate in the imperial cultic liturgy of Rome. Ruiz posits that this type of stance would have had profound political implications for the Johannine churches, yet the Apocalypse calls for such resistance at any cost. Revelation 19.1-10 reinforces this 'ethic of resistance' by placing the exhortation to praise God between 'the hymnic reassurance of the victory of divine justice' (19.1-4) and the 'hymnic anticipation of the eschatological consummation' (19.6-8).[156] Ruiz concludes that John's intentional use of liturgy provides an effective means of encouraging a strategy of resistance for his hearers.

VI. Conclusion

The purpose of this chapter has been to provide the reader with a review of contemporary scholarship related to the theme of worship in the Apocalypse. The first section of this literature review has revealed that relatively few scholarly works have been devoted to the theme of worship in the Apocalypse. At the time of this study, no monograph on the theme of worship has been produced. Instead, the worship scenes and the hymns of the Apocalypse are the focus of study. Of all the worship scenes, the one that has garnished the most attention is Revelation 4–5 due to the important place it occupies in the structure of the book. The final part of this survey has revealed that the remaining scenes are beginning to become the focus of scholarly interest. The scenes themselves have been analyzed through the lens of form, source and redaction criticism with profitable results; however, more recently, scholars have turned to literary criticism as a means of understanding the role and purpose of the worship scenes within the whole of the Apocalypse. A complete narrative reading of the worship scenes of the Apocalypse has yet to be done.

Strikingly, there has been no focused attention given to the worship in the Apocalypse by Pentecostal scholars. This review of literature demonstrates that worship is clearly recognized as a significant

---

[156] Ruiz, 'The Politics of Praise', p. 385.

aspect of the Apocalypse. Because Pentecostals have always placed a high value on worship, the Apocalypse should be a rich source of worship and liturgy for the Pentecostal church.

2

METHODOLOGY: A PENTECOSTAL READING STRATEGY

I. Introduction

In this study I will engage in a Pentecostal narrative reading of the worship material found in the Apocalypse and, as a result of this reading, I hope to make a contribution towards a Pentecostal theology of worship based on the Apocalypse. As demonstrated in chapter one, while many scholars recognize the pervasive theme of worship in the Apocalypse, no one has yet to produce a monograph-length narrative treatment of the theme of worship as a whole. Pertinent to the concerns of this study, the theme of worship has not been taken up by Pentecostal biblical scholars who have written on the Apocalypse. Pentecostals place a high value on worship; thus, the Apocalypse could be a rich source for Pentecostals. This chapter lays out the reading strategy employed in the subsequent chapters of this study. First, I will provide a brief history of North American Pentecostalism. Second, I will describe the developing field of Pentecostal hermeneutics. Third, I will use *Wirkungsgeschichte* as a way to explore how early Pentecostals were influenced by the worship found in the Apocalypse. Fourth, I will advocate that a narrative reading of the Apocalypse is most conducive for Pentecostals. Fifth, the results of these analyses will then be used to make overtures toward the construction of a Pentecostal theology of worship based on the Apocalypse.

II. Origins of Pentecostalism in North America[1]

Pentecostalism is a global movement whose adherents now number in the hundreds of millions.[2] Pentecostalism is experiencing its most explosive growth outside the United States, in places such as Asia, Africa, and Latin and South America.[3] The origins of the Pentecostal movement in North America are generally linked to two key leaders: Charles Fox Parham in Topeka, Kansas, and William J.

---

[1] In recognition of my own context, I am primarily concerned with Pentecostalism as it has grown and spread throughout North America. I realize, however, that Pentecostalism is not uniquely 'North American' and that prior to the outpouring at Topeka, Kansas and Azusa Street there were Pentecostal revivals happening around the globe, such as the Welsh, Korean, and Indian revivals, which played a key role in spreading Pentecostalism throughout the world. For a particularly helpful discussion of the role of international revivals, see A. Anderson, *An Introduction to Pentecostalism* (Cambridge: Cambridge University Press, 2004), pp. 35-38. See also W.J. Hollenweger, *The Pentecostals* (Peabody: Hendrickson, 1972), for his treatment of the spread of Pentecostalism in Europe, Latin America, Africa, Asia, and Australia (chs 5–20). See A. Anderson and W.J. Hollenweger (eds.), *Pentecostals After a Century: Global Perspectives on a Movement in Transition* (JPTSup 15; Sheffield: Sheffield Academic Press, 1999) for Pentecostalism in Africa, Chile, and Korea (pp. 67-163). Further, I acknowledge that Pentecostalism today is larger outside the United States. As Everett Wilson aptly writes,

> By almost any standard, Pentecostalism presently is not what Charles Fox Parham or any of his successors has pronounced it to be, but rather what contemporary Brazilians, Koreans and Africans demonstrate that it actually is. The future of the movement ... lies in the hands of people who because of their superior numbers, vitality and appreciation for its emphases will determine its course (p. 109).

E. Wilson, 'They Crossed the Red Sea, Didn't They? Critical History and Pentecostal Beginnings' in M. Dempster, B. Klaus, D. Petersen (eds.), *The Globalization of Pentecostalism: A Religion Made to Travel* (Oxford: Regnum Books International, 1999), pp. 85-115.

[2] For the origins and development of Pentecostalism, see H.V. Synan, *The Holiness-Pentecostal Movement in the United States* (Grand Rapids: Eerdmans, 1971); Hollenweger, *The Pentecostals*; D.W. Dayton, *Theological Roots of Pentecostalism* (Peabody: Hendrickson Publishers, 1987); H. Cox, *Fire From Heaven: The Rise of Pentecostal Spirituality and the Reshaping of Religion in the Twenty-First Century* (Reading: Addison-Wesley, 1995); D.W. Faupel, *The Everlasting Gospel: The Significance of Eschatology in the Development of Pentecostal Thought* (JPTSup 10; Sheffield: Sheffield Academic Press, 1996; Blandford Forum: Deo Publishing, 2009).

[3] S.J. Land, *Pentecostal Spirituality: A Passion for the Kingdom* (JPTSup 1; Sheffield: Sheffield Academic Press, 1993), p. 21. For further discussion concerning the globalization of Pentecostalism see also Anderson, *An Introduction to Pentecostalism*.

Seymour in Los Angeles, California.[4] On January 1, 1901, at Parham's Bethel Bible School in Topeka, Kansas, Agnes Ozman became the first of Parham's students to be baptized in the Holy Spirit and speak in other tongues. During the next few days, Parham and many others of his students also experienced Spirit Baptism.[5] Not until 1906 would the Pentecostal message and experience of Spirit Baptism explode onto the religious scene in the Azusa Revival led by Seymour, a black holiness preacher who had once sat under Parham's teaching on Spirit Baptism[6] before becoming the pastor of a small Los Angeles church. On April 9, 1906, several members of Seymour's Bible study began to speak in tongues. Seymour himself would experience Spirit Baptism on April 12, 1906.[7] Seymour and his congregation began what would become a three-year revival (1906–1909) at the Azusa Street Mission that would quite literally impact the world.[8]

---

[4] Hollenweger argues for Seymour as the founder of Pentecostalism (against Goff) and, further, suggests that the reason for the growth of Pentecostalism lies in its black roots. He supplies the following five aspects of Pentecostalism that is inherited from its black roots: 1) Orality of its liturgy; 2) Narrative theology and witness; 3) Maximum participation in decision-making; 4) Inclusion of dreams and visions into worship; and 5) Understanding the relationship between body and mind. Hollenweger, 'The Black Roots of Pentecostalism', *Pentecostals after a Century*, pp. 36-43. See also W. Vondey, 'The Making of a Black Liturgy: Pentecostal Worship and Spirituality from American Slave Narratives to American Cityscapes', *Black Theology: An International Journal* 10.2 (2012), pp. 147-68, who argues that the Pentecostalism and Pentecostal liturgy have their roots in the spirituality of African slaves and the open-air holiness camp meetings of the South. Both were transformed by the contexts of migration and urbanization. Vondey argues that the Azusa Mission kept alive the liturgical framework of the camp meeting in a new urban setting. He contends that Black liturgy is still at the heart of Pentecostalism which suggests that Pentecostalism 'is a liturgical movement based on spirituality and worship experience rather than doctrinal consensus' (p. 163).

[5] J.R. Goff, Jr., 'Parham, Charles Fox', in S.M. Burgess and E.M. van der Maas (eds.), *NIDPCM* (Grand Rapids: Zondervan, 2002), pp. 955-57.

[6] Parham had moved to Texas in 1905 and established a Bible school in Brunner, Texas. Because of the Jim Crow laws that were in force during this time, Parham allowed Seymour to sit outside the door in the hall to hear his lectures. C.M. Robeck Jr., 'Seymour, William Joseph', in S.M. Burgess and E.M. van der Maat (eds), *NIDPCM* (Grand Rapids: Zondervan, 2002), pp. 1053-57.

[7] E.M. Noble cites this date in the preface to the *AF* 1.1 (September, 1906).

[8] Robeck, 'Seymour, William Joseph', p. 1055. Parham will later reject the Azusa Revival. K.J. Archer, *A Pentecostal Hermeneutic: Spirit, Scripture and Community* (JPTSup 28; London: T&T Clark International, 2005; Cleveland, TN: CPT Press, 2009), p. 165 (Page numbers cited in this study are from the CPT Press edition).

The Azusa Revival brought changes to the religious landscape of North America. First in relation to theology, Spirit Baptism with tongues was embraced as a spiritual experience subsequent to regeneration and sanctification; thus, Jesus not only justifies and sanctifies, a position that the holiness churches of the day advocated, but also baptizes in the Holy Spirit, evidenced by tongues.[9] This theological understanding was also coupled with manifestations of healing[10] and the urgent message of the return of Jesus, producing what would come to be called the 'Five-fold Gospel'; that is, Jesus is Savior, Sanctifier, Spirit Baptizer, Healer, and Coming King.[11]

---

[9] 'Early Pentecostalism organized its understanding of the Christian life around the three "blessings" or "experiences" of justification, sanctification, and Spirit baptism'. Land, *Pentecostal Spirituality*, p. 82. The following testimony from *The Apostolic Faith* is representative of this understanding: 'In about an hour and a half, a young man was converted, sanctified, and baptized with the Holy Ghost, and spoke with tongues. He was also healed from consumption ...' *AF* 1.1 (September, 1906), p. 1, col. 3.

[10] The walls of the Mission were adorned with crutches and braces as a testimony to the fact that many who came in lame walked out healed. Even children were experiencing healing, as evidenced in the following description from the inaugural issue of *AF*: 'A little girl who walked with crutches and had tuberculosis of the bones, as the doctors declared, was healed and dropped her crutches and began to skip about the yard'. *AF* 1.1 (September, 1906), p. 1. People also were delivered from the bondages of tobacco and alcohol. Archer, *A Pentecostal Hermeneutic: Spirit, Scripture and Community*, pp. 42-43, writes, 'The countless reports of healings, trances (falling out in the spirit), tongues, and other tangible miracles functioned like a *life-changing sacrament* for those believers who witnessed and experienced these unforgettable moments of transforming grace' (emphasis mine).

[11] Land, *Pentecostal Spirituality*, p. 48. Dayton, *Theological Roots of Pentecostalism*, argues that only the gift of tongues set the Pentecostal movement apart from the Holiness movement and that the understanding of Jesus as Savior, Sanctifier, Healer, and Coming King were firmly established in the Holiness movement. He also notes the closeness between popular Evangelicalism at the turn of the century and Pentecostalism: 'Popular Evangelicalism was indeed at the time but a hairsbreadth from Pentecostalism. That hairsbreadth of difference was the experience of speaking in tongues' (p. 176). See also Faupel, *The Everlasting Gospel*, p. 30: 'The three-fold work of Christ on the cross assured justification, sanctification, and healing. The ascended Christ baptized the believer with the fullness of the Spirit. The returning Christ became the ultimate hope of the believer's destiny. *The sole Pentecostal contribution to this five-fold gospel was that the baptism of the Holy Spirit must be initially evidenced by speaking in an unknown tongue*' (emphasis mine). The issue of sanctification as a distinct experience caused a theological rift amongst early Pentecostals with the Wesleyan-Holiness Pentecostals maintaining sanctification as a distinct experience and the Finished-Work Pentecostals including sanctification under the rubric of salvation. This produced a 'Four-fold Gospel': Jesus as Savior, Spirit Baptizer, Healer, and Coming King.

Second, Azusa brought about social change as women and men of various ethnic backgrounds and socio-economic levels were drawn into the same worship service, and the Spirit was being poured out on all. This unprecedented sense of equality meant that anyone, regardless of race, gender, or class could play an active role in worship.[12] At Azusa, the marginalized and oppressed found acceptance, liberation, and a voice.[13] Theologically and socially, then, Pentecostalism broke new ground.[14] This is not to insinuate that racial, economic, or gender tensions were non-existent at Azusa; rather, the revival experienced a *radical equalizing* which set it apart from the religious mainstream of the time. Third, worship was a significant feature of Azusa. Cecil Robeck writes,

> There were those who, 'surrounded by [His] glory' at the mission, broke into dance. Others jumped, or stood with hands outstretched, or sang or shouted with all the gusto they could muster. Others were so full of awe when they encountered God that their knees buckled – they fell to the floor, 'slain in the Spirit'.

---

[12] C.M. Robeck, Jr., *The Azusa Street Mission and Revival: The Birth of the Global Pentecostal Movement* (Nashville: Thomas Nelson, Inc., 2006), pp. 136-37. See also D. Daniels, '"Everyone Bids You Welcome" A Multicultural Approach to North American Pentecostalism', in M. Dempster, B. Klaus, D. Petersen (eds.), *The Globalization of Pentecostalism: A Religion Made to Travel* (Oxford, Regnum Books International, 1999), pp. 222-52; Synan, *The Holiness-Pentecostal Movement*, p. 165,

> In an age of Social Darwinism, Jim Crowism, and general white supremacy, the fact that negroes and whites worshipped together in virtual equality among the Pentecostals was a significant exception to prevailing racial attitudes. Even more significant is the fact that this interracial accord took place among the very groups that have traditionally been most at odds, the poor whites and the poor blacks.

R. Mills, 'Musical Prayers: Reflections on the African Roots of Pentecostal Music', *JPT* 12 (1998), pp. 109-26, argues that Azusa was not unique because it was interracial (there were other interracial revivals); rather, it was unique because it was 'the first black revival which attracted white followers' (p. 123).

[13] Hollenweger describes Seymour's understanding of the significance of the Pentecostal experience in relation to society: 'For him pentecost meant more than speaking in tongues. It meant to love in the face of hate, to overcome the hatred of a whole nation by demonstrating that pentecost is something very different from the success-oriented American way of life.' W.J. Hollenweger, 'After Twenty Years Research on Pentecostalism', *International Review of Mission* 75 (January 1986), p. 5.

[14] This does not come without a price, and the early Pentecostal movement came under tremendous pressure from the largely segregated society at large. See Synan, *The Holiness-Pentecostal Movement*, p. 166.

Some spoke, rapid-fire, in a tongue they did not know, while others were struck entirely speechless.[15]

In addition to the singing of hymns and gospel songs from the Holiness movement, new songs in known and unknown tongues were sung in the wake of the coming of the Spirit.[16] A supernatural manifestation of angelic singing was also a frequent testimony of these early Pentecostals.[17] Fourth, from Azusa the message of Pentecost spread around the world. The outpouring of the Spirit was seen as the precursor to the pre-millennial return of Jesus Christ. This eschatological fervor and urgency launched a missionary movement as visitors to Azusa from around the world took the message of Pentecost back to their homelands. Some participants at Azusa received the 'gift of language' and saw it as a sign to travel to that land and evangelize.[18] In this way, Pentecostalism began to be spread around the globe in earnest.

---

[15] Robeck, *The Azusa Street Mission and Revival*, p. 131. Mills, 'Musical Prayers: Reflections on the African Roots of Pentecostal Music', pp. 118-22, argues that the bodily and rhythmic movements such as clapping, dancing, swaying and so on featured in Pentecostalism reflected the influence of the ring-shouts of the slaves and the black holiness movement.

[16] On the music of the Azusa Revival see S. Dove, 'Hymnody and Liturgy in the Azusa Street Revival, 1906–1908', *Pneuma* 31 (2009), pp. 243-63. Dove notes that the music of the revival is referenced in *The Apostolic Faith* more than any other communal practice (p. 243). He explores the liturgy of Azusa under three categories: 1) Singing in the Spirit; 2) New hymns composed by those at Azusa; and 3) The use of pre-existent hymns. Dove suggests that the music of Azusa was largely Christological in focus and served to balance out the pneumatological elements of the mission.

[17] 'No choir – but bands of angels have been heard by some in the spirit and there is a heavenly singing that is inspired by the Holy Ghost'. *AF* 1.3 (November, 1906), p. 1.

[18] F.D. Macchia, 'The Struggle for Global Witness: Shifting Paradigms in Pentecostal Theology', in M. Dempster, B. Klaus, D. Petersen (eds.), *The Globalization of Pentecostalism: A Religion Made to Travel* (Oxford: Regnum Books International, 1999), p. 16, writes:

[P]entecostalism began as a paradigm shift from an exclusive focus on holiness to an outward thrust that involved a dynamic filling and an empowerment for global witness ... It was thought that in these latter days the Spirit would grant the people of God the apostolic capacity revealed in Acts 2:4 to proclaim the mighty deeds of God in the many languages of the world. Tongues were thought, therefore, to be the most striking evidence of a Spirit baptismal experience that urged one to bear witness of the gospel of Jesus Christ to the nations. Tongues were the primary evidence because Spirit bap-

It was not long, however, until theological and social tensions began to divide the fledgling movement. Paradigm shifts over the purpose of tongues developed when missionaries found that they could not always communicate with people in foreign lands! Various theological positions developed around the understanding of tongues.[19] Competing understandings of soteriology, most notably in the 'Finished Work' and 'Oneness' theologies, developed and caused the movement to split into multiple Pentecostal denominations.[20] The racial equality so prevalent at Azusa early on unraveled, leading to the start of Pentecostal denominations that were racially segregated but still in 'fellowship' with one another. Despite these, or perhaps, because of these controversies, Pentecostalism has continued to grow and spread.[21]

Today, Pentecostalism is one of the largest Protestant groups in the world. Its impact upon the Church worldwide can hardly be over-stated. The influence of Pentecostalism has moved into historically non-Pentecostal churches with the advent of the Charismatic renewal as members of other branches of Christianity – Catholic, Episcopalian, Anglican, Orthodox, Methodist – began experiencing Spirit baptism with tongues. Similarly, the music and spirit of worship found in Pentecostalism has made its way into mainline churches and even into the mainstream of American culture. The global growth and nature of Pentecostalism resists any sort of

---

tism itself was viewed as an experience that thrust one into the challenges of a global witness that transcended established cultural boundaries.'

[19] Macchia, 'The Struggle for Global Witness', p. 17.

[20] Land, *Pentecostal Spirituality*, pp. 185-88.

[21] Robert Mapes Anderson observes that 'without the continuing stimulus provided by such agitation, the movement may have atrophied and died. Controversy became the very life and breath of the Pentecostal movement.' R. Anderson, *Vision of the Disinherited: The Making of American Pentecostalism* (Peabody: Hendrickson Publishers, 1979), pp. 192-93. On the issue of segregated Pentecostal denominations, Anderson notes that contact was maintained:

Pentecostals of different persuasions and affiliations have always had the custom of visiting one another's services and joining together in revival campaigns, conventions, and camp meetings. This practice of 'fellowshipping' often transcended racial barriers, especially in Northern urban areas, but elsewhere as well. Integrated Pentecostal meetings continued to be common even after the organizational separation of the races. Taken as a whole, Pentecostals have probably retained as much contact and friendship between racial and, it might be added, ethnic groups as have the adherents of any other religious community in America.

monolithic or generic label; thus, it seems more appropriate to speak of Pentecostal*isms* 'as there is no longer an adequate framework into which all Pentecostals easily fit'. The beliefs and practices of Pentecostal*isms* continue to have a tremendous impact around the world.[22]

III. Pentecostal Hermeneutics

Pentecostalism has generated a present and growing interest in the academy. One area of study that has emerged for Pentecostal scholars is the quest to define and flesh out how Pentecostals read and interpret Scripture. Pentecostal scholars are 'forging hermeneutical models' that reflect the ethos of Pentecostalism.[23] The rubric of Scripture, community, and Spirit resides at the heart of Pentecostal hermeneutics.[24] The goal of Pentecostal hermeneutics, however, is not just to understand a certain biblical text cognitively; rather, the goal is both to understand and be transformed by the biblical text.[25] Such an encounter with the Scripture is best done within the Pentecostal community under the direction of the Holy Spirit. Although theoretically each element of the rubric stands on its own, the reality is that Scripture, community, and Spirit are so integrated into the ethos of Pentecostalism that it is difficult to separate them into distinct categories. The Scriptures are a product of the Spirit; the community is formed by the Spirit and shaped by both the Scrip-

---

[22] K. Warrington, *Pentecostal Theology: A Theology of Encounter* (London: T&T Clark, 2008), p. 12. This brief description of the origins of Pentecostalism in North America is not meant to romanticize its origins or gloss over the issues and tensions that arose in and continue to plague Pentecostalism, particularly related to the inequality of race, class and gender. Rather, I seek to establish a context and ethos for my reading of the early Pentecostal periodical literature in chapter 3 of this study.

[23] See Green, *Toward a Pentecostal Theology of the Lord's Supper*, p. 183 where he lists eight general areas of consensus among Pentecostals.

[24] These categories have been used by a number of Pentecostal scholars, including R.D. Moore, 'Canon and Criticism in the Book of Deuteronomy', *JPT* 1 (1992), pp. 75-92; J.C. Thomas, 'Women, Pentecostals, and the Bible: An Experiment in Pentecostal Hermeneutics', *JPT* 5 (1994), pp. 41-56; A. Yong, *Spirit-Word-Community: Theological Hermeneutics in Trinitarian Perspective* (Eugene: Wipf & Stock, 2002); Archer, *A Pentecostal Hermeneutic: Spirit, Scripture and Community*.

[25] C. Bridges Johns, *Pentecostal Formation: A Pedagogy Among the Oppressed* (JPTSup 2; Sheffield: Sheffield Academic Press, 1993), p. 122.

tures and the Spirit. Nevertheless, there are important ideas that Pentecostals affirm about Scripture, the community, and the Holy Spirit.

Scripture

Pentecostals hold to a high view of Scripture; that is, the Bible is God's written revelation given to humanity, second only to the revelation of Jesus Christ.[26] Pentecostals read their Bible with an eye toward the whole; that is, the Old and New Testaments are viewed as a single story revealing God's involvement with humanity. At the center of that revelation is Jesus.[27]

Ellington defines the role of Scripture within the Pentecostal community by saying that 'the Bible is the basic rule of faith and practice and supplies the corrective and interpretive authority for all religious experience'.[28] While this is in keeping with many Christian traditions, Ellington contends that Pentecostals primarily base their understanding of biblical authority not on a doctrine of inspiration (which they would nevertheless affirm) but more so in their experience of God. Thereby, Scripture 'adds language to the relationship which exists between the believer and God'.[29] Scripture functions as 'word of God' precisely because Pentecostals experience God in the Scriptures; thus, '"what the Bible says" is identical with "what God says"'.[30]

---

[26] Pentecostals would give whole-hearted affirmation to Clark Pinnock's description of the Bible as 'the medium of the gospel message and the primary sacrament of the knowledge of God, his own communication, which is able to reconcile us to God so that we might come to love and obey him. Not a book wholly free of perplexing features, but one that bears effective witness to the Savior of all.' C.H. Pinnock, *The Scripture Principle* (San Francisco: Harper & Row, Publishers, 1984), p. xix.

[27] In agreement with Pinnock, *The Scripture Principle*, p. 16, who states, 'Christology, not Bibliology, occupies center stage in Christianity'.

[28] S.A. Ellington, 'Pentecostalism and the Authority of Scripture', *JPT* 9 (1996), p. 21.

[29] Ellington, 'Pentecostalism and the Authority of Scripture', p. 21. See also Warrington, *Pentecostal Theology*, p. 188, 'Pentecostals believe that the main purpose of the Bible is to help them develop their experience of and relationship with God, to be more available to the ministry of the Spirit and to be drawn closer to Jesus'.

[30] Ellington, 'Pentecostalism and the Authority of Scripture', p. 21. F.L. Arrington, *Christian Doctrine: A Pentecostal Perspective* (Cleveland: Pathway Press, 1992), I, p. 25, writes: 'An encounter with the Scriptures is an encounter with the living God'.

Scripture is made alive through the Spirit, who aids both the individual reader and the community in understanding, discerning, and applying it. The Spirit is 'centrally valued in the creation, transmission, reception and application of the text'.[31] Therefore, as Pentecostals read Scripture, it becomes 'an event of the Spirit in which the reader is transformed and made to experience what the bible puts forth as living truth'.[32] For Pentecostals, the fact that Scripture was originally written in a different historical setting does not limit its applicability to the present; rather, for Pentecostals there is a 'certain "present-tenseness" to the events and words of Scripture, so that what happened then, happens now'.[33] Pentecostals read the Scriptures not as observers but as participants in the stories. In this way, Pentecostals have an *experiential* relationship with Scripture as they relate to and participate in the *world* of the text.

Pentecostals focus on the final form of the Scriptures. The concerns of historical criticism, the world behind the text, are not as important to Pentecostals as the world within the text.[34] 'The final canonical form of the biblical narrative is what shapes the reader and enables the reader to develop a praxis-oriented understanding of life'.[35] The Scriptures are to be read as a single coherent story –

---

[31] Warrington, *Pentecostal Theology*, p. 199.

[32] F.D. Macchia, 'Theology, Pentecostal', in S.M. Burgess and E.M. van der Maas (eds.), *NIDPCM* (Grand Rapids: Zondervan, 2002), p. 1122.

[33] Macchia, 'Theology, Pentecostal', p. 1122. See also T.L. Cross, 'The Divine-Human Encounter: Towards a Pentecostal Theology of Experience', *Pneuma* 31 (2009), p. 5, 'At least part of what we are claiming when we say we have experienced God is that the God of the Bible is the one who encounters us in the history of our own lives'. J.B. Green, 'The (Re-) Turn to Narrative', in J.B. Green and Michael Pasquarello III (eds.), *Narrative Reading, Narrative Preaching* (Grand Rapids: Baker Academic, 2003), p. 23:

I take the claim, the Bible as Scripture, to refer to a theological stance whereby we recognize that *we* are the people of God to whom these texts are addressed. This leads us to the realization that the fundamental transformation that must take place is not the transformation of an ancient message into a contemporary meaning but rather the transformation of our lives by means of God's Word.

[34] L.R. Martin, *The Unheard Voice of God: A Pentecostal Hearing of the Book of Judges* (JPTSup 32; Blandford Forum: Deo Publishing, 2008), p. 14. See also A. Davies, 'What Does it Mean to Read the Bible as a Pentecostal?', *JPT* 18 (2009), p. 224.

[35] Archer, *A Pentecostal Hermeneutic*, p. 228.

the 'drama of salvation-history'.[36] Because of this understanding of the Scripture as story, Pentecostals are drawn to and privilege narrative portions of Scripture.[37] As readers and hearers, they become caught up in the stories of Scripture and, as a result, they are invited to experience transformation.[38]

Community

The Pentecostal community plays an important role in the interpretation of Scripture owing to the understanding that interpretation is a communal activity. The community reads and hears the Scriptures in particular ways, in light of its self-identity.[39] Reading and hearing the Scriptures within a community, rather than in isolation, shapes one's experience of the text. Together, the community appropriates the meaning of Scripture for its present day context.[40] Reading the Scriptures within a community of believers helps guard against interpretations that are 'dogmatic, divisive and thus ultimately and

---

[36] Green, *Toward a Pentecostal Theology of the Lord's Supper*, p. 189.

[37] Warrington, *Pentecostal Theology*, p. 191, writes that Pentecostals 'have related more easily to the Gospels and Acts than the epistles; they have enjoyed pausing with the historical books before Psalms more than the prophetic books that follow'. See C.H. Pinnock, 'The Work of the Spirit in the Interpretation of Holy Scripture from the Perspective of a Charismatic Biblical Theologian', *JPT* 18 (2009), p. 169, who suggests that Scripture is primarily written in narrative because narrative was 'needed if God is to be properly identified as a living and personal agent'.

[38] Pinnock, 'The Work of the Spirit in the Interpretation of Holy Scripture', p. 170:

> Scripture is less the demand to submit to God than it is an invitation to indwell the narrative of God's grace. The task is not an attempt to adapt the words of Scripture to our reality but an invitation to make sense of our reality within its purview of new creation. The reader, by means of interpretation, enters into and appropriates the world of meaning that the text projects. The text creates a space into which the reader is being invited for transformation.

[39] Archer, *A Pentecostal Hermeneutic*, p. 223, writes:

> Moral reasoning is always rooted in a particular narrative tradition which offers its version of reality to other communities. In the negotiating of meaning, one's community is an important and necessary component of the hermeneutical strategy. In order to produce a 'Pentecostal' reading of Scripture, one needs to identify with the Pentecostal community.

[40] Pinnock, 'The Work of the Spirit in the Interpretation of Holy Scripture', p. 166. See also Archer, *A Pentecostal Hermeneutic*, p. 181.

fundamentally flawed'.[41] It is the community of faith 'which facilitates the uniting of a myriad of contrasting, individualised, contextualised applications of meaning in an arena of mutual coherence and significance'.[42] This process of interpretation takes place in the community under the direction of the Spirit who is the 'ultimate arbiter of meaning and significance'.[43] The Pentecostal community is a context created by the Spirit, and it is a place in which Scripture is interpreted through the guidance of that same Spirit.[44] The interpretation of Scripture is shaped and enhanced by the experience of sharing Scripture *in* community.[45] It is the Pentecostal community that 'serves as the vital context for good interpretation' and that 'truly authors interpretations' of Scripture.[46]

---

[41] Warrington, *Pentecostal Theology*, p. 198. See also J.C. Thomas, 'What the Spirit is Saying to the Church' – The Testimony of a Pentecostal in New Testament Studies', in K.L. Spawn and A.T. Wright (eds.), *Spirit & Scripture: Examining a Pneumatic Hermeneutic* (London: T&T Clark, 2012), p. 121, who reflects on how the Pentecostal community aids the interpreter:

> Not only do the experiences of the worshipping Pentecostal community serve to prepare the interpreter for a number of aspects of the text that are sometimes foreign to some modernist interpreters (such as miracles, healings, exorcism, prophecy, and other forms of Spirit activity), but such formational experiences also encourage the hearers to respect the affective dimensions of the text. One aspect of such discerning reflection is an awareness of and responsiveness to ways in which the biblical texts are instruments in affective transformation, both in terms of what is in the text and what is generated or formed in the interpreter. Another aspect of such discerning reflection is sensitivity to the way in which the 'passions' reflected in biblical texts are not only identified as part of the text but become part of the Pentecostal interpretive process itself.

[42] Davies, 'What Does it Mean to Read the Bible as a Pentecostal?', p. 227.

[43] Davies, 'What Does it Mean to Read the Bible as a Pentecostal?', p. 228.

[44] Archer, *A Pentecostal Hermeneutic*, pp. 135-36, writes, 'The community must discern what the text means and how that meaning is to be lived out in the community. This decision making process is imperative for Pentecostals because Pentecostal interpretation includes an act of willful obedient response to the Scripture's meaning.' See also Pinnock, 'The Work of the Spirit in the Interpretation of Holy Scripture', p. 171: 'Interpretation stands in the service of obedience and worship'.

[45] Martin, *The Unheard Voice of God*, p. 61. See also J. Goldingay, *Models for Interpretation of Scripture* (Grand Rapids: Eerdmans, 1985), p. 233: 'We have access to scripture not merely on the basis of individual experience and involvement but also on the basis of corporate experience and involvement'. See also Green, 'The (Re-) Turn to Narrative', p. 23, 'No interpretive tool, no advanced training can substitute for active participation in a community of Bible readers'.

[46] Green, *Toward a Pentecostal Theology of the Lord's Supper*, p. 191.

In addition to my worshipping community, I am by training part of an academic community. Of special significance for this present work is that within the community of Pentecostal biblical scholarship, there has been a growing interest in the academic study of the Apocalypse. Within the last 25–30 years, Pentecostal biblical scholars have contributed chapter essays[47] and journal articles[48] related to the Apocalypse.[49] Monographs have come primarily in the form of single-volume commentaries on the Apocalypse[50] and published

[47] M. Wilson, 'Revelation 19.10 and Contemporary Interpretation', in M. Wilson (ed.), *Spirit and Renewal: Essays in Honor of J. Rodman Williams* (JPTSup 5; Sheffield: Sheffield Academic Press, 1994), pp. 191-202; R. Waddell, 'Revelation and the (New) Creation: A Prolegomenon on the Apocalypse, Science, and Creation', in A. Yong (ed.), *The Spirit Renews the Face of the Earth: Pentecostal Forays in Science and Theology of Creation* (Eugene: Pickwick Publications, 2009), pp. 30-50; J.C. Thomas, 'Pneumatic Discernment: The Image of the Beast and His Number', in S. Land, R. Moore, J.C. Thomas (eds.), *Passover, Pentecost and Parousia: Studies in Celebration of the Life and Ministry of R. Hollis Gause* (JPTSup 35; Blandford Forum: Deo Publishing, 2010), pp. 106-24; *idem*, 'The Mystery of the Great Whore: Pneumatic Discernment in Revelation 17', in P. Althouse and R. Waddell (eds.), *Perspectives in Pentecostal Eschatologies: World Without End* (Eugene: Pickwick Publications, 2010), pp. 111-38; R. Herms, 'Invoking the Spirit and Narrative Intent in John's Apocalypse', in K.L. Spawn and A.T. Wright (eds), *Spirit and Scripture: Examining a Pneumatic Hermeneutic* (London: T&T Clark, 2012), pp. 99-114.

[48] J.C. de Smidt, 'Hermeneutical Perspectives on the Spirit in the Book of Revelation', *JPT* 14 (1999), pp. 27-47; *idem*, 'A Meta-Theology of Ὁ ΘΕΟΣ in Revelations [*sic*] 1:1-2', *Neot* 38.2 (2004), pp. 183-208; *idem*, 'The First μακαρισμός in Revelation 1:3', *Acta Patristica et Byzantina* 15 (2004), pp. 91-118; R. Skaggs, and T. Doyle, 'Violence in the Apocalypse of John', *CBR* 5.2 (2007), pp. 220-34; I. Paul, 'Ebbing and Flowing: Scholarly Developments in Study of the Book of Revelation', *The Expository Times* 119.11 (2008), pp. 523-31; J. Newton, 'Reading Revelation Romantically', *JPT* 18 (2009), pp. 194-215; R. Skaggs, and T. Doyle, 'Lion/Lamb in Revelation', *CBR* 7.3 (2009), pp. 362-75; R. Waddell, 'What time is it? Half-past three: How to calculate eschatological time', *JEPTA* 31.2 (2011), pp. 141-52; C. Tanner, 'Climbing the Lampstand-Witness-Trees: Revelation's Use of Zechariah 4 in Light of Speech Act Theory', *JPT* 20 (2011), pp. 81-92; M.L. Archer, 'The Worship Scenes in the Apocalypse, Effective History, and Early Pentecostal Periodical Literature', *JPT* 21 (2012), pp. 87-112.

[49] For a full treatment of this see my 'Pentecostals and the Apocalypse: A Survey of Recent Pentecostal Biblical Scholarship on the Apocalypse', *JPT* (forthcoming). This survey does not include unpublished theses and dissertations.

[50] R.H. Gause, *Revelation: God's Sovereign Stamp on History* (Cleveland: Pathway Press, 1983); C.S. Keener, *Revelation* (NIV Application Commentary; Grand Rapids: Zondervan, 2000); M. Wilson, *The Victor Sayings in the Book of Revelation* (Eugene: Wipf & Stock Publishers, 2007); R. Skaggs and P. Benham, *Revelation* (Pentecostal Commentary Series; Blandford Forum: Deo, 2009); G.D. Fee, *Revelation* (NCCS; Eugene: Cascade Books, 2011); J.C. Thomas, *The Apocalypse: A Literary and Theological Commentary* (Cleveland: CPT Press, 2012).

PhD theses, such as those written by Ronald Herms,[51] Philip Mayo[52] and Robby Waddell.[53] This present study will make another

---

[51] R. Herms, *An Apocalypse for the Church and for the World: The Narrative Function of Universal Language in the Book of Revelation* (BZNW 143; Berlin; New York: Walter deGruyter, 2006). Herms addresses the fate of the nations in Revelation from both a literary-narrative and tradition-historical methodological perspective by putting Revelation's universal language related to the fate of the nations in conversation with other Jewish apocalyptic works addressing the same issue, namely Tobit, *Similitudes* of Enoch (1 Enoch 37–71), 4 Ezra, and the *Animal Apocalypse* (1 Enoch 85–90). Herms shows how John differs from other Jewish apocalyptic writings in his understanding of who constitutes the people of God – those from 'every tribe, tongue, people and nation' (Rev. 5.9; 7.9). Two key texts, Rev. 1.5 and 21.24-26, reveal that John is influenced by Davidic/Solomonic traditions in depicting Jesus. 'These biblical traditions contribute universal language and designations for earth's peoples that appear in visions depicting God's eschatological rulership' (p. 260). As for the fate of the nations, Herms concludes that John is consistent with other apocalyptic writings that show the nations participating in the age to come not because the nations are converted but rather because the people of God are vindicated. The use of 'universal language does not necessarily presuppose universal salvation; rather, it serves to vindicate the faithful community, and validate their present circumstances in light of a future reversal' (p. 260).

[52] P.L. Mayo, *Those Who Call Themselves Jews: The Church and Judaism in the Apocalypse of John* (PTMS 60; Eugene: Pickwick Publications, 2006). Mayo explores the relationship between Judaism and the early church. Mayo seeks to make a contribution to the study of Jewish-Christian relations during the years 70 and 150 CE, a time designated as 'the parting of the ways,' 'when the church was emerging as a religion apart from Judaism' (p. 1). Along with the Gospel of John and the book of Acts, Revelation stands as a text which seems to reflect an anti-Jewish tone – particularly in utilizing phraseology such as 'synagogue of Satan' (Rev. 2.9; 3.9). Despite this, Mayo sees John adopting and adapting Jewish scriptures and cultic imagery and applying it to the church. Employing both historical and literary critical approaches, Mayo examines first and second century Jewish and Christian sources as well as several passages in Revelation (2.9; 3.9; 7.1-17; 14.1-5; 11.1-13; 12.1-17; 21.1–22.5) in an attempt to 'understand how these apocalyptic texts and images function within the literary whole and how they portray John's particular perspective on Israel's and the church's place in God's economy' (p. 4). On the one hand, Mayo identifies the references to the 'synagogue of Satan' in Revelation 2.9 and 3.9 as pertaining to ethnic Jews who were persecuting the Christian community as well as the reference to the earthly Jerusalem (Rev. 11.1-13). On the other hand, the 144,000 and the innumerable multitude (Rev. 7.1-17), the heavenly woman (Rev. 12.1-17), and the heavenly Jerusalem are all symbols for the church – true Israel. The church, God's new spiritual Israel, is comprised of all those – both Jew and Gentile - who acknowledge God's plan as brought about in the person of Jesus Christ. John's perceived pejorative language ('synagogue of Satan') is used for any who are unfaithful to God and the Lamb. Mayo does not argue for a replacement theology; rather, he insists that for John, the church is the *fulfillment* of God's covenant promises.

[53] R. Waddell, *The Spirit of the Book of Revelation* (JPTSup 30; Blandford Forum: Deo Publishing, 2006). Waddell offers the first monograph-length study of the

contribution to Pentecostal studies of the Apocalypse. I choose to include my Pentecostalism as an important part of my reading strat-

---

pneumatology of the Apocalypse. The overall purpose of Waddell's work is to examine the pneumatology of Revelation while inquiring 'into the intertextual relationship' between his own 'confessional context in a Pentecostal interpretive community and the literary references to the Spirit in the Apocalypse' (p. 40). As such, Waddell is among the first to self-identify as a Pentecostal and use the Pentecostal community as a component in his interpretive strategy. Waddell also offers a sketch of a Pentecostal reader and hermeneutic. For Waddell, a Pentecostal hermeneutic should be theological, ecumenical, and done from the margins. It must be done in community and employ multiple strategies that are faithful to the tradition without doing 'violence to the text' (p. 118). The community not only hears and reads the words of Revelation but also participates in and discerns the prophecy of Revelation by means of the Holy Spirit. For Waddell, 'the integration of orthodoxy, orthopraxis and orthopathy within Pentecostalism finds resonance with the multiple intersections of literary and cultural (con)texts within the theory of intertextuality' (p. 131). He applies his method to Rev. 11.1-13 – a passage that he proposes as the intertextual center for the role of the Spirit in Revelation. Waddell identifies Zechariah 4 as the key intertext relating to the role of the Spirit. Waddell seeks to 'demonstrate that the double imagery of the two olive trees and the two lampstands complemented by the use of πνεῦμα and πνευματικῶς creates a textual fabric that enables John to express richly the role of the Spirit in the prophetic ministry of the church whose primary task is to bear witness to Jesus in the world' (p. 133). Waddell presents a verse by verse analysis of Rev. 11.1-13 in conversation especially [but not exclusively] with Zechariah 4. The two witnesses appear as those divinely commissioned [perhaps by the Spirit] to prophesy. The introduction of the two olive trees and two lampstands (Rev. 11.4) is an intertextual echo of Zechariah 4. This serves to reveal the identity of the two witnesses as well as reveal the role of the Spirit in the Apocalypse. For John, the church is represented in the symbolism of the two lampstands, two olive trees, and two witnesses. As a priestly, kingly, and prophetic community, the church bears witness to Jesus through the power of the Spirit. Because the Spirit operates within the church, the church plays a pivotal role in the Lamb's victory. The echo of Zechariah further serves to shed light on John's use of the seven spirits and links the seven spirits with the two witnesses. With the introduction of the beast into the narrative, the period of protection is over and the witnesses are killed. The ministry of the witnesses is seen to be a replica of Jesus' ministry, including his death, resurrection, and ascension, since the witnesses are also resurrected and taken up into heaven. The earthquake in Rev. 11.13 serves as the final proof of the vindication of the witnesses. Rev. 11.1-13 calls the Spirit-anointed church 'to participate in a faithful pneumatic witness' not unlike the two spirit-anointed witnesses (p. 191).

egy.[54] Just as all readers bring their experiences and pre-understandings to the interpretive process, I bring my academic training and my Pentecostal experience to my reading of Scripture.[55] By identifying my community and my self-understanding, I open myself up to the scrutiny of the text as well as other interpretive communities.

The Holy Spirit

The Holy Spirit is the 'Scripture's definitive interpreter'.[56] Scripture is a gift of the Spirit and is 'at the disposal of the Spirit for new and subtle uses'.[57] The community looks to and expects the Spirit to inspire the Scriptures for their own contexts.[58] Mark Cartledge suggests, 'Pneumatology provides the link between text and community, since the Spirit has both inspired the original text and inspires the reading of the text today'.[59] The Spirit works in concrete ways

---

[54] Whereas previous generations of Pentecostal scholars have had to suppress their faith tradition in the academy, the recent increased interest in Pentecostal studies has made it easier for Pentecostal scholars to acknowledge their tradition. On this see J.C. Thomas, 'Pentecostal Theology in the Twenty-First Century', *Pneuma* 20.1 (1998), pp. 3-19 (now in J.C. Thomas, *The Spirit of the New Testament* [Blandford Forum: Deo Publishing, 2005], pp. 3-22).

[55] Archer, *A Pentecostal Hermeneutic*, p. 224-25, writes,

> The Pentecostal hermeneut who is educated by the academy must also be a participant within the Pentecostal community; that is, she should understand her Christian identity to be Pentecostal … The Pentecostal story must be interwoven into her personal story. This does not imply that one cannot be concerned about the larger Christian community or attempt to understand the Scripture from a different perspective or interpretive strategy, but it does mean that one's identity is shaped and formed by participating in a Pentecostal community … In this way, the reader is an extension and participant of the community not an isolated individual.

[56] Green, *Toward a Pentecostal Theology of the Lord's Supper*, p. 184. Green further states that without the Spirit, the faithful and effective reading of Scripture as God's Word is, quite simply, impossible' (p. 186).

[57] Pinnock, 'The Work of the Spirit in the Interpretation of Holy Scripture', p. 165.

[58] John Wesley wrote, 'The Spirit of God not only once inspired those who wrote the Bible but continually inspires those who read it with earnest prayer'. Cited in Pinnock, 'The Work of the Holy Spirit in Hermeneutics', p. 4.

[59] M.J. Cartledge, 'Text-Community-Spirit: The Challenges Posed by Pentecostal Theological Method to Evangelical Theology', in K.L. Spawn and A.T. Wright (eds.), *Spirit & Scripture: Examining a Pneumatic Hermeneutic* (London: T&T Clark, 2012), p. 140.

through the Scriptures to speak to present situations.[60] The Spirit is closely connected with the worshipping community for Pentecostals fully expect to encounter the Spirit of God when they are gathered together. Pentecostal theologian Terry Cross writes that Pentecostals have a 'radical openness to the invasion and intervention of God's Spirit in our daily lives'.[61] This *invasion* by the Spirit leads to transformation.[62]

The Spirit operates in the community in various ways. The Spirit speaks to the corporate body through prophetic words,[63] the proclamation of testimonies, prayer, and through times of worship. Pentecostals attest to 'feeling the presence of the Lord' in the worshipping community. This sense of the Spirit's presence elicits wide-ranging and varying responses from individuals in the community, such as audible praise, shouting, hand-raising, clapping, dancing, running, prostration, and weeping. These responses to the moving of the Spirit are understood to be consistent with responses to God expressed in the Psalms and other places in Scripture and are thereby valid and appropriate for the community. The Spirit is not limited to its work with the worshipping community, for the Spirit is at work throughout the world; therefore, Pentecostals desire to discern where the Spirit is at work and hear what the Spirit is saying through voices outside the community.[64]

---

[60] The constructive work of Thomas on Acts 15 presents an instructive paradigm for viewing the interdependent roles of the Scripture, the community, and the Spirit that can aid Pentecostals in addressing present day concerns within the community, such as the issue of women in ministry. Thomas, 'Women, Pentecostals and the Bible', pp. 41-56. See also Archer, *A Pentecostal Hermeneutic*, pp. 196-200 who, in assessing Thomas' model for use by Pentecostals, notes, 'Thomas' hermeneutical paradigm captures both the dialogical and dialectical essence of Pentecostalism' (p. 200).

[61] Cross, 'The Divine-Human Encounter', p. 6.

[62] Cross, 'The Divine-Human Encounter', p. 7.

[63] The community recognizes the human component in claiming to speak for the Spirit, so the community is admonished to weigh and discern spiritual manifestations in the light of Scripture and the experience of the community with the Spirit. Archer, *A Pentecostal Hermeneutic*, p. 249.

[64] Archer, *A Pentecostal Hermeneutic*, p. 250.

IV. *Wirkungsgeschichte*

In this study I will also engage my Pentecostal context, in part, by means of *Wirkungsgeschichte*. History of effects, *Wirkungsgeschichte*, is a relatively recent methodology being applied to the interpretation of Scripture. This approach, put forth most notably in biblical studies by Ulrich Luz,[65] seeks to understand the impact, influence, or effect that biblical texts have had on the Church and society throughout the centuries. In Luz's view, while historical-critical methods seek to reconstruct the original meaning of a text, a history of effects approach seeks in an intentional way to connect the text with the reader. Because Christianity has a relationship with Scripture as its sacred text, the history between the texts and its reader cannot be separated because this history 'is an expression of the text's own power'.[66] Luz states,

> Whatever we say about the biblical texts presupposes that we already have a relationship with them – directly, because we already know, love, or hate them; or indirectly, because we take part in a culture dominated by Christianity and speak a language formed by the Bible. We too are a product of the effective history of the Bible.[67]

Wirkungsgeschichte thus frees the interpreter from the almost impossible task of seeking to approach the text from a purely distant and neutral stance.

Luz maintains that there is no *one* true interpretation of a biblical text. This in itself is contrary to the stance of historical-critical interpretations which maintain that a text can only have one intended meaning. While the text itself is stable and does not change, interpretations of texts do change as they are read in new situations or as a result of new experiences in the life of the interpreter.[68] These changing circumstances cause readers to study and interpret texts in new and meaningful ways. With this said, however, a text cannot be completely subjected to any and all interpretations. Texts have been

---

[65] Luz follows Gadamer, who is the first to use the term. U. Luz, *Matthew in History: Interpretation, Influence, and Effects* (Minneapolis: Fortress Press, 1994).

[66] Luz, *Matthew in History*, p. 24.

[67] Luz, *Matthew in History*, p. 25.

[68] Luz, *Matthew in History*, p. 26.

(and continue to be) misinterpreted. This, too, is an important part of effective history.[69]

A particular strength of the history of effects approach to Scripture is that it emphasizes the power that biblical texts possess as an expression of 'the living Christ'.[70] As such, Scripture is held in high esteem as a *living* word for the present, rather than a static book of norms belonging to the past. Interpretation, then, continues to bring the power of Scripture to bear on the constantly changing situations and circumstances in the life of the Church.

Emerson Powery sees *Wirkungsgeschichte* as a helpful method for Pentecostals in their reading of texts because it 'requires that we examine the effects of different interpretations, including our own, as a basis for judging the validity of particular readings of the sacred texts'.[71] What should concern Pentecostals, writes Powery, is 'the effects our readings have had throughout our history and in the present-day on the Pentecostal movement'.[72] *Wirkungsgeschichte* complements Pentecostal hermeneutics by offering Pentecostals a means for both 'appreciating Scripture' and 'the interpretive tradition of Scripture by the community'.[73]

Of recent, Pentecostal scholars have begun to examine the effective history of biblical texts. One of the first to do so was Heather Landrus in a 2002 article on the effective history of 3 John 2.[74] In it, Landrus traces the history of interpretation of this verse from ancient times to modern in light of its use by a number of key historical figures.[75] Landrus includes a brief biography for each figure and

---

[69] Luz, *Matthew in History*, p. 28.

[70] Luz, *Matthew in History*, p. 37.

[71] E.B. Powery, 'Ulrich Luz's *Matthew in History*: A Contribution to Pentecostal Hermeneutics?', *JPT* 14 (1999), p. 15. For Luz's response to Powery see U. Luz, 'A Response to Emerson B. Powery', *JPT* 14 (1999), pp. 19-26. The value of looking to history of effects for Pentecostal hermeneutics was first raised by John Christopher Thomas in his Presidential address to the Society for Pentecostal Studies. See Thomas, 'Pentecostal Theology in the Twenty-First Century', pp. 3-19.

[72] Powery, 'Ulrich Luz's *Matthew in History*', p. 15.

[73] Powery, 'Ulrich Luz's *Matthew in History*', p. 16.

[74] H. Landrus, 'Hearing 3 John 2 in the Voices of History', *JPT* 11.1 (2002), pp. 70-88.

[75] Landrus includes Tertullian, Augustine, Bede, Ambrosius Catharinus, Isaac-Louis Le Maistre De Sacy, John Bird Sumner, Albert Banes, Carrie Judd Mont-

then suggests how the experiences of each person surveyed 'might have influenced the hermeneutical process' resulting in divergent understandings of 3 John 2.[76]

In 2003, John Christopher Thomas and Kimberly Ervin Alexander published an article on Mark 16.9-20 that examined, among other things, the history of effects of this passage for early Pentecostals.[77] The authors issue a clarion call for Pentecostals to reappropriate Mark 16.9-20 in Pentecostal theology.[78] After providing a text-critical analysis of Mark 16.9-20 and comments about the structural, literary, and canonical function of this text, the authors lift up *Wirkungsgeschichte* as a means for recovering the significance of this passage for Pentecostalism:

> Owing to this text's unrivaled significance in early Pentecostalism, perhaps biblical scholars working in the tradition have been too quick to dismiss the role of this text in the canon, owing to its non-Markan origins ... Perhaps theologians working within the tradition should be more intentional about its importance in the articulation of contemporary Pentecostal theology.[79]

Thomas's 2005 article titled 'Healing in the Atonement: A Johannine Perspective' is another example of the valuable contribu-

---

gomery, Oral Roberts, Kenneth Hagin, Raymond Brown, Fredrick Price, and Paul Yonggi Cho.

[76] Landrus, 'Hearing 3 John 2', p. 87.

[77] J.C. Thomas and K.E. Alexander, '"And the Signs Are Following": Mark 16.9-20 – A Journey into Pentecostal Hermeneutics', *JPT* 11.2 (2003), pp. 147-70.

[78] Thomas and Alexander survey the early literature of Pentecostalism and note that the Mark 16 passage served the movement as a 'kind of litmus test for the authenticity of their experience' (p. 150). Further, the authors trace the response of early Pentecostals to the text-critical issues surrounding the passage by showing that they were aware of the issues and affirmed the passage as canonical.

[79] Thomas and Alexander, 'And the Signs are Following', p. 170. See also the response to this article by R.W. Wall who affirms *Wirkungsgeschichte* as a responsible methodology for dealing with contested passages of Scripture. R.W. Wall, 'A Response to Thomas/Alexander, 'And the Signs are Following' (Mark 16.9-20), *JPT* 11.2 (2003), pp. 171-83. He challenges Thomas and Alexander in their hope for a reappropriation of this passage for Pentecostals by extending an invitation to the entire Church: 'If a Pentecostal reading of Mk 16 helps to prove its canonicity (and all of what this implies theologically and experientially), then a Pentecostal reading of Mk 16 must be formative of the faith and practices of the whole church' (p. 180).

tion of *Wirkungsgeschichte* to biblical studies.[80] Thomas first explores the healing accounts in the Fourth Gospel for the connections between healing and salvation. Second, he treats the relationship between the narrative location of the Johannine signs with the textual referents to Jesus' exaltation on the cross. Third, he points out other passages in John's Gospel that are relevant to his study, particularly Jn 10.10. Finally, Thomas appeals to the early literature of the Pentecostal movement as testimony to the close connection between healing and the atonement, especially based on Jn 3.14-15. Thomas discovers that Jn 3.14 is used in the *Apostolic Faith* as part of a more 'comprehensive understanding of healing as a prominent part of Gospel proclamation'.[81] He cites numerous articles found in early Pentecostal literature that make explicit connections between healing and the atonement based on Jn 3.14,[82] noting that early Pentecostals were 'more appreciative of the holistic nature of the life which Jesus brings than many contemporary readers'.[83] By listening to the voices of early Pentecostals, Thomas suggests that a more robust theology of healing in the atonement can inform both Pentecostalism and the church at large.

In his commentary on the Apocalypse, Thomas examines the effective history of the Apocalypse.[84] To date, this is the most comprehensive treatment of the effective history of the Apocalypse within Pentecostal scholarship, and it demonstrates for the reader the tremendous impact of the Apocalypse. The inclusion of the history of effects in a commentary written by a Pentecostal scholar will do much to aid Pentecostals in discerning their own history with the book as well as understanding its expansive impact on society and culture.

Other biblical scholars have examined the effective history of the Apocalypse, demonstrating the growing interest in its effective

---

[80] J.C. Thomas, 'Healing in the Atonement: A Johannine Perspective', in *The Spirit of the New Testament* (Blandford Forum: Deo Publishing, 2005), pp. 175-89.

[81] Thomas, 'Healing in the Atonement', p. 185.

[82] Thomas, 'Healing in the Atonement', pp. 185-88.

[83] Thomas, ''Healing in the Atonement', p. 189.

[84] See Thomas, *The Apocalypse*, pp. 60-90, where he examines the effective history of the Apocalypse under the following categories: apocalyptic Johannine writings, art, music, film, and commentaries.

history. These include Craig Koester,[85] Jon Paulien,[86] and Christopher Rowland. Rowland has written two commentaries on the Apocalypse in which he gives attention to its effective history. In the first commentary, Rowland devotes a short section specifically to the Apocalypse's effective history.[87] He references Martin Luther's negative assessment of the Apocalypse as well as the pivotal role the Apocalypse plays in prophecy schematics of Hal Lindsey and others. Additionally, Rowland's commentary includes the prayers of Janet Morley and the contemporary drawings of Kip Gresham – an artist whose abstract interpretation of the themes of Revelation draws the reader into a deeper understanding of the passage. In a second commentary, Rowland and co-author Judith Kovacs[88] introduce each chapter of the Apocalypse through its historical context and relation to other ancient Jewish and Christian texts but also

---

[85] C.K. Koester, *Revelation and the End of All Things* (Grand Rapids: Eerdmans, 2001), pp. 1-2, writes of the value of exploring the effective history of Revelation:

> Sometimes intriguing, sometimes disturbing, the story of Revelation's checkered history of influence on previous generations provides contemporary readers with an opportunity to think about the kinds of questions that our predecessors have asked, the assumptions that shaped their reading, and the effects of their interpretations on their communities. As we consider the perspectives of others, we are challenged to consider the questions and assumptions that we ourselves bring to the text, as well as the effects that our interpretations might have on our own communities. Looking at the past is a prelude to the task of seeking faithful and compelling ways to read Revelation in the present.

In his effective history, Koester's examination includes Dispensationalism, David Koresh and the Branch Davidians, and the influence of the Apocalypse upon music and hymnody.

[86] J. Paulien, 'The Lion/Lamb King: Reading the Apocalypse from Popular Culture', in D.L. Barr (ed.), *Reading the Book of Revelation: A Resource for Students* (Atlanta: Society for Biblical Literature, 2003), pp. 151-62. Paulien offers an intriguing analysis of the Apocalypse's influence upon North American culture in such things as movies, news-reporting (particularly of war-time or economic events), music lyrics, and science. He posits that much of today's cultural allusions are nonsensical without knowledge of the content of the Apocalypse. As a book that deals with many of the same issues that are dealt with by today's culture, Paulien sees that the Apocalypse offers its readers 'both a warning of doom and a promise of hope' (p. 161).

[87] C. Rowland, *Revelation* (London: Epworth Press, 1993), pp. 26-31.

[88] J. Kovacs and C. Rowland, *Revelation* (Blackwell Bible Commentaries; Oxford: Blackwell Publishing Ltd, 2004). This commentary series is unique in that it is the first to be 'devoted primarily to the reception history of the Bible' (p. xi).

provide numerous examples of the reception history of those particular texts extending from ancient to modern times.[89] In addition to these works, there are numerous examples of effective history on the Apocalypse in the periodic literature.[90]

This short survey of the use of *Wirkungsgeschichte* by scholars points to the growing interest in exploring how texts affect readers and how readers interpret texts. As a methodological partner with biblical studies, it provides another way to experience the power of Scripture. For Pentecostals, a history of effects approach that accesses the early literature of Pentecostalism holds much promise for connecting the movement with its historical and theological roots and enabling contemporary Pentecostals to be in 'experiential continuity' with early Pentecostalism[91] as they hear the testimonies of their spiritual ancestors.[92]

---

[89] Kovacs and Rowland, *Revelation*, p. 248, state in a postscript:

One thing that becomes clear from a survey of the history of the reception of the Apocalypse is that it is not so easy to pin down one original meaning of the text and then use that to evaluate the later interpretations, for the exegesis of such an allusive text is always going to resist the desire for an authoritative interpretation.

[90] Examples include M. Barkun, 'Divided Apocalypse: thinking about the end in contemporary America', *Soundings* 66.3 (Fall 1983), pp. 257-80; R.K. Emmerson, 'Introduction: The Apocalypse in medieval culture', in R.K. Emmerson and B. McGinn (eds.), *Apocalypse in the Middle Ages* (Ithaca: Cornell University Press, 1992), pp. 293-332; P. Szittya, 'Doomesday bokes: The Apocalypse in medieval English literary culture', in R.K. Emmerson and B. McGinn (eds.), *Apocalypse in the Middle Ages* (Ithaca: Cornell University Press, 1992), pp. 374-97; C. Vander Stichele, 'Apocalypse, art and abjection: images of the great whore', in G. Aichele (ed.), *Culture, Entertainment and the Bible* (Sheffield: Sheffield Press, 2000), pp. 124-38.

[91] Land, *Pentecostal Spirituality*, p. 221 offers the following challenge to Pentecostals: 'Contemporary Pentecostals should explore what it would mean to be in experiential continuity with the early movement in light of the claim to be in continuity with the apostolic church'.

[92] For the foundational role that testimonies play in Pentecostal spirituality, see Johns, *Pentecostal Formation*, pp. 126-27:

Testimony is the means of meshing the realities of life with the ongoing story of the faith community. Among Pentecostals, testimony can serve as a way of 'decoding reality' in order to analyze it for further action and reflection. It serves as a corporate liturgy, in which all are invited to speak, for each person has a testimony – a story – which when offered to the community serves to empower others ... [Testimonies] offer alternative realities when placed in dialogue with the Christian story. When a person has experienced an encounter with God, they are usually asked to testify. This serves to submit individual

V. The Use of Narrative Analysis

The final methodological element for this study is the employment of a narrative approach for reading the Apocalypse.[93] Because narrative critics define narrative as 'any work of literature that tells a story',[94] the Apocalypse is a narrative.[95] For Pentecostals, a narrative reading is a very natural way to encounter the Apocalypse because Pentecostals 'have been conditioned to engage the whole of Scripture as story'.[96] Developed in response to historical criticism,[97] narrative criticism is based on the premise that biblical narratives can be analyzed in the same way that secular literary critics analyze

---

experience to corporate judgment (with Scripture being held as the final authority) and to allow for experience to be given interpretive meaning.'

See also Thomas, 'What the Spirit is Saying to the Church', p. 118, who advocates that the testimonies of early Pentecostals must also be heard within the present-day Pentecostal community:

I would suggest that for the Pentecostal interpreter the hearing of testimonies should not be limited to the contemporary voices of the Pentecostal community but be extended by means of *Wirkungsgeschichte* to include the voices of those who have preceded us in discerning their way on this narrative journey.

[93] The term 'narrative' is often indistinct from 'literary'. See M.A. Powell, *What is Narrative Criticism?* (Minneapolis: Fortress Press, 1990), p. 19, who notes that narrative criticism is a form of literary criticism that developed 'within the field of biblical studies without an exact counterpart in the secular world'. I will consistently identify my reading as a narrative reading.

[94] Powell, *What is Narrative Criticism?*, p. 23.

[95] D.L. Barr, *Tales of the End* (Salem: Polebridge Press, 1998), p. 1:

Because it is part of the Bible, because it is used in our culture to advocate political agendas both of the left and right, because it utilizes an obscure set of images and ideas, because it is all divided up into neat chapters and discrete verses, because we are so familiar with a few of its symbols (such as the four horsemen or 666), it is easy to miss *the most important thing for understanding the Apocalypse: it is a narrative* (italics mine).

See also S. Saunders, 'Revelation and Resistance: Narrative and Worship in John's Apocalypse' in J.B. Green and M. Pasquarello III (eds.), *Narrative Reading, Narrative Preaching* (Grand Rapids: Baker Academic, 2003), pp. 119-22; J.L. Resseguie, *The Revelation of John: A Narrative Commentary* (Grand Rapids: Baker Academic, 2009).

[96] Archer, *A Pentecostal Hermeneutic*, p. 226.

[97] M. Sternberg, *The Poetics of Biblical Narrative* (Bloomington: Indiana University Press, 1985), p. 7.

novels and short stories.[98] Biblical narratives possess literary characteristics common to literature: narrator,[99] point of view,[100] plot,[101]
characters,[102] setting,[103] and rhetorical discourse.[104] My approach to

---

[98] J.L. Resseguie, *Narrative Criticism of the New Testament: An Introduction* (Grand
Rapids: Baker Academic, 2005), p. 18.

[99] The *narrator* is the one who tells the story and may or may not be identical
to the implied author. The narrator guides the reader through the plot; as such,
the narrator is regarded as reliable and knowledgeable. In biblical narratives, there
are two basic types of narrators: 1) third-person narrators who are omniscient;
that is, they tell the story from outside, narrate both public and private events,
and even reveal the inner thoughts and motivations of characters within the story
(as in the Gospels or Acts); and 2) first-person narrators who are limited in their
knowledge and often are participants in the events they are narrating (as in the
'we' passages in Acts and in the 'I' of Revelation). Pertinent to the Apocalypse is
the idea that first person narration 'lends authority to what is written since the
narrator presumably is a witness to the events'. Resseguie, *Narrative Criticism of the
New Testament*, p. 168.

[100] The point of view is the 'norms, values, and general worldview' established
by the implied author/narrator to which the readers are to accept and adopt as
their own. See Powell, *What is Narrative Criticism?*, pp. 24-25. In addition to the
author's 'evaluative' point of view, biblical narratives establish God's evaluative
point of view which the reader is to accept as 'true and right' and, as in the case
with Revelation, the *alternative* evaluative point of view of the Dragon. Powell
expresses the impact of this upon the implied reader: 'the implied reader will tend
to empathize with those characters who express God's point of view and will
seek distance from those characters who do not. Thus, in the process of telling
these stories, the implied authors provide standards that govern their interpretation' (p. 25). Point of view is established by the implied author/narrator through
the 'actions of the characters, their dialogue, their rhetoric and the setting' of the
narrative. See Resseguie, *Narrative Criticism of the New Testament*, p. 167. For an
extended discussion of how the narrator establishes point of view through these
vehicles, see his chapter 5.

[101] Plot refers to the events taking place within the narrative. Plot is not limited to physical action; thus, elements such as speech and revealed thoughts
should be considered as part of the plot line. Powell, *What is Narrative Criticism?*,
p. 35. In a narrative, elements that make up the plot are linked together by some
sort of causal relationship, either explicitly stated or implied, that helps the reader
create meaning. Conflict is also key to plot development.

[102] Characters are the figures that carry out the plot. Characterization can be
revealed by the narrator telling the reader something about a character or showing something about the character, often through the viewpoint of other characters in the narrative. See Powell, *What is Narrative Criticism?*, pp. 52-33. Additionally, the readers make evaluations of the characters in light of the traits assigned to
them in the story. Characters can then be distinguished based on their traits: *round*
characters are those that have 'potentially conflicting traits,' *flat* characters are
those that are 'consistent and predictable,' and *stock* characters are those who
have a single trait. Characters can also be dynamic (those whose traits and/or
point of view change over the course of the narrative) or static (those whose
traits and/or point of view remain steady throughout the narrative). See Res-

the text of the Apocalypse is informed by such formal literary characteristics but does not consist of observations that are controlled by these formal categories; rather the close analysis of the narrative will follow the lead of the text, incorporating such formal observations where appropriate.

One of the key features of narrative analysis is its emphasis upon the final form of the biblical text. The text is viewed as an 'entire communication' that contains the sender (implied author),[105] message (narrative), and receiver (implied reader).[106] Narrative critics are concerned with the 'world of the text' rather than the 'world behind the text'.[107] Pheme Perkins writes, 'Narrative criticism seeks to facilitate entry into the complexity of the narrative world, not exit

---

seguie, *Narrative Criticism of the New Testament*, pp. 123-26. Readers either relate to or distance themselves from characters presented in the narrative based on the degree of empathy, sympathy, or antipathy created by the implied author/narrator. Powell, *What is Narrative Criticism?*, pp. 56-58.

[103] Setting refers to the context(s) in which the plot unfolds. Narratives can take place in one setting or, as in Revelation, multiple settings. In addition to spatial or temporal settings (whether real or symbolic), narratives can have social settings related to customs, cultures, political structures, and so forth. See Powell, *What is Narrative Criticism?*, pp. 69-83; Resseguie, *Narrative Criticism of the New Testament*, pp. 94-114 identifies six different types of settings in the New Testament: topographical, architectural, props (such as clothing), temporal, social and cultural, and religious.

[104] Narrative critics explore the way a story is told through the implementation of rhetorical elements such as symbolism, irony, repetition, chiasm, rhetorical questions, simile, metaphor, and numerous other literary devices employed by the implied author/narrator. The way in which the story is told is carefully designed to persuade the reader to adopt the point of view of the implied author/narrator. See Powell, *What is Narrative Criticism?*, pp. 32-33 for a listing of 15 categories found in biblical narratives. See Resseguie, *Narrative Criticism and the New Testament*, pp. 41-86.

[105] Powell, *What is Narrative Criticism?*, p. 5, identifies the implied author as the one 'reconstructed by the reader from the narrative'. P. Perkins, 'Crisis in Jerusalem? Narrative Criticism in New Testament Studies', *Theological Studies* 50 (1989), p. 300, maintains that the implied author and narrator are distinct entities.

[106] The implied reader may or may not be the same as the real reader or even the 'ideal reader' – the one 'who perceives the ironies and interconnections in the development of the plot and who shares the implied author's presentation of the various characters'. P. Perkins, 'Crisis in Jerusalem?', p. 301.

[107] Powell, *What is Narrative Criticism?*, pp. 4-5, summarizes the shift from historical criticism to literary criticism: 'The New Criticism rejected the notion that background information holds the interpretive key to a text'. In fact, Powell notes, 'it is now accepted as axiomatic in literary circles that the meaning of literature transcends the historical intentions of the author'.

from it into history or theology'.[108] This is conducive for Pentecostals because issues related to historical criticism are simply not at the heart of their worldview. Pentecostals enter into and experience the story of Scripture both through their reading and hearing of it. The goal is to *hear* the Word of God and encounter the God of the Scriptures, an experience not unlike John's in the Apocalypse.

The concept of *hearing* the Word of God resonates deeply with Pentecostals because of the largely oral nature of Pentecostalism.[109] Lee Roy Martin lifts up the biblical concept of *hearing* (שמע)[110] as an important and appropriate model for Pentecostals because a) It is a biblical term. b) It reflects the oral nature of both the biblical and Pentecostal contexts. c) It is 'relational, implying the existence of a "person" who is speaking the Word'. d) It 'denotes a faithful adherence to the Word, since in Scripture to hear often means to obey'. e) It encourages 'transformation' as one hears and obeys the Word. f) It 'demands humility because, unlike the process of "reading" Scripture, "hearing" entails submission to the authority of the Word of God'.[111] The Apocalypse was written to its audiences to be *heard*, thus, I will intentionally adopt the language of *hearing* and *hearers* in my approach to the text.[112]

---

[108] Perkins, 'Crisis in Jerusalem?', p. 300.

[109] On the oral theology and liturgy of Pentecostalism, see Johns, *Pentecostal Formation*, pp. 87-91; W.J. Hollenweger, 'The Black Roots of Pentecostalism' in A. Anderson and W.J. Hollenweger (eds.), *Pentecostals after a Century: Global Perspectives on a Movement in Transition*, p. 36.

[110] See also G. Kittel, 'ἀκούω', *TDNT*, I, pp. 219-20.

[111] Martin, *The Unheard Voice of God*, p. 53. See also L.R. Martin, 'Longing for God: Psalm 63 and Pentecostal Spirituality', *JPT* 22 (2013), pp. 54-76 for a Pentecostal hearing of Psalm 63 in which he advocates that the affective dimension of the psalms resonates with Pentecostal spirituality. In particular, Psalm 63, with its emphasis on longing for encounter with God accords well with Pentecostalism's emphasis on encounter with God. Such a hearing, Martin argues, requires four 'cooperative moves' by the hearer: 1) The hearer must 'identify and acknowledge the affective dimensions' of the text; 2) The hearer must 'acknowledge his or her own passions' brought to the task of interpretation; 3) The hearer must 'be open to the emotive impact' of the Scripture; and 4) The hearer must 'allow himself or herself to be transformed by the affective experiencing' of the text (pp. 59-60).

[112] The implementation of the language of hearing does not negate the obvious fact that I am also *reading* the text of the Apocalypse. The Apocalypse itself identifies both a reader and hearers (1.3), yet there is a clear emphasis placed on hearing, especially hearing what the Spirit has to say to the churches (Revelation 2–3). My commitment to hearing reinforces the oral/aural nature of Scripture as well as the oral/aural nature of my Pentecostal tradition.

An emerging consensus on the use of narrative as a fitting literary methodological approach for Pentecostals has produced a number of fresh interpretations of biblical texts. This is not to say that Pentecostals are the only ones using narrative approaches to Scriptures; rather, it is to say that many Pentecostal scholars are finding narrative methodological approaches to be quite conducive to the way in which Pentecostals approach texts.[113] Pentecostal biblical scholars who have made use of narrative approaches to texts include R.D. Moore, J.C. Thomas, L.R. McQueen, L.R. Martin, and R. Waddell.[114] As to the use of narrative with the Apocalypse specifically, two recent commentaries, one by Resseguie and the other by Thomas, offer narrative readings of the Apocalypse.[115] This study will continue both of these trajectories by employing narrative criticism to produce a fresh hearing of Revelation as a liturgical text. For my own Pentecostal tradition, this hearing, especially as combined with the effective history gleaned from early Pentecostal literature, will encourage a renewed appreciation and retrieval of the Apocalypse as *Spirit*ed and doxological.

VI. Overtures Toward the Construction of a Pentecostal Theology of Worship

Worship is a central feature of Pentecostalism. In worship, Pentecostals expect to encounter God. Of recent, there has been a move

---

[113] Archer, *A Pentecostal Hermeneutic*, p. 226, identifies narrative as the 'most helpful contemporary literary method that could be woven into a strategy for Pentecostals' because it 'allows for the dialectic interaction of the text and reader in the negotiation of meaning'. See also Martin, *The Unheard Voice of God*, pp. 14-15; Green, *Toward a Pentecostal Theology of the Lord's Supper*, pp. 183 and 189; S.A. Ellington, 'Locating Pentecostals at the Hermeneutical Round Table', *JPT* 22.2 (Fall 2013), pp. 206-25.

[114] Moore, 'Canon and Charisma in Deuteronomy'; Thomas, 'Women, Pentecostals and the Bible'; L.R. McQueen, *Joel and the Spirit: The Cry of a Prophetic Hermeneutic* (JPTSup 8; Sheffield: Sheffield Academic Press, 1995; Cleveland: CPT Press, 2009); Martin, *The Unheard Voice of God*; Waddell, *The Spirit of the Book of Revelation*; Thomas, *The Apocalypse*. Thomas' commentary is the first narrative approach to the Apocalypse by a Pentecostal.

[115] Resseguie, *The Revelation of John: A Narrative Commentary*; Thomas, *The Apocalypse*.

within scholarship to study and describe Pentecostal worship. The most thorough study is Daniel E. Albrecht's monograph, *Rites in the Spirit* in which he analyzes the worship practices of three North American Pentecostal/Charismatic churches.[116] Sociologists Donald E. Miller and Tetsunao Yamamori examine several facets of global Pentecostalism, including worship.[117] Keith Warrington likewise includes a descriptive account of Pentecostal worship in his work on Pentecostal theology.[118] Mark Cartledge's study on the Hockley Pentecostal Church in the UK provides insights into their worship practices and discusses the topic of a Pentecostal theology of worship.[119] This growing body of scholarship (more of which will appear in the final chapter) affirms the central role of worship in Pentecostalism across the globe. The contention of this study is that the Apocalypse is a liturgical text concerned with worship. As such, the Apocalypse has much to offer Pentecostals in this regard. The final chapter of this study will provide a summation of the central tenants concerning worship derived from the narrative reading of the Apocalypse. These findings will then be put into conversation with Pentecostal spirituality and praxis as a way to offer overtures toward the construction of a Pentecostal theology of worship based on the Apocalypse.

VII. Summary

This chapter has laid out the reading strategy that will be employed in the subsequent chapters of this study. First, my Pentecostal context provides an interpretive lens through which I will read Revelation. By way of brief orientation, I summarized the origins and development of Pentecostalism (particularly classical Pentecostalism)[120] in my North American context as well as provided an orien-

---

[116] D.E. Albrecht, *Rites in the Spirit: A Ritual Approach to Pentecostal/Charismatic Spirituality* (JPTSup 17; Sheffield: Sheffield Academic Press, 1999).

[117] D.E. Miller and T. Yamamori, *Global Pentecostalism: The New Face of Christian Social Engagement* (Berkeley and Los Angeles: University of California Press, 2007).

[118] Warrington, *Pentecostal Theology*, pp. 219-26.

[119] M.J. Cartledge, *Testimony in the Spirit: Rescripting Ordinary Pentecostal Theology* (EPPET; Farnham, UK: Ashgate Publishing Limited, 2010), pp. 29-54.

[120] Classical Pentecostal groups are the Assemblies of God, the Church of God (Cleveland, TN), the Church of God in Christ (Memphis, TN), the Interna-

tation to Pentecostal hermeneutics with its emphasis upon Scripture, community, and Spirit as dialogue partners. The second part of my reading strategy employs *Wirkungsgeschichte* as a way to explore the effective history of the worship found in the Apocalypse on early Pentecostals. I laid out a description of *Wirkungsgeschichte*, provided examples of Pentecostal scholars who have employed the method on various biblical texts, and briefly surveyed works that contain effective history pieces. Because the early literature of Pentecostalism is primarily testimonial in nature and because testimonies continue to have formational value in Pentecostalism today, a history of effects chapter that explores the early literature in search of the connection between its worship and the Apocalypse will provide a bridge between the text and the contemporary reader. The third element of the reading strategy is to utilize narrative criticism in reading the Apocalypse. This is a methodology conducive for Pentecostals, but it is also emerging as a methodological approach in recent treatments of the Apocalypse. The final piece of the study will be to integrate the central tenants of what the Apocalypse reveals about worship with Pentecostal spirituality and praxis in an effort to make a contribution toward a Pentecostal theology of worship.

---

tional Pentecostal Holiness Church, and the International Church of the Foursquare Gospel.

3

EFFECTIVE HISTORY: THE APOCALYPSE IN EARLY PENTECOSTAL LITERATURE

I. Introduction

The purpose of this chapter is to examine early North American Pentecostal literature to ascertain to what extent early Pentecostals were influenced in their worship by the Apocalypse. To this end, I will survey publications in the Wesleyan-Holiness and Finished Work traditions from the first decade (1906–1916) of the Pentecostal movement, which has been identified by some scholars as the 'heart' of the movement.[1] Part of the reason for limiting my reading to the first decade is due to the confines of space for this study; however, I would argue that the real spirituality of early Pentecostalism emerges primarily in the testimonies submitted to the newly formed Pentecostal periodicals by ordinary men and women who wrote to relate their experiences of Pentecost. I will first survey the Wesleyan-Holiness publications *The Apostolic Faith, Bridegroom's Messenger,* and *Church of God Evangel* followed by the Finished Work publications *The Pentecost, Latter Rain Evangel, Word and Witness,* and *The Christian Evangel.*

---

[1] Steve Land follows Hollenweger's assertion that the first ten years of the Pentecostal movement represent its 'heart' rather than its infancy. Land, *Pentecostal Spirituality*, p. 47; W.J. Hollenweger, 'Pentecostals and the Charismatic Movement', in C. Jones, G. Wainwright & E. Yarnold, SJ (eds.), *The Study of Spirituality* (London: SPCK, 1986), p. 551.

II. Wesleyan-Holiness Publications

The Apostolic Faith

The Apostolic Faith published by William Seymour was the paper that grew out of the Azusa Street revival.[2] It chronicles not only the events at the Azusa Mission but also includes testimonials and mission reports from all over the world as well as sermonic material and doctrinal instruction from William Seymour. The testimonies, emerging from recipients of the Pentecostal message, document the spread of Pentecostalism around the globe. Additionally, the testimonies relate supernatural healings and other manifestations taking place through the power of the Holy Spirit.

The Apostolic Faith is filled with references and allusions to the Apocalypse. One of the ways in which the early Pentecostal community saw themselves was as the bride of Christ preparing for the great Marriage Supper of the Lamb. H.M. Turney writes, 'I believe this movement is the last call that this world will receive before He comes for His bride. Rev. 19.7, 8'.[3] The early Pentecostals lived with the lively expectation of the soon return of Jesus Christ. Throughout the literature, Jesus' words in Revelation – 'Behold I come quickly' – are sounded as the rallying cry for spreading the good news of Jesus around the world.[4] They saw the multi-ethnic component of the revival at Azusa as a further indication that the Lord's

---

[2] Its first publication in September 1906 documented the outpouring of the Holy Spirit and the subsequent revival that ensued. The periodical was published free of charge from September 1906 until May 1908, and Seymour stated that by the end of 1907, the press was putting out 40,000 copies that were sent all over the world. *AF* 1.12 (January, 1908), p. 2.

[3] *AF* 1.3 (November, 1906), p. 2; *AF* 1.5 (January, 1907), pp. 1, 3. The early Pentecostals believed that only those who were saved, sanctified, and filled with the Holy Spirit would be invited to the marriage supper of the Lamb. William Seymour states in the same issue (p. 2, col. 1),

> Dearly beloved, the Scripture says, 'Blessed are they which are called to the marriage supper of the Lamb.' Rev. 19, 9. So they are blessed that have the call. Those that will be permitted to enter in are those who are justified, sanctified, and baptized with the Holy Ghost – sealed unto the day of redemption. O may God stir up His waiting bride everywhere to get oil in their vessels with their lamps that they may enter into the marriage supper. The Holy Ghost is sifting out a people that are getting on the robes of righteousness and the seal in their forehead. The angel is holding the winds now till all the children of God are sealed in their foreheads with the Father's name.

[4] *AF* 1.2 (October, 1906), p. 3.

return was near: 'One token of the Lord's coming is that He is melt-
ing all races and nations together, and they are filled with the power
and glory of God. He is baptizing by one spirit into one body and
making up a people that will be ready to meet Him when He
comes'.[5] Throughout the periodical, Jesus is identified as the Lamb,[6]
the one who walks among the candlesticks,[7] and the 'king of kings
and lord of lords'.[8] The millennial reign of Christ,[9] white robes,[10]
and the heavenly city, New Jerusalem,[11] are other key images from
the Apocalypse that surface in the periodical. A sermon by Seymour
on the seven messages to the churches of Revelation contains application to the fledgling Pentecostal movement.[12] An unsigned
sermon on being full overcomers based on Revelation 14 appears in
the January, 1908 issue.[13] Pentecostals saw themselves as overcoming 'by the blood of the Lamb and the word of their testimony'.[14] In
addition to those above, direct citations of Revelation appear
throughout the paper.[15]

While one might expect such use of the Apocalypse as a source
for eschatological imagery, the testimonial literature also provides

---

[5] *AF* 1.6 (February-March, 1907), p. 7.

[6] *AF* 1.2 (October, 1906), p. 4; *AF* 1.3 (November, 1906), p. 2; *AF* 1.8 (May,
1907), p. 1; *AF* 1.11 (October-January, 1908), p. 2; *AF* 1.12 (January, 1908), p. 4;
AF 2.13 (May, 1908), p. 3.

[7] *AF* 1.5 (January, 1907), p. 1; *AF* 1.9 (June-September, 1907), p. 2.

[8] *AF* 1.8 (May, 1907), p. 2; *AF* 1.10 (September, 1907), p. 4.

[9] *AF* 1.6 (February-March, 1907), p. 8; *AF* 1.9 (June-September, 1907), p. 4.

[10] *AF* 1.1 (September, 1906), p. 4; *AF* 1.7 (April, 1907), p. 3.

[11] *AF* 1.6 (February-March, 1907), pp. 4, 8; *AF* 1.7 (April, 1907), p. 4; *AF* 1.9
(June-September, 1907), p. 3; *AF* 1.11 (October-January, 1908), p. 2.

[12] *AF* 1.11 (October-January, 1908), p. 3.

[13] *AF* 1.12 (January, 1908), p. 2. In a later issue, readers are given the thirteen
promises to the overcomer as found in Revelation 2–3. *AF* 1.13 (May, 1908), p.
3.

[14] *AF* 1.4 (December, 1906), p. 3; *AF* 1.5 (January, 1907), p. 3; *AF* 1.7 (April,
1907), p. 4.

[15] *AF* 1.2 (October, 1906), p. 2 (Rev. 21.8; 20.10); p. 4 (Rev. 1.6, 7); *AF* 1.3
(November, 1906), p. 4 (Rev. 3.20); *AF* 1.4 (December, 1906), p. 1; *AF* 1.5 (January, 1907), p. 2 (Rev. 3.21, 22; 19, 20, 20.2, 10); p. 3 (Rev. 20.15), p. 4 (Rev.
20.14-15); *AF* 1.6 (February-March, 1907), p. 5 (Rev. 19.6); *AF* 1.8 (May, 1907),
p. 2 (Rev. 20.6), p. 4 (Rev. 3.15-22); *AF* 1.9 (June-September, 1907), p. 1 (Rev.
22.20); *AF* 1.10 (September, 1907), p. 4 (Rev. 2.17; 20.4); *AF* 2.13 (May, 1908), p.
3 (Revelation 2–3), p. 4 (Rev. 22.17).

glimpses into the worship of Azusa and the revivals it sparked around the world. Although these references to worship are almost made in passing or are simply a part of the narrative climax of relating an account of Spirit Baptism, they nonetheless reveal a connection to the Apocalypse that extends beyond eschatological longings. Sister J.S. Jellison's testimony is a prime example:

> Salvation has come. Hallelujah! God has come our way at last. Amen. Last Friday afternoon at Francis Jones' a few of us were gathered pleading for the baptism of the Holy Spirit and He gave us the desire of our hearts at last. Glory, O glory. Two of us received our baptism, Sister Leyden and I. The rest are hard after Him … There is quite a company of us. Sister Leyden lay under the power for several hours and talked and sang in the Spirit and the Lord let me join in the song and sing too. Glory, glory, hallelujah! Blessed be the name of Jesus. The song was 'Worthy is the Lamb' and nearly the whole chapter. She interpreted it afterwards.[16]

Jellison's testimony states that the song sung in the Spirit was '"Worthy is the Lamb" and nearly the whole chapter'. The odd reference to the 'whole chapter' implies that she is thinking of a chapter in the Bible. It must be a reference to Revelation 5 with the song of the Spirit arising from the song of Revelation 5.12, 'Worthy is the Lamb having been slain to receive power and wealth and wisdom and strength and honor and glory and praise'. Jellison does not explicitly state that the song comes from Revelation 5; however, it seems clear that this passage provides the context for her statement.

Another connection with the Apocalypse occurs in the testimony of Mrs. A.A. Boddy from Sunderland, England. She writes of her Spirit Baptism experience and includes the following description:

> Much to my astonishment, I began to speak fluently in a foreign language – Chinese I think. The Spirit sang through me. The joy and rapture of this purely spiritual worship can never be described. If for no other purpose, I felt at last satisfied that 'there was no difference between me and them as at the bginning,' [*sic*]

---

[16] *AF* 1.12 (January, 1908), p. 1.

Acts xi., 15. Then came a vision of the Blood. As the Spirit spoke that word I was conscious that ALL heaven oh glory! (myself included) was 'worshipping the Lamb, as it had been slain' ... Then came more words in 'tongues' with the interpretation, 'Worthy is the Lamb; Jesus is coming'.[17]

Once again, this testimony assumes familiarity with Revelation 5. Indeed Revelation 5.6 records John's vision of seeing a 'Lamb standing as slain,' and the rest of the chapter depicts the worship of the Lamb by all living creatures in heaven and on the earth. Coupled with the two interpreted 'words' 'Worthy is the Lamb' and 'Jesus is coming,' the link with Revelation seems clear.

While the preceding two testimonies provide a clear reference to the contents of Revelation 5, there are numerous testimonies that seem to contain illusionary references to the Apocalypse:

Many have received the gift of singing as well as speaking in the inspiration of the Spirit. The Lord is giving new voices, he translates old songs into new tongues, he gives the music that is being sung by the angels and has a heavenly choir all singing the same heavenly song in harmony. It is beautiful music, no instruments are needed in the meetings.[18]

When we receive the baptism with the Holy Spirit, we may sing in tongues, because the Lord drops down sweet anthems from the paradise of God electrifying every heart. Many times we do not need these song books of earth, but the Lord simply touches us by His mighty Spirit and we have no need of organs or pianos, for the Holy Ghost plays the piano in all our hearts, and then gives the interpretation of the song and sings it in the English language. It is so sweet. It is heaven below.[19]

Mildred composed a piece of music and sat down to play it yesterday. It took my soul almost out of this land, while she played it, and the power came on sister Reece and she began to sing words, O so sweet and in such harmony with the music. How God flooded our souls as she sang. She could not remember

---

[17] *AF* 1.11 (October-January, 1908), p. 1.

[18] *AF* 1.1 (September, 1906), p. 1.

[19] *AF* 1.4 (December, 1906), p. 2.

them, but yesterday afternoon the power came on her again and she wrote them down. O you could hardly stay here, when they sing and play that piece. It's from the Paradise of God. If nothing else had happened but this, it ought to convince people.[20]

Several aspects of these statements are significant for this study. First, these testimonies reveal that the early Pentecostals believed they were receiving and singing songs and anthems of heaven, the Paradise of God. The description of heaven as the 'Paradise of God' comes directly from Revelation 2.7b, 'To the one overcoming I will give to him to eat of the tree of life which is in the paradise of God'. While it is possible that in the minds of these speakers they would think of Isaiah 6 or Lk. 2.14 as places where the music of heaven is mentioned, it is more likely that they have Revelation in mind because of its specific language of song (ἡ ᾠδη) to identify the music of heaven (Rev. 5.9; 14.3; 15.3). Second, the testimonies also mention angels. The presence of angelic beings in heaven, also a feature of Isaiah and Luke, is likewise found in Revelation. Third, the testimonies clearly express the idea that Pentecostal services regularly featured what came to be called 'The Heavenly Anthem' – songs sung by angelic choirs. In another testimony, a writer states, 'No choir – but bands of angels have been heard by some in the Spirit and there is a heavenly singing that is inspired by the Holy Ghost'.[21] Still another writer states, 'One of the blessed privleges [*sic*] conferred upon me was a place in that heavenly choir, the songs of which defy all power of humans to imitate. Hallelujah for His unspeakable gift'.[22] This music is also closely connected with the Spirit as it is the Spirit who baptizes and bestows the gift of song. The connection between the Spirit and the music in the testimonials is a feature that tips the scale in favor of Revelation, for in the Apocalypse the Spirit is intimately connected to God and the Lamb in the throne room of heaven where music abounds.

---

[20] *AF* 1.4 (December, 1906), p. 4.

[21] *AF* 1.3 (November, 1906), p. 1.

[22] *AF* 1.3 (November, 1906), p. 3. See also *AF* 1.5 (January, 1907), p. 1, where H.M. Turney writes of a Mrs. Williamson: 'Sister Williamson has received her Pentecost and God has put her in His heavenly choir, to sing the heavenly songs for His glory'.

The following testimonies further demonstrate that early Pentecostals were influenced by the imagery of the worship scenes in Revelation:

> Our brother who recently received was praising the Lamb of God (under the power of the Spirit) when he began a song without words for a time (worshipping in the Spirit) then a few utterances in tongues, and so on till he spoke most fluently.[23]

> I shall never forget that night. Why, I was raised from the depths of despair to the very throne of our God. (Right here the Spirit stopped me and sang through me praises to my blessed Redeemer and King; my Master whom to serve is my greatest joy.).[24]

The writers appear to have been influenced by Revelation with their references to praising the Lamb of God and being before the throne of God. The second testimonial seems to suggest a participatory sensory experience of actually being before the throne of God. The idea of 'meeting at the throne'[25] suggests a collapse of the space between the earthly and the heavenly world.

Often singing in the Spirit was connected to visions of heaven. A lengthy account of a child who has a visionary experience of heaven seems to have been precipitated by the 'wonderful spirit of song' in which the Spirit 'sang the songs of Zion' through the lips of those gathered for worship. In recounting her vision she tells of riding in a clean car on the clean street to the 'beautiful city of God' and seeing Satan in a dirty car on a dirty street headed for the 'dark abyss'. She goes on to describe the beautiful houses in the beautiful city of God as well as the Palace of the King. She sees Jesus sitting on a throne made of diamonds and pearls and preparations for a 'beautiful Christmas feast' where her family is present, dressed in 'transformed' clothing. She ends her testimonial by noting, 'And all the host sang a most beautiful song of praise'.[26] While visionary language is found in various places in Scripture, the combination of terms and imagery appears to point to a dependence on the Apocalypse. John sees New Jerusalem coming down from heaven. While

---

[23] *AF* 1.8 (May, 1907), p. 1.

[24] *AF* 1.5 (January, 1907), p. 4.

[25] *AF* 1.2 (October, 1906), p. 3.

[26] *AF* 1.5 (January, 1907), p. 3.

it is not specifically called the 'beautiful city of God' it is described with imagery evoking beauty, such as a bride adorned for her husband (Rev. 21.2) and having a radiance like a 'precious stone, like jasper, being clear as crystal' (Rev. 21.11). In the child's testimony, the 'beautiful city of God' is juxtaposed with seeing Satan headed for the 'dark abyss'. Clearly this is a reference to Rev. 20.3. Her description of seeing Jesus on a throne brings to mind Revelation 5. The 'transformed clothing' her family wears is likely influenced by the white robes given to the overcomers (Rev. 7.13-14; 19.8). In light of all of this, is appears likely that her description of the 'beautiful Christmas feast' is an allusion to the Marriage Supper of the Lamb (Rev. 19.9).

Frequently songs sung through the Spirit were about the return of Christ. Clara Lum testifies,

> O, it was so sweet to have Him [the Holy Spirit] talk and sing through me ... Sometimes I sang for hours and in a new voice and it did not tire me. He also interpreted. He said, 'Jesus is coming.' It rejoiced me so much, and then He sang a song right from heaven about His coming.[27]

Similarly, Miss Lillian Keyes is noted as singing and interpreting in the Spirit. Her interpretation is recorded in hymnic fashion:

> Jesus is coming again,
> Coming again so soon,
> And we shall meet Him then.[28]

This short song seems to combine elements of 1 Thessalonians 4 along with the New Testament's message of the return of Jesus. However, for the writer the singing of the song as well as its interpretation is clearly connected with the Spirit of God. Coupled with Clara Lum's acknowledgement that the song the Spirit sang of Jesus' return is a 'song right from heaven' suggests that the background for Miss Keyes' song is Jesus's own words from Revelation, 'I am coming quickly' (Rev. 22.7, 12, 20).

---

[27] *AF* 1.6 (February-March, 1907), p. 8.
[28] *AF* 1.2 (October, 1906), p. 3.

The *Apostolic Faith* records poetry and/or song lyrics submitted by various authors.[29] Some of these are identified as songs while others are identified as poems. Individuals testify to receiving the gift of writing and reciting poetry, even in unknown languages.[30] This suggests that for early Pentecostals such activity was clearly Spirit-led and intended for worship. One such entry is 'When Jesus Comes' by Brother Alfred Beck. Beck's poetry reflects meditation on the Scripture and is filled with the imagery of the Apocalypse. Due to its length of thirteen stanzas, I will only highlight seven consecutive stanzas of the text that reflect on the Apocalypse:

The bloodwashed saints in robes of light
With bodies glorified,
With glad hosannahs [*sic*] on their lips
Shall then be Jesus' bride.

The cross laid down, our burdens gone,
And crown of life we'll wear,
And standing close by Jesus' side,
His glory we shall share.

The marriage supper shall begin,
The marriage bells shall ring;
Angels and archangels shout,
And help the saints to sing.

The praises of Immanuel
Who died for Adam's race,
Who purchased such ecstatic joys
For sinners saved by grace.

---

[29] See *AF* 1.4 (December, 1906), p. 2 ('Baptized with the Holy Ghost'); *AF* 1.4 (December, 1906), p. 4 ('A Message Concerning Christ's Coming' and 'Jesus is Coming'); *AF* 1.5 (January, 1907), p. 1 ('Pentecost Restored'); *AF* 1.5 (January, 1907), p. 2 ('Hark! The Moments They are Passing!' and 'Holy Spirit be My Guest'); *AF* 1.5 (January, 1907), p. 4 ('A Song of Prayer'); *AF* 1.6 (February-March, 1907), p. 4 ('The Warfare, the Rapture and Afterwards'); *AF* 1.6 (February-March, 1907), p. 5 ('Glory!'); *AF* 1.7 (April, 1907), p. 3 ('The Signs of the Times'); *AF* 1.8 (May, 1907), p. 2 ('The First Resurrection' and 'Jesus is Coming'); *AF* 1.8 (May, 1907), p. 3 ('Jesus Talking to His Bride: Song of Solomon, 4.7'); *AF* 1.12 (January, 1908), p. 2 ('Press Toward the Mark').

[30] *AF* 1.6 (February-March, 1907), p. 8.

O God, how wonderful it seems
That Thou shouldst deign to call
From out of earth's dark race of men
A bride for Thy dear Son.

Our hearts rejoice to think, dear Lord,
That Thou wilt soon appear,
We read the signs in earth and sky,
And know that Thou art near.

Amen, e'en so, dear Lord, we say,
Come Jesus, quickly come,
And end the awful conflict here,
And take Thy loved ones home.[31]

Another aspect of the worship of early Pentecostals which is a regular feature of their testimonies is the experience of being under the power of the Spirit. Individuals testify to 'being slain' under the power of God,[32] laid out,[33] 'fall[ing] prostrate' under the power of God,[34] and falling 'like dead men'.[35] This experience was sometimes accompanied by involuntary kinesthetic movements and could last for minutes or hours.[36] W.H. Durham, a Chicago evangelist, testifies to such an experience when he visited the Azusa Mission:

But on Friday evening, March 1, His mighty power came over me, until I jerked and quaked under it for about three hours. It was strange and wonderful and yet glorious. He worked my

---

[31] *AF* 1.5 (January, 1907), p. 2. Other poems by Brother Beck are found in the following issues: *AF* 1.6 (February-March, 1907), p. 4; *AF* 1.8 (May, 1907), p. 2; *AF* 1.8 (May, 1907), p. 3.

[32] *AF* 1.2 (October, 1906), pp. 1, 2; *AF* 1.3 (November, 1906), pp. 1, 4; *AF* 1.6 (February-March, 1907), p. 7; *AF* 1.8 (May, 1907), p. 2.

[33] *AF* 1.3 (November, 1906), p. 1; *AF* 1.6 (February-March, 1907), p. 3; *AF* 1.6 (February-March, 1907), pp. 4, 8; *AF* 1.7 (April, 1907), p. 4; *AF* 1.8 (May, 1907), pp. 1, 2.

[34] *AF* 1.3 (November, 1906), p. 1; *AF* 1.6 (February-March, 1907), p. 8; *AF* 1.9 (June-September, 1907), p. 1.

[35] *AF* 1.6 (February-March, 1907), p. 5; *AF* 1.7 (April, 1907), p. 1.

[36] Brother Levi R. Lupton testifies of being on the floor 'under His gracious power' for nine hours. *AF* 1.6 (February-March, 1907), p. 5. M.L. Ryan testifies that little children 'shook for some hours under the power of God.' *AF* 1.7 (April, 1907), p. 4.

whole body, one section at a time, first my arms, then my limbs, then my body, then my head, then my face, then my chin, and finally at 1 a.m. Saturday, Mar. 2, after being under the power for three hours, He finished the work on my vocal organs and spoke through me in unknown tongues.[37]

What is intriguing about the entirety of Durham's testimonial (not all of which is included here) is that he also testifies to hearing the 'Heavenly Chorus' which he clearly identifies as coming 'direct from heaven'. He states, '… and when about twenty persons joined in singing the "Heavenly Chorus," it was the most ravishing and un-earthly music that ever fell on mortal ears … I know it came direct from heaven'. The experience of March 1st (quoted above) is actual-ly Durham's third such experience during his stay at Azusa. He tes-tifies to being 'down under' the power of God for two hours on Tuesday and two more hours on Thursday before receiving his Spirit Baptism on Friday. He describes the working of God during these times by acknowledging that a 'wonderful glory' came into his soul.[38]

Often those who fell under the power of God experienced vi-sions of Jesus[39] or of heaven.[40] By May 1907, this concept of a 'di-vine trance' is being defended scripturally due to the acknowledge-ment that there are those who 'look with disfavor upon falling un-der the power and many regard with suspicion visions and revela-tions'. Various New Testament examples are appealed to including the following: 'John also in Revelations [sic] says: "I was in the Spirit on the Lord's day." He heard Jesus speaking and says: "When I saw Him, I fell at His feet as dead." Just as so many in this mission have seen a vision of Jesus and have fallen at His feet as dead.'[41] For early Pentecostals, this experience in the Spirit was clearly connected to worship with the Apocalypse serving as one of the primary models.

---

[37] *AF* 1.6 (February-March, 1907), p. 4.

[38] *AF* 1.6 (February-March, 1907), p. 4.

[39] *AF* 1.7 (April, 1907), p. 1; *AF* 1.3 (November, 1906), p. 4; *AF* 2.13 (May, 1908), p. 1.

[40] *AF* 1.6 (February-March, 1907), pp. 1, 2, 8; *AF* 1.9 (June-September, 1907), p. 1.

[41] *AF* 1.8 (May, 1907), p. 3. See also p. 4 where one sister testifies that when she was prostrate before the Lord she thought that she would die, and she had no strength.

Finally, *The Apostolic Faith* is filled with exclamatory words of praise. Testimonies are punctuated with 'Hallelujah', 'Praise God', 'Praise the Lord', 'Praise His name', 'Bless His name', 'Glory to God', and 'Glory to Jesus'. People testify to singing, shouting praises, and worshiping. Indeed, C.E. Foster testifies to shouting 'all over the house'.[42] Such acclamations as well as types of worship (singing, shouting, worshiping) are well known from the Psalms, but such language and expression is also very much at home in the Apocalypse.

Summary

The Apostolic Faith testifies to the fact that the early Pentecostals at Azusa were familiar with the text and images of the Apocalypse. While the testimonials found within its pages primarily describe individuals' experiences of salvation, sanctification, healing, and Spirit baptism, their testimonies also unveil the worship of the early revival.

An examination of this literature reveals that the worship of the early Pentecostals at Azusa was influenced by the Apocalypse in a number of ways. These early Pentecostals saw themselves as worshiping the Lamb on the throne and joining in the heavenly chorus of 'Worthy is the Lamb'. It is almost as if the space between the earthly and the heavenly realms collapsed in the context of worship. The other-worldly singing of the 'Heavenly Chorus' by choirs of angels and the conclusion that such singing was inspired by the Holy Spirit reflects further influence of the Apocalypse. The early Pentecostals recounted visions and dreams in which they experienced heaven or Jesus. Quite often such sensory experiences happened while being under the power of the Spirit. John's experiences on Patmos are appealed to as justification for such encounters by means of the Spirit. Even their written ascriptions of praise, such as 'Hallelujah', are at home in the world of the Apocalypse.

---

[42] *AF* 1.8 (May, 1907), p. 1.

The Bridegroom's Messenger

The publication of *The Bridegroom's Messenger* began in 1907 in Atlanta, Georgia, under the editorship of G.B. Cashwell.[43] In many respects, *The Bridegroom's Messenger* is identical to *The Apostolic Faith* in format and content. Like *The Apostolic Faith*, *The Bridegroom's Messenger* evidences the significant role of music in the early Pentecostal revivals. Many testimonials mention specific song titles and/or quote song lyrics.[44] A spirit of worship and praise seems to be a key feature of the Pentecostal revival. In a testimony from the Apostolic Faith Camp Meeting in Portland, Oregon, an anonymous writer states,

> For hours the power fell in the big tabernacle filled with saints and sinners. It was the Holy Ghost, and the place was like heaven. The very ground seems holy since then. The sound of the shouting, singing in the Spirit and praying was like the roar of a cataract. It sounded like the music and was heard at a distance, and sinners came to see what was going on … Eternity alone will reveal the results of this meeting. The power began to fall during the testimony meeting while some were on their feet waiting for an opportunity to speak and while the chorus was being sung over and over:
>
> 'Yes, I'll sing the wondrous story
> the Christ who died for me,
> Sing it with the saints in glory
> Gathered by the crystal sea.'
>
> It seemed as if the scene about the crystal sea and the one on earth blended, and the shouting began which lasted an hour … It was like heaven. That is all one can say to describe it. You

---

[43] In 1908, Cashwell turns the editorship of the paper over to Mrs. E.A. Sexton. Originally a minister in the Holiness Church of North Carolina, Cashwell travelled to the Azusa Mission in California in November, 1906, and received the Baptism of the Spirit when Seymour and others laid hands on him. He brought the Pentecostal message back to North Carolina and much of the American South. H.V. Synan, 'Cashwell, Gaston Barnabas', in S.M. Burgess, G.B. McGee, and P.H. Alexander (eds.), *DPCM* (Grand Rapids: Zondervan, 1998), pp. 109-10.

[44] Songs such as 'The Comforter has Come', 'Hallelujah, Thine the Glory', 'All Hail the Power of Jesus' Name', 'I Remember Calvary', 'Anchored in Jesus', 'Lean Upon the Arms of Jesus', and 'Mansions in Heaven' are but a few of the songs mentioned.

could feel the presence of heavenly visitors, the angels and the stately stopping of Jesus ...[45]

The reference to the crystal sea derives from Revelation 4 in the description of the heavenly throne room. In stating that the 'scene about the crystal sea and the one on earth blended', the writer suggests that the space between heavenly worship and their own worship collapsed and merged into a collective experience. From a report of a camp meeting in Stouffville, Ontario, comes the following testimony: 'The spirit of adoration and worship in song was very manifest. Spirit-filled hearts sang the glad songs of Zion until the tabernacle seemed filled with the glory of God.'[46] A testimony out of Sunderland, England, describes the music of the convention as 'glorious and inspiring' and goes on to say:

> Sometimes it would be a grand act of worship – 'Holy! Holy! Holy! All the saints adore Thee.' Sometimes it would be a triumphant song of the blood of Christ which cleanseth. Sometimes in happy mood it would be – 'O yes! O yes! There's something more, There's something more than gold. To know that Jesus saves you now, is something more than gold.' A railway gatekeeper said in his testimony: 'I was coming to the meeting one night and a man said to me, 'There's some grand singing going on in there; what does it all mean?' 'Why, man, the convention's on, won't you come in?' So he said he would and they were singing – 'He will hold me fast, He will hold me fast, For my savior loves me so, He will hold me fast,' and the Lord got a hold that night, and praise Him, He's holding him fast today. Hallelujah![47]

Also from England, A.A. Boddy writes about the on-going revival services, 'There is a wonderful adoration of the Lamb, a wonderful knowledge of the presence of our Christ, with His arms uplifted in blessing over His dear ones as they worship Him and we cry with tears of joy, "O, come let us adore Him, Christ the Lord"'.[48] Of

---

[45] *TBM* 2.45 (September 1, 1909), p. 4.

[46] *TBM* 3.65 (July 1, 1910), p. 4.

[47] *TBM* 6.136 (July 1, 1913), p. 3.

[48] *TBM* 7.156 (June 1, 1914), p. 3.

note is the recognition that the saints are worshipping the Lamb, Jesus Christ, who is present with them in their worship.

From the inaugural issue forward, however, early Pentecostals were also singing songs birthed by the Spirit in both known and unknown tongues. Mrs. H.H. Goff writes of her healing at Cashwell's revival in Dunn, North Carolina, and then states, 'God has given me twelve different languages, enabling me to write several, and play beautiful anthems with the words on the piano'.[49] Another testimony records, 'We have heard Heavenly music in sweet songs sung in unknown tongue and unknown tune by Spirit-filled saints'.[50] The phenomenon of the 'heavenly choir' is mentioned throughout the periodical and is clearly a regular feature of Pentecostal gatherings. One particular description of this is significant for this study. In a report from a Pentecostal convention in 1910, the following is written:

> We had read about the 'heavenly choir,' that the Spirit is forming, but we never imagined its power and sweetness until we actually heard its notes, sounding out like a grand oratio of angelic voices ... One anthem that was poured forth upon one occasion was rendered with all the runs and trills and variations of a practiced choir, not one of them knowing a word or tune until it burst forth from their lips. The words often ran as follows:
>
> First voice: 'Praise the Lord, praise the Lord, praise ye the Lord.'
> Second voice: 'For He is worthy to receive honor, and glory, and power, and blessing.'
> Third voice: 'For He was slain from the beginning.'
> Fourth voice: 'And let all the ends of the earth praise our God.'
> Fifth voice: 'Hallelujah, hallelujah, Amen!'
>
> At times several were singing together, yet in perfect harmony. The anthem began by one voice, was taken up by an alto or tenor, and rolled on in rapturous sweetness to the end, which seemed to die away in the distant heavens.[51]

---

[49] *TBM* 1.1 (October 1, 1907), p. 4.

[50] *TBM* 1.3 (December 1, 1907), p. 3.

[51] *TBM* 4.75 (December 1, 1910), p. 4.

This beautiful description indicates that the Spirit directed the voices to sing words taken primarily from the worship of the Lamb in Revelation 5.

Included in the descriptions of the worship and music of the Pentecostal revival are remarks both about vocal and kinesthetic manifestations in the worship service. That this was also written about in *The Apostolic Faith* suggests that such manifestations were a normative experience for the early Pentecostals. In an article titled 'The Pentecostal Worshippers' the author writes, 'Did they talk in unknown tongues? Yes, from a little maid of seven years to a gray-haired sire of 77 years. And did they jump and shout and move their hands? Yes, more or less in all their services.'[52] Pentecostal services were marked by shouts of praises to God and shouts of victory.[53] Cashwell reports that in one of his meetings in Florida people would be lying on the ground as dead, some crying, leaping, or laughing.[54] In Germany, it is reported that in the meetings 'some were knocked down to the floor, some were overflowed gently while sitting in their seats. Some cried with a loud voice, others shouted, Hallelujah, clapped their hands, laughed, shouted for joy.'[55] In Arkansas, 'some are shouting; some are praying with all their might; some are jumping and clapping their hands and some laying prostrate under the power of God'.[56] In Georgia, the following testimony is given:

In one service that I witnessed there were only two prayers offered that was all, no testimonies, preaching or anything except shouting, leaping, jumping, hopping, dancing, falling under the power, writhing under the power, speaking in tongues, and a few words interpreted by the Spirit, lasting about two hours.[57]

---

[52] *TBM* 1.3 (December 1, 1907), p. 4.

[53] *TBM* 1.9 (March 1, 1908), p. 1; *TBM* 1.16 (June 15, 1908), p. 1; *TBM* 1.22 (September 15, 1908), p. 1; *TBM* 2.44 (August 15, 1909), p. 2.

[54] *TBM* 1.19 (August 1, 1908), p. 2.

[55] *TBM* 2.30 (January 15, 1909), p. 3.

[56] *TBM* 2.33 (March 1, 1909), p. 2.

[57] *TBM* 2.45 (September 1, 1909), p. 4. See also *TBM* 3.50 (November 15, 1909), p. 3; *TBM* 3.52 (December 15, 1909), p. 4; *TBM* 3.59 (April 1, 1910), p. 1; *TBM* 5.109 (May 1, 1912), p. 2.

Similarly in a Florida revival, a saint testifies, 'The meeting was so good that at times there would be as many as 40 or 50 leaping and dancing, shouting and talking in tongues all at one time'.[58] Such expressions appear to be viewed as appropriate responses of worship. A final testimony from China is illustrative of this point: 'At every night's tarrying service, the power fell and the shouts and prayers and singing and speaking in tongues mingled and went up to God in a volume of praise like the sound of many waters'.[59] The reference to 'the sound of many waters' finds its origin in the volume of praise offered to God and the Lamb in Rev. 19.6. Although there are no references in the Apocalypse to leaping or dancing, there are indications that kinesthetic movement is a feature of worship. The great joy of the heavenly hosts in Revelation 19 provides a setting in which physical worship such as leaping and dancing would be appropriate. Exclamatory words and phrases of praise, such as 'Hallelujah',[60] and 'Glory to the Lamb forever and ever'[61] tighten the link between their own worship and the worship of heaven.

The Bridegroom's Messenger is filled with songs and poems written by early Pentecostals. The fact that these are included amongst the testimonials suggests that they, too, are testimonies – testimonies of worship. As in *The Apostolic Faith*, many of these songs and poems are based on the images and text of the Apocalypse. Elder A.W. Orwig's song, 'The Wedding in the Air', is a wonderful example. Along with the chorus, I will quote stanzas one, two, seven, and eight:

(Chorus) Hail, rapt'rous [*sic*] wedding in the air,
When Jesus' bride hath met Him there,
From ev'ry nation, tribe and tongue,
And bliss Immortal hath begun.

Oh, there's to be a wedding,
More glorious and fair,
Than any earthly pageant,
The wedding in the air.

---

[58] *TBM* 5.115 (August 1, 1912), p. 2.

[59] *TBM* 8.167 (February 1, 1915), p. 1.

[60] *TBM* 1.7 (February 1, 1915), p. 4.

[61] *TBM* 1.7 (February 1, 1908), p. 2.

The Bridegroom is the Saviour,
The bride, His saints, who wear
The garments that are spotless,
Blest wedding in the air!

O brother, are you ready?
That blissful scene to share,
To join the marriage supper,
The wedding in the air?

The Spirit's sealing only
Can fit us to be there;
Oh, what a royal banquet,
The wedding in the air.

Orwig's song is based on the Marriage Supper of the Lamb (Rev. 19.7-8). Here the saints, the Bride, are given clean, linen garments. The sealing of the Spirit, which alludes to Spirit Baptism for early Pentecostals, is likely a reference to the sealing of the saints in Revelation 7.

Agnes Semple submits her song titled 'Signal Bell' which draws from the Parable of the 10 Virgins, 1 Thessalonians 4, and various texts of Revelation:

Awake, behold the midnight cry:
The Bridegroom's at the door;
Come forth and greet our glorious King,
Arise and Christ adore.
The pierced hand loans on the latch,
His welcome voice we hear,
Saying, Come, my love, and be at rest;
I've heard thy sighs and tears.

Our garments now keep white and clean,
Be ready for the Groom,
For soon He'll clasp us in His love,
Our Lord is coming soon.
Come, trim our lamps, be ready,
The Bridegroom's now at hand
To gather all His loved ones
In one united band.

To join the marriage supper,
To walk the golden streets,
To meet with friends so long apart,
In love of God complete.
We're longing to behold Thy face,
Our hearts expand to Thee;
Dear Lord, Thy promise Thou hast said,
The Church is one with Thee.

We're waiting for the trumpet call,
The dead in Christ shall rise;
The Bride who waiteth for her Lord
Shall meet Him in the skies.
Away on wings as lightning's flash
We'll sweep through cloud and sky,
Our Lord will then present His Bride
Made free from groans and sighs.

In glory bright with jeweled crowns
Arrayed in spotless white,
Partaking of the banquet feast
In rapturous delight.
Our Lord and King will then appear,
On Zion's mount He'll stand,
With tens of thousands of His saints
He'll lead the glorious band.[62]

Like Orwig, Semple's primary imagery is that of the Marriage Supper of the Lamb. She clearly identifies Jesus as the Bridegroom and the Church as the Bride in stanzas one and four respectively. The Bride is bedecked in a spotless white garment and has a jeweled crown (stanza five). Such imagery finds its source in the Apocalypse where white garments adorn the saints (Rev. 7.13; 19.8), and the overcomers are promised a crown of life (Rev. 2.11). That union with Christ will lead to a time free from sighs, groans, and tears reflect Rev. 21.4. Finally, the song ends with an allusion to Revelation 19 in which the rider on the white horse leads the armies of heaven in victory over the beast.

---

[62] *TBM* 3.53 (January 1, 1910), p. 1.

Sister Ida Terry is reported as singing the following song in the Spirit:

Come to this city I have prepared for you,
It's just ahead, It's just ahead;
Oh, glory, the beautiful city of love!
He will shield and protect you,
Oh, glory, for this city above!
Look ahead, look ahead.[63]

Sister Terry's song speaks of a beautiful city above that is prepared for the saints. This appears to be a reference to the heavenly city, New Jerusalem, as portrayed in Revelation 21-22.

The song 'Behold, I Come Quickly' is noted as being based on Revelation 22.7. The lyrics are as follows:

Behold I come quickly!
Blessed is he that keepeth the sayings
Of the prophecy of this Book –
I am Alpha and Omega,
The beginning and the end,
The first and the last.

(Chorus) Glory! Hallelujah! He is coming soon,
Glory! Hallelujah! In your hearts make room,
Glory! Hallelujah! He is coming soon,
Coming to the children of men.

Behold I come quickly!
I, Jesus, have sent Mine angel to
Testify unto you these things in the churches;
I am the root and the offspring of David,
The bright, and morning star,
The Lamb slain from the foundation of the world.

Behold I come quickly!
Hold that which thou hast,
That no man take thy crown;
I am He that liveth and was dead,

---

[63] *TBM* 2.35 (April 1, 1909), p. 3.

And behold! I am alive forevermore,
Amen! And have the keys of Hell and of death.

Behold I come quickly!
My reward is with me to give every
Man according as his work shall be,
He that is unjust, let him be unjust still,
He that is filthy, let him be filthy still,
And he that is holy, let him be holy still.[64]

This poem clearly reflects on more than just Revelation 22.7. Much of its text derives from the opening chapters of Revelation. Stanza one juxtaposes the blessing on those who keep the words of the prophecy (Rev. 1.3) with the words of Jesus in Rev. 22.13. Stanza two comes directly from Revelation 22.16 where Jesus says that he sent his angel with this testimony for the churches. The description of Jesus as the 'root and the offspring of David, the bright and morning star' is from Rev. 22.16. Stanza three derives from Rev. 3.11 where Jesus admonishes the church at Philadelphia to hold fast so that no one steal their crown and from Rev. 1.18 where Jesus declares Himself to be the living one who holds the keys of Hell and death. The final stanza is from Rev. 22.11-12.

Like the songs, the poetry found in *The Bridegroom's Messenger* often reflects the Apocalypse. Consider the poem, 'The Coming Christ':

Lo! He comes with clouds descending
Once for favor'd sinners slain,
Thousand thousand saints attending,
Swell the triumph of His train;
Hallelujah!
God appears on earth to reign.

Yea, amen, let all adore Thee,
High on Thine eternal throne!
Savior, take the power and glory;
Claim the kingdom for Thine own;

---

[64] *TBM* 7.154 (May 1, 1914), p. 1. Under the title to the song, the writer states, 'This song was heard by the composer as sung by a great number of beautiful voices in a vision. No pen, or singer of this earth can describe perfectly the beauty and glory of the exquisite harmony of these voices singing God's Holy Word.'

Oh, come quickly!
Everlasting God, come down![65]

This poem begins with a reference to Rev. 1.7, a prophetic word about the return of Christ. It further alludes to the one who was slain and who is worshipped on the throne (Revelation 5). The acclamation 'Hallelujah' in the context of the poem finds its origin in Revelation 19 as the multitudes of heaven rejoice over the reign of God. Finally, the prayer of 'come quickly' with which the poem ends not only resonates with John's own prayer in Rev. 22.20 but also equates Jesus with the 'Everlasting God'. Another poem, untitled and anonymous, likewise reflects the longing for the return of Christ:

Lord Jesus, come!
Let every knee bow down,
And ev'ry tongue to Thee confess,
The Lord of all come forth to bless,
Lord Jesus, come!

Spirit and bride
With longing voice, say, 'Come;'
Yea, Lord, Thy word from that bright home
Is, 'Surely, I will quickly come.'
Even so, Lord, come. footnote?

The dependence on the Apocalypse is hard to miss as the poem clearly draws on Rev. 22.17, 20, and 21.

The spiritual experience of being slain in the Spirit is amply demonstrated in *The Bridegroom's Messenger*. This experience is variously described as being (slain) under the power of God,[66] laid out,[67] prostrate,[68] or even, dead.[69] Often saints were in this condition for lengthy periods of time. Mrs. J.Y. Clark reports of being 'down un-

---

[65] *TBM* 5.124 (January 1, 1913), p. 1.

[66] *TBM* 1.5 (January 1, 1908), p. 4; *TBM* 1.7 (February 1, 1908), p. 4; *TBM* 3.72 (October 15, 1910), p. 2; *TBM* 7.157 (June 15, 1914), p. 3; *TBM* 7.158 (July 1, 1914), p. 1; *TBM* 7.159 (August 1, 1914), p. 3.

[67] *TBM* 1.8 (February 15, 1908), p. 2.

[68] *TBM* 2.33 (March 1, 1909), p. 2.

[69] *TBM* 1.19 (August 1, 1908), p. 2.

der the power' for six hours,[70] and another saint testifies to 'laying prostrate' for eight hours.[71] Visions seen during these experiences are also documented. As in other publications, these recorded visions are often based on the Apocalypse. Ruth O'Shields writes, 'Another vision I had was the throne and Jesus on it with a gold crown on. His face was white as wax'.[72] At a Pentecostal convention in Fyzabad, India, a woman testifies of having a vision of the slain Lamb, hearing the songs of the angels, and seeing the twenty-four elders fall down before the Lamb'.[73] Mattie Dennis recounts her vision where first she sees people going to hell and then she sees heaven:

> Then I was carried, or led upward through a heavenly atmosphere with the light remaining over my head. Then I saw the walls of the great city of God. Oh, the beautiful colors can never be told! And it dazzled like the sun. I now saw many bands of angels flying over and about the city. Then the hand led me through a shining gate, and all the host of heaven were praising God with voices and with all the music of heaven. The hand then let go of me and I saw it was the Lord Jesus, and he said to me, 'You are home but not to stay'.[74]

A testimony from a Maria Woodworth-Etter revival in Dallas, Texas, states: 'Sunday, God came in slaying power and twenty-one, like Saul, were struck down by the power of God and lay from one to eleven hours. They had wonderful visions of Heaven and of Jesus and all got up with shining faces, filled with the love of God'.[75] In another testimony about the same revival, a report is given of a minister's vision of the Holy City and the hearing of angels. He says, 'I saw the innumerable company of angels singing around the throne and was permitted to join in the song'. Those who were around him testified, 'while he was lying prostrated on the floor under the power of God, we heard him singing in tongues at the same

---

[70] *TBM* 1.9 (March 1, 1908), p. 3.

[71] *TBM* 1.16 (June 15, 1908), p. 3. See also *TBM* 2.45 (September 1, 1909), p. 4.

[72] *TBM* 2.42 (July 15, 1909), p. 3.

[73] *TBM* 3.56 (February 15, 1910), p. 4.

[74] *TBM* 5.105 (March 1, 1912), p. 3.

[75] *TBM* 5.119 (October 15, 1912), p. 1.

time he was in the Spirit and singing with the angels around the Father's throne'.[76] This appears to reflect the music of the heavenly throne room as found throughout Revelation.

The Marriage Supper of the Lamb is also seen in visions. One testimony describes the vision of a 12-year-old boy who sees the Bride's table 'all set, and God standing by it, and while under the power he kept saying, "Sinners, get ready, Jesus is coming soon!" He says there was nothing on the table, only, all set, ready to be filled when the Bride gets ready'.[77] In a missionary report from China, the testimony comes forth of a man who, while under the power of the Spirit, 'was taken into a room where the tables and chairs were all arranged for a feast'.[78] Both of these testimonies underscore the importance of the Marriage Supper of the Lamb for the Pentecostal community.

Summary

The Bridegroom's Messenger is perhaps to be seen as the true heir to *The Apostolic Faith*. In format and content it replicates *The Apostolic Faith* and provides a record of the spread of Pentecostalism across the American South as well as around the world. Its testimonial nature documents the early Pentecostal outpouring from its grass-roots inception. Like *The Apostolic Faith*, it provides glimpses into the worship of the early Pentecostals. This worship is highly influenced by the liturgy of the Apocalypse. In their songs, poems and visions, these early Pentecostals were connecting their worship experiences to the heavenly worship of the Apocalypse.

Evening Light/Church of God Evangel[79]
Begun in 1910 under A.J. Tomlinson, this publication was and continues to be the official voice of the Church of God (Cleveland, TN) Pentecostal denomination. Unlike the *Bridegroom's Messenger*, another paper originating in the South, *The Church of God Evangel* does not provide as much detail concerning the worship of this early Pentecostal group. Although also largely testimonial in format,

---

[76] *TBM* 5.120 (November 1, 1912), p. 3.

[77] *TBM* 1.18 (July 15, 1908), p. 3.

[78] *TBM* 9.179 (February 1, 1916), p. 2.

[79] The publication, which released its first issue on March 1, 1910, was originally titled *The Evening Light and Church of God Evangel*; however, in March 1911, the name was shortened to *The Church of God Evangel*.

attention is more focused on recounting experiences of salvation, sanctification, Spirit-baptism, and healing.[80] A curious feature of the publication is the revelation that this Pentecostal group endured great suffering and persecution for its beliefs and practices.[81] It is not without significance, then, that many references to the 'overcomers' texts in Revelation are found throughout its pages.[82]

Although attention to the actual worship practices of the Church of God saints is infrequently mentioned, there is an early testimony of a Baptist minister who visits one of their services. His testimony contains many of the key features that marked early Pentecostal worship services:

> When we got there they were singing; soon they had an altar service. They went to the altar – or as you would call it, the mourner's bench – and such a noise I never before heard. I really thought at first the whole bunch had gone crazy. About twenty-five men, women, and children were praying, shouting, yelling, and speaking some unknown tongue. The noise was something fierce, and never to be forgotten. Some were jerking as if they would be torn asunder, some fell over as if dead, some leaped, others ran, and all hands yelled glory! glory! and other cries of praises, with many 'amens' and 'praise God'.[83]

The apparent 'chaos' of the Pentecostal service is justified in a later issue by appealing to the noise of the singing and shouting in heaven.[84] A meeting conducted by Brother Llewellyn is described as one in which 'the power fell and the house was filled with audible praises, shouting and dancing in the Spirit. Hallelujah!'[85] In another testimony, the writer states that the saints were 'rejoicing, dancing,

---

[80] As the denomination takes shape, much space in the paper is devoted to reports of general assemblies and the business transacted therein. Lengthy articles and editorials as well as a weekly Sunday School lesson are also prominent features of the periodical.

[81] On the history of the Church of God, see C.W. Conn, *Like a Mighty Army* (Cleveland: Pathway Press, 1977) who also chronicles the persecution of the fledgling church (ch. 3).

[82] See for example *COGE* 5.11 (March 14, 1914), p. 4.

[83] *COGE* 1.9 (July 1, 1910), p. 2.

[84] *COGE* 1.12 (August 15, 1910), p. 6.

[85] *COGE* 5.15 (April 11, 1914), p. 5.

praising and weeping at intervals'.[86] Mrs. Annie Brown writes of a Florida meeting: '[T]he power fell in a way I never witnessed before, I never saw such leaping, dancing, laughing and shouting – talking and singing in tongues'.[87] Further justification and rationale is provided in an article by Z.R. Thomas on 'Operations of the Holy Spirit' in which he expounds on the power of God:

> Dear reader, I don't wonder at people jumping, leaping, dancing, trembling, shaking or falling under the mighty power of God. While a great many people say it is indecent for people to fall about as some of the pentecostal people do, but now we want to see what the bible says about that … We see that John, when he met with Jesus fell at his feet as dead. Rev. 1:17. We see also that he saw a vision of heaven while on Patmos and saw four and twenty elders fall down before him that sat on the throne and worship Him that liveth forever and ever. Rev. 4:10,11.[88]

It is of interest to this study that Thomas justifies physical manifestations of worship by appealing to John's experience before Jesus as well as to the elders' worship of Jesus. Although Revelation does not mention dancing and leaping, it is clear that for Thomas such manifestations are not incongruent with the worship of heaven. A.J. Tomlinson provides a report of an Alabama meeting in which people were 'slain' under the power of God. He quotes from his journal: 'People lay under the power for hours. Some groan and moan, some froth at the mouth, many are jerked violently, while some dance, others shout, and still others cry and have many motions of the body'.[89] While Tomlinson does not appeal to Revelation as Thomas does, his description gives witness to the normative nature of such manifold manifestations connected with worship in the Pentecostal services.

---

[86] *COGE* 5.17 (April 25, 1914), p. 8.

[87] *COGE* 5.20 (May 16, 1914), p. 7. See also *COGE* 5.24 (October 17, 1914), p. 4; *COGE* 6.2 (January 9, 1915), pp. 2, 4; *COGE* 6.9 (February 27, 1915), p. 4; *COGE* 6.17 (April 24, 1915), p. 4; *COGE* 6.19 (May 8, 1915), p. 1; *COGE* 6.30 (July 24, 1915), p. 3; *COGE* 6.32 (August 7, 1915), p. 3; *COGE* 7.24 (June 10, 1916), p. 2; *COGE* 7.53 (December 30, 1916), p. 2.

[88] *COGE* 5.24 (June 13, 1914), p. 8.

[89] *COGE* 1.15 (October 1, 1910), p. 5.

Frank Brown's testimony reinforces a connection between worship and heaven perceived by these early Pentecostals: 'We all look forward to the time when we will shout around the great white throne and never have to part'.[90] Likewise, another writes, 'The power fell and some played under the power, others sang while others danced. Praise God for the real foretaste of heaven in our souls'.[91] T.J. Byerley writes, 'I feel the glory in my soul now, for I know there is soon coming a time when we shall meet around the great white throne and sing praises unto God and the Lamb forever'.[92] Such testimonies indicate that the worship portrayed in the Apocalypse was indeed pedagogical for the early Pentecostals.

While not as plentiful as in *The Apostolic Faith* or *The Bridegroom's Messenger*, *The Church of God Evangel* does mention songs sung in the early Pentecostal meetings. Songs such as 'Higher Ground',[93] 'I Need Thee, O I Need Thee',[94] 'Where the Healing Waters Flow',[95] 'I Have Heard of a City',[96] 'There is a Fountain Filled with Blood', and 'Nothing but the Blood of Jesus'[97] attest to the practice of congregational singing. C.B. Reynolds writes of his desire to start a 'singing school' because 'the song service is a grand way to praise the Lord'.[98] A saint comments on the singing at a state camp meeting in Florida: 'The singing was of such spirit and vigor that it was plain to see that the Lord was being worshipped in song, at times the songs were interspersed with shouts and praises'.[99] Included also are songs and poems written by the saints. Many of these deal with themes and ideas from the Apocalypse. One such song is a 'prophetic song' given to a sister in tongues and interpreted by another sister. The last stanza is as follows:

---

[90] *COGE* 6.46 (November 13, 1915), p. 2.

[91] *COGE* 7.12 (March 18, 1916), p. 3.

[92] *COGE* 7.13 (March 25, 1916), p. 3.

[93] *COGE* 1.8 (June 15, 1910), p. 6.

[94] *COGE* 1.9 (July 1, 1910), p. 6.

[95] *COGE* 1.13 (September 1, 1910), p. 3.

[96] *COGE* 5.49 (December 12, 1914), p. 4.

[97] *COGE* 6.24 (June 12, 1915), p. 1.

[98] *COGE* 6.34 (August 21, 1915), p. 4.

[99] *COGE* 7.23 (June 3, 1916), p. 3.

So come up, my children, I'll gather you home.
You've fought a good fight, your reward is a crown.
You are free from man's taunts, from the devil and beast,
Come sit at my table and eat at my feast.[100]

This song speaks of a crown given as a reward to those who fight the good fight. While this could be a reference to Paul's words to Timothy in 2 Tim. 4.7-8, it also finds a home in the Apocalypse as the overcomer in Rev. 2.10 is promised a crown of life. This connection is further strengthened by the mention of the devil and beast (Revelation 13), and the invitation to eat at the feast (Rev. 19.7-8).

Mrs. I.V. Powers contributes a poem titled 'My Pentecost' in which the second stanza draws on imagery from the Apocalypse:

I received my Pentecost, the bride adorned;
I received my Pentecost for the marriage more,
I received my Pentecost, the abundant life,
And I'll be crowned the Lamb's own wife.[101]

This poem reflects the understanding of early Pentecostals who saw themselves as the Bride of Christ, awaiting the Marriage Supper of the Lamb. Another poem (or perhaps a stanza of a song) bears the marks of the Apocalypse:

Shall I meet you up there?
Where loved ones are waiting,
No night will be there,
It is one endless day.
No tears will be shed,
God will wipe them away;
No sickness and dying,
No pain we shall bear,
No parting with loves.
Shall I meet you up there?[102]

---

[100] *COGE* 1.11 (August 1, 1910), p. 1.
[101] *COGE* 1.14 (September 15, 1910), p. 1.
[102] *COGE* 6.9 (February 27, 1915), p. 3.

This poem/song draws on descriptions of the wonderful reality of the new heaven and new earth where there will be no night (Rev. 22.5) and no more tears, sickness, pain, or dying (Rev. 21.4).

Homer Tomlinson writes an article titled 'Song Service – The Singing in Dr. Gush's Church' in which he admonishes the saints to sing and even join the choir. He states, 'We'll sing in heaven, O how we'll sing – the angels can not [*sic*] compare with us as we sing'. Tomlinson ends his article with the following musical stanza:

> I'm goin' to sing, eternally sing
> Where the river of life is flowing
> And the beautiful trees are growing,
> I'm goin' to sing, eternally sing.[103]

The lyrics to this stanza are based on the description of the river of life with the trees growing on either side (Rev. 22.1-2). Tomlinson's admonition to sing is no doubt based on the music of heaven as found throughout Revelation. Clearly for Tomlinson, the singing of the saints is a warm-up for the eternal singing that will be experienced in heaven.

Reports of visions, often occurring during the worship service, appear throughout the publication. Quite frequently these visions are of the Marriage Supper or other scenes from the Apocalypse. In an eleven day revival held in Alabama, it is reported that people lay prostrate on the ground for hours seeing visions. One girl had a vision of the Marriage Supper 'with the table spread and ready'.[104] A Sister Daniels went into a 'trance' for four hours and had a vision of Heaven and talked with the saints there.[105] Similarly, a woman in Florida 'fell under the power' and had a vision of Heaven and Hell.[106] In another testimony, a woman recounts the following visionary experience:

> In my dream, I was in a great company of saints, such as is mentioned in Rev. 7:9-14. They were searching through the crowd to find one worthy to be the bride, the Lamb's wife … To my surprise they caught me by the hand saying 'this one may do' and

---

[103] *COGE* 6.36 (September 4, 1915), p. 3.

[104] *COGE* 1.12 (August 15, 1910), p. 4.

[105] *COGE* 5.42 (October 17, 1914), p. 7.

[106] *COGE* 6.26 (June 26, 1915), p. 4.

they led me up to where they were getting the wedding garment ready...[107]

It is particularly interesting that this woman sees herself in the great gathering of saints described in Rev. 7.9-14. These saints, clothed in white robes, are clearly described as those having come out of the great tribulation (v. 14). Whether this identification reflects the persecution of this Pentecostal band of saints is unclear. The woman is deemed worthy to be the Lamb's wife and is taken to receive a wedding garment (Rev. 19.7-8).

An eleven-year-old girl, Laurice Wiggins, recounts a vision she had during the singing in a worship service. She testifies to being 'carried off in a trance' and seeing Jesus and the angels. Jesus, who is dressed in a white robe, takes her to heaven where she sees 'a beautiful green place and all kinds of musical instruments in gold'. She continues:

> I played on the golden harp and He showed me a robe and a crown with stars in it that I should wear when I came to stay in heaven ... I saw Jesus sitting on a snow-white throne in the midst of that beautiful green place. There were a lot of people around Jesus all dressed in white robes with crowns on their heads ...[108]

Laurice describes herself as being 'carried off' to heaven, an experience reminiscent of John's in Rev. 4.1. Like John, she sees a throne. Her depiction of the throne being snow-white is drawn from the great white throne in Rev. 20.11. Laurice sees the heavenly throne room populated with people dressed in white robes with crowns. John portrays the white-robed throng in Revelation 7, and crowns and white robes are also promised to the overcomers in Rev. 2.10 and 3.5, respectively. At the end of her lengthy testimony, she indicates that Jesus instructed her to write her vision down for others. This is similar to Jesus' instructions to John (Rev. 1.19).

---

[107] *COGE* 7.11 (March 11, 1916), p. 1.
[108] *COGE* 7.38 (September 16, 1916), p. 3.

Summary

The Church of God Evangel provides documentary evidence to the worship of the early Church of God denomination. Although not as plentiful as some of its contemporaries in its descriptions of worship, it nonetheless bears witness to the same types of things seen in the other publications. It portrays lively worship characterized by hearty singing and shouting, both in known and unknown tongues, and a variety of kinesthetic components such as leaping, jumping, and dancing. Further, the phenomenon of being slain or under the power of God is a regular feature of Pentecostal worship. Quite often such an experience is accompanied by visions of Jesus and various heavenly scenes. These visions, primarily of the throne of God, the Marriage Supper of the Lamb, and the new heaven and earth, show the remarkable influence of the Apocalypse upon this early Pentecostal group. Original music and poetry is often based on the Apocalypse as well. The publication of these continues to suggest that such Spirit-inspired compositions are indeed intended for the worship of God and the Lamb.

III. Finished Work Publications

The Pentecost

The Pentecost appeared in 1908 and was published first in Indianapolis, Indiana and then in Kansas City, Kansas, under the editorship of J. Roswell Flower. A.S. Copley, who was the associate editor until January 1910, assumed the editorship and eventually changed the name to *Grace and Glory*. The focus of *The Pentecost* is different than *The Apostolic Faith* and *The Bridegroom's Messenger* in that it contains less individual testimonials and more sermonic and teaching materials as well as missionary reports and descriptions. Despite these differences, one can clearly see that in *The Pentecost*, the influence of the Apocalypse is brought to bear upon the worship described within its accounts.

The Pentecost contains direct citations from Revelation. The inaugural issue cites Rev. 22.20 in an article titled 'The Blessed Hope' by C.J. Quinn.[109] Elsewhere, the texts of Rev. 7.23 and 19.7-9 are quoted in an article discussing Joseph and the seven years of plenty in

---

[109] *TP* 1.1 (August, 1908), p. 5.

Egypt which, for the writer, will lead up to the tribulation and return of Jesus Christ. The article concludes with a citation of Rev. 1.7, an admonition to be a part of the first resurrection, and a final appeal to Rev. 22.17.[110] A.S. Copley, who writes a five-part series on 'The Seven Dispensational Parables' of Matthew 13 cites extensively from Revelation.[111] In another teaching series on 'Pentecost in Type', Copley again turns to Revelation for much of his scriptural citations.[112] A writer using the pen name of Deborah has a teaching series titled 'Lessons from Genesis' in which she draws comparisons between Genesis and Revelation.[113] Lastly, J.R. Flower writes an article on 'The Bride of Christ' which opens with a citation of Rev. 21.9. The entirety of the article is drawn from Revelation and references such things as the Marriage Supper and robes washed white in the blood of the Lamb.[114]

In *The Pentecost* people testify to being laid out under the power of God in the midst of the worship service. One testimony states that saint and sinner alike were 'prostrate under the power of God at one time'.[115] A mother writes of her and her daughter's Spirit Baptism experience in which they both fell under the power of the Spirit and sang and talked in tongues.[116] These experiences were often accompanied by visions of Jesus and heaven. Ruth Angstead, who begins her story with 'Blessing and honor and glory and power unto Him that sitteth upon the throne and unto the Lamb forever and ever', a clear allusion to Rev. 5.13, testifies to being prostrate 'under the feet of the Son of God' and receiving a 'new vision of His Majesty'.[117]

---

[110] *TP* 1.2 (September, 1908), p. 6.

[111] *TP* 1.3 (November, 1908), pp. 1-2; *TP* 1.4 (December, 1908), pp. 9-10; *TP* 1.5 (January-February, 1909), pp. 7-8; *TP* 1.6 (April-May, 1909), pp. 7-8; *TP* 1.7 (June, 1909), p. 7.

[112] *TP* 1.9 (August, 1909), pp. 7-8; *TP* 1.10 (September, 1909), pp. 5-6; *TP* 1.11 (October 15, 1909), pp. 5-6; *TP* 1.12 (November 1, 1909), pp. 5-6; *TP* 2.2 (January 1, 1910), p. 5.

[113] *TP* 2.2 (January 1, 1910), pp. 2-3; *TP* 2.3 (February 1, 1910), pp. 2-3; *TP* 2.4 (March 1, 1910), pp. 2-3; *TP* 2.5 (April 1, 1910), pp. 2-3.

[114] *TP* 2.11-12 (November-December 1910), pp. 10-11.

[115] *TP* 1.2 (September, 1908), p. 2.

[116] *TP* 1.11 (October 15, 1909), p. 6.

[117] *TP* 1.2 (September, 1908), p. 1.

In another visionary experience, Angstead has a glimpse of the 'Celestial City of Glory' where a 'stream pure as crystal flowed from under the throne, winding about, with the trees of life on either side'.[118] Angstead's testimony undoubtedly draws on John's description in Rev. 22.1-2. On the morning after the vision Angstead writes about her worship:

> … I sank out of self in such glorious worship before the Father, far too deep for any utterance. There seemed to be many waters surging through my being, then the Holy Spirit sang through me four songs, such beautiful words and music. I never could sing much. I was a spell-bound listener to the songs bursting forth from the glorified Jesus through His Holy Spirit. The first three, as I sang them each time – often in English –were new to me, but the fourth was that glorious old song 'All glory and praise to the Lamb that was slain,' then I spoke in tongues, each time interpreting, magnifying Father, Son, and the precious blood.[119]

Angstead apparently understands herself to be singing songs given directly by the Spirit. Although the first three songs are new to her, she identifies the fourth as 'that glorious old song'. What she quotes appears to be the first line to the third verse of the hymn 'Revive Us Again'. This phrase draws on the imagery of Revelation 5 and gives further witness to the power of this chapter for early Pentecostals. Additionally, Angstead's connection of the songs with the Spirit fits well in the narrative world of Revelation 4–5 where the Spirit is before the throne of God, and music is issuing forth to God and the Lamb.

Singing, both in tongues and in one's native language, is reported in the pages of *The Pentecost*. Mrs. S.A. Smith reports about 'Pentecost in Tennessee' where people were singing in the Spirit and praising while 'under the power'.[120] Mary Friesen tells about the revival among the children of India. She writes:

> Oh, how they would shout and praise God all over the place! It seemed sometimes as though they could not stop praising God. The glory of God was upon them in such a manifest way, some

---

[118] *TP* 1.2 (September, 1908), p. 1.

[119] *TP* 1.2 (September, 1908), p. 2.

[120] *TP* 1.2 (September, 1908), p. 8.

would shout, others jump, dance, fall, laugh, cry, yet all so in the power of God. Sometimes the whole crowd would swing about with their singing. It made me think of a crowd of cherubs swinging around the throne. It really seemed, sometimes, as though we were in heaven, or as though heaven had come down.[121]

As with the sentiment expressed in the Wesleyan-Holiness publications, there is in *The Pentecost* a perceived collapsing of the space between earth and heaven that takes place within the context of Pentecostal worship. The mention of kinesthetic worship, singing, angelic beings (cherubs) and the throne points to the influence of the Apocalypse as each of these elements figure prominently there. E. Hildreth contributes a testimonial about the outpouring of the Holy Spirit in Ohio. She writes that at one point during the service 'one sister started to sing in the Spirit, but in English, "Worthy is the Lamb"'.[122] Finally, although only mentioned once, A.S. Copley identifies the 'Heavenly Chorus' as one of the manifestations of the Spirit: '... but the sublimest of all is the anthem of the so-called "heavenly choir"'.[123] These testimonies of angelic choirs and the Spirit's song ('Worthy is the Lamb') continue to document the Apocalypse's influence on Pentecostal spirituality.

Perhaps *The Pentecost's* greatest jewel is the following song called 'While the Years Roll On' by Jan M. Kirk:

I have read of a wonderful city on high,
There the saints gather home with the Lord in the sky;
Twelve gates made of pearl! Ever open we're told,
To that wonderful city that never grows old.

Our Savior we soon in that city shall meet,
And all of our loved ones again we shall greet.
There we'll all sing and play on harps of pure gold,
The only song written that never grows old.

---

[121] *TP* 1.5 (January-February, 1909), p. 5. For other references to singing see *TP* 1.10 (September, 1909), p. 1; *TP* 1.10 (September, 1909), pp. 2-3; *TP* 1.11 (October 15, 1909), p. 6.

[122] *TP* 1.7 (June, 1909), p. 9.

[123] *TP* 1.11 (October 15, 1909), p. 6, col. 1.

Saying blessing and honor and wisdom and power,
Thanksgiving and honor and might evermore;
Unto God and the Lamb and the Spirit three-fold,
Who forever unfolding can never grow old.

In that city, our feet shall be sandaled with light,
Our robes washed with blood shall be dazzling white;
There the fashions never change like the Hebrews we're told,
Our sandals and garments shall never grow old.

In that city of light where live the redeemed,
There's a strange tree that grows on both sides of the stream;
Twelve manner of fruit twelve times a year we're told,
And ever fresh manna that never grows old.

Life is reckoned down here by youth, man and age,
We order a shroud for the child or the sage;
And they never die there in that city we're told,
But they live on forever and never grow old.[124]

The stanzas of this song rely heavily upon the images and language of Revelation. The dominating theme of the city with gates of pearl (stanza one) and ever-fruitful trees along the river (stanza five) is reminiscent of Rev. 21.21 and 22.2 respectively. The ascriptions of praise in stanza three reflect the worship of God and the Lamb in Revelation 5. The addition of the Spirit as worthy of worship is not drawn directly from Revelation but seems to be inferred since the Spirit is intimately tied to both God and the Lamb. Stanza four speaks of the apparel of the saints in heaven. While it evokes the experience of the Hebrews in the wilderness as recorded in Deut. 29.5 – 'The clothes on your back have not worn out, and the sandals on your feet have not worn out' – it also reflects the blood-washed robes depicted in Rev. 7.14. The publication of this song suggests that it was sung by at least some early Pentecostals in their worship services, thus reinforcing the contention that the Apocalypse inspires and informs their worship.

Summary

Although *The Pentecost* is largely devoted to sermons, teachings and missionary reports, it nevertheless provides insight into the spiritu-

---

[124] *TP* 2.6 (May 1, 1910), pp. 1, 8.

ality of early Pentecostals that reveals the influence of the Apocalypse. Although differences in doctrine are becoming evident, it is revealing that the spirituality is consistent with that of the Wesleyan-Holiness groups. Testimonies, songs, poems, and visions of these Pentecostals continue to center around images originating in the Apocalypse. Further, these Pentecostals see continuity between their Spirit-led worship and the Spirit-revealed worship of heaven depicted in the Apocalypse.

The Latter Rain Evangel

A lesser known early Pentecostal periodical is *The Latter Rain Evangel* published between 1908 and 1911 by the Stone Church in Chicago, Illinois, under the leadership of Pastor William Piper. The first two issues offer a unique feature in that they contain transcripts of sermons preached at Stone Church, including manifestations of the Spirit. The inaugural issue describes an afternoon service on September 20, 1908, and records this testimony of what took place during the middle of the service: 'At frequent intervals the Holy Spirit strengthened and confirmed the message of the afternoon by speaking through many in the audience in the unknown tongue, followed by the interpretation'. The interpretation of three 'words of the Spirit' given in the service are printed, with the third 'word' identified as 'The Voice of the Spirit – in Song'. A portion of the lyrics is as follows:

> Glory to God, our God, the everlasting God.
> Glory and honor be unto His name, our Christ of God.
> Behold He cometh in the clouds; every eye shall see Him,
> And they also which pierced Him.
> Behold He cometh with clouds.[125]

The words to this portion of the song are clearly derived from Rev. 1.7, reflecting the conviction of the community that the Spirit sings about the return of Jesus Christ. In the second issue, a similar experience is recorded. At the conclusion of the sermon is a transcription of a word from the Spirit exhorting the congregation to make ready for Jesus' soon return for his Bride so that they can be a part

---

[125] *LRE* 1.1 (October, 1908), p. 7.

of the Marriage Supper of the Lamb.[126] Although only found in the first two issues, the transcription of words from the Spirit reveals their perception of the presence of the Spirit in their midst as well as their conviction that these words are relevant for all who read their periodical.

The Latter Rain Evangel gives ample witness to the same type of worship and manifestations of the Spirit published in the publications already examined. Various reports are given within its pages about services and camp meetings, and nearly all contain references to the experiences of worship. At the first Stone Church Convention, it is reported that 'sometimes He [the Spirit] lifted us up to the very throne, oftener did His hand lead us along the way of crucifixion to self. The same Spirit that carried us in song into the heavenlies, travailed and interceded'.[127] The language of being 'lifted' to the throne by the Spirit recalls John's experience of the Spirit in Rev. 4.1. Another writer makes the following comment about singing in known and unknown tongues during a service: 'It seemed as though in Spirit we soared up to the very gates of heaven, then back to earth again ...'[128] The perception of traveling back and forth between heaven and earth in the Spirit is reminiscent of Revelation.

Testimonies of men and women who 'received their Pentecost' are reported in *The Latter Rain Evangel*, albeit not as frequently as is other publications. The following examples are indicative:

> For about two hours He led me through physical motions, loud crying, joyous laughter, holy song and heavenly vision, breaking up the depths, letting the pent-up springs burst forth in rivers through my soul.[129]

> I began to praise Jesus and broke out in another tongue; a clear, distinct language; I also sang. One song was made up of different passages of Scripture joined together so that they rhymed. The oft-repeated chorus was, 'Jesus is coming soon.'[130]

---

[126] *LRE* 1.2 (November, 1908), p. 7.

[127] *LRE* 1.2 (November, 1908), p. 3.

[128] *LRE* 1.3 (December, 1908), p. 21.

[129] *LRE* 1.10 (July, 1909), p. 24.

[130] *LRE* 4.2 (November 1911), p. 11.

Significant to this study is that these testimonies of Spirit baptism are closely connected to worship and contain allusions to images and ideas found most often in the Apocalypse, such as loud sounds, songs, visions, and the soon return of Jesus. Dr. Wesley Myland writes of a vision he had in which he saw Jesus Christ 'away up in glory and in the midst of a great multitude'. In his vision he asks Jesus if he can join the 'great chorus of singers' and Jesus puts him in the choir. He continues, 'I began to sing with them a little and what do you suppose? I was singing the "latter rain" song in "tongues," which I afterwards interpreted, and wrote into English.' Myland ends his account by quoting Rev. 5.12 and 1.5.[131] Dr. Myland's vision places him in the midst of the great multitude (likely Revelation 7) where he joins the heavenly worship.

Songs and/or poems given by the Spirit are also found within this periodical and continue to evidence the deep connection these early Pentecostals had with the Apocalypse.[132] Mrs. Elizabeth D. Van Horn recounts her Spirit baptism experience and says that the Spirit 'spoke and jubilantly sang through me in an unknown tongue for a long time'. She also includes a song that the Lord gave to her titled 'At His Pierced Feet'. The fourth stanza reflects the influence of the Apocalypse:

> The wedding robe so clean and white
> He bought for me on Calvary's height,
> Nor spot nor wrinkle shall ever stay,
> For when I ask, He'll cleanse them away.
> He'll raise me up to stand at His side,
> Through His precious blood, a part of His Bride.[133]

This stanza draws on the imagery of the saints as the bride (Rev. 19.7; 21.2). The white robes reflects the imagery of both Rev. 7.13-14, where the saints are dressed in robes made white by the blood of the Lamb, and Rev. 19.7-8 where the bride is clothed in white linen. The combination of images gives indication as to how these early Pentecostals viewed themselves.

---

[131] *LRE* 2.3 (December, 1909), p. 6.

[132] See also *LRE* 1.5 (February, 1909), p. 24; *LRE* 1.7 (April, 1909), p. 11; *LRE* 2.2 (November, 1909), p. 16; *LRE* 3.8 (May, 1911), p. 23.

[133] *LRE* 1.6 (March, 1909), p. 10.

Another song published is by Alvin Branch, a Baptist minister, who receives Spirit Baptism and is given a song in tongues with the interpretation coming two weeks later. Two of the stanzas of this song, titled 'Looking Up to Jesus', reflect imagery from the Apocalypse:

> I am looking up to Jesus as He sits upon the throne,
> And gives me sweet assurance that I am His very own.
> My eyes are fixed on Jesus, and in His blessed face
> I see that He forgives me and saves me by His grace.
>
> I am looking up to Jesus for the strength I need each day,
> For the wisdom that shall guide me along the narrow way,
> That leads me up to glory where angel hosts sings praise,
> To the wondrous King of Glory as they look upon His face.[134]

These stanzas reflect the imagery of Jesus on the throne found throughout Revelation as well as the worship afforded to Jesus.

The Latter Rain Evangel has a great deal of teaching and sermonic material in which elements from the Apocalypse are discussed. This includes judgment[135] and tribulation,[136] the 144,000,[137] Babylon,[138] the return of Jesus (Revelation 19),[139] the first resurrection,[140] the millennial reign,[141] Armageddon,[142] the marriage supper of the Lamb,[143] and the New Jerusalem.[144] In an address delivered in the Gospel Tabernacle in Chicago, D. Wesley Myland uses imagery from Revelation to address the importance of worship in 'The Yielded Life':

---

[134] *LRE* 2.11 (August, 1910), p. 23.

[135] *LRE* 1.7 (April, 1909), p. 15.

[136] *LRE* 1.7 (April, 1909), p. 19; *LRE* 2.6 (March, 1910), p. 17; *LRE* 2.8 (May, 1910), pp. 3-9.

[137] *LRE* 2.12 (September, 1910), p. 6.

[138] *LRE* 3.1 (October, 1910), pp. 17-23.

[139] *LRE* 3.2 (November, 1910), p. 1, 16.

[140] *LRE* 1.7 (April, 1909), p. 18; *LRE* 2.3 (December, 1909), pp. 20-22; *LRE* 2.4 (January, 1910), pp. 23-24; *LRE* 3.7 (April, 1911), pp. 16-18.

[141] *LRE* 1.1 (October, 1908), p. 8; *LRE* 1.7 (October, 1908), p. 18; *LRE* 2.10 (July, 1910), p. 16.

[142] *LRE* 1.7 (April, 1909), p. 15; *LRE* 2.10 (July, 1910), p. 8.

[143] *LRE* 1.7 (April, 1909), p. 18.

[144] *LRE* 2.10 (July, 1910), p. 13.

If you want to give a perfect service, learn a perfect worship. We have never learned to worship perfectly, and because the coming of Jesus is so near, and we are soon to be ushered into the great temple of the skies, we must have knowledge of true worship. We must be in training now. This is an important phase of this Pentecostal Movement, for even if the Bride was perfect, she must have a real spirit of worship before she enters into the marriage feast.[145]

The mention of the great temple, the Bride, and the marriage feast clearly show the influence of the Apocalypse. Significant for this study is the connection of all of this imagery to worship. The earthly worship experiences are 'training' for the heavenly worship to take place when believers are ushered into the marriage feast.

Summary

The Latter Rain Evangel gives further testimony to the influence of the Apocalypse for early Pentecostals. A close connection between worship and the Spirit is a theme that runs throughout its pages. As the listing of sermon and teaching topics from the Apocalypse indicates, this group (or at least their leadership) also looked to the Apocalypse for perceived eschatological material, yet their experiences of, in, and as a result of worship are consistent with other groups, suggesting a normative pattern to early Pentecostal worship.

Word and Witness

The periodical *Word and Witness* was a pre-Assemblies of God publication edited by E.N. Bell initially out of Malvern, Arkansas.[146] Like other Pentecostal publications, *Word and Witness* contains testimonials of salvation, sanctification, Spirit Baptism, and healing experiences. Descriptions also reference singing in the Spirit,[147] being slain in the Spirit,[148] kinesthetic worship,[149] and loud shouting

---

[145] *LRE* 1.4 (January, 1909), p. 4.

[146] The location of the paper subsequently changes to Findlay, Ohio, in 1914, and to St. Louis, Missouri, in 1915.

[147] *WW* 8.10 (December 20, 1912), p. 1; *WW* 10.1 (January 20, 1914), p. 3.

[148] *WW* 8.8 (October 20, 1912), pp. 3, 4; *WW* 9.6 (June 20, 1913), p. 4; *WW* 10.1 (January 20, 1914), p. 1; *WW* 12.7 (July, 1915), p. 5.

[149] *WW* 9.1 (January 20, 1913), p. 3; *WW* 9.2 (February 20, 1913), p. 1.

and worshiping.[150] All of these are consistent with early Pentecostal worship as documented in other publications.[151]

The periodical records several visionary accounts, many of which take place during worship, that find their point of reference in the Apocalypse. A man who had been a preacher for forty-five years is described as being struck down by the power of God, baptized in the Holy Spirit, and given a vision. It is recorded as follows:

> Last Sunday morning he was carried away in the Spirit, like the Apostle John, and beheld the Holy City, the New Jerusalem, coming down from God out of heaven, prepared as a bride adorned for her husband, all exactly as described in the book of Revelation. He said: "I saw the innumerable company of angels, singing around the throne, and was permitted to join in the song." (We heard him singing in tongues at the time he was in the Spirit).[152]

This testimony explicitly cites Revelation, thus providing a clear context for the imagery of the vision. The man is described as being carried away in the Spirit like 'the Apostle John', suggesting that the writer views the Spirit working among them in the same manner. The vision of New Jerusalem that the man recounts is 'exactly as described' in Revelation. While this could simply reflect the man's thorough knowledge of this passage, the testimony points to the agency of the Spirit; that is, the man's testimony provides confirmation to John's writing.

Effie Hile testifies about her vision experienced during worship: 'I was also at the marriage supper in the skies with Jesus. I was al-

---

[150] *WW* 9.1 (January 20, 1913), p. 3; *WW* 9.2 (February 20, 1913), p. 1. An exhortation titled 'On Shouting' draws freely from the Apocalypse: 'There will be shouting like the voice of great multitudes, like the noise of many waters, like the sound of mighty thundering. They will all be shouting, "Hallelujah, the Lord God omnipotent reigneth".' *WW* 10.1 (January 20, 1914), p. 4.

[151] In an article titled "Sane and Insane Practices" the writer acknowledges that there are manifestations of worship practices that claim to be of the Spirit but are not. The writer then states: 'But the excesses we have in mind, however, are not shouting, dancing in the Spirit, the heavenly chorus, or speaking in tongues, for these are not excesses but are legitimate because Scriptural'. *WW* 12.7 (July, 1915), p. 5. This clearly demonstrates that these practices were normative for early Pentecostal worship, even if they were labeled as 'excessive' by outsiders.

[152] *WW* 8.8 (October 20, 1912), p. 3.

lowed to walk the golden streets in glory ... I saw the angels singing and shouting on the streets of gold and was allowed to sing with them the heavenly songs'.[153] In Sister Hile's vision she participates in the marriage supper (Rev. 19.7-8), walks the golden streets of New Jerusalem (Rev. 21.21), and then participates in heavenly worship. Her vision, like so many others, indicates that early Pentecostals had proleptic experiences of heaven in the Spirit.

A testimony from a meeting in San Antonio, Texas, relates visionary accounts experienced collectively by a group of individuals praying around an altar. The writer says that these people

> saw 'Him who is walking today among the Candlesticks, holding the stars in His right hand.' Numbers seemed to hear that voice as the sounding of 'great waters' and like John fell at his feet as dead. Oh glory! ... Many saw visions of Jesus coming in the clouds of heaven with power and great glory ... At the same time several in the Spirit were hearing the 'tramp, tramp' of a mighty army, and two saw the mighty armies of Heaven riding forth on White Horses ...[154]

This vision is filled with images from the Apocalypse. Jesus is the one like the Son of Man who walks among the candlesticks, whose voice is like the sound of many waters, who holds the seven stars in his right hand, and before whom John falls as dead (Rev. 1.9-17). The visions of Jesus coming in the clouds of heaven draws from Rev. 1.7,[155] and Rev. 19.14 describes the armies of heaven riding on white horses behind Jesus (Rev. 19.11-13). It is intriguing that this is compiled as a collective experience in which the Spirit reveals the same thing (or at least similar things) to groups of people at the same time.

Like other Pentecostal literature already surveyed, *Word and Witness* includes the publication of poems and songs. One song that appropriates images from the Apocalypse is 'Twill Last While the Ages Shall Roll' by Burt McCafferty. Despite their length, I will quote stanzas two through four:

---

[153] *WW* 8.10 (December 20, 1912), p. 3.

[154] *WW* 9.2 (February 20, 1913), p. 1

[155] This could also reflect Jesus' own words in Mk 13.26 (also Mt. 24.30; Lk. 21.27).

In that home of the blest, I'm longing to stand,
And gaze with sweet wonder and love
On scenery celestial – yea scenery so grand
That's fashioned by Father above.
O, precious the thought that from Him we'll never part;
By clear, living fountains we'll stroll,
And the joy that He gives will fill ev'ry heart,
And 'twill last while the ages shall roll.

No sighing o'er there; no sorrow and tears
Are known in the land of the blest,
For God in His mercy, hath banished all fears
And given the weary ones rest.
No parting with those who are dear to our hearts,
No longer we'll hear the sad toll.
O, soon the reunion in heaven will start,
And 'twill last while the ages shall roll.

We'll walk with the ransomed, the heavenly street;
We'll dwell in His presence for aye;
In sweetest communion we'll sit at His feet
And join in the angelic lay, -
On scenery celestial – yea scenery so grand
A lay that from sorrow and sighing is free,
A music enthralling the soul,
Whose melody reaches from sea unto sea,
And 'twill last while the ages shall roll.[156]

McCafferty's song draws on the Apocalypse for much of its content. In stanza two, the Father is the creator of the 'scenery celestial', an image which could reflect Revelation's depiction of the new heaven and earth or New Jerusalem (Revelation 21-22). The likelihood of this is strengthened as McCafferty writes of a fountain there (Rev. 22.1-2), as well as the absence of sighing, sorrow, and tears (Rev. 21.4). The eternality of worship is reflected in the last lines.

---

[156] *WW* 12.8 (August, 1915), p. 5.

Summary

Despite its short publication period, *Word and Witness* provides confirmation of the normative worship practices of early Pentecostals and the influence of the Apocalypse for their worship experiences. The periodical lifts up visions as an important experience and even gives testimony to corporate visionary experiences. The Spirit gives the visions which draw heavily from the Apocalypse, suggesting that Apocalypse functions as an important *present* word for the Pentecostal community.

The Christian/Weekly Evangel[157]

This early publication, begun in 1913 out of Plainfield, Indiana, will eventually become the *Pentecostal Evangel*, the primary publication voice for the Assemblies of God. Like the other Pentecostal publications, it provides testimonial evidence to the early Pentecostal revivals, including indications of the worship. Once again, the influence of the Apocalypse is clearly seen.

Several editorials reflect the influence of the Apocalypse, particularly in light of the advent of the First World War. In 1914, E.N. Bell, the managing editor, wrote a front-page editorial titled 'The Mark of the Beast' in which he draws heavily from Revelation.[158] Other editorials in that same year include 'Prophetic War Horses Sent Out'[159] based on Revelation 6, and 'The Great Tribulation'[160] on interpreting the three woes of Revelation. Also in 1914, three articles appear on the second coming of Jesus Christ, all of which cite Revelation.[161]

As in other publications, songs and poems are found throughout the pages of *The Christian Evangel*. This continues to build a case for viewing these as expressions of worship. Many of these reflect the influence of the Apocalypse. The thought of singing around the

---

[157] The name of the periodical will change in March, 1915 to the *Weekly Evangel*. The footnotes will reflect both titles.

[158] *CE* 49 (July 11, 1914), pp. 1-2.

[159] *CE* 56 (August 29, 1914), p. 1.

[160] *CE* 57 (September 5, 1914), p. 1.

[161] *CE* 58 (September 12, 1914), p. 3; *CE* 62 (October 10, 1914), p. 3; *CE* 72 (December 26, 1914), p. 1.

throne of God, an image drawn from Revelation, is found in John Morcum's poem 'Loving Service'. The last stanza declares:

> There with angel faces smiling,
> All around that happy throne;
> We shall join that heavenly chorus,
> Singing praise to Him alone.[162]

Burt McCafferty couples the throne-room imagery with the vision of the New Jerusalem in his song 'When We Meet Over Yonder' to be sung to the tune 'Meet Me in Heaven':

> (Chorus) When we meet over yonder the faithful and true
> In that home where no schism is known,
> With the saints of all ages – the Gentile and Jew –
> We will worship our King on the throne.
> When the Lord brings to earth in its beauty
> That fair city from Heaven above,
> 'We shall see eye to eye,' Hallelujah!
> And be one in the doctrine of love.[163]

The return of Christ, from the perspective of Revelation 19.11-14 is the subject of a song titled 'Rejoice and Be Glad' to be sung to the tune 'Revive Us Again'. Its fourth stanza is as follows:

> Rejoice and be glad for the Victor's in sight
> Conquering and to conquer, riding forth in His might.
> Hallelujah, sing His praise, Hallelujah, Amen!
> Hallelujah, give Him glory, for He's coming again.[164]

The imagery of the conquering rider on the white horse linked to the mentioning of His return is suggestive of Rev. 19.11-16. Along with the return of Christ, songs and poems depict the millennial reign (Rev. 20.1-6). The poem, 'The Morning Cometh' by Burt McCafferty, has as its last two lines:

> The day of Christ triumphant
> To reign a thousand years.[165]

---

[162] *WE* 139 (May 13, 1916), p. 15.
[163] *WE* 156 (September 9, 1916), p. 14.
[164] *WE* 136 (April 22, 1916), p. 5.
[165] *CE* 65 (October 31, 1914), p. 1.

Another poem, titled "The Night is Far Spent' by McCafferty continues this theme. The last stanza is as follows:

> The night, the dark night,
> Has forever gone,
> And gone are our sorrow and tears,
> For there we shall reign
> With Christ on His throne,
> A thousand, sweet, beautiful years.[166]

McCafferty connects the bliss of the millennial reign with the absence of sorrow and tears (Rev. 21.4).

Another favorite subject for the songs and poetry of early Pentecostals is the joyous marriage supper of the Lamb. Mrs. Ellen M. Winter writes about it in her poem 'The Bridegroom Cometh!':

> There'll be Hallelujahs round the throne
> And joys that Heaven has never known,
> When Jesus brings His dear bride home
> In that happy, crowning day.
> She's living now midst toil and pain –
> But earthly loss will be richest gain
> When she shares His throne and glorious reign
> In the Kingdom without end.[167]

The poem 'Are You Ready?' by Florence Burpee echoes this theme in its third stanza with the line 'Have you on the wedding garment through the blood made white as snow?' and in its fourth stanza with the line 'Soon will come the marriage supper and the wedding in the sky'.[168]

In addition to these individual reflections of worship, there are descriptions of corporate worship that reflect the influence of the Apocalypse. As has been observed in the other publications, singing, shouting, and kinesthetic movement are common features of the Pentecostal service. From Hartford, Arkansas, comes the following testimony:

---

[166] *WE* 125 (January 29 and February 6, 1916), p. 14. See also *WE* 100 (July 24, 1915), p. 3, for the song 'A Thousand Years'.

[167] *WE* 129 (March 4, 1916), p. 14.

[168] *WE* 130 (March 11, 1916), p. 14.

Such singing, such praying in the Spirit I never did hear before. As we sang, wave after wave of the Holy Spirit came down and swept through the church until it seemed the angels were in our midst taking part in the singing. Glory to our King![169]

A saint from Alabama testifies, 'God wrought wonderfully one night during praise service and let down the Heavenly Host to play and sing for us. Many of the saints and many sinners heard the heavenly choir'.[170] In a report of the General Council, the following is noted after the singing of the hymn 'All Hail the Power of Jesus' Name':

At the conclusion of the hymn, the congregation stood with up-lifted hands for ten or fifteen minutes, lost in wonder and praise, the heavenly chorus mounting up in a great overflow of ecstasy until the very windows of heaven seemed to be opened and the power and glory of God streamed down upon us.[171]

It is also reported that the saints were 'dancing, leaping, and pros-trating themselves' in the church services.[172] In a testimonial from a meeting led by Maria Woodworth-Etter in San Francisco, the writer states, 'Every meeting the heavenly choir is heard like the noise of many waters, and sometimes as many as fifteen dancing in the Spir-it'.[173] In this testimony it is interesting to note that the 'noise of many waters' is connected to the heavenly choir. This identification is also found in a testimony from China. The writer says, '... I never heard anything that sounded so much like the 'voice of many wa-ters' as the volume of praise that went up spontaneously to God that night'.[174] This imagery comes from Rev. 1.15 in describing Je-sus' voice and from Rev. 19.6 where it describes the worship of the great multitude. A connection between the description of Jesus' voice and worship might suggest a deep sense of the presence of Jesus in the midst of the Pentecostal worship service. The close

---

[169] *CE* 78 (February 20, 1915), p. 3.

[170] *WE* 107 (September 11, 1915), p. 4.

[171] *WE* 111 (October 16, 1915), p. 1.

[172] *WE* 109 (September 25, 1915), p. 1.

[173] *WE* 170 (December 23, 1916), p. 14. See also *WE* 168 (December 9, 1916), p. 15, for another report from a Woodworth-Etter revival in Salt Lake City in which the heavenly chorus was heard nearly every night.

[174] *WE* 103 (August 14, 1915), p. 4.

connection found in all of these testimonies between congregational worship and heaven is at home in the world of the Apocalypse where heavenly music and worship celebrate the power and glory of God.

The experience of being slain in the Spirit is also described. Frequently those slain in the Spirit are noted as falling as dead under the power of the Spirit.[175] From a meeting in Alabama, a writer testifies that 'some fell as dead and lie for hours and are given visions of things to come'.[176] Similarly in a report from Arkansas, a writer states, 'I saw many shake and tremble and fall as dead men under the mighty power of God'.[177] The visions granted to the saints while under the power of the Spirit show the remarkable influence of the Apocalypse. The testimony of L.G. Chandier is illustrative as it is replete with images from Revelation:

> The angel of the Lord showed me the Holy City that John saw coming down from heaven one night when I was praying at my little home. I went into the Holy City in a vision and I saw the seven angels standing before the throne of God with their trumpets ready to sound. God had taken His seat on the throne and I saw on the trumpet of the first angel written that the end should come in 19 __. The angel showed me my crown and it was beautiful. It had 130 stars in it. The Holy City was made of pure gold as clear as a crystal.[178]

In an extensive article titled 'The Gift of Tongues and the Pentecostal Movement', the author, W. Bernard, writes a section on seeing visions:

> Mrs. Helen Dyer, in her book on the recent revivals in India, gives the following account of visions seen by girls at the American Baptist Mission Station ... She tells of as many as twenty of the older girls going into a trance. She says 'They prayed, sang, laughed, clapped their hands, and were evidently for the time be-

---

[175] *CE* 1.3 (August 30, 1913), p. 8; *WE* 136 (April 22, 1916), p. 14.

[176] *WE* 115 (November 13, 1915), p. 4.

[177] *WE* 164 (November 11, 1916), p. 14.

[178] *CE* 2.13 (March 28, 1914), p. 8. The last two numerals of the date are left off but later in the issue the editor tells the reader that the date is 1933 but that it was left off so that people will not wait for a certain date to get right with God.

ing, in different scenes. After returning to consciousness, they spoke diffidently of what they had seen and some refused to tell. Some said the Revelation, chapters 4, 5, and 7, described what they saw. They also saw Jesus, who showed them His wounded hands, and the blood flowing from His side.' These visions are characteristic of the visions of the scenes of Revelations [*sic*] 4, 5, and 7 ... In my new Pentecostal experience, the reading of these chapters thrills one through and through.[179]

This report makes explicit the significance of Revelation, particularly chapters 4, 5, and 7 for early Pentecostals. It is clear that the Spirit guides these girls through 'different scenes' that are directly from Revelation. Also of interest is the final statement where the writer indicates that 'my new Pentecostal experience' enhances the reading of these chapters.

A final visionary account to be mentioned is that from J.M.L. Harrow, a missionary to West Africa who tells of a native woman who attends a service and has the following vision:

I was taken to such a lovely place, and I saw a wonderful Person sitting on a great seat, and out from under the seat came lots of beautiful water; the water was so beautiful that you wanted to drink it and to bathe in it, oh so much ...[180]

What stands out about this testimony is that fact that Harrow indicates that this native woman had no prior knowledge of Scripture before having this vision. It seems quite significant that the vision granted to her appears to be the 'lovely place' of New Jerusalem.

Summary

In its early years, *The Christian Evangel* is filled with testimonials that provide glimpses into the worship of the early Pentecostals even as it describes experiences of salvation, healing and Spirit baptism. Like the other publications examined, *The Christian Evangel* provides evidence that the worship found in the Apocalypse, particularly Revelation 4–5, functions at a deep level for these early Pentecostal saints. The consistency of the testimonies reveals a normative spirituality amongst Pentecostals. The advent of the great world war

---

[179] *WE* 143 (June 10, 1916), p. 5.
[180] *WE* 166 (November 25, 1916), p. 3.

leads to more speculative usage of Revelation in editorials and teachings but the testimonies nestled within show that the Apocalypse was also seen as a liturgical narrative that bore witness to their own experiences.

IV. Conclusion

This survey of early Pentecostal literature (1906–1916) reveals that the liturgy of the Apocalypse played a significant role in Pentecostal worship for both Wesleyan-Holiness and Finished Work streams of the tradition. To a large degree, the publications present a unified portrait of the worship of these early Pentecostals and demonstrate that they were clearly influenced in their worship by the Apocalypse in general and by the worship scenes in particular. Where other studies have documented significant theological differences between the two Pentecostal branches, particularly in relationship to healing[181] and eschatology,[182] this study reveals that in their descriptions of worship, both streams had very similar experiences. For both, worship is grounded pneumatologically and christologically. For both, their experience of worship is a real participation in the worship of heaven. The Holy Spirit transforms their worship and even transports them into the heavenly throne room, via the experience of being slain under the power of God. Further, the Holy Spirit 'speaks for Himself' the songs of heaven through the saints. The Spirit inspires original songs and poetry which often are based on images and themes found in the Apocalypse. Loud, exuberant music and shouting along with kinesthetic movement, such as leaping, jumping and dancing, are viewed across both branches of the tradition as normative expressions of worship. All of this for early Pentecostals is made possible by the Spirit of God.

The value in hearing the testimonies of early Pentecostals about their worship is that it opens the way for a retrieval of the Apocalypse for contemporary Pentecostals. Many Pentecostal groups have been influenced to one degree or another by Dispensationalism; unfortunately, this has led to a particular reading of the Apocalypse that fails to appreciate its spirituality. This Dispensational influence

---

[181] See Alexander, *Pentecostal Healing: Models in Theology and Practice*.

[182] See McQueen, *Toward a Pentecostal Eschatology*.

is already evident in the editorials and sermonic materials of the early Finished Work publications, but it does not present itself in the descriptions of worship as one might expect. If the early Pentecostals found within the pages of the Apocalypse a template for liturgy then perhaps a Pentecostal narrative reading of the Apocalypse will lead a new generation of Pentecostals from both sides of the tradition to (re)discover the deep spirituality of the Apocalypse.

4

LITURGICAL NARRATIVES: HEARING THE REVELATION OF JOHN

This chapter will provide a narrative reading of the Apocalypse. To facilitate this reading, the text will be divided up by means of the four ἐν πνεύματι ('in the Spirit') phrases found throughout the Apocalypse. As literary markers, these phrases guide the hearers through the phases of John's vision while at the same time providing continuity to the whole. These phrases also ground the Apocalypse pneumatologically by highlighting the role of the Spirit. Along with the prologue and epilogue, these phrases suggest the following large units as a way of structuring the narrative:[1]

   I. Prologue (1.1-8)
   II. ἐν πνεύματι – 'On the Lord's Day' (1.9–3.22)
   III. ἐν πνεύματι – 'In Heaven' (4.1–16.21)
   IV. ἐν πνεύματι – 'In the Wilderness: Babylon' (17.1–21.8)
   V. ἐν πνεύματι – 'On a Mountain: New Jerusalem' (21.9–22.5)
   VI. Epilogue (22.6-21)

---

[1] Many scholars recognize the ἐν πνεύματι phrases as having a significant role in the Apocalypse. Bauckham, *The Climax of Prophecy*, p. 3, identifies them as denoting 'three major transitions within the whole vision'. J.A. Filho, 'The Apocalypse of John as a Visionary Experience: Notes on the Book's Structure', *JSNT* 25.2 (2002), p. 229, suggests that the phrases indicate 'the most important moments in the visionary experience that the book presents, involving changes of place and subject'. For scholars who use the phrases to outline Revelation, see J.L. Trafton, *Reading Revelation: A Literary and Theological Commentary* (Macon: Smyth & Helwys, Inc., 2005), p. 10; Waddell, *The Spirit of the Book of Revelation*, pp. 148-49; Thomas, *The Apocalypse*, pp. 5-6.

The narrative reading of Revelation offered in this chapter will follow the outline provided above. At the conclusion of each section, I will offer summaries as a way not only to manage the large amount of text but also to reveal the continuous thread of worship woven throughout the Apocalypse.

I. Prologue (1.1-8)

The prologue sets the stage for the Apocalypse and provides the hearers with initial information in its opening verses:

Ἀποκάλυψις Ἰησοῦ Χριστοῦ ἣν ἔδωκεν αὐτῷ ὁ θεὸς δεῖξαι τοῖς δούλοις αὐτοῦ ἃ δεῖ γενέσθαι ἐν τάχει, καὶ ἐσήμανεν ἀποστείλας διὰ τοῦ ἀγγέλου αὐτοῦ τῷ δούλῳ αὐτοῦ Ἰωάννῃ, ὃς ἐμαρτύρησεν τὸν λόγον τοῦ θεοῦ καὶ τὴν μαρτυρίαν Ἰησοῦ Χριστοῦ ὅσα εἶδεν

The revelation of Jesus Christ which God gave to him to show to his servants what is necessary to happen quickly, which he showed by sending his angel to his servant John who testified to the things that he saw: the word of God and the testimony of Jesus Christ (Rev. 1.1-2).[2]

From this opening statement, John's hearers would likely understand that whatever is about to be *revealed* in this narrative is to be closely connected with the ultimate *revelation*[3] of and about Jesus

---

[2] The UBS 4th Revised Edition Greek text is used throughout this study.

[3] Aune, *Revelation 1–5*, p. lxxvii, indicates that this is the first occurrence of the term ἀποκάλυψις ('apocalypse') as a title in literature. He defines the apocalyptic genre in relation to Revelation in terms of form, content, and function as follows:

(1) Form: an a apocalypse is a first-person prose narrative, with an episodic structure consisting of revelatory visions often mediated to the author by a supernatural revealer, so structured that the central revelatory message constitutes a literary climax, and framed by a narrative of the circumstances surrounding the purported revelatory experience. (2) Content: the communication of a transcendent, usually eschatological, perspective on human experiences and values. (3) Function: (a) to legitimate the transcendent authorization of the message, (b) by mediating a reactualization of the original revelatory experience through a variety of literary devices, structures, and imagery, which function to 'conceal' the message that the text purposes to 'reveal,' so that (c) the recipients of the message will be encouraged to continue to pursue, or if necessary to modify, their thinking and behavior in conformity with transcendent perspectives (p. lxxxii).

Christ.[4] Despite its initial usage, the Apocalypse never again uses the term 'apocalypse', which suggests that this term is not being used as an indication of genre.[5] Whatever the hearers might have understood by 'apocalypse' is uncertain given the fact that it does not appear in Johannine literature. Perhaps the hearers would have understood it, as in the Pauline communities, as a manifestation of the Spirit (1 Cor. 14.6).[6] Perhaps they would have been familiar with Jewish and/or Christian apocalypses with similarities to Revelation.[7] Regardless, the simple yet startling introduction focuses attention on Jesus as both giver and content of the apocalypse. The Apocalypse consistently identifies itself as a prophecy (Rev. 1.3; 22.7, 10, 18-19).[8] The close proximity of 'apocalypse' and 'prophecy' in the opening verses would likely lead the hearers to *hear* what follows as apocalyptic *and* prophetic without concern to differentiate between the two ideas. God, identified as the ultimate source of the revelation, gives the revelation to Jesus who sends his angel to give it to

---

[4] Scholars debate whether ἀποκάλυψις Ἰησοῦ Χριστοῦ is a subjective genitive (the revelation *from* Jesus Christ) or an objective genitive (the revelation *of* or *about* Jesus Christ). M. Gorman argues, '... [L]ike every other New Testament book, Revelation is about Jesus Christ – "A revelation of Jesus Christ" (Rev 1:1)'. M. Gorman, *Reading Revelation Responsibly* (Eugene: Cascade Books, 2011), p. xv. Choosing one over the other is not necessary because both ideas are conveyed in Revelation. It is Jesus' revelation which he shows to John but it is also a revealing of the exalted Jesus, for this is the 'primary purpose' of the Apocalypse. Saunders, 'Revelation and Resistance', p. 120.

[5] M. Jauhiainen, 'ΑΠΟΚΑΛΥΨΙΣ ΙΗΣΟΥ ΧΡΙΣΤΟΥ (Rev. 1:1): The Climax of John's Prophecy', *Tyndale Bulletin* 54.1 (2003), pp. 99-117, who likewise argues that the term was not intended by John as a genre marker. In addition to pointing to the explicit identification of the work as prophecy, he also points to the two Old Testament style prophetic utterances (1.7-8) and the formal epistolary opening (1.4-6) and closing of the letter (22.21) as evidence against designating Revelation solely as apocalyptic literature.

[6] Waddell, *The Spirit of the Book of Revelation*, p. 123, believes that John uses ἀποκάλυψις ('apocalypse') not to identify his work but as a description of his experience in the Spirit.

[7] Bauckham, **The** *Climax of Prophecy*, pp. 38-91, provides an extensive chapter in which he compares Revelation with Jewish and Christian apocalypses. While he believes that John is aware of the apocalyptic traditions, he cautions that it is impossible to prove John's literary dependence on these traditions. See also Aune, *Revelation 1–5*, pp. lxxvii-xc.

[8] F.J. Murphy, *Fallen is Babylon* (Harrisburg: Trinity Press International, 1998), p. 37, 'John self-consciously writes a book of prophecy, which makes him unique among the known prophets of earliest Christianity'.

John.[9] The use of servant language to identify both John and the recipients could suggest that the seven churches of Asia are to see themselves as servants, or, in light of the later way that 'servants and prophets' will be linked in the Apocalypse, it could hint at prophetic figures in the churches, of whom John is likely one.[10] In this way, John 'mediates the revelation of Jesus Christ to his community, and he shares in its prophetic life'.[11] The same John who receives the revelation is the one who gives witness to the things that he saw concerning the word of God and the witness of Jesus Christ (1.2). This establishes for the hearers a close connection between John's witness and Jesus' witness.[12] Further, it establishes that John's writing is not a fictional account but is based on what he experienced.[13]

The prologue presents John as the implied author and narrator of the Apocalypse. The hearers would likely know who this John is, thus no further description is given. As the implied author and nar-

---

[9] G.K. Beale, 'The Purpose of Symbolism in the book of Revelation', *Calvin Theological Journal* 41 (2006), pp. 53-66, suggests that the verb ἐσήμανεν should be translated as 'he symbolized' based on its usage in the LXX of Dan. 2.28-29, 45. Adopting this meaning suggests that what occurs in Revelation is 'symbolic communication and not mere general conveyance of information'. Coupled with this understanding is the use of δεῖξαι (to show) since '"show" throughout the book always introduces a divine communication by symbolic vision' (4.1; 17.1; 21.9-10; 22.1, 6, 8). Thus, 'the reader is to expect that the main means of divine revelation in this book is symbolic' (p. 55). Beale looks to the Old Testament prophets' use of symbolism as a vehicle of communication when the people's hearts 'had become hardened to rational, historical, and sermonic warning methods'. When the prophet used symbolism it was a sign of impending judgment. Beale further notes that symbolic communication was only effective with the faithful remnant who could 'be shocked, by the unusual parables, back into the reality of their faith' (p. 57). Beale applies this to John's reality: '[B]y the time Revelation is written, John stands at the end of Israel's very existence. As a nation, they have rejected Christ and his warnings of judgment' (p. 60). See also G.L. Stevens, 'A Vision in the Night: Setting the Interpretive Stage for John's Apocalypse', in G.L. Stevens (ed.), *Essays on Revelation: Appropriating Yesterday's Apocalypse in Today's World* (Eugene: Pickwick Publications, 2010), p. 6, where he likens Revelation to 'sign language' for the persecuted believers.

[10] Bauckham, *The Climax of Prophecy*, p. 84, suggests that John was part of a group or school of Christian prophets. Contra Yarbro Collins who dismisses the idea of John as a *Christian* prophet and maintains that all references to prophets in Revelation can just as easily refer to Old Testament prophets. A. Yarbro Collins, *Crisis and Catharsis: The Power of the Apocalypse* (Philadelphia: Westminster, 1984).

[11] S.S. Smalley, *The Revelation to John* (Downers Grove: IVP, 2005), p. 8.

[12] Thomas, *The Apocalypse*, p. 89.

[13] D.A. deSilva, *Seeing Things John's Way: The Rhetoric of the Book of Revelation* (Louisville: Westminster John Knox Press, 2009), p. 120.

rator, all of the events in the book are understood to be presented from his perspective by the implied audience, the seven churches of Asia.[14] The specific location of the churches anchors the text historically and provides the earthly setting in which John's writing is received. That the work is addressed to a cluster of churches indicates that the writing is intended for communal and liturgical use in all of the churches. It is within the context of the worshipping church that an ἀποκάλυψις ('apocalypse') and προφητεία ('prophecy') can be given and received, heard and discerned.[15]

The prologue introduces the hearers to a divine cast of characters: God, Jesus Christ, and the seven-fold Spirit. While each is a separate character in the narrative, these divine characters are clearly inter-related. The initial relationship between God and Jesus in Rev. 1.1 is given further specificity in 1.6 as God is named as the Father of Jesus. The seven-fold Spirit is before the throne of God and thereby to be linked directly with God and Jesus (1.4). Johannine hearers would likely identify the seven-fold Spirit as the Holy Spirit given the tight connections between Father, Son, and Spirit throughout the Fourth Gospel (John 14–16).[16]

A final feature of the prologue is its pervasive use of liturgical language, beginning with the pronouncing of a liturgical blessing:[17]

---

[14] M.A. Powell, 'Narrative Criticism', in J.B. Green (ed.), *Hearing the New Testament: Strategies for Interpretation* (Grand Rapids: Eerdmans; Carlisle, UK: The Paternoster Press, 1995), pp. 240-41. See J.R. Michaels, *Revelation* (IVPNTC; Downers Grove: IVP, 1997), p. 18, who argues that in addition to being the implied author, John also functions as the implied reader 'by reacting to what he sees and hears in the way he expects *us* to react'.

[15] Gloer, 'Worship God! Liturgical Elements in the Apocalypse', p. 38; deSilva, *Seeing Things John's Way*, pp. 11-12.

[16] Contra Aune, *Revelation 1–5*, p. 40, who states, 'The "seven spirits who are before his throne" is not a phrase referring to the Holy Spirit, as so many commentators have claimed, but rather a reference to the seven archangels who stand continually in the presence of God (4:5; 5:6; 8:2)'. Resseguie, *The Revelation of John*, p. 66, uses the same references from Revelation as Aune to argue that John uses the number seven to describe the Holy Spirit. Such 'dynamic imagery emphasizes the active presence and power of the Spirit of God in the world'. For a thorough treatment of the Spirit in Revelation, see Waddell, *The Spirit of the Book of Revelation*, pp. 7-38.

[17] Thompson, *The Book of Revelation: Apocalypse and Empire*, p. 54; Gloer, 'Worship God! Liturgical Elements in the Apocalypse', p. 38. See also Peters, *The Mandate of the Church in the Apocalypse of John*, p. 47; O. Cullmann, *Early Christian Worship* (London: SCM, 1953), p. 23.

μακάριος ὁ ἀναγινώσκων
καὶ οἱ ἀκούοντες τοὺς λόγους τῆς προφητείας
καὶ τηροῦντες τὰ ἐν αὐτῇ γεγραμμένα,
ὁ γὰρ καιρὸς ἐγγύς

Blessed is the one reading
and the ones hearing the words of this prophecy
and the ones keeping the things having been written in it,
for the time is near (Rev. 1.3).

John's writing is intended to be experienced in a communal setting; that is, a reader or lector is to read it aloud to the community[18] as part of the worship service.[19] A blessing[20] comes not only to the reader but also to those who will hear/obey *and* keep the words of the prophecy.[21] All within the community are thereby invited to participate, and the use of the present participles suggests that reading, hearing, and keeping the prophecy are to be considered liturgical activities within the churches.[22] The prophecy functions as the Word of God for the churches – an urgent word owing to the belief that the time is near.

---

[18] In this way, the lector functions as a narrator. See Barr, *Tales of the End*, p. 29.

[19] Aune, *Revelation 1–5*, p. 20. Michaels, *Revelation*, p. 51, highlights the role of the lector, 'The only access that ordinary Christians had to the Gospels and letters that now make up the New Testament was public reading in worship services. The public reader therefore performed a ministry to the congregation far beyond what is normally the case today.' G.E. Ladd, *A Commentary on the Revelation of John* (Grand Rapids: Eerdmans, 1972), p. 23, says of the phrase 'those who hear': 'This is not a reference to private reading and study but to public worship'.

[20] This is the first of seven macarisms in Revelation (see 14.13; 16.15; 19.9; 20.6; 22.7, 14).

[21] C. Rotz, *Revelation: A Commentary in the Wesleyan Tradition* (Kansas City: Beacon Hill Press, 2012), p. 46, 'The mere reading of Revelation brings blessing, but hearing and obeying complete its purpose and result in greater blessedness'.

[22] Gorman sees 1.3 as the hermeneutical key to the book: 'Revelation 1:3 is thus the interpretive (or hermeneutical) key to the book with respect to our motivation for reading it and our basic strategy in doing so. We read Revelation as words from a prophet-pastor (and ultimately from God), in order to be formed and transformed, not merely informed.' Gorman, *Reading Revelation Responsibly*, p. 82. See also Thompson, *The Book of Revelation*, p. 72, 'Reading and listening to the Book of Revelation are themselves liturgical acts in the worship life of Christians in western Asia Minor'.

Second, the conventional epistolary greeting[23] utilizes liturgical language to extend grace and peace to the audience:

χάρις ὑμῖν καὶ εἰρήνη
  ἀπὸ ὁ ὢν καὶ ὁ ἦν καὶ ὁ ἐρχόμενος
καὶ ἀπὸ τῶν ἑπτὰ πνευμάτων
  ἃ ἐνώπιον τοῦ θρόνου αὐτοῦ
καὶ ἀπὸ ᾽Ιησοῦ Χριστοῦ, ὁ μάρτυς ὁ πιστός,
  ὁ πρωτότοκος τῶν νεκρῶν
καὶ ὁ ἄρχων τῶν βασιλέων τῆς γῆς

Grace to you and peace from the One who is and who was and who is coming and from the seven-fold Spirit which is before His throne and from Jesus Christ, the faithful witness, the firstborn of the dead and the ruler of the kings of the earth (1.4-5).

The expansive description of God is a paraphrase of the divine name found in Exod. 3.14-15[24] and provides for the hearers a poetic description of the eternality of God. It is God 'whose presence embraces all time: past and future, as well as present'.[25] The Spirit is next introduced as giving grace and peace to the churches. Third, grace and peace comes from Jesus. The three titles given to Jesus compliment the three-fold description of God. The three 'honorary' titles emphasize Jesus' relationship to the community as the eschatological faithful witness, the 'inaugurator and the representative of the new creation', and the ruler of the kingdoms of the earth.[26]

---

[23] For discussions of the epistolary features of Revelation see Aune, *Revelation 1–5*, pp. lxxii-lxxv; Murphy, *Fallen is Babylon*, pp. 48-49; Osborne, *Revelation*, pp. 12-13; R.W. Wall, *Revelation* (NIBC; NTS 18; Peabody: Hendrickson, 1991), p. 13.

[24] Smalley, *The Revelation to John*, p. 32.

[25] Smalley, *The Revelation to John*, p. 32.

[26] E. Schüssler Fiorenza, 'Redemption as Liberation: Apoc 1:5f and 5:9f', *CBQ* 36.2 (1974), p. 223. See Stevens, 'A Vision in the Night', pp. 8-10, who identifies the three titles as part of the biography of Jesus: '(1) Jesus crucified, (2) Jesus raised, and (3) Jesus glorified'. As such, these titles become paradigmatic for the believers. As Jesus is faithful witness, so too must believers continue in faithfulness even if it leads to death. That Jesus is firstborn from the dead holds out the promise of vindication for the faithful, and as ruler of the kings of the earth, Jesus is the one whom the believers must worship despite the pressures of the world around them.

Third, this identification of Jesus leads to a spontaneous doxological confession about Jesus:

Τῷ ἀγαπῶντι ἡμᾶς
καὶ λύσαντι ἡμᾶς ἐκ τῶν ἁμαρτιῶν ἡμῶν ἐν τῷ αἵματι αὐτοῦ
καὶ ἐποίησεν ἡμᾶς βασιλείαν, ἱερεῖς τῷ θεῷ καὶ πατρὶ αὐτοῦς
αὐτῷ ἡ δόξα καὶ τὸ κράτος εἰς τοὺς αἰῶνας [τῶν αἰώνως]·
ἀμήν

To the one who loves us
and who loosed us from our sins by means of his blood,
and made us a kingdom, priests to his God and Father,
to him be glory and might for ever.
Amen (1.5b-6).

The hymnic quality of this doxology is expressed through its use of participles to begin the phrases, the parallelism of the phrases, and the use of the temporal clause to conclude the doxology.[27] The triple use of ἡμᾶς ('us') unites John with his hearers as the beneficiaries of Jesus' actions. By means of the two dative participial phrases[28] with which the doxology begins, Jesus is worshipped as the one who loves the community and as the one who loosed them from their sins by means of his blood – a reference Johannine hearers would likely link to the cross.[29] The results of this sacrifice are expressed in the final verbal clause: the community is to see themselves as a kingdom[30] and as priests to God. This brief doxology is catechetic; it contains the salvific events central to the early followers of Jesus.[31] In structuring the doxology with the object of praise

---

[27] Deichgräber, *Gotteshymnus und Christushymnus in der frühen Christenheit*, p. 53; Thompson, *The Book of Revelation*, pp. 54-55.

[28] Aune, *Revelation 1–5*, p. 45 designates this as a double doxology because of the double dative participial phrases.

[29] Johannine hearers might reflect on statements made in the Fourth Gospel about Jesus' love, such as Jn 13.1, 34; 14.21; 15.9-12. Further, the connection between Jesus' love and his sacrifice is made explicit in 1 Jn 3.16.

[30] 'John considered the churches to be an alternative to the earthly rule of kings and emperors'. Freisen, *Imperial Cults and the Apocalypse of John: Reading Revelation in the Ruins*, p. 181.

[31] Aune, *Revelation 1–5*, p. 45.

preceding the ascription of praise, the worthiness of Jesus is emphasized.[32] That the doxology is addressed solely to Jesus is striking and serves to bolster the community in their worship of Jesus.[33] Indeed, the doxology is a song for the churches to sing.[34] The liturgical ἀμήν ('amen') concretizes the doxology and invites the hearers to respond in kind.

Fourth, the doxology is immediately followed by a prophetic word that has a liturgical form:[35]

> Ἰδοὺ ἔρχεται μετὰ τῶν νεφελῶν,
> καὶ ὄψεται αὐτὸν πᾶς ὀφθαλμὸς
> καὶ οἵτινες αὐτὸν ἐξεκέντησαν,
> καὶ κόψονται ἐπ᾽ αὐτὸν πᾶσαι αἱ φυλαὶ τῆς γῆς.
> ναί, ἀμήν

> Behold he comes with the clouds,
> and every eye will see him
> even those who pierced him,
> and all the tribes of the earth will mourn because of him.
> Yes, amen (1.7).

The presence of this prophetic word affirms the prophetic nature of the Apocalypse and the role of prophecy within the church. Its hymnic structure suggests that prophetic songs were likely a part of the liturgy of the community.[36] This prophetic word is centered on the second coming of Jesus.[37] Prophetic words from Dan. 7.13 and

---

[32] Thomas, *The Apocalypse*, p. 94.

[33] Bauckham, *The Theology of the Book of Revelation*, p. 61, 'Doxologies, with their confession that glory belongs eternally to the One who is addressed, were a Jewish form of praise to the one God. *There could be no clearer way of ascribing to Jesus the worship due to God*' (emphasis mine).

[34] Michaels, *Revelation*, p. 56.

[35] Thompson, *The Book of Revelation*, p. 55.

[36] Thomas, *The Apocalypse*, pp. 94-95, writes,

> It should perhaps be noted that the placement of these prophetic words within a context of worship in the prologue may indicate something about the way in which prophecy functioned within community gatherings … [I]t would appear likely that prophetic utterances came forth in the moments when the community was engaged in times of spontaneous praise.

[37] P. Prigent, *Commentary on the Apocalypse of St. John* (trans. W. Pradels; Tübingen: Mohr Siebeck, 2001), p. 121.

Zech 12.10 are conjoined into a *present* prophetic word about Jesus.[38] Despite the fact that Jesus is not named specifically, Johannine hearers would connect the phrase 'those who pierced him' with the death of Jesus where soldiers pierced (ἔνυξεν) his side (Jn 19.34). The use of present tense verbs coupled with the revelatory ἰδού ('behold') reinforce the expectancy of the community and confirm the earlier notification that the time is near (1.3). The prophetic word ends with the emphatic ναί ('yes') and benedictory ἀμήν ('amen').

Finally, the prologue concludes with a direct word from God: Ἐγώ εἰμι τὸ Ἄλφα καὶ τὸ Ὦ, λέγει κύριος ὁ θεός, ὁ ὢν καὶ ὁ ἦν καὶ ὁ ἐρχόμενος, ὁ παντοκράτωρ ('I AM the Alpha and the Omega, says the Lord God, the One who is and who was and who is coming, the Almighty') (1.8). This is fitting since the prologue opens with the notification that God is the ultimate source of the revelation pertaining to Jesus. The 'I AM' would likely remind the hearers of Jesus' use of these words in John's Gospel; however, here God, not Jesus, is the speaker. God is *the* Alpha and Omega, *the* Lord God, *the* one who is, was, and is coming, and *the* Almighty. Such self-revelation brings the sovereign and powerful God 'dangerously close' to the people of God.[39] Yet, this is the same God who extends to them χάρις καὶ εἰρήνη ('grace and peace') (1.4), suggesting God's involvement with and commitment to them. The voice of God would likely be experienced by the community as direct communication from God mediated to them through a prophetic word. This continues to strengthen the place of prophecy in the context of worship; that is, worship provides a receptive context for the giving and receiving of prophetic words.[40] The powerful words of God close out the prologue by taking the hearers back to the 'originating being of God'.[41]

---

[38] Michaels, *Revelation*, p. 57.

[39] J.L. Mangina, *Revelation* (BTCB; Grand Rapids: Brazos Press, 2010), p. 47.

[40] Aune, *Revelation 1–5*, p. 59, identifies v. 8 as an 'amplified oracle' which gives further explanation concerning the prophetic word of v. 7. He suggests that both oracles may be the products of the author or of others within John's prophetic circle.

[41] Smalley, *The Revelation to John*, p. 38.

II. ἐν πνεύματι – 'On the Lord's Day' (1.9–3.22)

A. John's Context and Commission (1.9-20)

The use of first person language in v. 9 alerts the hearers to a change in the narrative as John assumes the narration and consciously identifies himself as one of the characters in the story.[42] As such, he is a 'person of the present and a person of a recent and narrowly defined past, a witness to his own visions and to divine voices'.[43] John identifies himself in relation to his audience: Ἐγὼ Ἰωάννης, ὁ ἀδελφὸς ὑμῶν καὶ συγκοινωνὸς ἐν τῇ θλίψει καὶ βασιλείᾳ καὶ ὑπομονῇ ἐν Ἰησοῦ ('I John, your brother and participant in the tribulation and kingdom and patient endurance in Jesus') (1.9). Through the use of the terms ὁ ἀδελφὸς ('brother') and συγκοινωνὸς ('participant'), John associates himself with the churches relationally and through shared experience.[44] That θλίψις ('tribulation') occurs as the first of three arenas in which John shares in the experience of the churches gives likely indication of the pressing situation for the hearers.[45] John goes on to narrate his location on the island of Patmos. This change in setting locates John's experience in a specific location and time.[46] John gives the reason for his being on Patmos as διὰ τὸν λόγον τοῦ θεοῦ καὶ τὴν μαρτυρίαν Ἰησοῦ ('on account of the word of God and the testimony of Jesus'). This language recalls Rev. 1.2 and would likely remind the hearers that John is indeed a witness. Moreover, because

---

[42] Resseguie, *The Revelation of John*, p. 71.

[43] F. Bovon, 'John's Self-presentation in Revelation 1:9-10', *CBQ* 62.4 (Oct 2000), p. 695. He also states that the 'I' legitimizes John's witness throughout the rest of the book.

[44] Contra Aune who suggests that the two terms are a rhetorical device 'intended to foster compliance'. Aune, *Revelation 1–5*, p. 75. Mangina, *Revelation*, p. 48, rightly observes that John 'stands in complete solidarity with his listeners'. Bovon, 'John's Self-presentation in Revelation 1:9-10', p. 698: John 'refuses a hierarchical clerical order and states his communion with them'. Michaels, *Revelation*, p. 17: John 'stands alongside them' rather than standing over them. So also C. Gonzáles and J. Gonzáles, *Revelation* (Louisville: Westminster John Knox Press, 1997), p. 16.

[45] P.S. Minear, 'Ontology and Ecclesiology in the Apocalypse', *NTS* 13 (1966), p. 93, 'Common participation in suffering is as fully historical as the existence of the churches themselves'.

[46] John's use of ἐγενόμην ('I was') suggests that John was 'no longer on Patmos at the time of writing the book'. Ladd, *A Commentary on the Revelation of John*, p. 30.

Jesus is the faithful witness (1.5), the hearers would likely connect John with Jesus in this regard,[47] particularly if John is exiled on Patmos for his faith.[48]

John's visions on Patmos take place ἐν πνεύματι ἐν τῇ κυριακῇ ἡμέρᾳ ('in the Spirit on the Lord's Day') (1.10). Many scholars suggest that these events take place on Sunday, the day of Christian worship.[49] Thus, even though away from his hearers, John does not deviate from his practice of worship.[50] He shows solidarity with his brothers and sisters who likewise would be engaged in worship.[51] This strengthens the liturgical framework for what follows in the Apocalypse. John's narration that he was *in the Spirit* on the Lord's Day suggests that such an experience was a normal part of his worship;[52] that is, being *in the Spirit* was not abnormal for John. One could rightly argue that being ἐν πνεύματι ('in the Spirit') is a necessary prerequisite for the reception of an apocalypse.[53] Bauck-

---

[47] S.L. Homcy, '"To Him Who Overcomes": A Fresh Look at What "Victory" Means for the Believer According to the Book of Revelation', *JETS* 38.2 (June 1995), p. 199.

[48] For a discussion of Patmos and how John might have ended up there, see Aune, *Revelation 1–5*, pp. 77-80. See also I. Boxall, *The Revelation of St. John* (BNTC; London: Continuum, 2006), p. 10, on Patmos being an inhabited island with a large enough population to support a gymnasium and various trade guilds.

[49] Aune, *Revelation 1–5*, pp. 83-84; Murphy, *Fallen is Babylon*, p. 87; Osborne, *Revelation*, pp. 81-82.

[50] Thomas, *Revelation*, p. 100, noting the identical constructions of the phrases ἐγενόμην ἐν τῇ νήσῳ τῇ καλουμένῃ Πάτῳ ('I was on the island called Patmos') and ἐγενόμην ἐν πνεύματι ἐν τῇ κυριακῇ ἡμέρᾳ ('I was in the Spirit on the Lord's Day') states: 'While the identical construction with which these statements open clearly connects John's geographical location with his spiritual location, it also serves to contrast these two locations. Although John may be on an island, he is at the same time "in the Spirit".' See also Gorman, *Reading Revelation Responsibly*, p. 122.

[51] Peters, *The Mandate of the Church in the Apocalypse of John*, p. 49.

[52] J.N. Kraybill, *Apocalypse and Allegiance: Worship, Politics and Devotion in the Book of Revelation* (Grand Rapids: Brazos Press, 2010), p. 28, describes John as being in 'an attitude of waiting on God' as he normally would during regular worship ('on the Lord's day').

[53] R.H. Charles, *A Critical and Exegetical Commentary on the Revelation of St. John*, (Edinburgh: T&T Clark, 1920), I, p. 24, is representative of most early interpreters as he writes, 'In this passage, then, ἐγενόμην ἐν πνεύματι denotes nothing more than that the Seer fell into a trance. It was not until he was in this trance that Christ addressed him.' See G.B. Caird, *The Revelation of St. John the Divine* (New York: Harper & Row, 1966) who translates all the ἐν πνεύματι ('in the Spirit') phrases as 'in a trance'.

ham, who writes at length on John's being in the Spirit, states: 'John was ἐν πνεύματι in the sense that his normal sensory experience was replaced by visions and auditions given him by the Spirit'.[54] The phrase, for Bauckham, highlights the Spirit's role as 'agent of visionary experience'.[55] He further likens John's experience to other prophetic characters, such as Isaiah, Ezekiel, Zechariah and Enoch. Bauckham is correct in underscoring the important role of the Spirit as the source of John's vision, but I contend that more is being communicated in John's statement of being ἐν πνεύματι ('in the Spirit'). Johannine hearers might recall Jesus' statement about worship being ἐν πνεύματι καὶ ἀληθείᾳ ('in Spirit and in truth') (Jn 4.24). Perhaps in identifying himself as being ἐν πνεύματι, John is making a statement about the significance of worship as the point of contact between heaven and earth. John is *in* a state of worship *when* he receives the apocalypse. He did not worship ἐν πνεύματι in hopes of receiving an apocalypse; he worshipped ἐν πνεύματι because that is how worship takes place. This is not to take away from the significance of John receiving the revelation or the agency of the Spirit in giving the revelation; rather, it is to emphasize the *context* in which John received the revelation. Both John and the hearers receive the apocalypse in the context and setting of worship.[56] This initial use of the ἐν πνεύματι phrase reinforces the liturgical setting begun in the prologue by linking worship with the Spirit; that is, worship takes place *in the Spirit*.

As John is ἐν πνεύματι, he hears a great voice ὡς σάλπιγγος ('like a trumpet') commanding him to write in a βιβλίον ('book, scroll') what he sees and send it to the seven churches of Asia (Rev. 1.10b-11). The naming of each church here affords them individual identities even though they were collectively addressed in 1.4. Upon

---

[54] Bauckham, *Climax of Prophecy*, p. 152.

[55] Bauckham, *Climax of Prophecy*, p. 154. See also Prigent, *Commentary on the Apocalypse of St. John*, p. 128, who says the phrase 'undoubtedly refers to a phenomenon more or less resembling that of ecstasy'.

[56] R.L. Jeske, 'Spirit and Community in the Johannine Apocalypse', *NTS* 31 (1985), p. 458. However, Jeske sees the ἐν πνεύματι ('in the Spirit') statements as 'symbolic code for participation in the community of the Spirit' (p. 462).

turning to see the voice,[57] John sees something totally unexpected: seven golden lampstands and a figure in their midst. Although the hearers are immediately pressed to consider the figure in the midst of the lampstands, it is significant that John *first* sees the seven lampstands. These lampstands are one of the first symbols interpreted for John, for the figure John sees, the living Jesus, identifies the lampstands as the seven churches (1.20). What John sees is intended for the churches among whom Jesus walks.[58] Each of the seven churches is thereby intimately connected to Jesus.

In the description of the magnificent inaugural vision of Jesus (1.12-16), Old Testament texts and images pertaining to 'God, the Son of Man, and his servants' are combined in uniquely new ways to give the hearers a *revelation* of Jesus.[59] Even so, the repeated use of ὡς ('as, like') and ὅμοιος ('as, like') indicates that John is attempting to describe the indescribable.[60] At beholding this figure, John states: ἔπεσα πρὸς τοὺς πόδας αὐτοῦ ὡς νεκρός ('I fell at his feet as dead') (1.17). This response is not unlike the responses of Ezekiel or Daniel, both of whom fall facedown before the presence of a divine figure (Ezek. 1.28; Dan. 10.9). It is a response of awe and even terror at being in the presence of God.[61] However, as the hearers will soon learn in Revelation 4–5, prostration is also a litur-

---

[57] The Greek text is very emphatic and almost awkward: Καὶ ἐπέστρεψα βλέπειν … καὶ ἐπιστρέψας εἶδον ('And I turned to see … and after turning I saw').

[58] G.L. Stevens, 'One Like a Son of Man: Contemplating Christology in Rev 1:9-20' in G.L. Stevens (ed.), *Essays on Revelation: Appropriating Yesterday's Apocalypse in Today's World* (Eugene: Pickwick Publications, 2010), p. 20.

[59] See Thomas, *The Apocalypse*, p. 103, where he locates the OT referents for the images in the vision. He then writes, 'Yet none of these details on their own, nor simply an accounting for them from their OT texts, does justice to the vision. Such a convergence of elements and details indicate that the revelation of Jesus Christ continues in astounding fashion as he is seen and experienced in ways as never before.'

[60] Resseguie, *The Revelation of John*, p. 76; G. Biguzzi, 'A Figurative and Narrative Language Grammar of Revelation', *NovT* 45.4 (2003), pp. 382-402 identifies the description of Jesus as the first of many "description songs" in Revelation. The description songs function as a way for the author to introduce characters into the story for the following purpose: 'by describing the exterior appearance of each such character, John conveys its moral identity and physiognomy' (p. 384). John uses the physical features of the exalted Jesus to give the hearers an indication of Jesus' character.

[61] Resseguie, *The Revelation of John*, p. 79, calls it a '*stereotypical* response to the presence of the numinous' (italics mine); See also Mangina, *Revelation*, p. 51.

gical response modeled by the elders who worship before the throne of God. Although Jesus' first words to John are μὴ φοβοῦ ('Do not fear') (1.17), suggesting that John indeed is fearful, this does not negate the act of prostration as a proper response of worship to Jesus. Reverential fear is a necessary element of worship.[62] That Jesus places his right hand on John – the hand holding the seven stars – envelops John with the churches and evokes strong protection for both. Jesus' touch is also an act of blessing and commissioning as once again John is instructed to write.[63]

The second command to write in Rev. 1.19 forms an inclusio with 1.11 and provides the bookends for John's inaugural vision of Jesus. The use of οὖν ('therefore') clearly connects the command to the vision and words of the living Jesus. John is to write down ἃ εἶδες καὶ ἃ εἰσὶν καὶ ἃ μέλλει γενέσθαι μετὰ ταῦτα ('what you saw and what is and what is about to happen after these things'). The relative pronoun, here used three times, recalls Rev. 1.1 where John is to be shown ἃ δεῖ γενέσθαι ἐν τάχει ('what is necessary to happen quickly'). The use of such cryptic language in both verses would suggest to the hearers the need for careful hearing and discernment of what follows.[64]

The inaugural vision concludes with the identification of the seven stars and seven lampstands (1.20). The seven stars are identified as the seven ἄγγελοι ('angels, messengers') of the seven

---

[62] Waddell, *The Spirit of the Book of Revelation*, p. 130, sees this idea of reverential fear and worship as a necessary prerequisite for a Pentecostal interpretation of Scripture: 'Pentecostals believe they will encounter God when they read the Bible ... a reading of the biblical text, not unlike the christophany experienced by John, should involve a certain amount of fear and worship'.

[63] Smalley, *The Revelation to John*, p. 55.

[64] Rev. 1.19 has often been used as a way to structure the Apocalypse: what John 'saw' (Rev. 1.9-20); what 'is' (Rev. 2–3); and what 'will be' (Rev. 4–22). See Charles, *A Critical and Exegetical Commentary on the Revelation of St. John*, p. 33; R.L. Thomas, 'John's Apocalyptic Outline', *Bibliotheca Sacra* 123.492 (Oct-Dec 1966), pp. 334-41; M.E. Boring, *Revelation* (Louisville: John Knox Press, 1988), p. 84; G.A. Krodel, *Revelation* (ACNT; Minneapolis: Augsburg Press, 1989), pp. 97-98. Resseguie, *The Revelation of John*, p. 81, cautions on reading too much into this verse: 'Threes ... are so common in this first chapter that caution is advised. Rather than a chronological outline of the book, John uses the tripartite formula to underscore the importance of what is contained in the book for the past, present, and future.'

churches,[65] which are themselves the seven lampstands. By means of two images, stars and lampstands, the churches are closely connected to the living Jesus and are, along with John, the recipients of the revelation of Jesus.

The inaugural vision of Jesus strengthens the christological emphasis begun in the prologue. Gorman suggests that the inaugural vision serves as a portrait of security because Jesus is the powerful protector of the church; as a portrait of hope because Jesus is the conqueror of death; and as a portrait of discipleship as Christ calls the communities to obedience.[66] However, the strong presence of liturgy in the prologue coupled with the fact that what John experiences while *in the Spirit* is a revelation of Jesus suggests that the inaugural vision has a liturgical function. The churches are to be affirmed in their worship of Jesus. This Jesus, who is lauded doxologically in 1.5b-6, is now unveiled before them in all of his magnificence and splendor. Further, Jesus stands in the midst of his churches – this is what the Spirit reveals! The inaugural vision *is* a worship scene in the Apocalypse.

B. Seven Prophetic Messages (2.1–3.22)

In Revelation 2–3, each of the seven churches named in Rev. 1.11 receives a prophetic message[67] addressed to it specifically but in-

---

[65] For an excellent critical summary of the various interpretations see Aune, *Revelation 1–5*, pp. 108-12. The consensus of most modern commentators is that the seven stars are patron angelic figures or heavenly counterparts to the earthly churches. See for example Ladd, *A Commentary on the Revelation to John*, p. 35; J.P.M. Sweet, *Revelation* (Philadelphia: The Westminster Press, 1979), p. 73; Murphy, *Fallen is Babylon*, p. 100; Koester, *Revelation and the End of All Things*, p. 56; B.K. Blount, *Revelation: A Commentary* (Louisville: Westminster John Knox Press, 2009), p. 47; Resseguie, *The Revelation of John*, p. 83. R.H. Mounce, *The Book of Revelation* (Grand Rapids: Eerdmans, 1977), p. 85 identifies the ἄγγελοι as the prevailing spirits of the church. A.M. Enroth, 'The Hearing Formula in the Book of Revelation', *NTS* 36 (1990), p. 604, identifies the ἄγγελλοι as prophets in each community. So also G.L. Stevens, 'One Like a Son of Man', pp. 33-34. H. Kraft, *Die Offenbarung Des Johannes* (Tübingen: Mohr, 1974), p. 52, suggests that the angel is to be identified with a human figure who would understand the message and communicate it to the community.

[66] Gorman, *Reading Revelation Responsibly*, p. 83.

[67] Commentators often designate Revelation 2–3 as 'letters' to the seven churches. I am identifying them as 'prophetic messages' in order to be consistent with my understanding of the overall genre of the Apocalypse as apocalyptic prophecy. I see them as words of Jesus spoken to the community through the Spirit as words of prophecy. See Michaels, *Revelation*, p. 64, who identifies them as

tended for the seven churches collectively.[68] Each message is linked
to Jesus in two specific ways. First, each message is specifically addressed to the ἄγγελος ('angel, messenger') of the church (Rev. 2.1,
8, 12, 18; 3.1, 7, 14). Whatever the hearers might have understood
in this term, at the very least they would closely connect it to Jesus,
since he holds the seven stars in his hand (1.20). Second, each prophetic message comes from Jesus and draws upon elements found
in descriptions of Jesus from Revelation's opening chapter. The
narrative function of the messages is that they 'represent the "revelation of Jesus" promised by the opening voice (1:1)'.[69]

Ephesus (2.1-7)

In the first prophetic message, John is told to write to the angel of
the church in Ephesus. The hearers would recall that in Rev. 1.11,
John's instructions were to write in a book the things he saw and
send it to the seven churches. From 1.3, the hearers know that
John's writing is intended for public reading in the churches. Thus,
this prophetic message to Ephesus would have been read in the
context of the worship service and as part of *all* the churches' worship.[70] The prophetic message opens with imagery familiar to the
hearers from Revelation 1: Τάδε λέγει ὁ κρατῶν τοὺς ἑπτὰ
ἀστέρας ἐν τῇ δεξιᾷ αὐτοῦ, ὁ περιπατῶν ἐν μέσῳ τῶν ἑπτὰ
λυχνιῶν τῶν χρυσῶν ('Thus says the one holding the seven stars
in his right hand, the one walking in the midst of the seven golden
lampstands' [2.1]). The τάδε λέγει ('thus says') phrase indicates to
the hearers that the same Jesus who has been speaking to John
(1.17-20) is now speaking to the churches. Jesus is here identified to
the church by means of the imagery of the stars and golden
lampstands. Thus, although specifically addressed to Ephesus, the
opening words encompass *all* of the churches. Two subtle yet

---

'oracles of a prophet, given in the name of the divine Being who speaks through
them'.

[68] Bauckham, *The Theology of the Book of Revelation*, pp. 12-17; Homcy, '"To Him
Who Overcomes"', p. 194. Mangina, *Revelation*, p. 55, remarks: 'Even if the
churches previously had little in common, the fact of their being addressed together by Christ renders them mutually accountable, giving each an interest in the
lives of the others'.

[69] Barr, *Tales of the End*, p. 41.

[70] Thompson, *The Book of Revelation*, p. 72.

significant differences emerge in the way the imagery appears here in comparison to their initial usage in Revelation. First, in 1.16 Jesus *has* (ἔχων) the seven stars in his right hand, whereas in 2.1 Jesus is *holding* the seven stars in his right hand.[71] The verb κρατέω ('hold') has a stronger and more active sense of taking hold of or seizing;[72] thus, the churches are held firmly in the right hand of Jesus.[73] Not to be forgotten as well is that Jesus' right hand is also upon John (1.17). Second, in 1.13 Jesus is described as being ἐν μέσῳ τῶν λυχνιῶν ('in the midst of the lampstands'), but in 2.1, Jesus is depicted as ὁ περιπατῶν ἐν μέσῳ τῶν ἑπτὰ λυχνιῶν ('the one walking in the midst of the seven lampstands'). This subtle shift from *being* to *walking* suggests deliberate activity on the part of the resurrected Jesus.[74] Jesus is active in the churches; his presence is in their midst.[75] This ascription both connects with the inaugural vision of Revelation 1 and attests to the active involvement of Jesus in the churches as they worship.

After the opening ascription, the narrative switches from third person to first person direct speech. The hearers discover, along with John, that Jesus knows (Οἶδα) things about them, both good and bad, for which he offers commendation or reproof, respectively. Since Jesus' words are likely received by the hearers in the context of worship, the important place of prophetic words in worship continues to be affirmed.[76] Jesus begins with commendations to the Ephesian church (vv. 2-3). This listing of things that Jesus knows about the church assures them that he does truly walk in their midst. Jesus does not simply know of them; he discerns their

---

[71] Note the juxtaposition in 1.13 (καὶ ἔχων ἐν τῇ δεξιᾷ χειρι αὐτοῦ ἀστέρας ἑπτά, 'and having in his right hand seven stars') and 2.1 (ὁ κρατῶν τοὺς ἑπτα ἀστέρας ἐν τῇ δεξιᾷ αὐτοῦ, 'the one holding the seven starts in his right hand').

[72] Although this verb is not used in the Fourth Gospel, it is used in the Synoptic Gospels when opponents of Jesus attempt to seize him (see Mk 12.12; 14.1) or when they finally arrest Jesus (Mt. 26.57; Mk 14.46). See W. Michaelis, 'κράτος, κρατέω, κραταιός, κραταιόω, κοσμοκράτωρ, παντοκράτωρ', *TDNT*, III, p. 911.

[73] Ladd, *A Commentary on the Revelation of John*, p. 38, sees this as indicating the 'constant vigilance and watchful presence of Christ' over the churches.

[74] Prigent, *The Apocalypse of St. John*, p. 157; Thomas, *The Apocalypse*, p. 111.

[75] Rotz, *Revelation*, p. 63.

[76] Thompson, *The Book of Revelation*, p. 72.

actions. He knows of their works,[77] labor, and endurance; he knows that they cannot βαστάσαι κακούς ('bear evil people'); he knows that they have not grown weary but have endured and persevered (ἐβάστασας) on account of his name. The verb βαστάζω has the sense of carrying or lifting up, and it is used in the broader Johannine tradition (Jn 12.6; 16.12; 20.15) but without the weight that it receives here in Rev. 2.3. Here carrying or lifting up Jesus' name indicates that the community bears witness to Jesus. As believers in Jesus they bear witness through their proclamation of his death and resurrection (1.18) and his soon return (1.7). They are identified with him who is the 'faithful witness' (1.5). Perhaps this has come about through persecution or as a result of them not bearing evil people in their midst. Bearing witness encompasses more than words; it defines their life lived before the world.[78]

As Jesus has engaged in discernment, so too has the church itself, for Jesus knows that they have tested those calling themselves apostles and found them to be liars (2.2). It is apparent that the Ephesian church has exercised discernment which has resulted in the exposure of false apostles within the community. In the broader Johannine tradition discernment is a crucial task of the entire community as evidenced in 1 Jn 4.1, where the community is not to believe[79] every spirit but to test (δοκιμάζετε) the spirits to determine if they are from God because ψευδοπροφῆται ('false prophets') have gone out into the world. Discernment is necessary to determine whether or not individuals claiming to speak by means of the Holy Spirit are truly of God. Evidently the church in Ephesus engaged in a similar process of discernment and exposed the false apostles as liars.

Not only does Jesus reveal the things that please him, he also reproves the church for aspects of their life and worship that are displeasing to him (Rev. 2.4). Despite all their commendable works, Jesus' prophetic discernment reveals that the Ephesian church has

---

[77] Thomas, *The Apocalypse*, pp. 111-12, provides a good treatment of the term 'works' in the Apocalypse. He suggests that 'the idea of works is an integrative one which includes one's activity or actions, that carries with them a sign-like quality which reveals something about one's relationship with God and/or Jesus'.

[78] F. Büchsel, 'βαστάζω', *TDNT*, I, p. 596.

[79] The use of μη plus the present imperative implies the prohibition of an ongoing activity; thus, the author is calling for them to *stop believing* every spirit.

forsaken its first love. Such a revelation, on the heels of Jesus' earlier words of praise, is a shocking statement. In spite of the abundant usage of ἀγάπη ('love') in the Fourth Gospel[80] and Johannine Epistles,[81] this is the only occurrence of the noun ἀγάπη ('love') in Revelation. The verb form is found in the doxology in 1.5, suggesting that at the very least the hearers would connect their first love with Jesus, the one who loves them. Further, it is not without significance that in the Johannine Epistles 'love' for God is revealed in love for others (1 Jn 4.11).[82] This broader Johannine context could indicate that the Ephesian community in failing to love others is ultimately failing to love God. Whereas the church has correctly discerned those claiming to be apostles, they have failed to discern their own spiritual condition. Because of this Jesus calls the community to spiritual action. The community is charged with three things: 1) to remember (μνημόνευε) from where they have fallen; 2) to repent (μετανόησον); and 3) to do (ποίησον) their first works (Rev. 2.5). Jesus' earlier words of commendation have served to jog the community's memory as they are gathered together in worship. Clearly their past stands in contrast to their present condition, for Jesus indicates, by means of the perfect tense πέπτωκας ('you have fallen'), that they are spiritually falling away. By remembering their past, the community joins with Jesus in the task of discernment. By repenting, the community discerns and renounces their present condition. By doing their first works, which are left undefined but must be related to Jesus' earlier words in 2.2, the community demonstrates its repentance through obedience to Jesus' words and thereby keeps the words of Jesus' prophecy (1.3). This is the first use of μετανοέω ('repent') in Revelation, yet its imperatival form suggests that the hearers are familiar with the concept of repentance. Indeed, 'repentance' is strong language that demands a response. While it is difficult to say what form such repentance would take, it would seem that given the role that confession plays in 1 Jn 1.5-2.1, it would probably involve public confession. Further, given the concrete way that love functions in 1 John, the 'evidence' of

---

[80] John 5.42; 13.35; 15.9, 10, 13; 17.26.

[81] 1 John 2.5, 15; 3.1, 16, 17; 4.7, 8, 9, 10, 12, 16, 17, 18; 5.3; 2 Jn 3, 6.

[82] Conversely hating others is a sign that one does not love God (1 Jn 4.2).

repentance will be tangible; that is, the community will *do* its first works.[83] All of this suggests that repentance should be taken seriously.

The importance of repentance within the church is augmented by Jesus' next prophetic words, for they contain a threat of judgment: εἰ δὲ μή, ἔρχομαί σοι καὶ κινήσω τὴν λυχνίαν σου ἐκ τοῦ τόπου αὐτῆς, ἐὰν μὴ μετανοήσῃς ('but if not, I am coming to you and I will remove your lampstand from its place, if you do not repent') (Rev. 2.5b). Without repentance, the community places itself under the threat of judgment. The hearers would likely not miss that Jesus uses the present tense of ἔρχομαι ('I come') rather than a future tense. They know from the opening chapter that God is described in part as ὁ ἐρχόμενος ('the one coming') (1.4, 8) and Jesus is coming (ἔρχεται) with the clouds (1.7). Thus, while the notice that Jesus will come is not without precedent, there seems to be ominous implications associated with this particular coming.[84] Whereas a *future* coming might cause the church to be apathetic in their response to Jesus' call for repentance, the prospect of his *present* coming calls for an immediate and energetic response of true repentance.

Jesus' words of impending judgment are brief, suggesting that full obedience is expected. Jesus quickly resumes with words that reveal his prophetic discernment: ἀλλὰ τοῦτο ἔχεις, ὅτι μισεῖς τὰ ἔργα τῶν Νικολαϊτῶν ἃ κἀγὼ μισῶ ('but you have this [in your favor], that you hate the works of the Nicolaitans which I also hate') (2.6). Jesus commends the community for hating the works of the Nicolaitans. Despite the fact that the text does not make known the origins or teachings of such a group, *their works* are repugnant to Jesus and to the Ephesian church.[85] Thus, it appears

---

[83] Rotz, *Revelation*, p. 65.

[84] Blount, *Revelation*, p. 51: 'The one who walks in the midst of the lampstands and cares for them will remove this one, this Ephesian church, from its place with the others, and thus its place of eschatological relationship with God and Christ, unless the people whom it represents repent'. See also Rotz, *Revelation*, p. 65.

[85] Many scholars see the name as being symbolic. Bauckham, *The Theology of the Book of Revelation*, p. 124, sees John employing a wordplay between the key verb νικάω found in the letters and the Nicolaitans (νικολαϊτῶν). He writes, 'Their teaching made it possible for Christians to be successful in pagan society, but this was the beast's success, a real conquest of the saints, winning them to his

likely that the Ephesian church has again engaged in discernment. That Jesus *hates* the works of the Nicolaitans, while shocking in its vehemence, serves to affirm the community in the correctness of their discernment. Jesus' language further strengthens the need for repentance; that is, the community does not want to become a group whose works are hated by Jesus.

The next words found in the prophetic message might surprise the hearers: ὁ ἔχων οὖς ἀκουσάτω τί τὸ πνεῦμα λέγει ταῖς ἐκκλησίαις ('let the one having an ear hear what the Spirit says to the churches') (2.7a). While Jesus has been the one speaking in the prophetic message, now the hearers discover that *the Spirit* is speaking to the churches; that is, Jesus' words are presented as coterminous with the words of the Spirit.[86] The hearers recognize that the means by which Jesus is both present within the community and speaking to the community is through the Holy Spirit. Although the Spirit has only been mentioned twice to this point (1.4, 10), this notification of the Spirit speaking to the churches provides for a very active presence of the Spirit within the churches. Jesus' words are heard in the worshipping community as prophetic words from the Spirit.[87] The Spirit calls the church to discernment. While directly applicable to the Ephesian church, this call to discernment is for all the churches. That they are called to discern indicates that they *can* discern. The Spirit who mediates Jesus' words and message will help the church in discerning his words. The church, then, is charged with the task of *hearing* in the Spirit.[88] Because the community is

---

side, rather than the only apparent conquest he achieved by putting them to death'. See also Wilson, *The Victor Sayings in the Book of Revelation*, pp. 84-85, who agrees with Bauckham's assessment and adds,

> The Asian audience would appreciate the irony of these would-be victors over the people contrasted with the true spiritual victors over the beast and false prophet ... By mentioning the Nicolatians [sic], John establishes a contrast between two groups (at least) in the Asian churches – those victorious over the people and those victorious unto God.'

[86] Ladd, *A Commentary on the Revelation of John*, p. 40; R.J. Bauckham, 'The Role of the Spirit in the Apocalypse', *The Evangelical Quarterly* 52.2 (April-June 1980), p. 73.

[87] Bauckham, *The Theology of the Book of Revelation*, p. 117: 'He [the Spirit] inspires the prophetic oracles in which the prophet John speaks Christ's words to the churches'.

[88] Thomas, *The Apocalypse*, p. 122, defines 'hearing in the Spirit':

hearing the Spirit in worship, worship *in the Spirit* provides the context for receiving the words of Jesus. Worship becomes a pneumatic experience.

The Spirit's call to discernment is followed by an eschatological promise that closes out the prophetic message: τῷ νικῶντι δώσω αὐτῷ φαγεῖν ἐκ τοῦ ξύλου τῆς ζωῆς, ὅ ἐστιν ἐν τῷ παραδείσῳ τοῦ θεοῦ ('to the one who overcomes I will give to eat from the tree of life which is in the paradise of God') (2.7b). In the context of the prophetic message, the overcomers are those who obey Jesus' words. This would include things such as continuing to do their first works, continuing to discern as Jesus discerned, and continuing to practice repentance. To the overcomers, Jesus holds out a future reward of eating from the tree of life in the paradise of God. Although it is a future reward and the hearers will hear about the tree of life at the end of Revelation (22.2, 14, 19), its presence here in the narrative indicates that when the church is gathered in worship, the time and space between the present and future collapses. Worship becomes a proleptic experience where the future breaks into the present.[89] In worship, the eschatological Jesus, the one who will come, *comes* to the community and invites them to participate in the world to come. It is not yet a full participation, but a foretaste. Although the hearers might readily associate the tree of life in paradise with the tree of life in Eden, the imagery of eating from the tree might cause the hearers also to think about the Eucharist – the sacred meal they shared in anticipatory hope of the great eschatological banquet to come.[90] The eschatological promise

---

The hearing here called for is a specifically pneumatic activity. Owing to the fact that John is 'in the Spirit' when he sees (and writes!), the fact that these words are the prophetically spoken words of Jesus, and the fact that John and his hearers have already received divine interpretive assistance from Jesus himself, it stands to reason that the entire process from first encounter to discerning obedience is a pneumatic experience. In this activity, the hearers stand in solidarity with John, Jesus, and the Spirit. If John's role is to 'write in the Spirit', the role of others in this prophetic community is to 'hear in the Spirit'.

[89] Thompson, *The Book of Revelation*, p. 72.

[90] Although the Gospel of John does not contain a tradition about the Last Supper, Eucharistic overtones are found in John 6 where Jesus speaks of eating his flesh and drinking his blood. If the Apocalypse is particularly designed to be read aloud during Christian gatherings for worship, which would likely include the Eucharist, then the Johannine hearers might think of the reference to *eating* from the tree of life as a reference to the Eucharist. See Boxall, *The Revelation of St.*

that ends the prophetic message, like the ascription that begins the message, draws the community's attention to Jesus. In this way, the promise to the overcomers serves as another reason to worship Jesus, for He is the eschatological giver of life.

Smyrna (2.8-11)

The shortest of the prophetic messages is that addressed to Smyrna. Like the message to Ephesus, this message to Smyrna is also heard by all the churches. The opening τάδε λέγει ('thus says') announces to all the churches that Jesus is about to speak again. To the church in Smyrna, Jesus is identified as ὁ πρῶτος καὶ ὁ ἔσχατος, ὃς ἐγένετο νεκρὸς καὶ ἔζησεν ('the first and the last, who was dead and became alive') (2.8). The hearers would recall similar words from Jesus in 1.17. Hearing this at this point assures the church that the same Jesus who spoke to John ἐν πνεύματι ('in the Spirit') is speaking to them as they also are gathered for worship ἐν πνεύματι. It is likely as well that the worshippers would connect the language of 'first and last' with the Alpha and Omega language used of God in 1.8; thus, Jesus identifies himself with God. The hearers would also likely detect the reversal of words for living and dead in 2.8 from their order in 1.18. In 1.18, the double use of the participle ζῶν ('living') brackets the notification of Jesus' death, thereby reinforcing the crucial event of the resurrection. The change in order in 2.8 assures the church that the *living* Jesus is in their midst. The ascription connects the prophetic message to the inaugural vision of Jesus, provides the central tenet for the churches' worship of Jesus as the living God, and serves as part of the content of their witness and proclamation to the world.

The switch to first person signals the start of Jesus' words of prophetic discernment. Jesus identifies three things that he knows about the community: 1) their tribulation (θλῖψιν); 2) their poverty (πτωχείαν); and 3) the blasphemy (τὴν βλασφημίαν) they have endured by those calling themselves Jews (2.9). This combination of terms suggests that the Smyrna church has suffered for its witness

---

John, p. 15. On the Johannine community, see also J. Webster, *Ingesting Jesus: Eating and Drinking in the Gospel of John* (Atlanta: Society of Biblical Literature, 2003). Scholars who affirm the Eucharistic setting for the Apocalypse include Filho, 'The Apocalypse of John as an Account of a Visionary Experience', p. 214; Gloer, 'Worship God! Liturgical Elements in the Apocalypse', pp. 35-57; Prigent, *Commentary on the Apocalypse of St. John*, p. 113; Barr, *Tales of the End*, p. 144.

to Jesus. Hearing that Jesus is aware of their situation not only attests to the presence of Jesus in their midst but also affirms them in their witness. Although Jesus knows about their situation, he does not intervene to alleviate their tribulation or poverty,[91] nor does he indicate that one has caused the other.[92] The community has learned from John's experience that faithful witness can lead to tribulation (1.9). Jesus' most pointed discernment relates to an external threat from those who call themselves Jews but who are exposed by Jesus as a synagogue of Satan (συναγωγὴ τοῦ Σατανᾶ) (2.9b). The Smyrna church is to discern properly those *calling themselves* Jews but who are not. That they *call themselves* Jews but Jesus *calls* them a *synagogue* of Satan indicates that at issue is religious identification. By using the terms συναγωγὴ ('synagogue') and ἐκκλησία ('church'), Jesus contrasts not two ethnic identities but rather two arenas of worship. Jesus praises the Smyrna believers for what they are not; that is, they are *not* a synagogue of Satan because they are a church aligned with Jesus who was dead and now lives.[93] Because those calling themselves Jews are blaspheming the church, their actions are clear evidence that they are not the true people of God; rather the true people of God are those who, regardless of ethnicity, align themselves with the living Jesus.[94] The use of the religious term

---

[91] G.R. Beasley-Murray, *Revelation* (Grand Rapids: Eerdmans, 1981), p. 81.

[92] Blount, *Revelation*, p. 53.

[93] I am grateful to my colleague Dr. Lee Roy Martin for this observation.

[94] Many scholars interpret this to be referencing ethnic Jews. See Thompson, *Book of Revelation*, p. 83; Osborne, *Revelation*, p. 131; Smalley, *The Revelation to John*, p. 63; Beasley-Murray, *Revelation*, p. 82; G. Carey, *Elusive Apocalypse* (Macon, GA: Mercer University Press, 1999), pp. 20-21; Prigent, *Commentary on the Apocalypse of St. John*, p. 167-68; Murphy, *Fallen is Babylon*, pp. 123-24; Koester, *Revelation and the End of All Things*, pp. 63-64; Wall, *Revelation*, p. 73; Blount, *Revelation*, p. 54. Mayo, *'Those Who Call Themselves Jews': The Church and Judaism in the Apocalypse of John*, pp. 60-61, argues that John is using the term Ἰουδαῖοι to refer to ethnic Jews, and he is addressing the conflict between ethnic Jews and Jewish Christians at Smyrna. He writes,

> Some of the Jews of Smyrna and Philadelphia are labeled a 'synagogue of Satan' because they oppose God's people and have allied themselves by default with God's arch-nemesis. This is not to imply that all Jews are of Satan in John's eyes or that John is intending here to be anti-Semitic or even anti-Jewish. John himself is a Jew. He does not use the appellation 'Jew' in any derogatory sense. He wants to claim the title for those who are 'true Jews' regardless of ethnicity. The 'true Jews' for John are the believers who are suffering on behalf of God and the Lamb.

'blasphemy' reinforces the idea that what is at issue is a religious claim. Perhaps the church is being slandered for its claims about the resurrection of Jesus. This claim would likely have put them at odds with other religious groups. The ascription, then, becomes all the more significant as it serves to affirm them in their understanding, confession, and worship of Jesus despite opposition from other religious groups.[95]

If the issue at stake is religious identification, the naming of the synagogue as a synagogue of Satan exposes the true source of opposition against the church.[96] This is the first mention of Satan in Revelation. By means of Jesus' discernment, the church is made aware of Satan's malevolent activity.[97] This is reinforced by the immediate notification of pending suffering and the imprisonment of some within the community by the Devil (v. 10). Whatever the hearers might understand by this, they would likely think of John's situation on Patmos. That Jesus commissions John on Patmos to write to the churches suggests that John has been forcibly separated from them, perhaps as an exiled prisoner.[98] The Smyrna church is about to witness some of their own members becoming prisoners as well. The purpose of this specific θλῖψις ('tribulation'), which is here limited to a ten-day period of time,[99] is for testing (ἵνα πειρασθῆτε). Where the Ephesian community had tested those calling themselves apostles, the Smyrna community will find themselves being tested. Ominously, although the *time* of testing is short and thereby limited, the community is to understand that this suffering

---

See also C. Hemer, *The Letters to the Seven Churches of Asia in their Local Settings* (JSNTS 11; Sheffield: JSOT Press, 1986), p. 67, who also argues that John uses the term 'Jew' to designate the true people of God and not an ethnic group. For the position that John is addressing Judaizing Gentiles, see Michaels, *Revelation*, p. 74.

[95] Blount, *Revelation*, p. 54

[96] Resseguie, *The Revelation of John*, p. 89, 'The name-calling is harsh perhaps because the danger is so great'. See also Fee, *Revelation*, p. 31; Skaggs and Benham, *Revelation*, p. 36.

[97] Thomas, *The Apocalypse*, p. 128.

[98] Hemer, *The Letters to the Seven Churches of Asia*, p. 29.

[99] Aune, *Revelation 1–5*, p. 166, suggests that such a phrase might be used because it is 'the sum of the fingers of both hands'. Murphy, *Fallen is Babylon*, p. 124, notes that ten is always a negative number in Revelation. Thomas, *The Apocalypse*, p. 40, suggests that the number ten may have reminded the hearers of Dan. 1.12, 14 where it is clearly connected to testing.

and testing might lead to death (v. 10).[100] Jesus calls them to remain faithful *even* unto death.[101] The call to faithfulness alerts the church that their witness to and about Jesus is a life and death issue from which they must not shrink back.[102] Rather, they are called publically to imitate Jesus, the faithful witness (1.5).

Although Jesus talks about death, he ties it directly to the promise of life: γίνου πιστὸς ἄχρι θανάτου, καὶ δώσω σοι τὸν στέφανον τῆς ζωῆς ('be faithful unto death, and I will give to you the crown of life') (2.10). That such a promise comes from the one who was dead and now lives assures the church that the resurrected Jesus is indeed able to give life, for he holds the keys of death and Hades (1.18). As Murphy rightly notes, the resurrection 'imparts ultimate significance to Christian suffering'.[103] The crown, a symbol of victory, is the eschatological reward for being faithful even unto death. The promise of life, the church learns, is not found in escaping tribulation but by being faithful *in* tribulation.[104]

The Spirit's second call for discernment goes out to all the churches as again the words of Jesus and the Spirit converge (2.11). The church of Smyrna is called to discern its context, its own public witness, and the source of its opposition. As in the first prophetic message, this call to discernment indicates to all of the churches that they *can* discern the words of this prophecy. The context of worship, again, is the place for the giving and receiving of prophetic messages.

The Spirit's call to discernment is followed by the concluding eschatological promise to the overcomers – those who heed the words of Jesus. In the present context, this would include continuing to worship the living Jesus and continuing to live a life of faithful witness even in the face of suffering and death. In doing this, the overcomers are to be closely identified with Jesus, the one who

---

[100] Beasley-Murray, *Revelation*, p. 82.

[101] Rotz, *Revelation*, p. 68, sees the testing as a means for the church to 'prove their own authenticity'.

[102] Koester, *Revelation and the End of All Things*, p. 65.

[103] Murphy, *Fallen is Babylon*, p. 120.

[104] Resseguie, *The Revelation to John*, p. 90.

overcame death and now lives. The promise to the worshipping community is that they will in no way[105] be hurt or injured by[106] the second death (2.11b). Jesus has already promised a crown of life to those who remain faithful unto death. Now the community discovers that Jesus' reward, the crown of life, is not a temporary reward. Although death is a very real possibility for those who remain faithful, Jesus has the keys to Death. Whatever the 'second death' is, the hearers know without a doubt that they will never be affected by it, even though they may be facing the 'first death' very soon.[107] As with the first eschatological promise, this promise of life is received proleptically in the worship experience of the community. It is perhaps here, at the end of the prophetic message, that the community is able to discern Jesus' earlier words that despite their condition of poverty they are rich. They are rich because of what they receive from Christ. Therefore, the eschatological promise, like the ascription, draws the attention of the community away from their immediate situation to Jesus who is in their midst by the Spirit and who is to be worshipped as the giver of life.

Pergamum (2.12-17)

The third prophetic message is for the church in Pergamum specifically and all the churches in general. The τάδε λέγει ('thus says') indicates that Jesus is about to speak again. Jesus is identified ὁ ἔχων τὴν ῥομφαίαν τὴν δίστομον τὴν ὀξεῖαν ('the One having the double-edged sword') (2.12). The double-edged sharp sword is the only piece of weaponry associated with Jesus in the inaugural vision. That the sword comes from Jesus' mouth speaks to the power and accuracy of his discerning words.[108]

---

[105] Note the use of the emphatic οὐ μή ('never, certainly not') with the aorist subjunctive ἀδικηθῇ ('hurt, injured').

[106] G. Schrenk, 'ἄδικος, ἀδικία, ἀδικεω, ἀδίκημα', *TDNT*, I, p. 161.

[107] Wall, *Revelation*, p. 74. Murphy, *Fallen is Babylon*, p. 126, does not deny the reality of the first death but sees the eschatological promise as providing a different perspective on impending death. He writes, 'For the Smyrneans, the first death is not real, for it leads to escape from the second death and to the attainment of the crown of life'.

[108] Stevens, 'One Like a Son of Man: Contemplating Christology in Rev 1:9-20', p. 35: 'The words of the Son of Man are his chosen weapon of offense'.

Jesus reveals what he knows about the Pergamum church:

Οἶδα ποῦ κατοικεῖς, ὅπου ὁ θρόνος τοῦ Σατανᾶ, καὶ κρατεῖς τὸ ὄνομά μου καὶ οὐκ ἠρνήσω τὴν πίστιν μου καὶ ἐν ταῖς ἡμέραι Ἀντιπᾶς ὁ μάρτυς μου ὁ πιστός μου, ὃς ἀπεκτάνθη παρ' ὑμῖν, ὅπου ὁ Σατανᾶς κατοικεῖ

I know where you live, where the throne of Satan is, and you are holding fast to my name and did not deny my faith even in the days of Antipas my faithful witness, who was put to death among you, where Satan lives (2.13).

Jesus' discernment, like the sword coming from his mouth, is pointed and sharp. He explicitly identifies their dwelling place with the place where Satan dwells and has his throne.[109] The hearers would recall Satan's work against the church in Smyrna. Here they discover Satan's stronghold in Pergamum. The two-fold reference to Satan brackets further discernment from Jesus. The church demonstrates faithful witness by holding fast to Jesus' name. Coupled with holding fast is the acknowledgement that they have not denied[110] their faith in Jesus even in the days of Antipas. The aorist tense of ἀρνέομαι ('deny') stands in contrast to the present tense of κρατεῖς ('hold fast'), indicating that Jesus knows of a particular time, identified by reference to the days of Antipas, when the believers' confessed and did not deny their faith. Jesus singles out Antipas, one of their own who was put to death, as an example of faithful witness. Antipas, who is identified by Jesus as my faithful witness is described in language reminiscent of Jesus (1.5).[111] Thus,

---

[109] The use of ὁ θρόνος ('the throne') might suggest a particular throne, whether literal or symbolic, that the readers would recognize. Aune, *Revelation 1–5*, p. 182. See his discussion of possible suggestions for identifying the throne (pp. 182-84). Fee, *Revelation*, p. 34, sees this as 'John's now-Christian epithet for a city where Christian blood is first known to have been spilt'.

[110] H. Schlier, 'ἀρνέομαι', *TDNT*, I, pp. 469-71, indicates that this verb relates primarily to a person rather than an object, and it implies 'a previous relationship of obedience and fidelity' that can 'take place only where there has first been acknowledgment and commitment' (p. 470). Conversely, Blount, *Revelation*, pp. 56-57 takes 'my faith' as a subjective genitive (the faith that Jesus bore) rather than an objective genitive (faith in Jesus). He sees that the believers are commended for not denying Christ's 'faith in his own lordship, to which he testified and for which he died on the cross'. Blount's argument is unconvincing in the context of the prophetic message itself.

[111] Beale, *The Book of Revelation* (NIGTC; Grand Rapids: Eerdmans, 1999), p. 247, discusses the awkward Greek construction that surrounds the name Antipas.

Jesus, the faithful witness, calls Antipas *my* faithful witness. The double use of the pronoun μου ('my') is emphatic and closely connects Antipas to Jesus.[112] That Antipas' death took place where Satan dwells – the place where they live! – indicates that Antipas was killed for his belief in Jesus and Satan is behind that death.[113] The warning of death in Smyrna (2.10) takes on added urgency as does the admonition to be faithful unto death. Antipas serves as an exemplar for the churches as one who embodied faithful witness as an act of worship. It is perhaps here, with the notice of the first martyr to this point in Revelation, that the eschatological promises from the messages to Ephesus and Smyrna become the foundation for the hope of the believing communities. In bearing witness to Jesus unto death, Antipas is now in the presence of Jesus – the paradise of God – where he wears a crown of life and eats from the tree of life. For Antipas, as for all who overcome, the second death is rendered powerless.

Jesus' words of discernment to the worshipping community also include words of reproof. Jesus' discernment reveals that there are those within the church who are holding to both the teachings of Balaam and the Nicolaitans. The reappearance of κρατέω ('holding fast') creates a patent contrast with those whom Jesus has just commended for holding fast to his name (2.13). The double use of the noun διδαχή ('teaching') indicates that both 'Balaam' and the Nicolaitans are giving instruction within the community. The use of διδαχή ('teaching') suggests that teaching and instruction was a part of the church's gatherings, yet the community has apparently failed in its discernment as false teachers are operating in its midst. Jesus identifies one of the false teachers symbolically as the biblical char-

---

Where it should be in the genitive case ('Αντιπᾶς) following ἐν ταῖς ἡμέραις ('in the days'), John employs a nominative phrase ('Αντιπᾶς ὁ μάρτυς ... ὁ πιστός, 'Antipas the faithful witness'). John does the same thing in Rev. 1.5 when he uses the nominative phrase ὁ μάρτος ὁ πιστός ('the faithful witness') following the genitive 'Ιησοῦ Χριστοῦ ('of Jesus Christ') (which Beale indicates is to draw attention to the allusion to Ps. 88.38 (89.37). Beale suggests that John does this intentionally in 2.13 to make clear the identification of Antipas with Jesus as a faithful witness.

[112] Murphy, *Fallen is Babylon*, p. 130. Blount, *Revelation*, p. 58, sees Antipas as the 'ultimate representative of non-violent resistance'.

[113] Sweet, *Revelation*, p. 88.

acter Balaam.[114] This suggests that the community knows the biblical story and, more importantly, should be able to discern the 'Balaam' within their midst.[115] 'Balaam' is identified as the one teaching Balak to throw a snare before the Israelites in the form of eating food sacrificed to idols and engaging in sexual immorality.[116] The church is to heed the lesson of the Israelites who were ultimately led into idolatry with the Moabites in order that the same thing not happen to them. As with 'Balaam', the same must surely be said about the Nicolaitans. The use of ὁμοίως ('in the same way') links the teachings of the Nicolaitans to the teachings of 'Balaam', suggesting either two distinct groups or, more likely, that 'Balaam' is a part of the Nicolaitans.[117] Where their works were condemned in 2.6, here it is their teaching (2.15). Where the Ephesian church was praised for hating the Nicolaitans, the Pergamum church is rebuked for allowing them to operate within the community.[118] As Israel's faith was corrupted by idolatry and sexual immorality, the church, likewise, is to realize that its faith is in danger of being corrupted. This teaching and the behavior resulting from it, if indeed the church is actually engaging in idolatry and immorality, will invalidate the faithful witness of the church. As Jesus has discerned, the church in Pergamum must also engage in proper discernment both of those who instruct as well the content of their instruction.

Following Jesus' prophetic discernment, Jesus calls the church to repent (μετανόησον) (2.16). This imperatival call to repentance is brief yet pointed. The postpositive οὖν ('therefore') links it directly

---

[114] Blount, *Revelation*, p. 58. Blount also suggests that it is likely that Balaam was an 'identifiable leader within the Nicolaitans' since the two groups are closely connected in the text. Mounce, *Revelation*, p. 98, states that 'Balaam became a prototype of all corrupt teachers who betrayed believers into fatal compromise with worldly ideologies'.

[115] Koester, *Revelation and the End of All Things*, p. 59, 'Calling one of the teachers at Pergamum "Balaam" warned the congregation about what the teacher was doing'.

[116] In Num. 25.1-2, the Israelites do engage in sexual immorality and idolatry with the Moabites but this is not directly attributed to Balaam until Num. 31.16. Aune notes that Revelation, like Jude and 2 Peter, seems to follow the haggadic traditions about Balaam that developed in Judaism. Aune, *Revelation 1–5*, p. 187.

[117] Mounce, *The Book of Revelation*, p. 98; Murphy, *Fallen is Babylon*, p. 130; Trafton, *Reading Revelation*, p. 39.

[118] Murphy, *Fallen is Babylon*, p. 127.

to Jesus' discerning words concerning false teachers. The church is to recognize its situation and rid itself of this false teaching immediately. The utter seriousness of their repentance is heightened by Jesus' threat to come to them quickly (2.16). The use of the present tense verb ἔρχομαί ('I come') coupled with ταχὺ ('quickly') provides a sense of urgency and immediacy. If he comes to them, says Jesus, he will make war with them using the sword of his mouth. The aggressive language of war indicates to the hearers that the living Jesus who is walking in their midst as they worship will bring immediate judgment upon them.[119] Jesus is prepared to 'do battle against those who would pervert his pure gospel into something else'.[120] Because the sword comes from his mouth, the 'war' is verbal; that is, the church will be confronted with 'his truthful word of witness and, consequently, condemnation'.[121] All of this makes repentance a crucial act of worship within the community. With the Balaam story in mind, one might imagine that repentance would take the form of public confession of sin as well as the expulsion of the false teachers and their followers from the church.

Jesus' threatening words are followed by the third call of the Spirit for discernment (2.17). Once again, the church is to discern that Jesus is speaking to them through the Spirit. The call goes out for them to examine their private and public witness and to reject any teaching that does not align itself with Jesus' teaching. The appeal to the stories of Scripture suggests that the reading and hearing of Scripture is an important activity of worship within the churches. Above all, the church must repent or face the consequences of their rebellion.

The eschatological promise to the overcomers concludes the prophetic message. It is the longest promise to this point (2.17). Jesus promises hidden[122] manna to the overcomers. Once again,

---

[119] Rotz, *Revelation*, p. 73.

[120] Fee, *Revelation*, p. 36.

[121] Bauckham, *The Theology of Revelation*, p. 122.

[122] The use of the perfect κεκρυμμένου ('having been hidden') indicates that Jesus has hidden away provisions for them. Thomas, *The Apocalypse*, p. 141. Wilson, *The Victor Sayings in the Book of Revelation*, p. 123, writes, 'The promise of the bread of heaven/life is a realized one in the Fourth Gospel, while the promise of hidden manna in Revelation is future, though the second is obviously predicated on the first'. Mounce, *Revelation*, p. 99, writes, 'While the promise is primarily eschatological, it is not without immediate application for a persecuted people'.

Jesus appeals to scriptural stories and thereby affirms the church in the use of Scripture for teaching and instruction. The manna stands in sharp contrast to the mention of food sacrificed to idols in v. 14.[123] Jesus fully expects the church to heed his words, repent, and be overcomers. It is in worship that the church partakes of the hidden manna – the food which sustains them. Perhaps this constitutes another allusion to the Eucharist.[124] Jesus also promises a white stone[125] with a new name written upon it that will only be known to the ones receiving it.[126] Whatever else this promise might indicate, it is not insignificant that Jesus has praised them for holding fast to his name (2.13). At the very least there is a continuing connection between Jesus' name and the name he will give to the overcomers.[127] It is also likely that since Jesus has given Antipas the name 'my faithful witness' that the believers are to realize that in holding fast to Jesus' name, they *are* Jesus' faithful witnesses. That this name has already been written[128] expresses Jesus' expectation that the church will be faithful witnesses to his name. The eschatological promises are proleptically experienced by the church as they are gathered together in worship.

Thyatira (2.18-29)

The fourth prophetic message to the church at Thyatira is also being read and heard in all of the churches. This prophetic message begins with the now familiar τάδε λέγει ('thus says') and proceeds to identify Jesus in three ways (2.18b). First, Jesus is ὁ υἱὸς τοῦ θεοῦ ('the Son of God'). Remarkably this designation is not found in the inaugural vision of Jesus; in fact, it is not found in Revelation prior to this point. Second, Jesus is ὁ ἔχων τοὺς ὀφθαλμοὺς

---

[123] Murphy, *Fallen is Babylon*, p. 131.

[124] P. Richard, *The Apocalypse: A People's Commentary on the Book of Revelation* (Maryknoll: Orbis Books, 2005), p. 58; Thompson, *Revelation*, p. 72; Sweet, *Revelation*, p. 90.

[125] For a listing of possible interpretations of the word ψῆφος ('stone') see Wilson, *The Victor Sayings in the Book of Revelation*, p. 125.

[126] Ladd, *A Commentary on the Revelation of John*, p. 49, sees that both the white stone and new name are symbols representing admission to the messianic feast.

[127] Beale, *The Book of Revelation*, p. 255, writes that 'believers already possess Christ's name before death (or the parousia)' and 'the future promise of the name refers to the time when they will be identified with Christ in a fuller way because of their perseverance'.

[128] The Greek perfect γεγραμμέον ('having been written').

αὐτοῦ ὡς φλόγα πυρὸς ('the One having his eyes as a flame of fire'). This description of Jesus' eyes returns to the portrayal in the inaugural vision but with one slight difference. Jesus says he is the one *having* his eyes like a flame of fire. By means of this subtle shift away from the purely descriptive statement of 1.14 (his eyes as flames of fire), Jesus becomes the subject of the participle. The hearers wait in expectation of what Jesus has honed his eyes upon as his gaze penetrates the community. Third, and in continuity with the inaugural vision (1.15), Jesus is identified as having feet like burnished brass. This imagery suggests 'strength and stability'.[129] By combining elements from the inaugural vision with the title 'Son of God', the ascription serves definitively to identify the 'one like a son of man' that John saw and who now speaks to the church as *the* Son of God.

As the narrative switches from third to first person, the hearers prepare for Jesus' prophetic words: Οἶδά σου τὰ ἔργα καὶ τὴν ἀγάπην καὶ τὴν πίστιν καὶ τὴν διακονίαν καὶ τὴν ὑπομονήν σου, καὶ τὰ ἔργα σου τὰ ἔσχατα πλείονα τῶν πρώτων ('I know your works and love and faith and service and your perseverance, and your last works are greater than the first') (2.19). Jesus makes double mention of the works of the church without describing them in any detail. The subtle positioning of σου ('your') before the first use of τὰ ἔργα ('the works') rather than after it, as in the second half of the verse (see also 2.2), emphasizes that Jesus knows the works specific to the church in Thyatira.[130] Jesus also commends them for possessing love, faith, righteousness, and perseverance. Aside from the term τὴν διακονίαν ('service') the hearers have heard these terms used in the earlier prophetic messages (2.2, 3, 13). Unlike Ephesus, the church at Thyatira is lauded for its last works being greater than its first works.

The words of commendation from Jesus stand in stark contrast to the extensive rebuke that Jesus gives to the church. It is here where Jesus' flaming eyes provide prophetic illumination. Jesus' rebuke centers around their tolerance of and adherence to the teachings of a self-proclaimed προφῆτιν ('prophetess') whom Jesus calls

---

[129] Stevens, 'One Like a Son of Man', p. 30.

[130] See also 2.9 where Jesus says to the Smyrna church Οἶδά σου τὴν θλῖψιν ('I know your tribulation'). The possessive pronoun precedes the noun rather than follows it. Again, this could be for emphasis.

'Ιεζάβελ ('Jezebel') (2.20). This 'Jezebel' διδάσκει καὶ πλανᾷ τοὺς ἐμοὺς δούλους πορνεῦσαι καὶ φαγεῖν εἰδωλόθυτα ('teaches and deceives my servants to commit sexual immorality and to eat food sacrificed to idols') (2.20). Several things stand out here. First, Jesus indicates that this woman calls herself a prophetess. It would seem that such a title would connote a position of authority not unlike those who called themselves apostles in the Ephesian community (2.2). That it is the feminine form is all the more striking. If the church permits her to teach, this suggests that a woman could function as a prophetess in their community.[131] She does not seem to be rebuked because she is a woman but because she is claiming to speak for God things that are antithetical to the beliefs and practices of the believing community. Second, 'Jezebel' is presently teaching *and* deceiving the community.[132] Third, Jesus links himself with the church by identifying the members of the church who are falling prey to 'Jezebel' as τοὺς ἐμοὺς δούλους ('*my* servants'). Fourth, the content of Jezebel's teaching is expressed in exactly the same terms, albeit in reverse order,[133] as that of 'Balaam' (2.14). As with the story of Balaam, the appeal to the Old Testament story of Jezebel is intended to jolt the hearers into recognizing compromising and sinful activities taking place even within the church. As the Pergamum church failed in their discerning of 'Balaam', so too has the Thyatira church failed to discern the 'Jezebel' in their midst. In doing so, they have also failed in discerning their own spiritual situation.

Where the hearers expect Jesus to issue a call to repentance as in the previous messages to Ephesus and Pergamum, Jesus' next words are unanticipated: καὶ ἔδωκα αὐτῇ χρόνον ἵνα μετανοήσῃ, καὶ οὐ θέλει μετανοῆσαι ἐκ τῆς πορνείας αὐτῆς ('I gave her time to repent, and she did not wish to repent of her immorality') (2.21). What is clear is that Jesus has already warned this prophetic figure to repent (perhaps through a prophetic word spoken in the context of the worshipping community or through John

---

[131] Skaggs and Benham, *Revelation*, p. 42. See also Richard, *Apocalypse*, p. 58, who states, 'Although the prophetess Jezebel is seen negatively here, her presence provides positive testimony to the existence of women prophets'.

[132] While the idea of (false) teaching has been seen in the messages to Ephesus and Pergamum, this is the first explicit reference to deception or deceit.

[133] Smalley, *The Revelation to John*, p. 74.

himself), but she does not wish to repent of her immorality.[134] For the first time in the prophetic messages, the hearers encounter blatant rebellion to the Son of God who walks in the midst of the community by one within the community. No doubt as the worshippers are receiving *this* prophetic word, the two previous calls to repentance take on added urgency. Additionally, where the hearers might expect Jesus to announce his coming (as in 2.5, 16), he does not; rather, Jesus acts in other ways with respect to 'Jezebel' and her followers. Jesus states: ἰδοὺ βάλλω αὐτὴν εἰς κλίνην καὶ τοὺς μοιχεύοντας μετ᾿ αὐτῆς εἰς θλῖψιν μεγάλην, ἐὰν μὴ μετανοήσωσιν ἐκ τῶν ἔργων αὐτῆς, καὶ τὰ τέκνα αὐτῆς ἀποκτενῶ ἐν θανάτῳ ('Behold I am throwing her on a sickbed and the ones commiting adultery with her into great tribulation, unless they repent of her works, and her children I will kill with death') (2.22-23). The shift in verb tenses from present βάλλω ('I throw) to future ἀποκτενῶ ('I will kill') is striking. The use of the present tense points to the immediacy of Jesus' action; that is, because of her rebellion, 'Jezebel' and her partners are being judged *now*. The future tense is for her 'children' – those who are led into sin. It is in his *action* that Jesus' coming is realized. For the partners of 'Jezebel', the judgment – referred to here as great tribulation – is intended to lead them to repentance. To this point in Revelation, tribulation has been connected to one's witness about Jesus (1.9; 2.9-10). Here, however, those committing adultery with 'Jezebel' will receive tribulation from Jesus if they do not repent.[135] Their works stand in sharp contrast to the works which Jesus has commended the church for in v. 19. Once again, the necessity of repentance as a crucial part of the church's worship is underscored. To refuse is to put oneself in danger of judgment. This is reinforced as Jesus states that he will kill Jezebel's children. As with the idea of tribulation, the concept of being killed has been in connection with one's witness. Further, it is something done to a faithful witness by those opposing them (2.13). Here, Jesus says that he himself will kill Jezebel's 'children'. If the phrase ἐν θανάτῳ ('with death') is translated

---

[134] Ladd, *A Commentary on the Revelation of John*, p. 54.
[135] Thomas, *The Apocalypse*, p. 150.

as 'with a plague'[136] then perhaps the hearers are to understand that this is the sickbed onto which Jezebel is cast. If so, then her followers will share in her fate.

This strong word of condemnation and judgment, while directed at Thyatira, is intended as a warning for all the churches.[137] All the churches are to know that Jesus searches the minds and hearts and gives to each according to their works (2.23b). The importance of discernment within the community, particularly as it concerns those who minister in their midst, is underscored.[138] It is Jesus, the Son of God, who stands as judge over all the churches. He will give to them in accordance with their works, whether good or bad.

In v. 24, Jesus shifts his gaze to those in Thyatira who have discerned properly and have not been deceived by false teaching, here called 'the deep things of Satan'. If 'Jezebel' is claiming to speak for God, Jesus reveals the true origin of her teaching.[139] By this, those who have not been deceived are affirmed in their discernment. Jesus admonishes them to hold fast (κρατήσατε) to what they have until he comes (2.25). This admonition connects with the faithful witness of the church.

As the prophetic message to Thyatira comes to a close, the call for discernment to the voice of the Spirit follows rather than precedes the promise to the overcomer. The promise to the overcomer is more expansive than the previous messages:

καὶ ὁ νικῶν καὶ ὁ τηρῶν ἄχρι τέλους τὰ ἔργα μου, δώσω αὐτῷ ἐξουσίαν ἐπὶ τῶν ἐθνῶν καὶ ποιμανεῖ αὐτους ἐν ῥάβδῳ σιδηρᾷ ὡς τὰ σκεύη τὰ κεραμικὰ συντρίβεται ὡς κἀγὼ εἴληφα παρὰ τοῦ πατρός μου, καὶ δώσω αὐτῷ τὸν ἀστέρα τὸν πρωϊνόν

---

[136] This phrase can convey two meanings: 'I will kill in death' or 'I will kill with a plague'. Aune, *Revelation 1–5*, p. 198.

[137] Ladd, *A Commentary on the Revelation of John*, p. 52 suggests that 'Jezebel' was widely known throughout all the churches of Asia.

[138] Skaggs and Benham, *Revelation*, p. 43. Sweet, *Revelation*, p. 95, writes that the crucial issue of discernment is raised 'in its sharpest form'.

[139] Koester, *Revelation and the End of All Things*, p. 62, states that the 'deep things of Satan' is a parody of Jezebel's possible claim to teach 'the deep things of God'. Beasley-Murray, *Revelation*, p. 92, sees this as indication that Jezebel and her followers were conscious of their 'emancipation from traditional ethics and their boldness in religious expression. The order of Jezebel claimed the freedom of the spiritual world, of hell as well as of heaven.'

And the one who overcomes and the one who keeps my works until the end, I will give authority over the nations to shepherd them with an iron rod – as when clay pots are shattered, even as I received from my Father, and I will give the morning star (2.26-28).

Strikingly, Jesus' promise is given to the one who overcomes *and* the one who keeps Jesus' works until the end. The hearers would not forget the opening blessing of the Apocalypse where these two ideas are linked (1.3). Jesus exhorts the Thyatira church to keep his *works*. Works have heretofore been associated with the activities of the churches, most recently in Rev. 2.23 where the works serve as the basis for judgment, yet here the hearers learn about Jesus' works. Thus, the hearers have a choice to keep the works of 'Jezebel' or the works of Jesus.[140] To the overcomers, Jesus promises authority over the nations, to shepherd them with an iron rod, and the morning star (2.26b-28). The contrast between 'Jezebel' and Jesus is clear. 'Jezebel', an authority figure within the church, will lead her followers to destruction. Jesus, the Son of God, will lead his followers to victory. By drawing on images from Ps. 2.8-9, the community is to discern that they will participate in activities of Jesus himself; that is, believers will shepherd the nations with Christ.[141] As Jesus received authority from the Father, so he gives authority to believers. Jesus also promises the morning star. Although the text does not give any explanation as to what the morning star is, the hearers know that at the very least it is connected with Jesus. The promise to the overcomers points the worshippers to Jesus who comes to them and enables them to experience proleptically his gifts in worship.

The prophetic message ends with the fourth call to heed the words of the Spirit (2.29). Its position at the end takes in the entirety of the message, including the promise to the overcomer. The present word of the Spirit, again co-terminus with the words of Jesus, must be heard and obeyed by all the churches. As in previous letters, the key issue of false teaching – an activity taking place within the worshipping community by pseudo-prophetic figures – takes center stage. The Spirit's call for discernment requires the church to

---

[140] Murphy, *Fallen is Babylon*, p. 139.

[141] Wilson, *The Victor Sayings*, p. 135.

discern the words of Jesus from the words of those like 'Jezebel' who claim to speak prophetically. The giving, receiving, and discerning of the word – all elements of the church's worship – must take place under the guidance of the Holy Spirit.

Sardis (3.1-6)

The fifth prophetic message for the churches is the message to the Sardis church. As the hearers have come to expect, the τάδε λέγει ('thus says') signals that Jesus is about to speak again. Jesus is identified by means of two images: ὁ ἔχων τὰ ἑπτὰ πνεύματα τοῦ θεοῦ καὶ τοὺς ἑπτὰ ἀστέρας ('the One having the seven Spirits of God and the seven stars') (3.1). The mention of the seven Spirits of God takes the hearers back to John's greeting from the Spirit (1.4) as well as John's testimony of being ἐν πνεύματι ('in the Spirit'). Further, the prophetic messages are clearly identified as the words of the Spirit. Therefore, in this opening address to Sardis, the intimate connection between Jesus, the Spirit, and the community is prominent. Smalley maintains that in this opening, 'the Lordship of Christ is asserted in the strongest possible way'.[142] While this is certainly correct, perhaps this connection between Jesus, the Spirit, and the community is also intended to add reinforcement to the important role that the Spirit plays in the Apocalypse. The ascription affirms the presence of Jesus within their midst, who is intimately connected with the Spirit *and* holds the churches close to himself. If the ascriptions are worshipful expressions about Jesus, perhaps this connection between Jesus and the Spirit supplies a rationale for the Spirit being a legitimate object of worship within the churches.

With the use of οἶδά ('I know'), the hearers recognize that Jesus is about to unveil his discerning assessment of the church: Οἶδά σου τὰ ἔργα ὅτι ὄνομα ἔχεις ὅτι ζῆς, καὶ νεκρὸς εἶ ('I know your works that you have a name that you are alive, but you are dead') (3.1b). Jesus knows them; however, he offers no commendation for their works. By contrasting the concepts of life and death, Jesus pulls back the veneer of their external reputation (ζῆς, 'you are alive') to reveal how he sees them (νεκρὸς εἶ, 'you are

---

[142] Smalley, *The Revelation to John*, p. 80.

dead').[143] Further, Jesus indicates that there are some things on the verge of death (3.2a).[144] Jesus does not indicate *how* or *why* they are dead nor does he give any hints as to what things are about to die. By means of an explanatory γὰρ ('for'), Jesus links these rather cryptic statements back to their works: οὐ γὰρ εὕρηκά σου τὰ ἔργα πεπληρωμένα ἐνώπιον τοῦ θεοῦ μου ('for I have not found your works to be complete before my God') (3.2b). The perfect tense εὕρηκά ('I have found') signifies that Jesus has been observing the community for some time and has found that the works which they are doing are not complete before God. Jesus calls God '*my* God', which indicates an intimate relationship between Jesus and God. Since Jesus and the Spirit are clearly connected in 3.1, the relationship between God, Jesus, and the Spirit, already seen in 1.4 and 2.8, is implicitly strengthened.

Jesus' discerning words call for a response from the church. As to Ephesus, Jesus calls the Sardis church to remember (μνημόνευε) what they have received and heard, to keep (τήρει) these things, and to repent (μετανόησον) (3.3). Remembering what they received and heard could be a reference to the gospel message and suggests that something has been forgotten along the way. In addition to the gospel message, they have also heard the words of the Spirit speaking to the churches of Ephesus, Smyrna, Pergamum and Thyatira. The church, therefore, is called to remember what they have received and heard as they have gathered for worship. Further, they are also to keep these things. Keeping demonstrates that the community has remembered. Keeping will ensure that those things about to die will instead begin to live. Third, Jesus calls them to repent. Repentance is the evidence that the community has discerned that Jesus is indeed speaking to them. In assessing their spiritual condition, the church must change its ways and align itself with him. Communal repentance must be demonstrated in the strengthening of those things about to die. Such a change will enable the church truly to have a testimony of being alive.

---

[143] Murphy, *Fallen is Babylon*, p. 144, 'The appearance of spiritual health masks spiritual decay and death'.

[144] Murphy, *Fallen is Babylon*, p. 145.

Jesus' next words pick up on the earlier admonition to keep watch in 3.2: ἐὰν οὖν μὴ γρηγορήσῃς ἥξω ὡς κλέπτης, καὶ οὐ μὴ γνῷς ποίαν ὥραν ἥξω ἐπὶ σέ ('therefore if you do not keep watch, I will come as a theif, and you will certainly not know at what hour I will come to you') (3.3b). The οὖν ('therefore') connects this statement to the series of imperatives in the first half of the verse but indicates that if they do not keep watch Jesus will come to them suddenly, like a thief. The οὐ μὴ plus aorist subjunctive construction ('you will certainly not know') emphasizes the absolute unexpected nature of Jesus' coming in judgment if they fail to keep watch.[145] The hearers have learned from Thyatira what happens when there is a refusal to repent (2.21-23). This threat of judgment continues to elevate the utter necessity of repentance as an on-going activity of worship within the community.

The ἀλλά ('but, rather') of v. 4 marks a transition in the bleak message to Sardis. Here the tone softens as Jesus reveals that there are some within the community who have engaged in proper spiritual discernment: ἀλλὰ ἔχεις ὀλίγα ὀνόματα ἐν Σάρδεσιν ἃ οὐκ ἐμόλυναν τὰ ἱμάτια αὐτῶν ('but you have some in Sardis who have not soiled their garments'). The reiteration of 'name' (ὀνόματα) sets up a contrast with 3.1 where Jesus commented on the ὄνομα of the community as being alive when in reality it is dead. That this was a general statement and not indicative of each and every member of the community is attested in v. 4. Within the community, there are a few who have not soiled their garments. The verb μολύνω ('defilement') is used in the sense of 'religious and cultic defilement'; thus, it is at this point that the reader understands why Jesus described the community as dead.[146] While many have defiled themselves, a few have remained faithful. Those who have not soiled their garments will walk with Jesus in white garments because they are worthy (3.4b). The color white reminds the hearers of the description of Jesus' hair (1.14) as well as the promise of the white stone (2.17). These faithful few are those who will walk

---

[145] Rotz, *Revelation*, p. 80, 'Because it is dependent on the church's response, this unexpected visit probably refers to an intermediate coming in judgment although all visitations include an anticipation of the Parousia'. See also Ladd, *A Commentary on the Revelation of John*, p. 37.

[146] F. Hauck, 'μολύνω, μολυσμός', *TDNT*, IV, p. 736.

in fellowship with Jesus. The future tense expressed in περιπα-τήσουσιν ('they *will* walk') stands in tension with the present tense ἄξιοί εἰσιν ('they *are* worthy'). Their future activity will be a result of their present state. The promise of fellowship with Jesus provides additional motivation for heeding the call to repentance. Failure to repent will result in loss of fellowship with Jesus.

The promise to the overcomers in Sardis is three-fold:

ὁ νικῶν οὕτως περιβαλεῖται ἐν ἱματίοις λευκοῖς καὶ οὐ μὴ ἐξαλείψω τὸ ὄνομα αὐτοῦ ἐκ τῆς βίβλου τῆς ζωῆς καὶ ὁμολογήσω τὸ ὄνομα αὐτοῦ ἐνώπιον τοῦ πατρός μου καὶ ἐνώπιον τῶν ἀγγέλων αὐτοῦ

The one who overcomes will likewise be clothed in white garments and I will not remove his or her name out of the book of life and I will confess his or her name before my Father and before his angels (3.5).

The promise is connected to the faithful believers in Sardis by means of οὕτως ('likewise, in this way'). Like those who will walk with Jesus in white, the overcomers will be clothed in white garments and will be worthy. Further, Jesus promises never to remove the names of the overcomers from the book of life.[147] The realization that one's name can be removed serves again as motivation for repentance. That Jesus has access to this book and the authority to remove names accentuates his power.[148] Additionally, Jesus' promise to confess the names of the overcomers before his Father and before the angels serves as verification that their names indeed are inscribed in the book of life.[149] The language of confession is featured through the Johannine literature where it relates primarily to individuals making a confession about Jesus; here, the imagery is inverted. 'The power of this promise, that the confessed one will do the confessing, indicates something of the faithfulness which Jesus feels towards those who have been faithful to him'.[150] The promise to the overcomers draws the attention of the church back to Jesus who walks in their midst and who calls them to renewed relation-

---

[147] See Exod. 32.32; Ps. 69.28; Dan. 12.1.
[148] Beasley-Murray, *Revelation*, p. 98
[149] Resseguie, *The Revelation of John*, p. 97.
[150] Thomas, *The Apocalypse*, p. 169.

ship with him. Hearing the promises in the context of worship continues to indicate that believers can experience a foretaste of what is to come in the present.

The prophetic message ends with the fifth call of the Spirit to discernment (3.6) by which the hearers are confronted with the coterminus words of Jesus and the Spirit. This connection is most explicit in this prophetic message owing to the fact that it opens with Jesus *having* both the Spirit and the stars in his right hand.

Philadelphia (3.7-13)

The sixth prophetic message is to the church in Philadelphia. With τάδε λέγει ('thus says') the hearers know that Jesus is about to speak again. Jesus is identified as: ὁ ἅγιος, ὁ ἀληθινός, ὁ ἔχων τὴν κλεῖν Δαυίδ, ὁ ἀνοίγων καὶ οὐδεὶς κλείσει καὶ κλείων καὶ οὐδεὶς ἀνοίγει ('the holy One, the true One, the One having the keys of David, the One opening and no one can shut and shutting and no one can open') (3.7). The use of the substantive adjectives, the Holy One and the True One, introduces into the narrative two new descriptors for Jesus. Their appearance here expands the christological focus of the Apocalypse. In the inaugural vision Jesus holds the keys of Death and Hades (1.18); now the hearers discover that Jesus holds the key of David. This reference to Israel's most famous king carries with it messianic hopes and expectations, of which Jesus is the fulfillment. As the key-holder, Jesus exercises the sole power of opening and closing, or perhaps locking and unlocking.[151] His actions cannot be undone. This lengthy ascription continues to inform the hearers about Jesus, the one who walks in their midst as they are gathered for worship.

As in previous messages, Jesus' use of οἶδά σου τὰ ἔργα ('I know your works') (3.8) signals the start of his discernment into the spiritual life of the church. Rather than enumerating their works, however, Jesus makes three revelatory statements introduced with ἰδοὺ ('behold'). In the first statement, the hearers learn that Jesus has placed before them an opened door which no one is able to close (3.8).[152] This seems to tie in with the key of David imagery at the beginning of the prophetic message. The perfect verbs (δέδωκα,

---

[151] See Isa. 22.22.

[152] For a concise summary of interpretive options for the door imagery, see Osborne, *Revelation*, p. 188.

'I have placed'; and ἠνεῳγμένην, 'I have opened') indicate to the hearers that they are to see that this door has already been opened and even now is open before them.[153] Jesus has placed the opened door before them because they have little power (μικρὰν δύναμιν). Jesus does not seem to be speaking disparagingly about them in this assessment because he joins this acknowledgment with two positive elements: they have kept (ἐτήρησάς) Jesus' word and have not denied (οὐκ ἠρνήσω) Jesus' name (3.8). Their lack of power cannot be connected to their spiritual condition since they have proven themselves to be faithful in these other areas. Jesus commends them for their faithful witness, which likely reminds all the churches that faithful witness is an act of worship. The hearers recall that the Pergamum community did not deny Jesus' faith even in the time of persecution (2.13). Although not stated explicitly, the hearers can perhaps infer that the Philadelphian church also made a confession of their faith in Jesus during a period of persecution. It would seem that the opened door has been placed before them because of their faithful witness to Jesus.

The other occurrences of ἰδοὺ ('behold') appear in v. 9 where Jesus indicates his activities on behalf of the struggling church. Here Jesus declares that he will make those from the synagogue of Satan who call themselves Jews bow (προσκυνήσουσιν)[154] before them and know that Jesus loves the Philadelphian church. The reference to the synagogue of Satan and those who call themselves Jews but are not recalls the prophetic message to Smyrna (2.9). The reappearing of the description here in the message to the Philadelphian church strengthens the idea that the believing community has experienced persecution from their Jewish neighbors.[155] Although they call themselves Jews, Jesus, as he did in the message to Smyrna, calls them liars. Here, as there, the true people of God are those who embrace Jesus as Messiah, the one who has the key of David. The church, thereby, understands that they are the true people of God not necessarily by ethnicity but because they have been faithful to Jesus. Because they have *kept* Jesus' word concerning endurance, Jesus ensures that he will *keep* them from the hour of trial that is

---

[153] Thomas, *The Apocalypse*, p. 174.

[154] 'This is submission, not worship ...' Osborne, *Revelation*, p. 191.

[155] Mayo, *'Those Who Call Themselves Jews'*, p. 68.

about to come upon the earth (3.10). In the message to Smyrna, Jesus revealed that the Devil was going to throw some of them into prison so that they may be tested (2.10). Now, to the Philadelphian church Jesus announces that they will be kept from, or perhaps preserved during,[156] the hour of testing that is coming to test all the inhabitants of the earth.[157]

The impetus for maintaining their witness comes in Jesus' announcement that he is coming quickly (ἔρχομαι ταχύ) (v. 11). This announcement 'holds no threat' of impending judgment for the church; nevertheless, they have 'the responsibility of continued vigilance'.[158] Because of Jesus' coming, the believers are to hold on (κράτει) to what they have so that no one can take their crown (3.11). That the community is not to let anyone take their crown is an interesting twist since the crown has appeared as a (future) reward to the overcomers at Smyrna (2.11). This reinforces the concept of worship as a proleptic eschatological experience. *Already* they have a crown! However, Jesus' words also indicate that the crown can be taken from them if they are not engaged in discerning their life in community.

Jesus continues his message with words to the overcomers. To them, Jesus promises two things. First, Jesus will make them a στῦλον ἐν τῷ ναῷ τοῦ θεοῦ μου ('pillar in the temple of my God') (3.12a). This is the first occurrence of temple language in the Apocalypse. Jesus identifies the temple as belonging to his God (τοῦ θεοῦ μου); thus, it contrasts sharply with the synagogue of Satan. Temples are places of worship; pillars are a permanent part of the temple's architecture. The overcomers therefore have the promise of permanent connection to God's presence.[159] Second, Jesus promises to write three things upon the overcomers: τὸ ὄνομα τοῦ θεοῦ μου καὶ τὸ ὄνομα τῆς πόλεως τοῦ θεοῦ μου,

---

[156] Resseguie, *The Revelation of John*, p. 98. See also Smalley, *The Revelation to John*, p. 92; Blount, *Revelation*, p. 77, 'Though Christ vows to keep the Philadelphians out of the hour of testing, he does not say that he intends to spare them from it'.

[157] Trafton, *Reading Revelation*, p. 49, says that in light of the way testing has occurred in Rev. 2.2 and 2.10, that the hour of testing is 'that which will verify once and for all that the ungodly are truly such'.

[158] Rotz, *Revelation*, p. 85.

[159] Ladd, *A Commentary on the Revelation of John*, p. 63.

τῆς καινῆς Ἰερουσαλὴμ ἡ καταβαίνουσα ἐκ τοῦ οὐρανοῦ ἀπὸ τοῦ θεοῦ μου, καὶ τὸ ὄνομά μου τὸ καινόν ('the name of my God and the name of the city of my God, the New Jerusalem coming down from heaven from my God, and my new name') (3.12b). The repetition of the pronoun μου ('my') continues the theme of Jesus' connection with the Father, who is identified as 'my God'. The writing upon the pillars speaks to identity and belonging. The overcomers belong to God, to God's community (the New Jerusalem), and to Jesus himself. Blount writes, 'How appropriate that "the ones who did not deny Christ's name, even in the face of opposition," are in the end inscribed with Christ's name'.[160] The first reference to New Jerusalem, identified as God's city, at the very least indicates that the overcomers are to see themselves as residents of the very place where God dwells. It is Jesus, the one in their midst, who does all of these things for the church. Despite their circumstances and lack of power, the church is to maintain their witness and worship of Jesus precisely because they are partakers now, if but in a limited sense, of God's realm to be revealed in all its fullness.

The prophetic message concludes with the sixth call of the Spirit for discernment (3.13). This continues to confirm for the hearers the connection between Jesus and the Spirit, who speak the same thing. It also confirms the connection between the Spirit and the community, for it is within the worshipping community that the voice of the Spirit is heard. Because this community has little power in and of themselves, they must rely fully on the power of the Spirit as they continue to hold fast to what they have. That they can lose their crown serves as a reminder that they must continue to hear what the Spirit says to the churches.[161] Continuing to heed the Spirit's direction in the community enables them to identify themselves proleptically as citizens of another city, God's New Jerusalem.

Laodicea (3.14-22)

The final prophetic message read, heard, and received in the churches is to the Laodicean church. As the seventh of seven, it

---

[160] Blount, *Revelation*, p. 79.

[161] Osborne, *Revelation*, p. 199.

serves as the culmination of the prophetic messages.[162] The final use of τάδε λέγει ('thus says') signals that Jesus is ready to speak to the churches again. The message begins with a three-fold description of Jesus as ὁ ἀμήν, ὁ μάρτυς ὁ πιστὸς καὶ ἀληθινός, ἡ ἀρχὴ τῆς κτίσεως τοῦ θεοῦ ('the Amen, the faithful and true witness, the ruler of God's creation') (3.14). The hearers would likely recognize that none of these descriptions come from the inaugural vision of Jesus. Thus, this last message is the first message to describe Jesus in ways wholly separate from the inaugural vision. First, Jesus is identified as 'the Amen'.[163] Johannine hearers might think of the Fourth Gospel where Jesus often prefaced his words with the ἀμὴν ἀμήν ('amen, amen') formula to validate the trustworthiness of his statements; therefore, 'the one who uses this "amen, amen" formula does so because he is the "Amen"'.[164] That Jesus begins his message to the Laodiceans by identifying himself as *the* Amen serves to validate at the outset the significance and trustworthiness of his prophetic message to *all* the churches. Its presence here might also remind the hearers of the double usage of the liturgical ἀμήν ('amen') found in 1.6-7 where it is used to affirm and conclude two statements about Jesus. The use of this liturgical word as a title for Jesus serves to deepen the connections between the person of Jesus and worship.[165] Second, Jesus is the faithful and true witness. While each of these adjectives has been used for Jesus (1.5; 3.7), the double adjectives create a new title for Jesus, *the* Faithful *and* True Witness. Jesus is *the* faithful witness who stands as the model for all the churches. Third, Jesus is the ἀρχὴ ('beginning') of the creation of God. The hearers of the text are immediately struck by the use of the feminine noun ἡ ἀρχὴ ('the beginning'), usually translated as 'origin' or 'beginning'. Earlier, in 1.5 the masculine noun ὁ ἄρχων ('the ruler') was used to say that Jesus is the *ruler* of

---

[162] Resseguie, *The Revelation of John*, p. 100.

[163] This is the only titular usage of 'Amen' in the New Testament. See Smalley, *The Revelation to John*, p. 96, who connects it to Isa. 65.16 where it is used of God. 'That such a description, "Amen", only otherwise associated with God, should be applied to Jesus, is an indication of John's high (if balanced) Christology'.

[164] Thomas, *The Apocalypse*, p. 186.

[165] Blount, *Revelation*, p. 81.

the kings of the earth. The two terms share the same semantic sub-domain thereby opening the possibility that ἡ ἀρχὴ ('the beginning') contains within it the idea of ruling.[166] In addition to being the ruler of the kings of the earth, Jesus is also the ruler of God's creation. In this way, Jesus' sovereignty and authority is established in convincing fashion. This final ascription reassures the church that the same Jesus identified in the opening of Revelation is the one who walks in their midst.

For the final time, the hearers encounter the familiar words of Jesus that signify the start of his discernment: Οἶδά σου τὰ ἔργα ('I know your works') (3.15). The emphatic placement of the pronoun signals Jesus' intimate knowledge of this particular church. What Jesus knows about this local church is perhaps the most well-known to modern readers of the Apocalypse: Οἶδά σου τὰ ἔργα ὅτι οὔτε ψυχρὸς εἶ οὔτε ζεστός ('I know your works that you are neither cold nor hot'). The use of οὔτε coupled with the two substantive adjectives contrasts two states of existence: the church is neither cold nor hot. The hearers would probably recall a similar technique in Jesus' description of Sardis as ζῇς ('living') and νεκρὸς ('dead'). Here the contrast is equally stark. Jesus follows up on his opening charge by saying that he wishes they were cold or hot. This suggests that neither state, hot *or* cold, is objectionable.[167] However, the fact that they are neither has implications for this church: οὕτως ὅτι χλιαρὸς εἶ καὶ οὔτε ζεστὸς οὔτε ψυχρός, μέλλω σε ἐμέσαι ἐκ τοῦ στόματός μου ('because you are lukewarm and neither hot nor cold, I am about to spit you out of my mouth') (3.16). Jesus discerns the true state of the church as being neither hot nor cold,[168] but lukewarm. Such a condition cannot be tolerated by Jesus; indeed, he is about to spit or vomit them out of his mouth. Although the warning is reminiscent of that given to the Ephesian church (2.5),[169] the graphic imagery intensifies the idea that the works of the Laodicean church make Jesus sick! The intolerable state in which Jesus views the community seems to stem

---

[166] Louw-Nida, *Greek-English Lexicon of the New Testament* (New York: United Bible Societies, 1989), I, pp. 478-79.

[167] Blount, *Revelation*, p. 82.

[168] Smalley, *The Revelation to John*, p. 98, notes the chiastic use of the three paired terms ('cold and hot') in an AB/AB/BA pattern in vv. 15-16.

[169] Blount, *Revelation*, p. 82.

from their confession about themselves (λέγεις 'you say') which indicates that their works are not just acts or deeds but, in this case, declarations.[170] The Laodicean church says, Πλούσιός εἰμι καὶ πεπλούτηκα καὶ οὐδὲν χρείαν ἔχω ('I am rich and have become rich and I have need of nothing') (3.17). The adjective πλούσιος ('wealth') and its related perfect verb πεπλούτηκα ('I have become rich') imply that the community sees itself as self-sufficient wealth-makers. Jesus unveils reality: σὺ εἶ ὁ ταλαίπωρος καὶ ἐλεεινὸς καὶ πτωχὸς καὶ τυφλὸς καὶ γυμνός ('You are miserable and pitiful and poor and blind and naked') (3.17). This piling up of adjectives paints a pathetic picture of a community ignorant of its own spiritual plight. Their pursuit of wealth has left them spiritually impoverished.[171] In hearing Jesus' discerning words, the Laodicean church is to recognize that they have failed in discerning their own spiritual condition.

Despite such an assessment and despite Jesus' warning that he is about to spit them out of his mouth, Jesus offers the church three ways to remedy its situation (3.18). Jesus' counsel is something the community cannot afford to ignore. First, Jesus counsels them to buy[172] from him gold so that they might become rich (ἵνα πλουτήσῃς). His counsel for them to buy from him, as opposed to anyone else, points to Jesus' ability to provide the best possible things (gold having been refined by fire) for the church. Second, Jesus counsels them to buy white garments so that they might be clothed. Such garments are needed to cover the shame of their nakedness. White garments are the attire of the overcomers (3.5); thus, the offer of white garments indicates that the Laodicean church, despite its present shameful condition, can be counted among those who overcome *if* they take Jesus' counsel. Third, Jesus counsels them to buy salve to anoint their eyes so that they might be able to see. The hearers know that Jesus' eyes are like flames of fire (1.14), which are capable of searching the minds and hearts of the churches (2.18, 23). Jesus' eyes do not miss a thing; conversely, the Laodiceans' eyes

---

[170] Ladd, *A Commentary on the Revelation of John*, p. 66.

[171] Murphy, *Fallen is Babylon*, p. 162.

[172] The aorist infinitive ἀγορᾶσαι ('to buy') governs the three commodities of gold, garments, and salve. Additionally, the reason for each commodity is provided in the form of a ἵνα + subjunctive clause.

have missed everything. The salve which Jesus has will cure their blindness if they will take his counsel and look to him for provision.

In his next words, Jesus says ἐγὼ ὅσους ἐὰν φιλῶ ἐλέγχω καὶ παιδεύω ('I reprove and discipline those whom I love') (3.19a). To a community exposed as wretched, pitiable, poor, blind and naked, this unexpected word of Jesus' love is remarkable. This statement speaks specifically to the Laodicean church; however, because this is the final message, it speaks to all the churches. In this, the hearers understand that Jesus' words to all of the churches come out of his love for them. The acknowledgment of Jesus' love would likely remind the hearers of 1.5 and 3.9. Although Jesus uses φιλέω ('I love, have affection for') rather than ἀγαπάω ('I love'), the two terms clearly function as synonyms. Johannine hearers would recall that in the Fourth Gospel, Jesus uses both ἀγαπάω and φιλέω to speak of the Father's love for the Son (Jn 3.35; 5.20). Just as the Father does not exhibit any lesser form of love for the Son, neither does the Son of God exhibit any lesser form of love for the churches. It is out of this love that Jesus hands out 'educative discipline'.[173] What follows are two commands that Jesus gives to the church: ζήλευε οὖν καὶ μετανόησον ('therefore be zealous and repent') (3.19b). Grammatically, the commands speak to two types of actions; therefore, as a present continuous imperative, ζήλευε ('be zealous') stands in tension with the punctiliar aorist imperative μετανόησον ('repent'). Further, the order of the commands is curious. One would expect Jesus to call them to repentance first so that they could then be zealous, yet Jesus first exhorts them to be zealous. Although the Laodiceans are lukewarm and ignorant of their own spiritual condition, they are still a community of believers who can burn with zeal for Jesus if they will take his counsel and respond to his reproof and discipline.[174] Responding to Jesus' discipline demands that the worshipping community engage in corporate confession and repent of their nauseating works. Their repentance must be evidenced in their works and attested by the Spirit. That this is the final call to repentance in the prophetic messages serves to heighten the importance of repentance for all of the communities. All the churches face the prospect of being spit out if they do not heed the message of Jesus.

---

[173] Aune, *Revelation 1–5*, p. 260.

[174] Ladd, *A Commentary on the Revelation of John*, p. 67.

It is at this point in the message that the hearers expect Jesus to announce he is coming to them, but what they discover is that Jesus is already there: Ἰδοὺ ἕστηκα ἐπὶ τὴν θύραν καὶ κρούω· ἐάν τις ἀκούσῃ τῆς φωνῆς μου καὶ ἀνοίξῃ τὴν θύραν, (καὶ) εἰσελεύσ- ομαι πρὸς αὐτὸν καὶ δειπνήσω μετ' αὐτοῦ καὶ αὐτὸς μετ' ἐμοῦ. ('Behold I stand at the door and knock; if anyone hears my voice and opens the door, I will come to him or her and eat with him or her and s/he with me') (3.20). In this statement Jesus reveals that he has been standing at the door to the church[175] and knocking. The hearers would probably remember Jesus' words to the Phila- delphian church that he placed before them an opened door that no one can shut (3.8). The door to the Laodicean church, however, appears to be shut. The one who walks among the candlesticks stands at their door and knocks, waiting to be invited in. Although Jesus has the ability to walk through this door (as Johannine hearers would recall, Jn 20.19, 26), he chooses not to do so; rather, he stands and continues to knock. Their inability to discern their own condition has not only blinded their eyes but also plugged their ears to Jesus' knocking. Nevertheless, they are still, barring a refusal to repent, his church.[176] The persistent pursuit of Jesus is further por- trayed in his calling out to the church. His voice, described as the sound of many waters in 1.15, thunders to his beloved church. If they will hear his voice, he will come to them and eat with them. Again, such a statement is meant not just for the Laodicean church but also for all the churches who have heard Jesus' voice through the Spirit. The use of the subjunctive mood (ἐάν τις ἀκούσῃ) in- dicates that it will be up to the hearers to hear. If they do, Jesus will come and will eat with them – a 'promise of the most intimate fel- lowship possible'.[177] The idea of sharing a meal gathers up the earli- er imagery of eating from the tree of life and partaking of the hid- den manna; thus, language related to eating forms an inclusio

---

[175] 'The meaning is not individualistic and about internal feelings (Jesus knocking at the door of the soul), but related to community'. Richard, *Apocalypse*, p. 63.

[176] Rotz, *Revelation*, p. 89, 'The church at Laodicea is in the worst condition of the seven churches ... Yet, the exalted Christ promises those who repent fellow- ship and eschatological reward'.

[177] Ladd, *A Commentary on the Revelation of John*, p. 68.

around the prophetic messages. In light of the liturgical setting of the Apocalypse and Jesus' messages to the churches, it is plausible that this imagery would be understood as referencing the Eucharist.[178] In such a setting, this final plea from Jesus becomes all the more striking. While they *eat* and *drink* the flesh and blood of Jesus (John 6), the very one whose presence they invoke stands outside.[179]

For the final time Jesus makes a promise to the overcomers: ὁ νικῶν δώσω αὐτῷ καθίσαι μετ᾽ ἐμοῦ ἐν τῷ θρόνῳ μου, ὡς κἀγὼ ἐνίκησα καὶ ἐκάθισα μετὰ τοῦ πατρός μου ἐν τῷ θρόνῳ αὐτοῦ ('The one overcoming I will grant to sit with me on my throne, just as I overcame and sat with my Father on his throne') (Rev. 3.21). Jesus' promise to give them a seat on his throne holds out the possibility for them to be identified with Jesus not unlike the way Jesus is identified with God; that is, the Laodicean church has the potential to sit with Jesus on his throne if they repent. Their ability to overcome is possible because Jesus walks among them as the model overcomer (ἐνίκησα, 'I have overcome'). As the final promise, these words also serve as a comprehensive promise for all the churches who maintain their worship of Jesus. The final promise to the overcomers collapses the space between the present and the eschatological future so that worship creates the context for the proleptic experience of sitting on the throne with Jesus.

The message closes with the Spirit's final call to discernment. For a final time, the churches are reminded that the Spirit communicates the words of Jesus. For a final time, the churches are to be encouraged to engage in discernment. Laodicea can remedy its spiritual condition by recognizing their intolerable state, by looking to Jesus for provision, and, above all, by repenting. Further, all the churches must discern who is knocking at their door and calling to them. The Spirit assures them that Jesus himself is knocking, calling, and waiting to be invited in for fellowship. The understanding of the on-going presence of the Spirit within the churches serves to

---

[178] Sweet, *Revelation*, pp. 109-10; Smalley, *The Revelation to John*, p. 102.

[179] Gonzáles and Gonzáles, *Revelation*, p. 37, 'When that church gathers for communion, Christ is standing outside, knocking at the door! The call to open the door means that in the very central act of the church's worship, Christ has been left out!'

reassure the churches that the Spirit will continue to speak the words of Jesus to them.

Summary

The opening chapter of the Apocalypse is comprised of a liturgy-filled prologue, a description of how John received the visions he records while in worship, and a vision of the living Jesus who both comes to and commissions John to record all that he sees. The opening chapter makes clear that the Apocalypse is for the seven churches of Asia Minor. The churches are of singular importance for Jesus for they are symbolized as the lampstands among which he walks and the stars which he holds in his hand. These images speak to Jesus' relationship, fellowship, and connection to the communities, for they are *his* churches. That the opening chapter is filled with worshipful confessions suggests that the worship in the churches must be an extension of their self-understanding. They must confess that they are loved by Jesus and freed from sin by Jesus' blood (1.5b), and that they are constituted as a kingdom of priests (1.6). They must testify, like John, that God is the Alpha and Omega (1.8) and that Jesus is the First and the Last, the Living One (1.17-18). Additionally, the churches are an eschatological community waiting for the return of Jesus (1.7) who is *now* the exalted Lord of all the churches. The churches' shared experience of θλίψις, βασιλεία, and ὑπομονή ('tribulation, kingdom, and patient endurance') (1.9) because of their witness about Jesus must not dampen their proclamation of Jesus' return nor skew their self-understanding as an eschatological community.[180] This opening chapter reveals that all that is to follow in the Apocalypse is to be read, seen, and heard *in the Spirit* in the context of the Christian community.

The seven prophetic messages of Revelation 2–3 are evidence of John's obedience to write the words of Jesus to the seven churches of Asia. The messages likely would have been read and heard within each worshipping community as part of their worship. As John is ἐν πνεύματι ('in the Spirit') so too are the churches. In the churches, worship is an encounter with the living Christ that takes place 'in the Spirit' (Revelation 1). Reading the prophetic messages

---

[180] Minear, 'Ontology and Ecclesiology in the Apocalypse', p. 93.

with an eye toward worship that began in the first chapter of Revelation reveals five aspects related to worship in the Spirit.

First, the presence of the living Jesus is in the midst of the churches. One of the ways that Jesus' presence is expressed is through the ascriptions in each message (2.1, 8, 12, 18; 3.1, 7, 14). Each ascription is a description of or declaration about Jesus that takes on meaning particular to each message. Coupled with the specificity of what Jesus knows about each church, the ascriptions demonstrate that Christ indeed *is* in the midst of each community. Collectively, the ascriptions create a liturgy – a doxological confession about Jesus. As each message unfolds, the churches discover another reason to worship Jesus. The presence of Jesus in their midst is further expressed in Jesus' statements of judgment if the church does not respond to his words of rebuke. These statements are found in four of the seven messages and are often connected to repentance (2.5, 16, 22-23; 3.3). In three of the four statements, Jesus indicates that he will come to them if they do not repent. This suggests that the hearers must give urgent and immediate attention not only to Jesus' words but also to his presence among them.

Second, repentance is a liturgical activity. In five of the seven messages, the church is called to repent (2.5, 16, 22; 3.3, 19). Repentance indicates that they indeed have heard the voice of Jesus in their midst and that they are obedient to his words. The implications of ignoring Jesus' call to repentance are also demonstrated in the messages, most notably in the figure 'Jezebel'. That the churches are called to repentance as they are gathered in worship indicates that repentance is a corporate liturgical activity of the community that must involve confession. Repentance calls for action on behalf of the community; that is, repentance must be evidenced in the works of each church for Jesus *knows* their works.

Third, worship creates a context for prophetic words and discernment. The messages themselves are prophetic oracles of Jesus given through the Spirit that reveal Jesus' intimate knowledge of the churches (2.2-3, 9, 13, 19; 3.1, 8, 15). The community hears the voice of Jesus as they worship *in the Spirit*. Prophetic speech, therefore, is an essential element of worship. Not all prophetic words come from the Spirit; therefore, there are words that are not to be received within the community. The Spirit reveals that false prophets with false messages have infiltrated the churches. The Spirit aids the community in proper discernment and assures the churches that the words they are hearing *are* the words of Jesus, thereby testifying to their validity. Not only must the church be able to discern words of prophecy, they must also be able to discern their own spiritual condition. Jesus' evaluations serve as a model for the type of self-discernment which must take place when the church is gathered for worship. The call of the Spirit, addressed to all of the churches, indicates that the churches *can* discern if they will listen to the Spirit. Taken collectively, the churches are challenged to hear the comprehensive message of the Spirit. Thus, one message cannot be heard in isolation from the others; the messages together are Jesus' words mediated through the Spirit to the worshipping communities.

Fourth, faithful witness is worship. This is found to some degree in all seven messages. It is often expressed in the idea of endurance or perseverance (2.2, 19), of being faithful (2.10, 13; 3.14), and of not denying Jesus (2.13; 3.8). Faithful witness is also modeled for the churches in the death of Antipas, Jesus' faithful witness. It is not insignificant that the final prophetic message identifies Jesus as the faithful witness, the one whom the churches are to emulate.

Fifth, worship *in the Spirit* collapses the *time* between the present and the future. This is expressed in the eschatological promises to the overcomers (2.7, 11, 17, 26-28; 3.5, 12, 21). These rewards are not 'put off' until the end of the book, where John sees the new heaven and earth and the New Jerusalem; rather, the eschatological promises are a present reality for those keeping the words of this prophecy (1.3). In worship, the church receives a foretaste of what awaits them. It is this foretaste that enables them to continue in their worship and witness to Jesus. While every message contains a promise specific for each church, together the promises form a collective store-house of rewards for all the faithful worshippers of Jesus.

III. ἐν πνεύματι – 'In Heaven' (4.1–16.21)

Revelation 4.1–16.21 is the largest section of the Apocalypse. Contained within this section is the inaugural throne room scene (4–5), the opening of the seven seals (6.1–8.5), the seven trumpet judgments (8.2–11.19), the cosmic story of the conflict of God's people

(12.1–15.4), and the seven bowl judgments (15.1–16.21). In addition, this section continues the book's theme of worship as several worship scenes are embedded into the narrative.

A. Revelation 4–5

After Jesus' piercing evaluation of the seven churches in Revelation 2–3, the hearers are summoned, along with John, to the throne room of heaven.[181] If the worship practices of the churches were the focus of Revelation 2–3, it almost goes without saying that the focus of Revelation 4–5 is also worship as the hearers are privileged to behold acts of heavenly worship, listen to hymns of heavenly worship, and participate in the heavenly liturgy. These chapters, which belong 'inseparably together',[182] have been described as the 'heart' of the Apocalypse,[183] as 'the interpretive key to understanding the Apocalypse',[184] and as its 'cosmic center'.[185] Smalley sees them as a means for the hearers to 'reflect upon and to recapitulate the scenes immediately preceding and following them'.[186] Fee, who regards Revelation 2–3 as the 'immediate background' for chapters 4–6, notes that no matter what condition in which each of the churches was found to be, all of them are invited to see the throne room of heaven.[187] He sees Revelation 4–5 as happening simultaneously with Revelation 2–3; thus, John's hearers, who have received Christ's 'view from below' in terms of his evaluation of them are now given 'a view from above, the eternal context in which they are to understand their own present existence, and in light of which

---

[181] See Aune, *Revelation 1–5*, pp. 276-79 for an excellent summary of the 'throne-vision report' in prophetic and apocalyptic contexts. See also Hurtado, 'Revelation 4–5 in the Light of Jewish Apocalyptic Analogies', pp. 105-109. For the view that in the background to chapters 4–5 is the imperial throne room of the Roman Emperor, see especially D. Aune, 'The Influence of Roman Imperial Court Ceremonial on the Apocalypse of John,' pp. 99-119. According to Aune, everything that is found in John's throne room scene has parallels in the Roman imperial court and is comprehensible only in light of this background. Such a view presupposes that John had intimate and thorough knowledge of the imperial court and ceremonial procedures, which is speculative at best.

[182] Gorman, *Reading Revelation Responsibly*, p. 102.

[183] Koester, *Revelation and the End of All Things*, p. 71; Murphy, *Fallen is Babylon*, p. 169.

[184] Resseguie, *The Revelation of John*, p. 105.

[185] deSilva, *Seeing Things John's Way*, p. 100.

[186] Smalley, *The Revelation to John*, p. 109.

[187] Fee, *Revelation*, p. 65.

they are to understand everything that follows'. In this way, heaven and earth are seen 'in light of each other' and the church is called to worship.[188]

Revelation 4 opens with a transitional marker: μετὰ ταῦτα εἶδον ('after these things I saw'). This is the first occurrence of this phrase in the narrative, but the hearers will soon discover that John employs it frequently throughout his visions (see 7.1, 9; 15.5; 18.1; 19.1). The opening verse is tied to the preceding chapters in several ways. First, the phrase μετὰ ταῦτα was heard in the words of the risen Jesus as he commissioned John to write of the things which are and the things which are about to happen *after these things* (1.19). Second, door imagery was found in the final two prophetic messages (Rev 3.8; 20). Here, however, it is John who sees an opened door. The verb εἶδον ('I saw') was last used in 1.12 and 1.17 where John *saw* the risen Christ in the midst of the lampstands. Its reoccurrence here suggests that John is now seeing something new. Third, John identifies the voice he is hearing with the voice he heard at the start of his vision (1.10). Since Jesus is the one who speaks to John (1.17-20), the hearers are led to surmise that Jesus is the one speaking to him in 4.1 from heaven. Fourth, just as John was summoned to action in the command to write what he saw and send it in a book to the seven churches (1.11), so also is John now summoned to action in the command to come up (ἀνάβα ὧδε) to heaven. Fifth, John is to see the things which must happen next, which not only connect back to Jesus' words in 1.19 but also to the opening of the Apocalypse (1.1).

The summons for John to come to heaven is made possible by means of the Spirit: εὐθέως ἐγενόμην ἐν πνεύματι ('at once I was in the Spirit') (4.2). This notification of being 'in the Spirit' continues the narrative thread begun in Revelation 1; that is, John has been and still is 'in the Spirit' since nothing in the text indicates otherwise to the hearers.[189] The ἐν πνεύματι phrase thus provides continuity with the previous chapters. Whereas John was ἐν πνεύματι and received a revelation of and commissioning from the risen Jesus in 1.9, so now the words of the risen Jesus result in

---

[188] Fee, *Revelation*, p. 66.

[189] Thomas, *The Apocalypse*, p. 203.

John being ἐν πνεύματι, thus strengthening the idea revealed in the seven prophetic messages of the close connection between the Spirit and Jesus. The use of εὐθέως ('immediately') indicates that John is transported at once in his vision to the throne room in heaven.[190] This signals a dramatic shift in venue for John and his hearers. The earthly settings of Patmos and the seven churches of Asia now give way to another setting, simply identified as *heaven*, 'a setting both remote and surreal'.[191] John does not describe his ascent to heaven, as this does not seem to be his intent.[192] That John is there – he who is a brother with those in the seven churches, he who has seen the risen Jesus and communicated his words to the churches – suggests that there is a close link between heaven and earth[193] and, more specifically, between the churches and the realm of heaven.

Once in heaven, John sees a throne and one sitting on the throne. The imagery of thrones would be fresh in the minds of the hearers from the opening greeting (1.4) and from the prophetic message to Laodicea (3.21).[194] John describes the one who sits on the throne in surprisingly brief fashion by likening God's appearance to the precious stones, jasper and carnelian (4.3).[195] God as the one on the throne is unquestioned. Perhaps the emphasis on the throne serves to contrast the other 'occupied' throne mentioned to

---

[190] In this, Revelation differs from other Jewish literature in which individuals ascend through the levels or layers of heaven. See, for example, 2 Enoch 1–22 where Enoch journeys through seven levels of heaven to reach the throne room of God. In each level, Enoch sees different aspects of the world of heaven (elders in the first heaven, condemned angels in the second heaven, Grigori in the fifth heaven, etc.). F.I. Andersen, '2 (Slavonic) Apocalypse of Enoch' in J.H. Charlesworth (ed.), *The Old Testament Pseudepigrapha* (Garden City: Doubleday & Co., 1983), pp. 103-40. See also 'Testament of Levi' where Levi is shown three levels of heaven. H.C. Kee, 'Testaments of the Twelve Patriarchs' in J.H. Charlesworth (ed.), *The Old Testament Pseudepigrapha* (Garden City: Doubleday & Co., 1983), pp. 788-90.

[191] Barr, *Tales of the End*, p. 62.

[192] Hurtado, 'Revelation 4–5 in the Light of Jewish Apocalyptic Analogies', p. 111.

[193] Murphy, *Fallen is Babylon*, p. 170.

[194] Smalley, *The Revelation to John*, p. 114.

[195] Howard-Brook and Gwyther, *Unveiling Empire: Reading Revelation Then and Now*, p. 203.

this point – namely, the throne of Satan (2.13).[196] By focused attention on the throne of God, the awesomeness and majesty of the throne – and of God – dwarfs any other supposed throne or ruler. It is God on the throne who rules and reigns.[197] It is this sovereign ruler of the world that the churches are aligned with and worship, despite any and all suffering or persecution.[198]

The central location of the throne of God in heaven provides further attestation to God's universal sovereignty.[199] John describes the throne as being encircled (κυκλόθεν) by a rainbow that looks like an emerald (4.3), but, more significantly, the throne is also encircled (κυκλόθεν) by 24 thrones upon which the 24 elders sit (4.4).[200] This clustering of thrones around *the* throne of God underscores the supreme authority of God while introducing the hearers to new characters in the heavenly court. The appearance of the 24 elders comes without preamble or fanfare, significant in light of the fact that the elders are unique to John's vision when compared to other visionary accounts. Their proximity to the throne hints at their importance for John. Hurtado, in fact, suggests that the elders 'may be the point of emphasis in the scene, second only to the throne of God'.[201] They are residents of heaven (whether human or

---

[196] Saunders, 'Revelation and Resistance', p. 136, observes that the throne of God 'displaces all other contenders as the defining center of human perception of reality and identity construction … Recentering the audience's imagination on the heavenly throne thus entails dislocation from whatever alternative center holds them in thrall'.

[197] Resseguie, *The Revelation of John*, p. 107.

[198] Richard, *Apocalypse*, p. 66,

God's throne is a symbol of God's power. On earth, in the world organized and controlled by the Roman Empire, the emperor's throne holds sway. Christians are familiar with this power and endure it. The great hope that the apocalyptic vision transmits is that in heaven God's power holds sway. That is the basis for Christian hope and what makes it possible to resist the empire.

[199] Smalley, *The Revelation to John*, p. 115.

[200] Ellul observes that 'God is not isolated in infinity, like the God of the philosophers'. J. Ellul, *Apocalypse: The Book of Revelation* (trans. G.W. Schreiner; New York: The Seabury Press, 1977), p. 236.

[201] Hurtado, 'Revelation 4–5 in the Light of Jewish Apocalyptic Analogies,' p. 112.

angelic John does not say),[202] yet their name – elders – suggests that they function in a leadership or supervisory role.[203] It will be up to the ensuing narrative to define the role of the elders. Their proximity to God and God's throne indicates a unique relationship between the elders and God. Although John does not provide any physical description of the 24 elders, the hearers would likely see continuity between the elders and the overcomers in the prophetic messages; for, in addition to sitting on thrones (as the overcomers are promised in 3.21), the elders have been clothed (περιβεβλημένους) in white garments, like that promised to the overcomers in 3.5, and they have golden crowns, like those promised in 2.10. In this way, the vision of the elders 'seems to be assurance of the heavenly reality of the promises'.[204]

Next, John states that out from the throne of God comes ἀστραπαὶ καὶ φωναὶ καὶ βρονταί ('lightning and sounds and thunders') (4.5), theophanic elements which distinguish God's throne from all others and add to its awe and mystery. Furthermore, John sees seven flaming torches identified as τὰ ἑπτὰ πνεύματα τοῦ θεοῦ ('the seven Spirits of God')[205] burning before the throne.

---

[202] Various attempts have been made at identifying the 24 elders. Charles, *A Critical and Exegetical Commentary on the Revelation of St. John*, pp. 129-33, summarizes the following positions: 1) the elders as glorified men, either representatives of Jewish or secular communities or as representatives of the OT (12 patriarchs) and NT (12 apostles) communities; 2) a college of angels originating out of the 24 Babylonian star-gods; 3a) angelic representatives of the 24 priestly orders; and 3b) heavenly representatives of the faithful who are priests and kings. Aune, *Revelation 1–5*, pp. 288-91, lists seven proposals: 1) heavenly counterparts to the 24 priestly orders; 2) the 24 divisions of Levitical musicians; 3) heavenly representatives of Israel and the Church; 4) martyred Christians who are now participating in heavenly life; 5) OT saints, based in part on Heb. 11.2 where exemplary Israelites are called πρεσβύτεροι; 6) angelic members of the heavenly court; and 7) figures from astral mythology or the zodiac. For similar categories, see Beale, *The Book of Revelation*, pp. 323-26.

[203] Hurtado, 'Revelation 4–5 in the Light of Jewish Apocalyptic Analogies', pp. 113-14, suggests that the first hearers would have most likely associated the term with the leaders in the synagogues and churches of the first century.

[204] Hurtado, 'Revelation 4–5 in the Light of Jewish Apocalyptic Analogies,' p. 113. He further suggests that the elders are 'heavenly archetypes, which serve as counterparts and representatives of the earthly saints … and are intended to show that the promises to the elect are based on heavenly realities'. See also Trafton, *Reading Revelation*, p. 60, who suggests that they represent the 'twenty-four angelic priestly families that serve in the heavenly Temple'.

[205] Zech 4.2-14 most likely stands behind John's reference to the Spirit here and in Rev. 5.6. In Zech 4.2, the prophet sees seven lamps (LXX: ἑπτὰ λυχνία)

This reinforces what the hearers have already learned about the close connection between God and the Spirit in 1.4. In addition to the Spirit being before the throne, John also sees something like a crystal sea of glass before the throne (4.6).[206] Finally, John notes that in the midst of the throne and around the throne are τέσσαρα ζῷα ('four living creatures') (4.6b).[207] Here again, John's description continues to give attention to the throne of God even while introducing new characters – the four living creatures – into the narrative.

John offers the hearers a physical description of the four living creatures that is reminiscent of the creatures in Ezekiel's vision (Ezek. 1.5-14); however, John's attention appears riveted less on their appearance and more on their *activity*. John states that the living creatures offer worship night and day (4.8a). By the use of the hendiadys ἡμέρας καὶ νυκτὸς ('day and night'), John reimagines the concept of time.[208] The living creatures sing[209] the first of many hymns that will appear in the Apocalypse:

Ἅγιος ἅγιος ἅγιος
κύριος ὁ θεὸς ὁ παντοκράτωρ,
ὁ ἦν καὶ ὁ ὢν καὶ ὁ ἐρχόμενος

Holy, holy, holy

---

which, in Zech 4.10 (LXX) are identified as ἑπτὰ οὗτοι ὀφθαλμοὶ κυρίου εἰσὶν οἱ ἐπιβλέποντες ἐπὶ πᾶσαν τὴν γῆν ('these are the seven eyes of the Lord which are looking upon the whole earth'). On this see especially Bauckham, *The Climax of Prophecy*, pp. 162-63, who contends that the Zechariah passage functions as 'the key Old Testament passage for John's understanding of the role of the Spirit in the divine activity in the world' (p. 162).

[206] Howard-Brook and Gwyther, *Unveiling Empire*, p. 204, sees the sea as 'the divider between God's abode and John's vantage point' and suggests that 'even John must keep some distance from the spectacular panorama upon which he has been allowed to gaze'.

[207] For a concise summary of the various ways these creatures have been identified, see Osborne, *Revelation*, pp. 233-34.

[208] Saunders, 'Revelation and Resistance', p. 136.

[209] I am choosing to translate the participle λέγοντες ('saying') in this way because it is followed by hymnic material. The hymns of the Apocalypse are regularly preceded by λέγοντες.

is the Lord God, the Almighty One,
the One who was and who is and who is coming (4.8c).[210]

The liturgical language of Revelation 1 has prepared the hearers for this heavenly liturgy. Source critical issues related to whether or not this liturgy emulates the Roman court,[211] comes from early Jewish or Christian worship,[212] or is John's own composition are issues which cannot be resolved with any degree of certainty or satisfaction. The narrative testifies of the heavenly throne room of God being a place filled with the sound of music. It is not insignificant that the first song John hears draws its source from the Scriptures (Isa. 6.3). Jörns suggests that the notification that the creatures sing it day and night is a conscious way for John to link the song to the praise of God in Isaiah 6. In this way, John presents the same picture as that found in Isaiah.[213] Although the song of the four creatures begins the same as that which Isaiah hears, it continues with two descriptions of God familiar to the hearers from Revelation.[214]

---

[210] Although see Jörns, *Das hymnische Evangelium*, p. 26, for his suggestion that the hymn should be arranged in two lines like the hymn in Isa. 6.3.

[211] See Laws, *In the Light of the Lamb*, p. 76, who describes the *humnodoi* as a group of musicians tasked with composing songs and choruses to honor the emperor. Friesen, *Imperial Cults and the Apocalypse of John*, p. 105, states that the *humnodoi* 'sang hymns to the imperial family, participated in imperial sacrifices, led celebrations, and hosted banquets'.

[212] Piper, 'The Apocalypse of John and the Liturgy of the Ancient Church', *Church History* 20.1 (1951), pp. 10-22, maintains that Revelation 'presupposes a definite type of worship in the churches to whom John wrote' whose 'order was largely borrowed from contemporary Jewish worship in temple and synagogue' (p. 19); O'Rourke, 'The Hymns of the Apocalypse,' pp. 399-409, sees John borrowing from preexisting liturgical sources, both Jewish and Christian, most notably in Rev 1.4, 5, 8b; 4.8b; 7.12, 15-17; 11.15, 17-18; 19.5, 6b-8. 'If he did use liturgical hymns [a claim he admits cannot be absolutely proven], we see how rich was the doctrinal expression used in the singing of early churches …' (p. 409); J.D.G. Dunn, *Unity and Diversity in the New Testament* (London: SCM Press, 1977), p. 145, sees the hymns as a whole as 'typical expressions of the praise of Hellenistic Jewish Christians', yet he notes that the songs to the Lamb might be John's own construction 'modelled on the acclamations of God and may well have been part of the language and worship of the community to which the seer belonged'.

[213] Jörns, *Das hymnische Evangelium*, p. 26: 'Dem Seher zeigt sich dasselbe Bild wie Jesaja' ('the Seer sees the same picture as Isaiah').

[214] See the interesting suggestion by Harris, *The Literary Function of the Hymns in the Apocalypse of John*, pp. 73-74, that John's omission of the last part of Isa. 6.3 signaled the 'depravity of John's narrative world'. 'The omission of the second half of the intertext in the hymn in 4:8 has the effect of placing the omitted textual fragment in the foreground. Isaiah 6:3b is thus present via negative'.

First, God is identified as 'Lord God, the Almighty'. This divine title, which will occur throughout the rest of the narrative (11.17; 15.3; 16.7; 21.22), first occurs in 1.8, albeit as separate titles. Second, God is described as 'the one who was and is and the one coming', familiar to the hearers from 1.4, 8. Thus, it is entirely appropriate that Revelation's first song is both ancient and yet familiar. What Isaiah heard, John hears and more. What the heavenly hosts sing, the churches are to sing.[215] The hymn has a pedagogic function as it emphasizes the person and character of God.[216] The theocentricity of their song accords with the singular focus of John's vision of the throne room; namely, God is unrivaled in sovereignty and majesty. In making such a claim, the worship of God is for the hearers nothing less than a political statement of allegiance. To worship God as the Lord God Almighty is to deny that status to any other ruler or deity. As such, worship is a subversive activity.[217] John's notification that the living creatures sing without ceasing indicates that worship is an on-going activity in heaven. That this is the *first* thing that the hearers *hear* in John's vision of heaven provides affirmation for their own worship and creates continuity between their worship and the worship of heaven. The collapsing of time and space, a key feature within the prophetic messages, occurs once again as the hearers experience the worship of heaven.

As the living creatures worship God in song, the 24 elders join in the worship in their own unique way. John records that the elders πεσοῦνται ('fall') before the throne, προσκυνήσουσιν ('worship') the one living forever,[218] βαλοῦσιν ('cast') their crowns before the throne,[219] and sing (λέγοντες) their own song (4.10). The hearers would recall John's own action of falling before the risen Jesus

---

[215] Deichgräber, *Gotteshymnus und Christushymnus in der frühen Christenheit*, p. 49. See also Aune, *Revelation 1–5*, pp. 303-306, for a thorough summary of the use of the *Trisagion* in Jewish and Christian liturgy, prayers, and magical texts.

[216] Harris, *The Literary Function of the Hymns in the Apocalypse of John*, p. 71.

[217] Howard-Brook and Gwyther, *Unveiling Empire*, p. 206.

[218] When προσκυνέω ('worship') is followed by the dative as here (τῷ ζῶντι, 'to the living One'), it usually is an indication that 'true Deity is the object of worship', D. Wallace, *Greek Grammar Beyond the Basics* (Grand Rapids: Zondervan Publishing House, 1996), p. 172.

[219] The casting of crowns is unique in the NT and may reflect Greco-Roman customs, Jörns, *Das hymnische Evangelium*, pp. 33-34.

(1.17). That the 24 elders likewise fall before God and worship confirms the appropriateness of this action as a bodily response of worship that expresses submission and allegiance to God.[220] The song of the 24 elders is the second song in heaven that John hears and records. It is an antiphonal response to the song of the living creatures.[221] Like their song, the elders' song is theocentric in its focus and pedagogic in its content:

Ἄξιος εἶ, ὁ κύριος καὶ ὁ θεὸς ἡμῶν,
λαβεῖν τὴν δόξαν καὶ τὴν τιμὴν καὶ τὴν δύναμιν,
ὅτι σὺ ἔκτισα᾽ τὰ πάντα
καὶ διὰ τὸ θέλημά σου ἦσαν καὶ ἐκτίσθησαν

You are worthy, our Lord and God,
to receive the glory and the honor and the power,
for you created all things
and by your will they existed and were created (4.11).

In their hymn, the 24 elders sing of God as the Worthy One,[222] who is to receive glory, honor and power because of God's role as Creator of all things.[223] Not to be missed is the personal and direct nature of the hymn noted by the second person pronouns. The hymn is an antiphonal response to v. 9 with the echoing of δόξα ('glory') and τιμή ('honor'). The hymn continues with δύναμις ('power') followed by the ὅτι ('for') clause, a construction indicating that the emphasis is on δύναμις ('power'); that is, God is connected with *power* in his role as Creator.[224] This stress on God as Creator is new to the Apocalypse, yet John's hearers would likely recognize this central tenant of both Judaism and Christianity. It is this One whom the elders proclaim as 'our' Lord and God. That the heavenly elders speak of God as their Lord and God encourages John's hearers

---

[220] Friesen, *Imperial Cults and the Apocalypse of John*, pp. 196-97.

[221] Laws, *In the Light of the Lamb*, p. 75. See also Jörns, *Das hymnische Evangelium*, p. 31; Harris, *The Literary Function of the Hymns in the Apocalypse of John*, p. 78.

[222] Prior to this point, the term 'worthy' has only been used of the faithful in Sardis who will walk with Jesus in white because they are ἄξιοί (3.4).

[223] 'The "all things" is absolute: angels, men, devils, heaven, earth and hell.' Gause, *Revelation: God's Stamp of Sovereignty on History*, p. 93.

[224] Jörns, *Das hymnische Evangelium*, p. 37. Ladd, *A Commentary on the Revelation of John*, p. 78, notes that the song 'asserts that behind all creation is the active sovereign will of the Creator'.

in their identification of God; that is, John's hearers are affirmed in their identification with and worship of God, who is Lord and Creator.

The events of Revelation 5 flow uninterrupted from the events of Revelation 4 as indicated by the opening καὶ εἶδον ('and I saw'). In chapter 4, John's attention is centered upon the throne of God and the worship of God given by the four living creatures and the 24 elders. Now as John looks, he sees at the right (ἐπὶ τὴν δεξ-ιὰν)[225] of the one sitting on the throne a βιβλίον ('book, scroll') (5.1). As throne language dominated chapter 4, so now does scroll language dominate Rev. 5.1-10. John describes the scroll as γε-γραμμένον ἔσωθεν καὶ ὄπισθεν ('having been written on the inside and on the back') and κατεσφραγισμένον σφραγῖσιν ἑπτά ('having been sealed with seven seals'). John's use of the perfect suggests that John is seeing a scroll that has already been prepared and now awaits its opening.[226] To such an end, John sees (καὶ εἶδον) a strong angel κηρύσσοντα ('proclaiming/preaching')[227] in a loud voice, Τίς ἄξιος ἀνοῖξαι τὸ βιβλίον καὶ λῦσαι τὰ σφραγῖδας αυτοῦ; ('Who is worthy to open the scroll and to loose its seals?') (5.2). The question proclaimed by the angel is perplexing; after all, the 24 elders have just sung that God is *worthy*. If God, who is supremely worthy, is not going to open the scroll in his

---

[225] R. Stefanovic, 'The Meaning and Significance of the ἐπὶ τὴν δεξιὰν for the Location of the Sealed Scroll (Revelation 5:1) and Understanding the Scene of Revelation 5', *Biblical Research* 46 (2001), pp. 42-54, argues that the phrase should be translated as the 'right side' rather than 'in the right hand' as is common among most translators. He states that translating it as 'in the right hand' is dependent upon Rev. 5.7 which uses the preposition ἐκ. Further, as attested in Greek literature up to the 7th century CE, this phrase functioned as an idiom having to do with the right side rather than the right hand (p. 51). The scroll, says Stefanovic, is on the throne on the right side or hand of God. This, combined with other key terms and phrases in the chapter to describe Jesus, point to the Messiah who would sit on the throne of David (p. 52). 'That the sealed scroll is described as lying on the throne at the right side of the Deity, might indicate an unoccupied place on the throne at the right hand of God waiting for a "worthy" candidate to take the scroll and occupy the place on the throne' (p. 53). The taking of the scroll at the right hand/side of God is an indication of 'the bestowal of royal authority' upon Jesus, the Lamb (p. 54).

[226] Trafton, *Reading Revelation*, p. 67, suggests that the scroll is the book of life.

[227] The present tense of the participle serves to draw attention to the proclamation of the angel. The same is true of the use of the present tense verbs that preface the hymns in 5.9-10, 12, and 13. D. Mathewson, 'Verbal Aspect in the Apocalypse of John: An Analysis of Revelation 5', *NovT* 50 (2008), p. 67.

hand, then perhaps the hearers would anticipate that one of the faithful, such as those in Sardis who are identified as *worthy*, might open the scroll. That no one is found who is able to open the scroll or look at it (5.3) elicits an emotional response from John: καὶ ἔκλαιον πολύ ('and I was weeping greatly') (5.4). The imperfect tense of the verb suggests that John is in this state of despair for some time before one of the elders speaks to him: Μὴ κλαῖε, ἰδοὺ ἐνίκησεν ὁ λέων ὁ ἐκ τῆς φυλῆς ᾿Ιούδα, ἡ ῥίζα Δαυίδ, ἀνοῖξαι τὸ βιβλίον καὶ τὰς ἑπτὰ σφραγῖδα᾽ αὐτοῦ ('Stop weeping, behold the Lion from the tribe of Judah, the Root of David, has overcome in order to open the scroll and its seven seals') (5.5). The position of the verb νικῶ ('overcome') at the beginning of the clause would likely stand out to the hearer; after all, this verb was the dominant verb used for the overcomers in the prophetic messages, and even Jesus used it of himself in 3.21. The subject of the verb, however, is not a particular person but rather an animal – the Lion of Judah. John's use of symbolism would perhaps be discerned by his hearers as a reference to Gen. 49.9, a text with messianic overtones. This Lion is further described as the root of David, perhaps reflective of Isa. 11.1-16. Such an association to David is not without precedent in Revelation, as Jesus identified himself with reference to David in 3.7.[228] That the Lion *overcomes* encourages the hearer to recognize that the Lion is a symbol for Jesus (Rev. 3.21; Jn 16.33).

While John *hears* about a Lion, he sees something entirely different:

Καὶ εἶδον ἐν μέσῳ τοῦ θρόνου καὶ τῶν τεσσάρων ζῴων καὶ ἐν μέσῳ τῶν πρεσβυτέρων ἀρνίον ἑστηκὸς ὡς ἐσφαγμένον ἔχων κέρατα ἑπτὰ καὶ ὀφθαλμοὺς ἑπτὰ οἵ εἰσιν τὰ [ἑπτὰ] πνεύματα τοῦ θεοῦ ἀπεσταλμένοι εἰς πᾶσαν τὴν γῆν

And I saw in the midst of the throne and the four living creatures and in the midst of the elders a Lamb standing as slaughtered having seven horns and seven eyes which are the [seven] Spirits of God being sent into all the earth (5.6).

---

[228] Unlike the Synoptic Gospels, 'Son of David' language is strikingly absent from the Johannine corpus. The only mention of David is in Jn 7.42 where the Messiah is said to be a descendant of David.

Now in the midst of all the thrones in heaven stands a Lamb! This 'psychedelic-like morphing of one form into another' is likely a sur- prise to the hearers.[229] Perhaps Johannine hearers would think of how Jesus is called ὁ ἀμνὸς τοῦ θεοῦ ὁ αἴρων τὴν ἁμαρτίαν τοῦ κόσμου ('the Lamb of God who takes away the sin of the world') (Jn 1.29, 36).[230] That this Lamb stands as slain indicates that 'the victory of the Lion has been won through the sacrificial death of the Lamb'.[231] The perfect verbs (ἑστηκὸς, 'standing' and ἐσφαγμένον, 'having been slaughtered') highlight the extraordinary nature of this Lamb for though he was slain, he now lives.[232] Jesus' own acknowledgement that he was dead but now lives (1.18; 2.8) gives added confirmation that this Lion-Lamb is Jesus,[233] the one who is praised for 'loving us and loosing us from our sins by his blood' (1.5). The Lamb has seven horns, which symbolizes com- plete power. Barr rightly calls this an 'oxymoron' as lambs are not powerful animals.[234] Moreover, the Lamb has the fullness of the Spirit because his seven eyes are the seven Spirits of God being sent out into all the earth. The hearers would recall the prominent place of the Spirit before the throne of God (1.4; 4.5) as well as the close connection between Jesus and the Spirit displayed in the prophetic messages. The use of ἀποστέλλω ('I send') could suggest the con- cept of being sent on mission; thus, the Spirit, as the eyes of the Lamb, is sent out into all the earth,[235] including the seven churches. This is why Jesus knows what is happening in the seven churches. Conceiving of the eyes of the Lamb as the Spirit reveals the deep

---

[229] Thomas, *The Apocalypse*, p. 224.

[230] However, it should be noted that the term used in Revelation (ἀρνίον) is a dimunitive of the usual term ἀμνός. The only other occurrence of ἀρνίον is in Jn 21.15 where Jesus instructs Peter, Βόσκε τὰ ἀρνία μου.

[231] Thomas, *The Apocalypse*, p. 227.

[232] Mathewson, 'Verbal Aspect in the Apocalypse of John', p. 71.

[233] By intentionally combining the contrasting imagery of a conquering Lion and slaughtered Lamb, John forges a completely new symbol for the Christian community. See Bauckham, *The Climax of Prophecy*, pp. 179-85; *idem, The Theology of the Book of Revelation*, p. 64; Friesen, *Imperial Cults and the Apocalypse of John*, p. 200, 'Even as John synthesized in Jesus such images as the Davidic ruler, Servant of the Lord, and the sacrificial Lamb, he refused to homogenize them. Instead, we are left with startling, unresolved juxtapositions …'

[234] Barr, *Tales of the End*, p. 69.

[235] Howard-Brook and Gwyther, *Unveiling Empire: Reading Then and Now*, p. 207.

relationship between Jesus and the Spirit[236] while it also communicates to the churches the importance of heeding the Spirit.

As John watches, the Lamb receives (εἴληφεν) the scroll from the right hand of the one sitting on the throne (5.7). The use of the perfect tense of λαμβάνω ('I receive, take') brings focused attention to this important event.[237] While the hearers might expect the Lamb immediately to open the scroll, what transpires is *un*expected. John sees the elders and the living creatures fall (ἔπεσαν) before the Lamb. Earlier, the elders alone fell before the throne of God in worship when the living creatures offered vocal praise unto God (4.10). Now *both* the elders and the living creatures engage in this kinesthetic act of worship. They also have with them harps and golden bowls full of incense which are the prayers of the saints (5.8). That the prayers of the saints are held, so to speak, in *golden* bowls is perhaps indicative of their value and worth. The hearers would likely connect their own prayers with those John sees. That their prayers are in the throne room of God where unceasing worship takes place reveals that prayer is to be counted as worship. Further, the location of the prayers of the saints at this particular point in the narrative connects their prayers with the Lamb's reception of the scroll; that is, in some way, their prayers have helped to bring about this momentous event. The elders and living creatures sing ᾠδὴν καινὴν ('a new song'). Considering that John has already heard two songs to this point, both of which have been sung to God, the notification that this song is *new* adds to the extraordinary event unfolding.[238] For the *Lamb*, only a new, spontaneous, song is appropriate:

Ἄξιος εἶ λαβεῖν τὸ βιβλίον
καὶ ἀνοῖξαι τὰς σφραγῖδας αὐτοῦ,
ὅτι ἐσφάγης καὶ ἠγόρασας τῷ θεῷ ἐν τῷ αἵματί σου
ἐκ πάσης φυλῆς καὶ γλώσσης καὶ λαοῦ καὶ ἔθνους

---

[236] Ladd, *A Commentary on the Revelation of John*, p. 88.

[237] Mathewson, 'Verbal Aspect in the Apocalypse of John', pp. 71-74, sees the perfect tense being used here to highlight the central event of the chapter: the Lamb's reception of the scroll (p. 74).

[238] Even granting that John is drawing on the form of a 'new song' from the Psalms (33.3; 40.3; 96.1; 98.1; 143.9; 144.9; 149.1), the notice that a new song is sung to the Lamb is most appropriate. Ladd, *A Commentary on the Revelation of John*, pp. 90-91.

καὶ ἐποίησας αὐτοὺς τῷ θεῷ ἡμῶν βασιλείαν καὶ ἱερεῖς,
καὶ βασιλεύσουσιν ἐπὶ τῆς γῆς

You are worthy to take the scroll
and to open its seals,
for you were slaughtered and you purchased for God by means
of your blood
people from every tribe and tongue and people and nation
and made them a kingdom and priests for God,
and they will reign on the earth (5.9-10).

Whereas the opening two words echo the opening of the song
sung in 4.11, this song is sung to the Lamb, as the rest of the first
line makes clear. That Jesus is being worshipped is momentous in
light of the monotheistic worship presented in Revelation 4. Bauckham states that 'the worship of Jesus must be understood as indicating the inclusion of Jesus in the being of the one God defined by
monotheistic worship'.[239] The *new* song makes explicit for the hearer
the significance of the Lamb; namely, the Lamb is worthy to open
the book because of his work of redemption through his blood. It is
a song celebrating salvation.[240]

The opening lines of the hymn provide an emphatic final answer
to the question proclaimed in 5.2. The ὅτι ('for') clause supplies
both the rationale for the opening affirmation and links the Lamb
to John's doxological praise of Jesus in 1.5b-6. The scope of the
Lamb's work provides for a *global* people of God as those from *every*
tribe *and* tongue *and* people *and* nation are formed as a kingdom and
priests for God. No doubt John's use of βασιλείαν ('kingdom')
would likely conjure up images of Empire, yet this song speaks of
an *alternative* kingdom brought into existence by the work of Jesus

---

[239] Bauckham, *The Theology of the Book of Revelation*, p. 60. Bauckham suggests
that the worship of Jesus is a development that occurs within Jewish Christianity
'where consciousness of the connexion between monotheism and worship was
high'. Bauckham states that John, who 'stands within this Jewish Christian tradition [which included Jesus "in the reality of the one God"] and, still within a
thoroughly Jewish framework of thought, has reflected deliberately on the relation of Christology to monotheism' (p. 61).

[240] Jörns, *Das hymnische Evangelium*, p. 52, identifies this hymn as a 'soteriologi-
cal' song. Deichgräber, *Gotteshymnus und Christushymnus in der frühen Christenheit*, p.
52, states that there are no Jewish elements in this song.

and inhabited by all those from every people and nation who pledge their allegiance to God and the Lamb.[241] The churches, localized in Asia Minor, are part of the global community of the Lamb. The triumphant conclusion to the song introduces a new element in the Apocalypse; that is, the community of the Lamb will reign on the earth. What an extraordinary 'reality' for the churches who have already or will likely face the *reality* of oppression and suffering (2.9-10, 13; 3.8-10). This song, as Allen Boesak rightly states, 'overturns the present reality and becomes a prophecy of another reality, God's reality'.[242]

The song of the elders and living creatures leads to another song as John sees and hears the voices of an innumerable group of angels who form yet another circle radiating out from the throne of God (5.11). With a loud voice (φωνῇ μεγάλῃ), they now sing:

Ἄξιόν ἐστιν τὸ ἀρνίον τὸ ἐσφαγμένον λαβεῖν
τὴν δύναμιν καὶ πλοῦτον καὶ σοφίαν καὶ ἰσχὺν
καὶ τιμὴν καὶ δόξαν καὶ εὐλογίαν

Worthy is the slaughtered Lamb to receive
the power and wealth and wisdom and strength
and honor and glory and blessing (5.12).

The hymn of the angels mirrors the previous song in that it is exclusively sung about the Lamb. The repetition of the adjective ἄξιος ('worthy') also joins the two songs together and reinforces the central concept of the *worthiness* of the Lamb. Further, the hearers would not miss that the second song sung to God likewise began with ἄξιος, thus equating God and the Lamb. The reiteration of 'the Lamb having been slain' elevates the salvific event of the cross and resurrection. Where the first hymn sung to the Lamb spells out the scope of the Lamb's work for humanity, this one provides worshipful ascriptions as appropriate responses to the Lamb's

---

[241] Friesen, *Imperial Cult and the Apocalypse of John*, p. 201; for a thorough discussion of the fourfold formula for the nations, see Bauckham, *The Climax of Prophecy*, pp. 326-37.

[242] A. Boesak, *Comfort and Protest: The Apocalypse from a South African Perspective* (Philadelphia: Westminster Press, 1987), p. 60

work. The seven ascriptions, three of which were heard in the hymn sung to God in 4.12, link the worship of the Lamb with God.

The angels' song leads to another spontaneous song as *all* of creation now sings a doxological hymn:[243]

Τῷ καθημένῳ ἐπὶ τῷ θρόνῳ καὶ τῷ ἀρνίῳ
ἡ εὐλογία καὶ ἡ τιμὴ καὶ ἡ δόξα καὶ τὸ κράτος
εἰς τοὺς αἰῶνα᾽ τῶν αἰώνων

To the One sitting on the throne and to the Lamb
be blessing and honor and glory and might
forever (5.13).

While John does not *see* all of the singers of this song, he hears their song as it resounds around him and under him. The whole of creation is expanded from its earlier listing in 5.3 where three divisions – heaven, earth, and under the earth – were explored in a search for one worthy to open the scroll. Now the sea becomes an arena of creation that joins in the eschatological hymn of praise to God and the Lamb.[244] John *hears* all of this from heaven, indicating that heaven is open to and aware of the activities on earth and under the earth. Just as the churches have been reassured that Jesus is in their midst and knows their situations, so now the churches are to understand that *their* worship is heard in heaven as John hears all of creation sing to God *and* the Lamb. God and the Lamb, each worshipped in individual songs of praise, are now worshipped jointly and equally.[245] To both belong blessing, honor, glory, and might

---

[243] Deichgräber, *Gotteshymnus und Christushymnus in der frühen Christenheit*, p. 53.

[244] Jörns, *Das hymnische Evangelium*, p. 54. P. Achtemeier, 'Revelation 5:1-14', *Interpretation* 40.3 (2001), pp. 285-86 expresses this most creatively: 'Every creature in every nook and cranny, wet or dry; every creature bathed in light or hid in darkness; every creature covered with scales or clothed in fur or feathers; every creature crawling, walking, running or flying; every creature now joins in the climax of praise …'

[245] Bauckham, who wants to maintain the monotheistic thrust of Revelation, points out that the worship of the Lamb leads to the worship of God. 'John does not wish to represent Jesus as an alternative object of worship alongside God, but as one who shares in the glory due to God. He is worthy of divine worship because his worship can be included in the worship of the one God.' Bauckham, *The Theology of the Book of Revelation*, p. 60. See also Ladd, *A Commentary on the Revelation of John*, p. 94, who writes that John was an 'inflexible monotheist; there is and can be only one God. Yet the Father is God, and the Son shares equally the divine prerogatives and the worship and adoration which God alone can receive'.

forever. It is noteworthy that two of the ascriptions – honor and glory – are also found in the individual songs to God (4.11) and to the Lamb (5.12). At a basic level, these terms serve as a verbal link tying together the songs of heaven; yet, at a deeper level they function as proclamations that God and the Lamb together *is* worthy of glory and honor. The hymn concludes with the formulaic expression of eternity indicating that forever and ever God and the Lamb will be worshipped. This extraordinary song thus becomes a fitting climax to the first scene of heavenly worship that John both sees and hears.

The worship scene ends with the four living creatures pronouncing the liturgical ἀμήν ('amen') (5.14). The imperfect tense of λέγω ('say') hints at repetition as if the living creatures had been offering up the ἀμήν as they listened to the songs of worship. To this point in Revelation, the ἀμήν has served as a concluding element to liturgical material (1.6, 7; also 3.14) and it does so here as well. With the pronouncement of the benedictory ἀμήν, the elders ἔπεσαν καὶ προσεκύνησαν ('fell and worshipped'). This is the third time that John records their kinesthetic worship (4.10; 5.8). If John's hearers would most likely identify with the elders, then the worship activities of the elders continue to be a model of appropriate worship for the churches.

Summary of Revelation 4–5

Revelation 4–5 transports the hearers along with John from the world of the seven churches to the heavenly throne room where John sees God and the Lamb. These chapters form the 'hinge' between the prophetic messages and the visions to follow; thus, they supply an indispensable 'interpretive lens' for the hearers as they continue through the Apocalypse.[246] Because this scene follows the prophetic messages to the churches, the hearers would connect the Lamb with the risen Jesus, the one speaking to them through the Spirit (Revelation 2–3) as well as the one appearing to John as he worshipped (1.9-20). The Spirit is also present and intimately linked

---

Trafton, *Reading Revelation*, p. 68, understands this differently: 'This juxtaposition of the one who sits upon the throne and the Lamb is astonishing. There is to be no distinction between them as recipients of praise. They are to be praised together, equally.'

[246] Saunders, 'Revelation and Resistance', pp. 140-41.

to God and the Lamb as the seven lamps before the throne (4.5) and the seven eyes of the Lamb (5.6). By means of such rich symbolism, this scene continues to emphasize the divine interrelationality of God, Jesus, and the Spirit begun in 1.4-5. John's experience comes to him ἐν πνεύματι ('in the Spirit'), thus reinforcing for the hearers the significance of the Spirit as a facilitator of worship.

These chapters also build on the theme of worship established in Revelation 1–3. In the throne room John experiences the liturgy of heaven offered to God and to the Lamb by the inhabitants of heaven. This makes an important and foundational point: worship belongs to God and the Lamb alone. A second point is that all of creation is to engage in worship to God and the Lamb. This is depicted in these chapters as John sees and hears the worship of the elders, the living creatures, the angels, and all of creation. A third point is that worship takes a variety of forms. The most recognizable element of worship in these chapters is its five hymns. The hymns are theological songs embedded into the surrounding narratives. In chapter 4, they give voice to the extraordinary person and character of God as Creator, as holy, and as worthy. In chapter 5, they celebrate the Lamb as Redeemer, making clear why the Lamb is worthy to take the scroll of God. They reveal Jesus' activities on behalf of humanity for God (5.9b-10). The hymns heard in heaven are to be the liturgy of the churches on earth. It is the power of liturgy to connect heaven and earth in such a way that 'the faraway heaven and the awaited future are fully present before God as of now' and can be experienced presently in worship.[247] In addition to the hymns, these chapters point out other liturgical activities that are to be part of the churches' worship. The elders' practice of falling before the throne indicates that prostration represents bodily worship and is fitting. Their harps, likely used to accompany the songs of worship, indicate the appropriateness of instrumental worship. The prayers of the saints, brought before God in golden bowls, are also to be viewed as a liturgical activity. Lastly, the use of ἀμήν in 5.14 indicates that it is a liturgical response appropriate for the worship of God.

---

[247] Prigent, *Commentary on the Apocalypse of St. John*, p. 32.

B. Revelation 6.1–8.5

The incredible worship scene of Revelation 4–5 segues without pause into the opening of the seven seals by the Lamb. Between the opening of the sixth and seventh seals is the second scene of heavenly worship (7.9-17).

The descriptions of the first four seals are tightly structured. First, the Lamb opens each of the four seals. Second, one of the living creatures issues the command: Ἔρχου ('Come') (6.1, 3, 5, 7). Third, at that word of command, John sees a horse. Each horse is identified by color: white (6.2), red (6.4), black (6.5), and pale (6.8).[248] Fourth, each horse has a rider, identified in seals 1–3 as ὁ καθήμενος[249] ἐπ᾽ αὐτὸν ('the one sitting upon it') and in seal four as ὁ θάνατος ('death'). Fifth, each rider is given[250] a specific task that results in destruction upon the earth. The first rider has a bow, is given a crown (symbol of authority), and goes forth conquering in order to conquer (νικῶν καὶ ἵνα νικήσῃ) (6.2). The second rider is given permission to take peace from the earth and a great sword (μάχαιρα). The result of the taking of peace from the earth has devastating consequences: ἵνα ἀλλήλους σφάξουσιν ('in order that they might slaughter one another') (6.4). The third rider is given a scale. A voice from the midst of the four living creatures announces increased prices for wheat and barley, a sign of famine, but prohibits the destruction (μὴ ἀδικήσῃς) of the oil and wine, which speaks to a partial famine (6.6). The fourth rider, Death, is followed by Hades. They are given authority over one-fourth of the earth to kill by sword, famine, death, and wild animals. The fourth seal envelops the activities of the first three riders and adds death and wild animals to the tools of destruction used by Death and Hades to kill one-fourth of the earth's population.

The opening of the fifth seal is different from the first four seals, for when the Lamb opens the seal, John sees ὑποκάτω τοῦ θυσιαστηρίου τὰς ψυχὰς τῶν ἐσφαγμένων διὰ τὸν λόγον τοῦ θεοῦ καὶ διὰ τὴν μαρτυρίαν ἣν εἶχον ('under the altar the souls

---

[248] John appears to draw on Zech. 1.7-11 and 6.1-8 for the four horses.

[249] But note the dative τῷ καθημένῳ ('to the one sitting') in 6.4. Gonzáles and Gonzáles, *Revelation*, pp. 46-47, suggest that the unusual way that the riders are described could suggest that they represent false thrones or seats of power.

[250] The use of the aorist passive ἐδόθη ('he was given') implies that God (or the Lamb) is the one giving.

of those having been slaugthered on account of the word of God and their testimony') (6.9). Perhaps this scene would unsettle John's hearers more than the first four scenes for they have been prepared in the narrative to identify with what John now sees. John himself is on Patmos διὰ τὸν λόγον τοῦ θεοῦ καὶ τὴν μαρτυρίαν Ἰησοῦ ('on account of the word of God and the testimony of Jesus') (1.9). The prophetic messages have warned of the possibility of death and admonished faithfulness (2.10); indeed, Antipas, Jesus' faithful witness, has been put to death (2.13). The reality that the faithful – those who hold fast to the word of God and the testimony of Jesus – will likely be *slain* like Jesus (5.6) is brought to bear upon the hearers. John sees these souls under[251] the altar, which is mentioned here for the first time. Because John is viewing all of this in the heavenly throne room, the hearers would likely understand that the souls are in the presence of God.[252] The cry of the slain souls – Ἕως πότε, ὁ δεσπότης ὁ ἅγιος καὶ ἀληθινός, οὐ κρίνεις καὶ ἐκδικεῖς τὸ αἷμα ἡμῶν ἐκ τῶν κατοικούντων ἐπὶ τῆς γῆς ('How long, holy and true Master, until you judge and avenge our blood from the inhabitants of the earth') (6.10) – is a direct plea to God and/or the Lamb,[253] identified only here in Revelation as 'Master', to avenge their deaths. Their cry is a plea for justice and vindication.[254] This is the first reference to the blood of the saints, and the hearers would likely connect it with the images of Jesus' blood and sacrifice (1.5, 5.9). The location of the martyrs – under the altar

---

[251] Ladd, *A Commentary on the Revelation of John*, p. 102, suggests that John's use of 'under' has 'nothing to do with the state of the dead or their situation in the intermediate state; it is merely a vivid way of picturing the fact that they had been martyred in the name of their God'.

[252] S. Pattemore, *The People of God in the Apocalypse: Discourse, Structure and Exegesis* (SNTSMS 128; Cambridge: Cambridge University Press, 2004), p. 77, discusses the use of ψυχή ('life, soul') and helpfully notes, 'It does not seem necessary to invoke an anthropology involving separable bodies and souls. The souls are people, clearly here people who have died ... and whose death represents in some sense a sacrifice to God'.

[253] Thomas, *The Apocalypse*, p. 282, 'The fact that on this occasion it is not altogether clear to whom this title has reference would not be lost on John and his hearers, as the intricate nature of the relationship between and identity of God and Jesus is becoming more and more apparent'. See also Pattemore, *The People of God in the Apocalypse*, p. 83.

[254] Pattemore, *The People of God in the Apocalypse*, p. 84. See also Richard, *Apocalypse*, p. 70; Gorman, *Reading Revelation Responsibly*, pp. 155-58.

– suggests that 'their deaths are given a sacred, sacrificial significance'.[255] Not to be missed is the distinctive terminology – οἱ κατοικοῦντοι ἐπὶ τῆς γῆς ('the inhabitants of the earth')– employed here (v. 10) that effectively dichotomizes humanity into two categories; thus, the souls under the altar – the martyrs – represent the faithful followers of God and the Lamb, and the inhabitants of the earth represent those who have rejected God and the Lamb.[256] Further, that heretofore worship has been the only thing the hearers have heard in heaven to this point in the Apocalypse intimates a link between their plea and worship, so that worship serves as the proper context for lifting up a cry for justice to God.[257] In response to their plea, the martyrs are given (ἐδόθη) white robes and told to rest until the full number of the faithful that are about to be killed are indeed killed (6.11). The hearers would not forget that white robes were promised to the worthy ones in Sardis who will walk with Jesus (3.5) nor that Jesus counseled the Laodicean church to buy from him white garments (3.18). 'Thus, the gift of a white robe conveys the idea that the promises made to those who overcome are being fulfilled before their very "eyes".'[258] Additionally, the hearers are to understand that there will be more martyrs – perhaps even from among the seven churches.

As John watches[259] the opening of the sixth seal, a series of events takes place. A great earthquake occurs, the sun becomes black, the moon becomes as blood, the stars fall to the earth, the heavens split apart, and the mountains and islands are moved from their places (6.12-14). If these horrific events are in response to the cry of the souls under the altar, the hearers are not told; however, the sheer terror of the events is revealed by the activity of the

---

[255] Thompson, *Revelation*, p. 104. See also B.K. Blount, *Can I Get a Witness? Reading Revelation Through African American Culture* (Louisville: Westminster/John Knox Press, 2005), p. 51, who sees that the altar is a symbol of God's judgment. 'The symbolism of the altar assures them that transformative, liberating justice is coming. This is why John locates them there; he wants his readers to be more focused on God's justice than on their own sacrifice'.

[256] Pattemore, *The People of God in the Apocalypse*, pp. 85-86. See also Rev 3.10.

[257] Gorman, *Reading Revelation Responsibly*, p. 156.

[258] Thomas, *The Apocalypse*, p. 284; Boesak, *Comfort and Protest*, p. 70.

[259] The first and sixth seal are identical in their opening: Καὶ εἶδον ὅτε ἤνοιξεν ('And I saw when he opened'). Seals two through five omit the verb εἶδον ('I saw').

inhabitants of the earth[260] who hide in the caves and in the rocks of the mountains. Their cry to the rocks – Πέσετε ἐφ᾽ ἡμᾶς καὶ κρύψατε ἡμᾶς ἀπὸ προσώπου τοῦ καθημένου ἐπὶ τοῦ θρόνου καὶ ἀπὸ τῆς ὀργῆς τοῦ ἀρνίου ('Fall on us and hide us from the face of the One sitting on the throne and from the wrath of the Lamb') – clearly reveals that the inhabitants of the earth know that the disaster taking place around them has its source in God and the Lamb (6.16a).[261] Further, they recognize that the events signify the coming of the great day of the wrath of God and the Lamb. While John's hearers might recognize these events as signaling the Day of the Lord likely familiar to them from Scripture, here it is the inhabitants of the earth who make this connection – 'because the great day of their wrath has come' (6.17). This signals a sharp contrast between the churches who experience the *discipline* of the Lamb (3.19) and the inhabitants of the earth who experience the *wrath* of the Lamb. The Lamb who is worshipped is the Lamb who metes out judgment.[262] Rather than turning to the Lamb in repentance, the inhabitants of the earth seek self-preservation in the rocks and caves. Their last words – τίς δύναται σταθῆναι ('Who is able to stand?') – constitute the second question raised in the seal openings; however, unlike the souls under the altar who are given white robes and an assurance of vindication, the inhabitants of the earth are given no answer.

While the hearers brace themselves for the opening of the final seal, the first of several interludes is introduced into the narrative.[263] The interlude contained in 7.1-17 delays the opening of the seventh seal in order that the servants of God be sealed (σφραγίσωμεν) upon their foreheads (7.1-3). The sealing of the people of God is an event of great importance as evidenced by the concentration of

---

[260] Here identified with a string of nominatives as the kings of the earth and the great ones and the military leaders and the rich and the strong and all slaves and free (6.15). They represent 'seven distinct classes of human society'. Thomas, *The Apocalypse*, p. 288.

[261] Thomas, *The Apocalypse*, p. 289.

[262] Trafton, *Reading Revelation*, p. 77; D. Guthrie, 'The Lamb in the Structure of the Book of Revelation', p. 65, 'Clearly the character of the Lamb is not intended to be seen as meekness and gentleness, otherwise the reference to the wrath of the Lamb would be inappropriate. But the wrath is entirely in line with a Lamb who carries out judgment.'

[263] Bauckham, *The Climax of Prophecy*, p. 11.

'seal' vocabulary (7.3, 4 [2x], 5, 8). John hears that 144,000 people, 12,000 from each tribe of Israel,[264] are sealed (7.4-8). It is quite likely that those who are sealed are the ones who will become martyrs, as told to the souls under the altar (6.11).[265] The use of 'servant' language in both texts would likely encourage the hearers to make this connection. The sealing of the servants of God serves as the catalyst for an eruption of worship in heaven.

Revelation 7.9-17

John sees an innumerable multitude consisting of people from παντὸς ἔθνους καὶ φυλῶν καὶ λαῶν καὶ γλωσσῶν ('every nation and tribe and people and tongue') (7.9). Once again one image morphs into another as the 12 tribes of Israel converge with the innumerable multitude to create a grand portrait of the people of God made up of *all* people, regardless of ethnicity, who follow God and the Lamb.[266] Echoing in the background are the words of the hymn in 5.9 where the Lamb is worshipped for purchasing for God people from πάσης φυλῆς καὶ γλώσσης καὶ λαοῦ καὶ ἔθνους ('every tribe and tongue and people and nation'). This verbal thread ties this scene with the worship scene of Revelation 4–5 and thereby advances the theological implications of the Lamb's redemptive work. This great multitude *stands* (ἑστῶτες, also 5.6) before the throne and before the Lamb[267] having been clothed in white robes

---

[264] Bauckham, *The Climax of Prophecy*, pp. 215-24, maintains that John is drawing on the tradition of the messianic army. Rather than being a purely symbolic number, Bauckham argues that John's audience might have taken this idea literally. 'It would be quite natural to think of an army of all Israel, assembled for the messianic war, as composed of twelve equal tribal contingents' (p. 218). He discusses several texts (Isa. 11.14, *Sibylline Oracle* 2.170-176, *4 Ezra* 13) which contain the idea of the ten tribes returning to take part in the messianic war. See also D.E. Aune, *Revelation 6–16* (WBC 52b; Nashville: Thomas Nelson, 1988), pp. 464-65.

[265] Murphy, *Fallen is Babylon*, pp. 221-22, suggests that the 144,000 do not represent historic Israel or even Jewish Christians but rather the martyrs, 'who form a special group among the total number of Christians' (p. 222). See also Bauckham, *The Theology of the Book of Revelation*, p. 79, who suggests that the sealing is to mark those who will be martyred.

[266] Sweet, *Revelation*, p. 150.

[267] Guthrie, 'The Lamb in the Structure of the Book of Revelation', *Biblical and historical essays from London Bible College* (London: the London Bible College, 1981), p. 66, observes that the linking of the throne with the Lamb suggests that 'there is no possibility of the Lamb being separated from the purposes of God'.

and holding palm branches, traditional symbols of victory.[268] That this international throng *stands* before God and the Lamb provides the people of God with a definitive answer to the question posed by the inhabitants of the earth (6.17). That these have been clothed in white robes like those given to the souls under the altar suggests that they too have given their lives for the Lamb. As Pattemore insists, the portrait of the church in Revelation is that of a martyr church – those willing to follow their Lord in death and, thereby, become overcomers.[269]

In a great voice the innumerable multitude cries out in song:

'Η σωτηρία τῷ θεῷ ἡμῶν τῷ καθημένῳ
ἐπὶ τῷ θρόνῳ καὶ τῷ ἀρνίῳ

Salvation to our God sitting
upon the throne and to the Lamb (7.10).

Unlike the hymns of Revelation 4–5 which are all introduced by a participial form of λέγω, ('saying, singing') this short hymn is also prefaced with the verb κράζω, ('cry out') which was also used to describe the cry of the souls under the altar (6.10).[270] This verbal repetition reinforces that the singers of this song belong to the group of the martyrs. Further, the force of the verb, which connotes crying out or shouting, gives indication of their emotional response to God's actions on their behalf. The great multitude jubilantly announces that salvation belongs to[271] God and to the Lamb.

---

[268] Beale, *The Book of Revelation*, p. 428. For a more extensive discussion of palm branches in Judaism and the Greco-Roman world, see Aune, *Revelation 6–16*, pp. 467-70.

[269] See his excellent discussion of this in *The People of God in the Apocalypse*, pp. 114-16. See also Trafton, *Reading Revelation*, p. 75. Harris, *The Literary Function of the Hymns in the Apocalypse of John*, draws attention to the honor-shame context and observes that 'in the reversed social system of the Apocalypse, not to have a white garment – or not to be a martyr – is a shameful event in the sight of God and the Lamb, even though from the perspective of normal Mediterranean social standards to be physically affronted in such a radical way is precisely a shameful act'.

[270] Smalley, *The Revelation to John*, p. 192, notes that in the Fourth Gospel, this verb is often used 'to introduce sayings of Jesus which involve a crucial disclosure (as at 7.28, 37; 12.44)'.

[271] Most likely a dative of possession. See Wallace, *Greek Grammar Beyond the Basics*, pp. 149-51.

In this context, ἡ σωτηρία ('salvation') encompasses victory, deliverance or justice/vindication. The cry of the martyrs for justice is enfolded in the prophetic declaration of the hymn: Salvation – victory – *belongs to* God *and* the Lamb!

The anthem of praise from the great multitude moves the angels, the elders, and the four living creatures around the throne to fall on their faces before the throne and worship God with their own anthem. The description of the heavenly residents as well as the repetition of throne language calls to mind Revelation 4–5. By this cue, the two worship scenes are mutually to inform one another as well as interpret the seal openings which they bracket. The song of the heavenly residents is an antiphonal response (prefaced with the familiar λέγοντες) to the hymn of the martyrs:

Ἀμήν, ἡ εὐλογία καὶ ἡ δόξα καὶ ἡ σοφία καὶ
ἡ εὐχαριστία καὶ ἡ τιμὴ καὶ ἡ δύναμις καὶ
ἡ ἰσχὺς τῷ θεῷ ἡμῶν εἰς τοὺς αἰῶνας τῶν αἰώνων·
ἀμήν

Amen, blessing and glory and wisdom and
thanksgiving and honor and power and
strength be to our God forever and ever.
Amen (7.12).

Although this hymn is addressed to God, the hearers have been encouraged to worship God and the Lamb together in previous hymns (5.13; 7.10). That the hearers should continue to think of God and the Lamb in this hymn is reinforced in two ways: 1) The content of this hymn consists of attributes earlier ascribed to the Lamb in 5.12 (wisdom, power, strength)[272] and to God and the Lamb in 5.13 (blessing, glory, honor). 2) The eternity formula used here is the same as that found in the hymn to God and the Lamb in Rev. 5.13. The worship of God includes the worship of the Lamb. That the song opens with ἀμήν ('amen') confirms the truthfulness of the song just sung by the great multitude; the closing ἀμήν is a benediction to their own hymn. The hymn, like those in the first worship scene, affirms the character of God; yet, in light of the martyrs' experience, the hymn's theological focus is all the more

---

[272] Of these three, δύναμις is the only one to previously have been ascribed to God in 4.11.

important. What happens to the faithful on earth does not take away from the character of God; that is, God is always to be worshipped. *Hearing* the hymn while *seeing* the martyrs redefines what it means to be a part of the community of the Lamb.

As the worship scene unfolds, John becomes a participant when one of the elders asks him about the identity of this group he has been observing (7.13). John's answer is to defer back to the elder: Κύριέ μου, σὺ οἶδας ('My lord, you know') (7.14). Indeed, the elder does know for he proceeds to identify the great multitude as οἱ ἐρχόμενοι ἐκ τῆς θλίψεως τῆς μεγάλης καὶ ἔπλυναν τὰς στολὰς αὐτῶν καὶ ἐλεύκαναν αὐτὰς ἐν τῷ αἵματι τοῦ ἀρνίου ('the ones coming out of the great tribulation and who washed their robes and made them white in the blood of the Lamb') (7.14). The elder does not define this 'great tribulation' but the hearers would likely reflect on Jesus' words concerning the ten days of tribulation mentioned in 2.10 or the trials about to come upon the inhabitants of the earth (3.10). If the referent to this great tribulation is somewhat vague, the identification of the multitude as a martyr church is clear. This is suggested by the use of the present tense οἱ ἐρχόμενοι; that is, the ones clothed in white *are* the ones (perhaps even from the seven churches)[273] coming out of the great tribulation. It is the 'efficacy' of the Lamb's blood that brings them through the time of duress and enables them to stand before the throne with garments made white by the blood of the Lamb.[274] The notice that the martyrs washed their robes expresses the idea that 'salvation is not effected without their co-operation'.[275] It is in the sharing of the Lamb's blood and the participating in his victory that the overcomers are made pure. The remainder of the elders' words are arranged as a hymn:

> διὰ τοῦτό εἰσιν ἐνώπιον τοῦ θρόνου τοῦ θεοῦ
> καὶ λατρεύουσιν αὐτῷ ἡμέρας καὶ νυκτὸς ἐν τῷ ναῷ αὐτου,
> καὶ ὁ καθήμενος ἐπὶ τοῦ θρόνου σκηνώσει ἐπ' αὐτούς.
> οὐ πεινάσουσιν ἔτι οὐδὲ διψήσουσιν ἔτι οὐδὲ μὴ πέσῃ ἐπ' αὐτοὺς

---

[273] Trafton, *Reading Revelation*, p. 85.

[274] Thompson, *Revelation*, p. 110.

[275] Sweet, *Revelation*, p. 153.

ὁ ἥλιος οὐδὲ πᾶν καῦμα,
ὅτι τὸ ἀρνίον τὸ ἀνὰ μέσον τοῦ θρόνου ποιμανεῖ αὐτοὺς
καὶ ὁδηγήσει αὐτοὺς ἐπὶ ζωῆς πηγὰς ὑδάτων,
καὶ ἐξαλείψει ὁ θεὸς πᾶν δάκρυον ἐκ τῶν ὀφθαλμῶν
    αὐτῶν

For this reason they are before the throne of God
and they are serving him day and night in his temple,
and the One sitting on the throne will spread a tent over them.
They will hunger no longer nor thirst any longer
nor will the sun fall on them nor any scorching heat,
for the Lamb in the midst of the throne will shepherd them
and lead them to springs of the water of life,
and God will wipe every tear from their eyes (7.15-17).

This, the longest hymnic piece of Revelation to this point, is the climatic song of the second worship scene. The jubilant song of the multitude (7.10) and the ascriptionary song of praise rendered by the heavenly residents now give way to a lengthy anthem that anticipates and celebrates God's care for his people. The martyrs have been faithful witnesses to God and the Lamb; God and the Lamb will faithfully provide for them in heaven. There they will be granted a place before the throne and will render worship unto God day and night, in continuity with the four living creatures (4.8). Their worship before God, expressed here in the verb λατρεύω, indicates service or ministry to God befitting the designation of the people of God as priests (1.6; 5.10). In recalling that this group is comprised of people from all nationalities (7.9), the hearers would likely be struck by this redefinition of priesthood as available to all people. With them, God will dwell. The language of 'dwelling' evokes the tent of meeting by which God's presence journeyed with Israel, or Ezek. 37.26-28 where God speaks to the exiles of a time when God will dwell in the midst of his people. Johannine hearers would likely equate the verb σκηνώσει with Jesus, the Logos who became flesh and ἐσκήνωσεν ('pitched a tent') amongst his people (Jn 1.14). God's divine presence will provide shelter and protection for the people of God.[276]

---

[276] Thomas, *The Apocalypse*, p. 275.

In addition to abiding in the presence of God, the overcomers will not be in need; that is, they will not hunger or thirst nor experience the scorching of the sun (7.16). While the imagery of food might also cause the hearers to recall Israel's wilderness experience where water, manna and quail were provided by God, perhaps they would also think of Jesus' promises to the overcomers of eating from the tree of life (2.7) and receiving hidden manna (2.17). They might also think of their own partaking of the bread and wine of the Eucharist. As such, the meal of the Eucharist provides nourishment for their earthly journey and anticipates the provision that awaits them in heaven. Further, the Lamb will shepherd them and guide them to streams of living water. Johannine hearers would likely recall Jesus' words recorded in the Fourth Gospel: Ἐγώ εἰμι ὁ ποιμὴν ὁ καλὸς ('I am the good shepherd') (Jn 10.11, 14). As shepherd, Jesus provides for and protects his sheep. He lays down his life for them, and they cannot be snatched from him (Jn 10.28).[277] The final line of the hymn perhaps gives voice to the present painful condition of the faithful in the midst of a hostile world, yet they are to be assured that God will wipe away their tears. In this way, 'the concerns of theodicy are answered'.[278] John's churches are thus encouraged to sing about what awaits them and in doing so experience a foretaste of what is to come.[279] Faithful endurance – even if it leads to death – will be rewarded with *final* salvation.

The hymn flows directly into the opening of the seventh and final seal without so much as an ἀμήν ('amen') to mark its conclusion. The hearers would likely be astonished that with the opening of the seventh seal comes a half-hour of silence (8.1).[280] With all that has taken place in the heavenly realm, this time of silence is deafening. It is as if all of heaven pauses, waiting. Coming on the heels of worship given to God and the Lamb, this period of silence

---

[277] Kelly, 'Revelation 7:9-17', p. 293.

[278] Wall, *Revelation*, p. 121.

[279] deSilva, *Seeing Things John's Way*, p. 217, expresses this well: 'There is restoration, healing, and blessedness after the storms of life; therefore, disciples can brave those storms faithfully'.

[280] Contra Ladd, *A Commentary on the Revelation of John*, p. 122, who says that the seventh seal 'has no content'. See Beale, *The Book of Revelation*, pp. 446-54, for an exposition on 'silence' in the Old Testament and in Judaism. See Aune, *Revelation 6–16*, pp. 507-508, for evidence of a time of silence as part of the temple and/or early Christian liturgy.

should perhaps be viewed as another time of worship. After, or even during, the time of silence, John sees seven angels with seven trumpets (8.2). Although John sees the seven angels, he nonetheless first describes an angel with a golden censer standing before the altar with a great amount of incense. This incense, along with the prayers of all the saints, is placed on the altar before the throne, and its smoke rises up with the prayers before God (8.3-4). The angel then hurls (ἔβαλεν) fire taken from the altar upon the earth which results in βρονταὶ καὶ φωναὶ καὶ ἀστραπαὶ καὶ σεισμός ('thunders and sounds and lightning and an earthquake') (8.5). The use of altar imagery ties this scene to the fifth seal while the mention of the prayers of the saints takes the hearers back to 5.8. The reappearance of the prayers of God's people in light of all that has occurred since 5.8 elevates prayer as a liturgical act with eschatological significance, for through prayer, the church is 'intimately linked with the real world, the world of God'.[281] God's response to the prayers of the saints is marked in two ways. First, the hurling of fire upon the earth indicates God is continuing to execute judgment. Second, the theophanic elements, which first occurred in 4.5 are expanded to include an earthquake. The hearers would not forget that the inhabitants of the earth have hidden themselves in caves and implored the rocks to fall upon them (6.15-16). Perhaps the mentioning of the earthquake signals that indeed the rocks have fallen.

Summary of Revelation 6.1–8.5

Revelation 6.1–8.5 narrates the first of Revelation's judgment cycles – the opening of the seven seals. Embedded within this section is an interlude which delays the action between the openings of the sixth and seventh seals. The interlude consists of the sealing of the servants of God (7.1-8) and the worship scene that follows (7.9-17). The worship scene is tied to Revelation 4–5 in a number of ways: 1) It takes place before the throne and in front of the Lamb. 2) The elders, living creatures, and angels are present. 3) Worship is offered up to God and the Lamb by means of hymns, spoken words of praise, and kinesthetic movement. The worship scene also interprets the narrative in which it is embedded. In the midst of the

---

[281] Boring, *Revelation*, p. 133.

wrath of God and the Lamb being unleashed, salvation for the martyrs is realized. The great multitude sings of salvation belonging to God and to the Lamb (7.10), and all the heavenly residents respond with an antiphonal song of praise to God (7.12). Their song, in light of the martyrs' experience, infuses the worship of God and the Lamb with added significance. Worship is not a frivolous activity as it might demand the very life of the worshipper. Within this worship scene, the idea of being an overcomer is defined in light of tribulation and martyrdom. These experiences intimately link the overcomers with the Lamb whose blood provides salvation. Martyrdom is not in vain, for the elder sings of the provision that awaits the people of God as well as the reality that God's people will be present with God and the Lamb forever. Such songs of hope are to inspire the churches to persevere even in the face of opposition.

The significance of prayer as an activity of worship is further developed in this section. Whereas in Revelation 5, the prayers of the saints are presented before the Lamb, here the prayers of the saints are offered up on the golden altar before the throne of God. That the prayers of the saints go up before God in the throne room is extraordinary. God hears the prayers of the saints – including their petitions for justice – and responds to them.

The final element that pertains to worship is the time of silence (8.1). It is during this time that the prayers of the saints are heard. Gonzáles and Gonzáles write, 'What are we to say about this? Perhaps we would do best to say nothing and to respect the silence – to learn that God's time is not our time and to take this as a lesson on what it means to wait on God.'[282] Perhaps it is in the silence that the hearers can best *hear* the rhythms and cadence of heaven.

C. Revelation 8.6–11.19

Revelation 8.6–11.19 narrates the seven trumpet judgments. As in the seal openings, an interlude occurs between the sounding of the sixth and seventh trumpets (10.1-14). The third worship scene (11.15-19) occurs at the conclusion of the interlude. As with the opening of the seven seals, at the sounding of the trumpets terrible events unfold that affect the earth and its inhabitants. Many of these events would likely remind the hearers of the ancient plagues on

---

[282] González and González, *Revelation*, p. 59.

Egypt (Exod. 7.14-10.29).[283] The trumpet judgments, however, bring greater devastation to creation than that experienced in the seal openings. Whereas one-quarter of the earth is affected by various events in the seal openings, one-third of the earth is affected by the events in the trumpet soundings.

The first four trumpet blasts, like the first four seal openings, occur in rapid succession in the narrative and unleash destruction upon the earth (8.7), the sea (8.8-9), the waters (8.10-11), and the luminaries (8.12). The results appear nearly catastrophic as one-third of the earth and trees are burned, one third of the sea creatures die, one third of the sea vessels are destroyed, and one third of the luminaries are darkened. Despite this wide-spread devastation, the cry of the eagle in 8.13 prepares the hearers for an intensification of judgment.[284]

The descriptions of the fifth and sixth trumpets are more extensive in length and thus cannot be treated in detail here.[285] What is germane to this study is what John records after the sixth trumpet. At the sounding of the sixth trumpet, John hears the golden altar speak (9.13). The reference to the altar reminds the hearers of the fifth seal where the souls *under* the altar cry out to God for justice and vindication (6.9). Here, it seems that the altar itself 'comes to life' and speaks. It is the altar that issues a command to the sixth angel: Λῦσαν τοὺς τέσσαρας ἀγγέλους τοὺς δεδεμένους ἐπὶ τῷ ποταμῷ τῷ μεγάλῳ Εὐφράτῃ ('Loose the four angels having

---

[283] G.K. Beale, *John's Use of the Old Testament in Revelation* (JSNTSup 166; Sheffield: Sheffield Academic Press, 1998), p. 208, writes, 'The Exodus plagues are probably understood by John as typological foreshadowings of punishments on the ungodly during the eschatological church age, which precedes the final Exodus of God's people from this world to the new creation'. See also M.E. Boring, 'The Theology of Revelation: "The Lord Our God the Almighty Reigns"', *Interpretation* 40.3 (2001), pp. 263-64; Trafton, *Reading Revelation*, pp. 91-92.

[284] Trafton, *Reading Revelation*, p. 94, sees four purposes for the eagle's words: 1) to separate the first four trumpets from the last three; 2) to provide a 'dramatic pause'; 3) to identify the last three trumpets; 4) to show that the woes are targeted at those who live on earth. Specifically in light of his final point, Trafton argues that the people of God, who are distinguished from those who live on earth in the narrative, will not be 'harmed' by the events of the last three trumpets.

[285] When the fifth trumpet is sounded, an army of locust is unleashed from the Abyss and given power to torment for five months those without the seal of God on their forehead (9.1-11).

been bound at the great river Euphrates') (9.14). The four bound angels that are loosed by the trumpeting angel have an appointed assignment to kill a third of humanity.[286] Although John *hears* of four angels, he *sees* a vast army of cavalry, two million strong. As with the locusts in the fifth trumpet, John provides ample description of the horses and their riders (9.17-19). One third of humanity is killed by the fire, smoke, and sulfur bellowing forth from the mouths of the horses. In the fifth trumpet, death was not to be found by those who sought for it (9.6); in the sixth trumpet, death comes. John concludes the sixth trumpet narrative by relating that those who were not killed by the plagues did not repent (οὐδὲ μετενόησαν) of the works of their hands nor did they stop worshipping (μὴ προσκυνήσουσιν) demons and idols. Furthermore, they did not repent (οὐ μετενόησαν) of their murders, sorceries, fornication, or thefts (9.20-21). The mention of repentance is surprising to the hearer as there has been no linking of repentance and the judgments prior to this point. In fact, the language of repentance has only been found in the prophetic messages to the churches.[287] This notification that repentance has not been achieved indicates that repentance is the desired outcome of God's judgments. This is instructive for the churches as repentance becomes another mark of distinction between the followers of the Lamb and the inhabitants of the earth. By this, the repeated calls to repentance found in the prophetic messages to the church take on added significance and urgency. The recalcitrant nature of humanity toward God indicates the hardness of their hearts. Further, the use of προσκυνέω ('worship') in connection with demons and idols reminds the hearers that the worship of anything or anyone other than God and the Lamb constitutes idolatry and is demonic in origin.[288]

---

[286] The only other mention of a group of four angels is in 7.1-3 where John tells of four angels who are given power to damage the earth and the sea. Aune, *Revelation 6–16*, p. 537, notes that apart from these two texts, 'no groups of four angels of *punishment* are known in Jewish apocalyptic literature'.

[287] Trafton, *Reading Revelation*, p. 99.

[288] D.A. deSilva, 'Honor Discourse and Rhetorical Strategy of the Apocalypse of John', *JSNT* 71 (1998), p. 95, provides an insightful comment on the use of idolatry: 'The majority of people in Greco-Roman society would have been regarded by John as idolaters ... Jews and Christians, who opposed the worship of idols, formed a distinct minority in the empire. As John's vision unfolds, however, it is the worshipper of idols who is in the minority. All the host of heaven and

With the judgment and devastation of the six trumpets firmly in mind, the hearers await the seventh and final trumpet. It appears as if nothing short of complete destruction will assuage the wrath of God and the Lamb. For John's hearers, the *intrusion* of the interlude that follows the sixth trumpet would likely have been experienced with both relief and dread.

The second interlude appears in Rev. 10.1–11.14. Its sheer length gives evidence to its importance for the Apocalypse; however, an extensive treatment lies outside the scope of this study.[289] In this interlude, John again becomes a participant in the drama he is narrating. John sees ἄλλον ἄγγελον ἰσχυρον ('another strong angel') coming down from heaven, whom he describes in language heretofore reserved for Jesus (1.7, 15; 5.5).[290] Waddell suggests that this angelic figure is the Holy Spirit, and although he admits its conjectural nature, his suggestion accords with John's concern to show the inter-relationship between God, the Lamb, and the Spirit.[291] When this divine being (the Spirit?) cries out, the seven thunders also speak (10.3) and John prepares to write their words; however, he is immediately commanded *not* to write but rather to seal up (σφράγισον) their message (10.4). For the first time in the vision, John's hearers are denied access and left to wonder about the role and message of the seven thunders.[292] The prohibition against John writing is limited to the message of the seven thunders, for John records the angel's proclamation that there will be no more delay as the mystery of God is about to be accomplished in the sounding of the seventh trumpet (10.5-7). In spite of this announcement, the

---

'every creature in heaven and on earth and below the earth' know where the true center of the cosmos is, and thus where worship and adoration are properly directed'.

[289] For an excellent treatment of this text, see Waddell, *The Spirit of the Book of Revelation*, pp. 132-91.

[290] Waddell, *The Spirit of the Book of Revelation*, p. 155. See Beale, *The Book of Revelation*, pp. 522-26, for his contention that what John sees is a Christophany.

[291] Waddell, *The Spirit of the Book of Revelation*, p. 159.

[292] Michaels, *Revelation*, p. 134: 'If anything, the seven thunders are more mysterious and more frightening for *not* being described in detail'. Bauckham, *The Theology of the Book of Revelation*, pp. 82-83 suggests that the seven thunders would likely have been the next series of judgment and would have affected one half of the earth. He reasons that the seven thunders are sealed up because God's judgments have not produced repentance, and, therefore, final judgment awaits.

seventh trumpet is delayed by two events: John's ingesting of the scroll (10.8-11) and the story of the two witnesses (11.1-13).

John becomes an active participant in the drama as he is instructed to eat the scroll in the hand of the divine being (10.8-10), an experience the hearers would likely recognize as similar to that of the prophet Ezekiel (Ezekiel 2–3). This act of eating the scroll, which is bitter in his stomach yet sweet in his mouth, confirms John's role as a prophet. To the prophets, God reveals his plans and unveils his mysteries (10.7). While John has not called *himself* a prophet, his status is confirmed by this divine being. If Waddell's tantalizing suggestion that the divine being is the Spirit is taken seriously, then the close connection between prophecy and the Spirit evidenced especially in the prophetic messages is reaffirmed.[293] The hearers can trust John to speak on behalf of God; the hearers can trust God to reveal his will through John. Like the prophets of old, John engages in the 'hermeneutical ministry' of interpreting the 'historical deeds of Yahweh'. John's 'prophetic role binds him to his present as its interpreter'.[294] The scroll that John ingests is likely the same scroll that the hearers first learned about in Revelation 5; hence, John now has access to the scroll received by the Lamb.[295] Because he has received the scroll, John is told that it is necessary (δεῖ) for him to prophesy again concerning[296] many[297] peoples,

---

[293] Waddell, *The Spirit of the Book of Revelation*, p. 162.

[294] Boring, 'The Theology of Revelation: "The Lord Our God the Almighty Reigns"', pp. 262-63.

[295] The scroll is identified as βιβλίον (10.8) and βιβλαρίδιον (10.9). Despite the use of different terms, it seems best to understand the terms as synonymous and identical to the scroll of the Lamb. See Bauckham, *Climax of Prophecy*, p. 266, who states that the scroll which John consumes is the revelation '*in nuce*'. Waddell, *The Spirit of the Book of Revelation*, p. 161, connects this to Revelation 4–5: '… John suspends his call narrative which he began in 4:1–5:14 in order to record the breaking of the seals. Once the seals have been broken, the divine angel of the Lord, distinct from John's visionary guide, delivers the opened scroll to John. What follows on the heels of the call narrative is the prophecy, or better put, *the* revelation (11:1-13)'.

[296] The key to this phrase hinges on the translation of the preposition ἐπί. Aune, *Revelation 6–16*, p. 573, gives two possible meanings for this proposition when it is followed by the dative case as here: 'against' or 'concerning'. He opts for 'against' because of the typically negative attitude of apocalyptic literature toward the ungodly nations of the world. As Bauckham, *Climax of Prophecy*, pp. 326-37, points out, however, this four-fold designation is not wholly used in this way in Revelation. Its first occurrence in 5.9 links these people groups with the conquest of the Lamb. Furthermore, the seven-fold Spirit of God is sent out into

nations, tongues and kings (10.11). John's re-commissioning links this chapter with what is to follow in 11.1-13 and provides a context for the appearance and significance of two more prophetic figures – the two witnesses.

The lengthy narrative of the two witnesses can only receive brief treatment here. John is given a measuring rod and told to measure the temple[298] of God, the altar, and those worshipping at the altar. 'The worshipers represent the priestly aspect of the saints as they offer up their prayers as incense before God'.[299] The believers are to see the activity of measuring, most likely drawn from Ezekiel 40, to be an indication of divine protection. In this way, the measuring is similar to the sealing of the saints in Revelation 7. John is not to measure the courtyard because it and the holy city are to be trampled upon for forty-two months (11.1-2). During this same time frame,[300] God will give authority to his two witnesses to prophesy (11.3). These two witnesses are not the first witnesses in Revelation. The hearers know that Jesus is the faithful witness (1.3) and that Antipas, Jesus' faithful witness (2.13), has been killed. These witnesses, clothed in sackcloth, are specifically identified by means of allusions to Zechariah 4 as the two olive trees and the two lampstands standing before the Lord. Aside from this Old Testament allusion, the hearers would most certainly recall John's inaugural vision of Jesus walking among the seven lampstands, specifically identified as the churches. In short, the two witnesses are thereby to be identified as *Christian* prophets, symbolic of the prophetic

---

all the earth (5.6). It is the intended outcome of God that the prophetic witness of the church lead to the conversion of the nations. The preposition, therefore, is better translated as 'about' or 'concerning'.

[297] Despite the fact that πολλοῖς is at the end of the phrase, it modifies all four nouns.

[298] John uses ναὸς ('temple') exclusively in Revelation in reference to the heavenly temple (11.19; 15.5, 6, 8; 16.1, 17; 21.22).

[299] Waddell, *The Spirit of the Book of Revelation*, p. 167.

[300] John uses 42 months and 1260 days to designate the same time period from different perspectives. Waddell, *The Spirit of the Book of Revelation*, p. 169 states, '... the span of three and a half years serves as a symbolic amount of time in which the church will face the threat of the beast (forty-two months), yet throughout this same span of time, the church can trust that she will be protected by God (1260 days)'.

mission of the believing community to proclaim the word.[301] Their garments of sackcloth reflect their message of repentance to which they call all who will listen.[302]

The two witnesses deliver their testimony and are protected by God for the duration of their witness (11.5-6); however, when their witness is complete, four unexpected sets of events occur. First, the beast from the Abyss[303] makes war with the witnesses, overcomes (νικήσει) them, kills them, and lays their corpse (πτῶμα αὐτῶν)[304] in the place *pneumatically* called Sodom and Egypt where[305] their Lord was crucified (11.7-8).[306] Second, the inhabitants of the earth celebrate the death of the witnesses (here called prophets) for three days with gift giving (11.9-10). Third, after three days, the πνεῦμα

---

[301] Waddell, *The Spirit of the Book of Revelation*, p. 174, 'The witnesses serve as a synecdoche for the entire church …' See also Waddell, *The Spirit of the Book of Revelation*, p. 175, footnote 144 where he writes, 'Faithful members of the church [in Revelation] are prophetic not because they deliver a charismatic word for the community but rather because they bear a prophetic witness of Jesus to the world'. See also Trafton, *Reading Revelation*, pp. 107-108.

[302] Gonzáles and Gonzáles, *Revelation*, p. 72.

[303] This is the first appearance of the beast in Revelation. The use of the definite article suggests that the hearers are familiar with such this image, perhaps from Daniel where the fourth beast makes war with the saints and overcomes them (Dan. 7.21). The beast emerges from the Abyss which was unlocked during the fifth trumpet (9.1-2). Waddell, *The Spirit of the Book of Revelation*, p. 180, indicates that the Abyss attests to the demonic origin of the beast. Blount, *Revelation*, 213 sees the term 'beast' as an 'apocalyptic cipher for the historical Rome'.

[304] Note the singular noun instead of the plural. Their witness is viewed as a singular activity. See Thomas, *The Apocalypse*, p. 335.

[305] Beale, *Book of Revelation*, p. 592, suggests that John uses 'where' as a way to introduce 'symbolic, spiritual geography'.

[306] Thomas warns against automatically identifying the Great City as Jerusalem because of the way in which the church is called to discern the location as Sodom and Egypt. He further points out that the Great City in Revelation is identified with Babylon (16.19; 17.18; 18.10, 16, 18, 19, 21). On the term πνευματικῶς, he writes, 'While this term is often translated as "figuratively", "metaphorically", "symbolically", or even "spiritually", none of these translations are adequate for they fail to bring out the fact that this identification comes by means of the Spirit. Just as Jesus has earlier revealed the identity of the seven lampstands and the seven stars (1.20), so now the Spirit reveals the identity of this Great City'. See also Waddell, *The Spirit of the Book of Revelation*, pp. 181-83; Trafton, *Reading Revelation*, pp. 109-10; Gonzáles and Gonzáles, *Revelation*, pp. 72-73: 'This may mean Jerusalem; but most probably it means the entirety of society as presently ordered, which is a society of corruption and oppression and which therefore is worthy of the symbolic names of "Sodom" and "Egypt"'.

ζωῆς[307] ἐκ τοῦ θεοῦ ('Spirit of life from God) enters into them and they are raised to life, resulting in great fear falling upon all who see them (11.11).[308] Finally, the onlookers *hear* the two witnesses being summoned to heaven by a great voice saying: Ἀνάβατε ὧδε ('come up here') and *see* them ascending into heaven in a cloud (11.12). A great earthquake[309] ensues resulting in a tenth of the city falling and 7,000 people dying (11.13a).[310] This earthquake is not unlike the great earthquake that accompanied the opening of the sixth seal; thus, it is to be regarded as divine judgment upon the inhabitants of the earth. In a surprising twist, the hearers discover something heretofore unprecedented in Revelation: καὶ οἱ λοιποὶ ἔμφοβοι ἐγένοντο καὶ ἔδωκαν δόξαν τῷ θεῷ τοῦ οὐρανοῦ ('and the rest were fearful and gave glory to the God of heaven') (11.13b). Where God's judgments to this point have been met with defiance and a refusal to repent, this judgment produces a different result because it is coupled with the effectual witness of the church.[311] In giving glory to the God of heaven, the newly-repentant join their voices with those in heaven (4.11; 5.12; 7.12). In the story of the two witnesses, the church is to see that the desired outcome

---

[307] Waddell, *The Spirit of the Book of Revelation*, p. 184, states that the phrase 'breath of life' is likely a 'double-entendre referring both to the breath of life (cf. Gen. 2:7) and to the Spirit of life'. The hearers might also recognize an illusion to Ezek. 37.5 (LXX) where the 'Spirit of life' occurs in connection with the resurrection of the dry bones. However, see Blount, *Revelation*, p. 215, who argues that John is not referring to the divine Spirit. He indicates that John always uses the definite article when referencing the divine Spirit, and since the noun is anarthrous in this text, John is likely referencing it as a particular quality, 'the empowering force of that Spirit'. Blount's argument puts unnecessary weight on the presence or absence of the definite article as the Spirit is *from* God. On this see Thomas, *The Apocalypse*, p. 339.

[308] deSilva, 'Honor Discourse and Rhetorical Strategy of the Apocalypse of John', p. 97, sees the raising of the witnesses as an indication of their honor and suggests that it is 'intimately linked with God's establishment of God's own honor' in 11.13.

[309] See also Smalley, *The Revelation to John*, p. 285.

[310] John inverts the Old Testament imagery of remnant by stating that only one-tenth of the population dies from the earthquake while the remnant (οἱ λοιποί) is the nine-tenths that are left. Bauckham, *Climax of Prophecy*, p. 283, notes, 'Not the faithful minority, but the faithless majority are spared, so that they may come to repentance and faith'.

[311] Resseguie, *The Revelation of John*, p. 166. Contra Trafton, *Reading Revelation*, p. 111.

of their witness is the conversion of the nations, even if the vehicle of such witness is martyrdom. Bauckham writes,

> The church was not redeemed from all nations merely for its own sake, but to witness to all nations. Martyrdom is not simply the church's deliverance from the world, but the culmination of the church's witness to the world. Where judgments alone have failed to bring the nations to repentance, the church's suffering witness, along with judgments, will be effective to this end. Thus God's kingdom will come, not simply by the deliverance of the church and the judgment of the nations, but primarily by the repentance of the nations as a result of the church's witness.[312]

The hearers would likely not miss the many parallels between the story of Jesus and the story of the two witnesses. They might also recall Jesus' words to his disciples concerning the hatred of the world toward them: 'If they persecuted (ἐδίωξαν) me, they will persecute (διώξουσιν) you' (Jn 15.20). Like Jesus, his followers most likely will be put to death, but as the story of the two witnesses reveals they, like Jesus, also will experience vindication through resurrection and dwell with God for eternity (7.9-17).

The second interlude concludes with the ominous declaration: Ἡ οὐαὶ ἡ δευτέρα ἀπῆλθεν· ἰδοὺ ἡ οὐαὶ ἡ τρίτη ἔρχεται ταχύ ('The second woe has passed; behold the third woe is coming quickly') (11.14). The first woe, tied to the fifth trumpet (9.12), follows a scene of terror; however, the second woe contains a glimmer of hope as the witness of the church leads some of the inhabitants of the earth to repentance. Now, the hearers await the coming of the third woe. Because 'coming' has been associated most notably with God (1.4, 8; 4.8) and Jesus (1.7; 2.5, 16, 26; 3.11), it is possible that the hearers would connect the 'soon coming of the third woe and the soon coming of Jesus himself'.[313]

---

[312] Bauckham, *The Climax of Prophecy*, p. 258.

[313] Thomas, *The Apocalypse*, p. 343. There is much discussion among scholars as to the 'third woe' in Revelation. For the view that it is what unfolds in Revelation 12–22.17, see Charles, *A Critical and Exegetical Commentary on the Revelation of St John*, p. 292. For the view that the third woe is the material found in Rev. 12.1–15.8 (of which 11.15-19 introduces and is thereby included in the third woe), see Smalley, *The Revelation to John*, p. 287; Resseguie, *The Revelation of John*, p. 167. For the view that the seventh trumpet is the third woe, see Beale, *The Book of Revela-*

Revelation 11.15-19

Revelation 11.15-19 is the third worship scene in the Apocalypse. It is a unique worship scene in that the scene itself *is* the seventh trumpet. In this way it both concludes the narrative cycle of the trumpet judgments and reveals the content of the seventh and final trumpet. John introduces the sounding of the seventh trumpet with the simple connective καὶ ('and') followed by the formulaic expression of introduction found in the trumpet series: ὁ ἕβδομος ἄγγελος ἐσάλπισεν ('the seventh angel trumpeted') (11.15). Although the hearers might expect the seventh trumpet to result in incalculable devastation and destruction, their prior experiencing of the seventh seal would likely encourage them to expect something similar here. In contrast to the *silence* of the seventh seal, at the sounding of the seventh trumpet, John hears *loud* voices in heaven singing another anthem of praise:

Ἐγένετο ἡ βασιλεία τοῦ κόσμου τοῦ κυρίου ἡμῶν
καὶ τοῦ Χριστοῦ αὐτοῦ,
καὶ βασιλεύσει εἰς τοὺς αἰῶνας τῶν αἰώνων

The kingdom of the world has become that of our Lord
and of his Christ,
and he will reign forever and ever (11.15b).

The hymn opens with the verb ἐγένετο ('become'). Its placement at the beginning of the phrase emphasizes that what is truly important is that the kingdom of the world *has become* our Lord's. This futuristic use of the aorist suggests that despite the fact that this event has not yet come in its fullness,[314] it is experienced in worship as having already happened. The hymn thus prophetically announces the *true* reality for the people of God. The phrase ἡ βασιλεία τοῦ κόσμου ('the kingdom of the world') is found here for the first (and only) time in Revelation. To this point, kingdom language has been primarily associated with believers. Thus, because of the work of the Lamb, believers are a kingdom for God (1.6, 9; 5.10). Here, 'the kingdom' is linked with God and the Lamb. The hymn veers

---

tion, pp. 609-10. See also Thomas, *The Apocalypse*, pp. 343-44 who argues that the woes are being transformed in Revelation.

[314] Ladd, *A Commentary on the Revelation of John*, p. 161; Resseguie, *The Revelation of John*, p. 167, aptly notes that the narrative continues for eleven more chapters.

from the normal language used in the hymnic material in reference to God (the One who sits on the throne) and Jesus (the Lamb) by using the terms κύριος ('Lord') and Χριστός ('Christ'). Since 'Christ' has thus far been used in reference to Jesus (1.1, 2, 5) and because it is followed by the third person pronoun, 'Lord' appears here to refer to God. John's churches are unequivocally to declare in their worship and in their witness that Jesus is both the Lamb and the Christ of God. The hymn ends with the acknowledgment that *he* will reign, but it is grammatically unclear as to whom the pronoun refers. The most natural subject for the verb is Christ (i.e. Christ shall reign) but the subject could just as easily be God. It is also possible that the ambiguity is an intentional way for John to refer to the 'singularity of God and Jesus':

> Thus, the hearers may be encountering this phenomenon for one of the first times with reference to the phrase, 'and he will reign forever and ever'. As such it appears that the Greek grammar is not sufficient to convey the theological reality of the identity of God and Jesus. Consequently, the breaking apart of the grammar conveys something of the depth of the theological reality here described.[315]

In this short hymn, John's hearers have heavenly confirmation of what they already know: God and the Lamb are reigning[316] and will continue to reign forever and ever. Like the two witnesses, this reality fuels the witness of the church to the world around them.

Much like in previous worship scenes, the hymn of worship is not the singular mode of expressed worship. Here the 24 elders, identified by their proximity to the throne (which ties the worship scene to the two prior worship scenes) respond with both physical and verbal worship. Such responses are what the hearers have come to expect of the 24 elders (4.10; 5.8, 14; 7.11); thus, their actions

---

[315] Thomas, *The Apocalypse*, p. 345. See also Osborne, *Revelation*, p. 441. Aune, *Revelation 6–16*, p. 639, also feels that God and Jesus are the subject and that the verb should be plural but he allows for the possibility that *christos* is the implied subject of the verb.

[316] Boring, 'The Theology of Revelation: "The Lord Our God the Almighty Reigns"', p. 266: 'God rules, but God has definitively manifested his rule in Jesus (11:15!) who turned out not to be the Lion who devoured our enemies but the Lamb who was slain'.

continue to be paradigmatic for John's churches. The elders sing yet another hymn to God:

Εὐχαριστοῦμέν σοι, κύριε ὁ θεὸς ὁ παντοκράτωρ,
ὁ ὢν καὶ ὁ ἦν,
ὅτι εἴληφας τὴν δύναμίν σου τὴν μεγάλην
καὶ ἐβασίλευσας.
καὶ τὰ ἔθνη ὠργίσθησαν,
καὶ ἦλθεν ἡ ὀργή σου
καὶ ὁ καιρὸς τῶν νεκρῶν κριθῆναι
καὶ δοῦναι τὸν μισθὸν τοῖς δούλοις σου τοῖς προφήταις
καὶ τοῖς ἁγίοις καὶ τοῖς φοβουμένοις τὸ ὄνομά σου,
τοὺς μικροὺς καὶ τοὺς μεγάλους,
καὶ διαφθεῖραι τοὺς διαφθείροντας τὴν γῆν

We give you thanks, Lord God Almighty,
the One who is and who was,
for you have taken your great power
and have reigned.
And the nations were wrathful,
but your wrath came
and the time for the dead to be judged
and to give rewards to your servants, to the prophets
and to the saints and to the ones fearing your name,
the small and the great,
and to destroy the ones destroying the earth (11.17b-18).

Several interesting features stand out in this hymn. First, this is the only explicit hymn of thanksgiving, as suggested by the verb εὐχαριστοῦμέν ('we give thanks'), among all the hymns sung in Revelation.[317] The offering up of thanksgiving is the response to the proclamation of the coming kingdom of God and Christ. The fact that the heavenly elders offer thanksgiving for this points to the extraordinary nature of this scene, which, as the hearers are to understand, is predicated on the faithful witness and worship of the church (11.1-13). Further, the present tense of the verb indicates the continual nature of their thanksgiving and invites the hearers to

---

[317] Aune, *Revelation 6–16*, pp. 640-41, notes that the verb phrase is the only certain liturgical formula found in the hymns of Revelation. He further suggests that John might have preserved liturgical traditions dealing with the celebration of the Eucharist.

join in the celebration. Second, the hymn employs a number of terms for God. God is addressed as κύριε, παντοκράτωρ, and ὁ ὢν καὶ ὁ ἦν ('Lord, Almighty, and the One who is and who was'). The four living creatures gave a similar ascription to God in 4.8. The hymns of worship, thereby, reinforce the nature of God. Perhaps the hearers would be surprised that the phrase ὁ ὢν καὶ ὁ ἦν ('the who is and who was') is not followed by καὶ ὁ ἐρχόμενος ('and the One coming') as in 1.8 and 4.8. The kingdom has come (11.15), has God come as well? Third, God is worshipped *because* of his reign. The hymn spells out the implications of this reign, not only with respect to the saints but also with respect to the nations of the earth who have been 'filled with wrath' (v. 18). Although it is likely that Psalm 2 stands as the backdrop to this phrase, the hearers do not have to look back any further than to the unrepentant attitude of the inhabitants of the earth in response to the seal judgments. There the acknowledgement of the wrath of God and the Lamb came from the lips of the inhabitants of the earth (6.16). Here, it is the elders who acknowledge the wrath of God. It is possible that this statement of the wrath of God as a response to the wrath of the nations is at least a part of the third woe of 11.14; that is, the coming of the kingdom spells doom for the unrepentant nations of the earth. The use of the aorist tenses suggest that both the rage of the nations and the rage of God are past events; however, the connection of ὀργή ('rage, wrath') with ἔρχομαι ('coming') indicates the eschatological character of God's wrath and points to a futuristic sense for the aorist in creating a realized eschatological framework for John's hearers. Fourth, the hymn announces that 'the time' has come for the dead to be judged, for rewards to be given, and for the destroyers of the earth to be destroyed. Osborne rightly suggests that the use of ὁ καιρὸς ('the time') refers to eschatological time – a time 'filled with the sense of God's judgment on those who do evil and his salvation for those who live for righteousness'.[318] The judging of the dead is linked with God's wrath here by the connective καὶ ('and'); but that does not mean that the dead being judged are necessarily wicked. It seems that based on the appearance of the martyrs in heaven (7.14-17) and the two witnesses

---

[318] Osborne, *Revelation*, p. 445.

(11.1-13), judging the dead could also be interpreted as divine vindication for the righteous who are put to death. This serves both to comfort and confront the hearers with the assurance that God *will judge* the dead.[319] It is also time for rewards to be given to God's servants, the prophets, and to the saints, and to the ones fearing God's name. The terms all appear to describe the one 'believing, witnessing, prophetic' people of God.[320] The contrast between the followers of God and the nations is stark. The nations will receive wrath; the followers of God will receive a reward. The hearers would most likely think back to the prophetic messages where the overcomers were promised rewards. Even though the term μισθός ('reward') is not used in Revelation 2–3, the implication of reward is understood.[321] God's reward is for God's people, both small and great. The equity expressed here is astonishing. Smalley aptly notes, '… the "insignificant and mighty" represent those in the Christian Church who are at opposite ends of the social and economic spectrum, for such disparities have no meaning within the community of faith to which the saints inclusively belong'.[322] Included as recipients of God's rewards are the newly repentant who have joined the community of the Lamb because of the faithful witness of the church (11.13). The final line – destroying the destroyers of the earth – is ominous. It is likely that ἡ γη ('the earth') functions as a metonymy for the 'people of the earth'[323] or the saints worldwide,[324]

---

[319] Ladd, *A Commentary on the Revelation of John*, p. 163.

[320] Thomas, *The Apocalypse*, p. 349; also Beale, *The Book of Revelation*, p. 617; Smalley, *The Revelation to John*, pp. 292-93; Prigent, *Commentary on the Apocalypse of St. John*, p. 523, '… [O]ur author has little concern for distinguishing clear-cut categories within the Church of God. What matters to him above all is to show that the Christian life is a whole that cannot be considered separately … It is plausible to assume that certain of the faithful play a particular role among the people of God. But this point is never highlighted; to the contrary, it is affirmed that every Christian has the calling of witness, saints, servant of God, and perhaps even prophet.'

[321] Thomas, *The Apocalypse*, p. 348, suggests that 'the reward' is a comprehensive term having reference to all those things promised to those who overcome'.

[322] Smalley, *The Revelation to John*, p. 293. He notes that in the OT and early Jewish literature, the phrase 'least and greatest' is used 'as an idiom to denote social inclusivity (e.g. Gen. 19.11; Deut. 1.17; 1 Kgs 22.31; Job 3.19; Jer. 6.13; Judith 13.4; *Wis.* 6.6-7; *1 Macc.* 5.45)'. He sees the NT continuing this notion in texts such as Acts 8.10; 26.22; Heb. 8.11.

[323] Aune, *Revelation 6–16*, p. 645.

[324] Osborne, *Revelation*, p. 447.

thus hinting at more judgment to come. The hymn thereby is both celebratory and anticipatory. It celebrates the reign of God and provides consolation for the hearers that God indeed will bring vindication to the people of God; at the same time, it anticipates events yet to come. The hearers must discern their own condition and endure faithfully to the end.

The conclusion to the worship scene alerts the hearers that despite the way that the seventh trumpet has seemed to signal the end of all things (i.e. God has come, the time for judging and giving rewards has come), there is still more to follow. Indeed, the final verse continues to move the story forward. John writes of the opening of ὁ ναὸς τοῦ θεοῦ ('the temple of God') in heaven (11.19). This re-emergence of temple imagery creates an *inclusio* with 11.1-2 and connects the story of the two witnesses with the seventh trumpet. Within the temple, John sees ἡ κιβωτὸς τῆς διαθήκης αὐτοῦ ('The Ark of his Covenant'). The Ark of the Covenant, one of Israel's most sacred objects, was lost when the Babylonians destroyed Solomon's temple in 586 BCE More than any other cultic object, the Ark came to be associated with the very presence of God.[325] That it is called God's Ark of the Covenant emphasizes its close connection to God. By its appearance, and with the understanding that the heavenly temple symbolizes God's people, John's hearers are to understand that *God's very presence* is among them. In this way, the Ark functions as a 'sacramental presence'.[326]

Along with the revealing of the Ark of the Covenant, John further develops the list of theophanic elements that were introduced in 4.5 and expanded upon in 8.5. Now, John describes ἀστραπαὶ καὶ φωναὶ καὶ βρονταὶ καὶ σεισμὸς καὶ χάλαζα μεγάλη ('lightning and sounds and thunders and an earthquake and great hail') (11.19). Hail is added to the list as yet another indication of the gathering storm associated with the coming of God. These elements are clearly associated with God and the throne room since

[325] R. Briggs, *Jewish Temple Imagery in the Book of Revelation* (New York: Peter Lang; 1999), p. 87.

[326] A. Spatafora, *From the Temple of God to God as the Temple: A Biblical Theological Study of the Temple in the Book of Revelation* (Rome: Gregorian University Press, 1997), p. 185.

they come from 'the innermost part of God's heavenly temple'.[327] Rather than providing a sense of closure to the narrative of the seventh trumpet, their presence alerts the hearers that the story is not yet complete.

Summary of Revelation 8.6–11.19

Revelation 8.6–11.19 narrates the second judgment cycle – the blowing of the seven trumpets. Six of the seven trumpets result in devastating calamity for both creation and humanity. The lack of repentance by the inhabitants of the earth after the sixth trumpet underscores the importance of repentance in the prophetic messages. The lengthy interlude between the sixth and seventh trumpet lifts up the importance of prophecy within the churches. John is re-commissioned to prophesy and the church is depicted as God's two witnesses giving witness both with their words and with their lives. The outcome of the story of the two witnesses, where repentance from at least some of the inhabitants of the earth is achieved, reminds the church of the importance of its witness to the world. Thus, the church is not to insulate itself from the world; rather, it must witness to the world about God and the Lamb.

The worship scene found in 11.15-19 is unique in that it *is* the content of the seventh trumpet. This speaks to the profound importance of worship as *the* response to God and the Lamb! Through the hymns, the worshippers of heaven declare the coming of God's kingdom and the eternal rule of God and the Lamb (11.15). Their song is to become the churches' song – a prophetic proclamation to the world! The hymns in this scene look both backward and forward; that is, God and the Lamb are exhibiting their reign (11.17-18) yet there is more to come, such as the giving of rewards and the judgment of the dead.[328] Worship is thereby also a prophetic proclamation of those things yet to come. The kinesthetic response of the elders, who fall on their faces and worship, validates the orthodoxy of the hymns and functions as a fitting liturgical response for the people of God.

---

[327] Beale, *The Book of Revelation*, p. 618. See also Smalley, *The Revelation to John*, p. 294.

[328] Harris, *The Literary Function of the Hymns in the Apocalypse of John*, p. 151.

D. Revelation 12–14

Revelation 12.1–14.20 is a unique unit in John's vision that functions as an interlude between the trumpet and bowl judgment cycles.[329] That it is different from the rest of the Apocalypse is signaled by the vocabulary of 'sign' (σημεῖον) which brackets the narrative at 12.1 and 15.1. With 15.1, the narrative announces the resumption of God's judgments (albeit they are not carried out until chapter 16). This *sign* language serves as a textual cue to alert the hearers to pay particular attention to what unfolds in these chapters. The hearers are presented with a kaleidoscope of images in which the past, present, and future all converge into one story. It is in these chapters that the hearers are introduced to a new cast of characters – the Dragon, the beast from the sea, and the beast from the land – who form a satanic trinity. These chapters, which provide 'the narrative rationale for the movement of his visionary plot', [330] delve into the origins of evil, the cosmic conflict between God and Satan, and the role of the people of God in the midst of evil.[331]

Revelation 12.1 opens in a way quite distinct from anything to this point in the narrative. John describes two great signs[332] seen in heaven. The first sign is a magnificent woman clothed with the sun with the moon under her feet and a crown of twelve stars on her

---

[329] Beasley-Murray, *Revelation*, p. 191 sees Revelation 12–14 as the central portion of the book: 'Not only do [these chapters] come at the middle of the work, they provide an understanding of the nature of the conflict in which the Church is engaged, and into which John sees she is to be drawn to the limit'.

[330] Blount, *Revelation*, p. 223.

[331] Bauckham, *The Climax of Prophecy*, p. 288, sees 12–14 as a 'much fuller exposition of the conflict between the forces of evil and the witnessing church, to which 11:7 briefly alludes … In 11:3-13, the role of the church is that of faithful witness, following Jesus Christ the faithful witness. But in chapters 12–14 the church's role is portrayed primarily by means of the image of warfare with the forces of evil'. I. Paul, *The Value of Paul Ricoeur's Hermeneutic of Metaphor in Interpreting the Symbolism of Revelation Chapters 12 and 13* (unpublished PhD study, Nottingham Trent University, 1998), p. 208, maintains that Revelation 12 forms the narrative of the community before the challenge presented by the beast in Revelation 13; thus 'the community is equipped with its story and identity before it faces the crisis of decision'.

[332] The language of 'sign' would be familiar to Johannine hearers as the Gospel of John utilized seven signs performed by Jesus (John 1–11). Such signs revealed Jesus' glory (2.11) and were intended to lead to belief in Jesus as the Son of God (20.31).

head (12.1). Aside from the description of 'Jezebel' in Rev. 3.20, female characters have been noticeably absent from the narrative. Now John sees this un-named woman[333] about to give birth (12.2). The second sign John sees is a fiery red Dragon having seven heads, ten horns, and seven crowns (12.3). That the dragon is a malevolent figure is indicated by his actions: First, he drags down with his tail a third of the stars of heaven and casts them to the earth; and, second, he stands before the woman in labor in order to devour (ἵνα καταφάγῃ) her child (12.4).[334] The woman gives birth to a υἱὸν ἄρσεν ('male son') who is to shepherd the nations with an iron scepter. The hearers would certainly recall the promise to the over-comers in Thyatira to shepherd the nations with an iron scepter (3.27) as well as the hymn in 7.17 where the Lamb will shepherd his people. Such clues in the narrative assist the hearers in identifying this male child as Jesus. Thus, it appears that Jesus' birth is inferred here.[335] Although the Dragon stands ready to devour the child, the child is snatched up to God and his throne (12.5) – a likely reference to the ascension of Jesus.[336] The location – God and his throne – serves to connect this child with God, the One on the throne (Revelation 4). Blount observes, 'It is only after we read this passage that we know how the Son/Lamb – standing as *slain* – arrived at the throne in chapter 5'.[337] From Revelation 5 the hearers know that the

---

[333] For a summary of the various ways that the woman has been identified, see Aune, *Revelation 6–16*, pp. 680-81. See also Barr, *Tales of the End*, p. 112, who sees that in the woman elements of three images – Eve, Israel, and the queen of heaven – create a composite character of 'woman as ancestor' of the community. Richard, *Apocalypse*, p. 101, sees the woman and the Dragon as signs of life and death respectively.

[334] Barr, *Tales of the End*, p. 106: 'The dragon's one goal seems to be to de-stroy'. See P. Minear, 'Far as the Curse is Found: The Point of Revelation 12:15-16', *NovT* 33.1 (1991), p. 72 who sees Rev. 12.2 as a reference to the curse of Gen. 3.16: 'As soon as John introduced the woman, he acknowledged the opera-tion of this curse … This curse was as essential to her identity as the heavenly clothing'. Minear argues that in Rev. 12.15-16 John reverses the curses of Genesis 3 as the earth comes to the aid of the woman and her seed.

[335] Barr, *Tales of the End*, pp. 123-24; contra Trafton, *Reading Revelation*, p. 119, who states that John shows no interest in the birth of Jesus.

[336] Smalley, *The Revelation to John*, p. 320, 'In this case, the life and earthly min-istry of Jesus appear in a very truncated form, with a jump in timescale from the birth to the exaltation of the Messiah, and with everything in between (including the passion) omitted'. See also Beasley-Murray, *Revelation*, p. 200.

[337] Blount, *Revelation*, p. 231.

Lamb is worthy because of his work on the cross and his subsequent resurrection; thus, although not directly mentioned here, the cross and resurrection stands in the background of the story.[338]

After the child is taken up to heaven, the woman flees to the desert to a place God has prepared for her in order that she might be nourished (τρεφεται) for 1,260 days (12.6).[339] Her time of protection, 1,260 days, is the same time frame as the protection extended to the two witnesses in 11.3 (there expressed as 42 months). This links these two narratives together at a deeper level for the hearers and aids them in identifying the woman with the Christian community[340] as well as reminding them that the protection is for a specific period of time; that is, protection does not mean complete exemption from suffering as evidenced in the story of the witnesses.[341] Nonetheless, the community is to see that like the woman, they too are nourished by God. The language of nourishment, in light of the imagery of eating from the tree of life (2.7), partaking of the hidden manna (3.17), and the provisions for the martyrs (7.16) might allude to the Eucharist; that is, as the churches partake of the Eucharist they are nourished by God in ways not unlike the woman.[342] If so, then the hearers would also likely think of Jesus' words of *eating* his flesh to find life (Jn 6.53) in stark contrast with the Dragon's attempt to devour the child.

John interrupts this story by providing a flashback[343] that gives the hearers more information about this Dragon. The hearers learn

---

[338] Blount, *Revelation*, p. 231; Trafton, *Reading Revelation*, p. 119; Richard, *Apocalypse*, p. 102. See also Sweet, *Revelation*, p. 197, who suggests that the cross and resurrection are not explicitly mentioned because John is writing to the churches who already know this. The center of the story, therefore, is about the church that is being attacked by Satan and called to share in Jesus' sacrifice through their faithful witness.

[339] Barr, *Tales of the End*, p. 118, notes that in the verb tenses of Rev. 12.6 (aorist, present, subjunctive) John is indicating what elements of the story are 'in the past for the narrator, what parts are in the present, and what is yet to come'.

[340] Smalley, *The Revelation to John*, p. 320. Gonzáles and Gonzáles, *Revelation*, p. 77.

[341] Boxall, *The Revelation of St. John*, p. 181.

[342] P. Duff, *Who Rides the Beast? Prophetic Rivalry and the Rhetoric of Crisis in the Churches of the Apocalypse* (New York: Oxford University Press, 2001), p. 103; Gonzáles and Gonzáles, *Revelation*, p. 79.

[343] Barr, *Tales of the End*, p. 106.

of a war in heaven between Michael[344] and his angels and the Dragon and his angels,[345] resulting in the Dragon and his angels being
cast out of heaven to the earth (12.7-9).[346] The hearers would not
miss the repetition found in these verses: Forms of the word πό-
λεμος ('war') occur three times in v. 7, and the aorist passive of ἐκβάλλω ('cast out') is used three times in v. 9. This flashback is important because it aids the hearers in resisting a purely linear understanding of the events John is relating. The Dragon stands before
the woman having *already* been cast out of heaven in a great cosmic
battle, thus past and present blur for the hearers.[347] This war in
heaven is 'a heavenly and symbolic counterpart of the historical
achievement of the cross'.[348] The Dragon who has been cast out is
identified in full as ὁ δράκων ὁ μέγας, ὁ ὄφις ὁ ἀρχαῖος, ὁ κα-
λούμενος Διάβολος καὶ ὁ Σατανᾶς, ὁ πλανῶν τὴν οἰκου-
μένην ὅλην ('The great dragon, the ancient serpent, the one called
the Devil and Satan, the one deceiving the whole world') (12.9).[349]
The repeated use of the definite article before each *name* indicates
that the hearers know of this evil one: indeed, Jesus has spoken to
the churches of his activity against them (2.10, 13). That the Dragon
is '*the* ancient Serpent' would likely cause the hearers to associate
him with the serpent in Genesis 3 where he deceived Adam and
Eve.[350] Now he is named as the one deceiving the whole world –
an indication of 'the universal scope' of the Dragon's power.[351]

---

[344] The hearers would likely be familiar with Michael from the book of Daniel
(10.13, 21; 12.1).

[345] Smalley, *The Revelation to John*, p. 324, suggests that the Dragon 'parodies
the position of the archangel Michael, for he has minions under him, who do his
bidding'.

[346] Blount, *Revelation*, p. 226, comments on why Michael fights the Dragon:
'for all the dragon's great strength, it is never, even narratively, on a par with
God. God need not engage the battle directly because God's representatives are
sufficient for the task; they handle the eschatological "light work"'.

[347] Barr, *Tales of the End*, p. 120.

[348] Smalley, *The Revelation to John*, p. 323.

[349] Beasley-Murray, *Revelation*, p. 201, 'The great dragon is given his full titles –
not in his honour, but as an expression of the prophet's exultation that at last the
ancient foe has been overthrown'.

[350] Barr, *Tales of the End*, p. 106.

[351] Smalley, *The Revelation to John*, p. 325.

Despite the fearsome power of the Dragon, he does not have even the power to defeat Michael but instead is thrown down to earth![352]

Revelation 12.10-12

The manifestation of God's sovereignty and power exhibited in the expulsion of Satan from heaven garners worship from φωνὴν μεγάλην ἐν τῷ οὐρανῷ ('a great voice in heaven'). Although John does not identify the 'great voice' who sings the hymn, it is likely to be viewed as representative of all the saints, especially the martyrs.

Ἄρτι ἐγένετο ἡ σωτηρία καὶ ἡ δύναμις
καὶ ἡ βασιλεία τοῦ θεοῦ ἡμῶν
καὶ ἡ ἐξουσία τοῦ Χριστοῦ αὐτοῦ,
ὅτι ἐβλήθη ὁ κατήγωρ τῶν ἀδελφῶν ἡμῶν,
ὁ κατηγορῶν αὐτοὺς ἐνώπιον τοῦ θεοῦ ἡμῶν
ἡμέρας καὶ νυκτός.
καὶ αὐτοὶ ἐνίκησαν αὐτὸν διὰ τὸ αἷμα τοῦ ἀρνίου
καὶ διὰ τὸν λόγον τῆς μαρτυρίας αὐτῶν
καὶ οὐκ ἠγάπησαν τὴν ψυχὴν αὐτῶν ἄχρι θανάτου.
διὰ τοῦτο εὐφραίνεσθε, οἱ οὐρανοὶ
καὶ οἱ ἐν αὐτοῖς σκηνοῦντες.
οὐαὶ τὴν γῆν καὶ τὴν θάλασσαν,
ὅτι κατέβη ὁ διάβολος πρὸς ὑμᾶς
ἔχων θυμὸν μέγαν,
εἰδὼς ὅτι ὀλίγον καιρὸν ἔχει

Now has come the salvation and power
and the kingdom of our God
and the authority of his Christ,
because the accuser of our brothers and sisters has been cast down,
the one accusing them before our God
day and night.
And they overcame him through the blood of the Lamb
and through the word of their testimony
and they did not love their life even in the face of death.
For this reason, rejoice, you heavens
and the ones dwelling in them.

---

[352] The aorist passive ἐβλήθη ascribes the activity ultimately to God. Aune, *Revelation 6–16*, p. 695.

Woe to the earth and the sea,
because the Devil has come down to you
having great anger,
knowing that he has little time (12.10-12).

Several things stand out in this hymn. First, the hymn announces that *now* the salvation, the power, and the kingdom of God have come. The use of ἐγένετο ('comes') bears striking similarity to 11.15 where the kingdom of God has come,[353] yet here the presence of ἄρτι ('now') delivers a sense of *finality*. The use of the definite article before each noun furthers this sense of finality.[354] *The* salvation, *the* power and *the* kingdom of God and *the* authority of God's Christ (11.15) have come because Satan has already been defeated in heaven.[355] Salvation, a term used in the hymn of 7.10 and ascribed to God and the Lamb, is here connected to God and Christ. It is interesting that in the hymns of 11.15 and here in 12.10 that Jesus is called χριστός ('Chirst') rather than the familiar τό ἀρνίον ('the Lamb'). Clearly, salvation – deliverance, victory[356] – comes by the authority of Jesus as God's Messiah. Second, the reason all of this has come about is because Satan has been thrown out of heaven. This is the fourth use of the aorist passive of ἐκβάλλω ('cast out') in the span of two verses. The repetition points to the overwhelming power and authority of God, reminding the hearers that the Dragon is in no way God's equal. With his expulsion, 'Satan has lost his power in the transcendent and spiritual realm'.[357] Johannine hearers would likely recall Jesus' words about Satan in the Fourth Gospel, 'Now the ruler of this world has been cast out (ἐκβληθήσεται)' (Jn 12.31b). Significantly Jesus' words appear in the context of his pending death and exaltation on the cross (Jn

---

[353] Thomas, *The Apocalypse*, p. 369.

[354] Jörns, *Das hymnische Evangelium*, p. 112.

[355] Aune, *Revelation 6–16*, p. 700, raises the question as to why John appears to use duplicate statements (11.15 and 12.10) about the coming of the kingdom and suggests that 'the answer must be that in the present text [12.10] the coming or occurrence of the kingship of God is described proleptically'.

[356] Aune, *Revelation 6–16*, p. 700, suggests that σωτηρία is best translated as 'victory' since it is set in the context of the battle between Michael and the dragon.

[357] Richard, *Apocalypse*, p. 106.

12.27-34). Jesus' victory over Satan was won on the cross.[358] Not to be missed is the final descriptor for the Dragon: the accuser of the saints[359] who accuses them before God day and night. By this, the hearers understand Satan's nefarious actions against *them*, for the anonymous voices in heaven sing of *our* brothers and *our* God.[360] 'Though the accuser will no doubt continue to bring accusation against the brothers on earth, as 12.10 will reveal, his days of accu-sations in heaven are over'![361] Third, despite the onslaught of accu-sations, the saints can overcome the Devil by means of the blood of the Lamb *and* the word of their testimony.[362] The key verb νικάω ('overcome') is tied to the saints in the prophetic messages (chs. 2–3), to Jesus (5.5), and most recently to the beast who overcomes the two witnesses (11.7). Here, it is the saints who are victorious against the Devil. Their victory is not achieved with weapons but through their identification with the Lamb and their witness.[363] The hearers are again confronted with the efficacy of Jesus' blood as the means of victory over Satan. It is by the blood that the saints are loosed from their sins (1.5); it is by his blood that humanity is purchased for God (5.9); it is by his blood that the robes of the martyrs are made clean (7.14); and it is by the blood that the saints are victori-ous over the Devil. Further, the hearers are confronted with the efficacy of their witness. It is through the witness of the church that God's salvation will be proclaimed, even if that witness leads to death (2.13; 11.1-13). Prigent states it correctly: 'According to Rev 12:10, God's reign is made openly manifest in the world when

---

[358] Beasley-Murray, *Revelation*, p. 203; contra Harris, *The Literary Function of the Hymns in the Apocalypse of John*, p. 158, who links the defeat of Satan with the mar-tyrdom of the saints.

[359] Jörns, *Das hymnische Evangelium*, p. 113, notes that it is for his activity against the saints rather than for who he is that Satan is cast out of heaven.

[360] Du Rand, '"Now the Salvation of our God Has Come": A Narrative Per-spective on the Hymns in Revelation 12-15', p. 322.

[361] Thomas, *The Apocalypse*, p. 371.

[362] Ladd, *A Commentary on the Revelation of John*, p. 172, identifies the testimony of the saints as the 'secondary means of victory'. As Bauckham, *The Theology of the Book of Revelation*, pp. 75-76 notes, the death of the martyrs does not have an 'in-dependent value of its own. Its value depends on its being a continuation of his [the Lamb's] witness'.

[363] W. Klassen, 'Vengeance in the Apocalypse of John', *CBQ* 28.3 (1966), p. 306.

Christians put their faithfulness before their very lives'.[364] It is in 'holding fast' to the blood of the Lamb and their own testimony even if it leads to death (11.1-13) that the saints become victors.[365] The hymn confronts the people of God with a radical definition of what it means to identify with Christ. It is not presented as *a* way to follow Jesus but rather the *only* way to follow Jesus.[366] Fourth, the expulsion of Satan from the heavens and the victory of the saints over Satan are cause for the heavens and all who dwell in them to rejoice (12.12). The verb εὐφραίνω ('rejoice, be glad'), used in 11.10 to describe the celebration of the inhabitants of the earth over the death of the two witnesses, is used here as the inhabitants of *heaven* are called on to celebrate God's victory wrought through the work of the Lamb.[367] Yet, given that διὰ τοῦτο ('for this reason') immediately follows the victory of the saints over the Devil, it would seem that the heavens are called upon to include the victory of the saints in their celebration. Fifth, the hymn announces woe upon the earth and sea in light of the wrath of the Devil. If this is the third woe, it serves to announce 'to the world and its inhabitants that Satan exercises his oppressive power on earth'.[368] While the war may be over in heaven, the battle on earth is still operational. The churches must understand that the earth is now the theater for the spiritual war and be resolved to stand firm.

In v. 13, the setting shifts from heaven to earth as the Dragon, now confined to the earth, pursues (ἐδίωξεν)[369] the woman, who is sent to a place of protection. Unable to pursue the woman, the Dragon proceeds to make war against her offspring – those who are keeping the commandments of God and holding on to the testimony of Jesus (12.17). The time of persecution is limited; that is, the woman's offspring will experience Satan's wrath for 'a time, times

---

[364] Prigent, *Commentary on the Apocalypse of St. John*, p. 26.

[365] deSilva, 'Honor Discourse and the Rhetorical Strategy of the Apocalypse of John', p. 108.

[366] Boesak, *Comfort and Protest*, p. 89.

[367] Smalley, *The Revelation to John*, p. 328.

[368] E. Schlüssler Fiorenza, *Revelation: Vision of a Just World* (Minneapolis: Fortress Press, 1991), p. 82.

[369] The verb ἐδίωξεν is an ingressive aorist indicating the beginning of a continued action. See C. Moule, *An Idiom Book of New Testament Greek* (Cambridge: Cambridge University Press, 1953), p. 10.

and half a time' – a period of time that the hearers might recognize from Dan. 7.25 and the same amount of time as in 11.3 and 12.6. John's hearers are to see themselves as part of the woman's offspring[370] and fully recognize the origin of the spiritual conflict in which they find themselves. By identifying with the Lamb, the saints are combatants in a war that will likely require their very lives.[371]

Revelation 13

In exploring the topic of worship in the Apocalypse, chapter 13 is pivotal as the hearers are introduced to the two beasts who work in conjunction with the Dragon. These 'bestial acolytes'[372] continue to wage the war initiated by the Dragon against the followers of the Lamb. Additionally, these characters serve as counterfeits to God, the Lamb, and the Spirit.[373] Worship plays a significant role in this chapter.

The first beast rises up from the sea. Perhaps the hearers would surmise that the Dragon, left standing at the seashore (12.18), has summoned this beast. The beast is very powerful as attested by his ten crowned horns and seven heads (13.1). That the beast has the same number of heads and horns as the Dagon reveals a close connection between them. The beast has blasphemous names on his

---

[370] Smalley, *The Revelation to John*, p. 334. Paul, *The Value of Paul Ricoeur's Hermeneutic of Metaphor*, p. 207, suggests that as the offspring of the woman, the readers 'share with her the vulnerability (12.2) and struggle (12.4, 13.7) and protection (12.6, 14) of the faithful messianic people of God. Whatever the ethnic disruptions in identity, there is a clear continuity of theological identity.'

[371] Blount, *Revelation*, p. 242. See also Pattemore, *The People of God in the Apocalypse*, p. 97, who notes that John's communities must understand that 'ethical obedience to God and witness to Jesus are both inescapably tied up with suffering'.

[372] So Smalley, *The Revelation to John*, p. 335.

[373] Beasley-Murray, *Revelation*, p. 207; Richard, *Apocalypse*, p. 111, 'The dragon, the beast, and the false prophet constitute a perverse Trinity. The relationship between the three is like that of the Father, the Son and the Holy Spirit. Satan is the anti-Father, the beast is the anti-Son, and the false prophet is the anti-Holy Spirit'. See also Thomas, *The Apocalypse*, particularly pp. 382-403. Yet see Trafton, *Reading Revelation*, pp. 131-32 who argues that one must be cautious in reading 'trinitarian theology' here. While agreeing that the dragon and first beast are 'cheap imitations' of the Father and Son, he argues that the close ties between the narrative of the two witnesses and the description of the second beast suggest that the second beast is an imitation of the Church.

seven heads.[374] The hearers would likely recall the *blasphemy* of those who call themselves Jews but whom Jesus calls a synagogue of Satan in 2.9. The verbal link between blasphemy and Satan aids the hearers in understanding both Jesus' ire in 2.9 as well as the insidious nature of this beast. To this beast the Dragon gives his power, his throne, and great authority (13.2). The throne of the Dragon would likely cause the hearers to identify it with the throne of Satan, known to them from the prophetic message to Pergamum (2.13). Heretofore, δύναμις (power) and ἐξουσία (authority) have been attributes designated exclusively for God and the Lamb. That the Dragon and *now* the beast have power and authority serves as warning to the believers not to underestimate their opponent. This power is revealed most pointedly in that one of the beast's heads is healed of a fatal wound (ἐσφαγμένην εἰς θάνατον, ('having been slaughtered to death') (13.3). The verb ἐσφαγμένην would no doubt remind the hearers of the Lamb ἑστηκὸς ὡς ἐσφαγμένον ('standing as slaughtered') in the midst of the throne, the living creatures, and the elders (5.6). The aorist passive ἐθεραπεύθη ('was healed') (13.3) suggests that it is the Dragon that has healed the wound of the beast! In this way, the Dragon and the beast parody God and the Lamb. The response of the whole world to this miracle is two-fold: First, they are filled with wonderment (ἐθαυμάσθη); and second, προσεκύνησαν τῷ δράκοντι, ὅτι ἔδωκεν τὴν ἐξουσίαν τῷ θηρίῳ, καὶ προσεκύνησαν τῷ θηρίῳ ('they worshipped the Dragon, because he gave authority to the beast, and they worshipped the beast') (13.3-4). The sense of wonder created by the healing of the beast's wound captivates the entire world. In terms of the linear telling of the story, the hearers would have to be themselves *amazed* at this response from the inhabitants of the world! After all, many awe-inspiring events have been wrought by God and the Lamb that have not led to awe or worship; indeed, the inhabitants of the world have blasphemed God! The worship now given to the Dragon and his beast attests to their power to deceive the inhabitants of the world. Additionally, the verb προσκυνέω ('worship'), which is used twice in v. 4, has to this point in Revelation been directly solely at God and the Lamb (with the exception

---

[374] deSilva, 'Honor Discourse and the Rhetorical Strategy of the Apocalypse of John', p. 96, sees the blasphemous names as 'the divine names which adorned the [Roman] emperor'.

of 9.20) and has explicitly been used in connection with the 24 elders (4.10; 5.14; 11.16) and the residents of heaven (7.11). The Dragon is worshipped for giving authority to the beast; the beast is worshipped for his use of such authority as expressed in the acclamation: Τίς ὅμοιος τῷ θηρίῳ καὶ τίς δύναται πολεμῆσαι μετ' αὐτοῦ; ('Who is like the beast and who is able to make war with him?') (13.4). The use of this acclamation coupled with the double use of προσκυνέω ('worship') indicates that, as the Dragon and beast are a parody of God and the Lamb, so too is this acclamation to be experienced as a hymn of worship to the beast parodying the worship of God and the Lamb. Echoing Exod. 15.11, the hymn sung to the beast is 'an explicit mockery of biblical traditions of praise of YHWH'.[375] Thus, for the first time in Revelation, a hymn of worship is sung to someone other than God or the Lamb![376] Prophetic discernment is necessary to distinguish between true and false worship; that is, 'only those committed to worship of the true Power see past the facade to the satanic reality'.[377] While the whole world celebrates in their song the power of the beast and their perceived notion that no one can war against him, the churches have learned through the true songs of worship presented in the narrative that worship is only to be given to God and the Lamb, who exercise all power and authority.

The beast is empowered for 42 months to war against the saints and gain victory (νικῆσαι) over them (13.7).[378] As in the story of the two witnesses, identification with God and the Lamb makes the people of God combatants in this war. Simultaneous to his warfare with the saints, the beast is given authority by the Dragon over all

---

[375] Howard-Brook and Gwyther, *Unveiling Empire: Reading Revelation Then and Now*, p. 215; also Smalley, *The Revelation to John*, p. 339.

[376] Ladd, *A Commentary on the Revelation of John*, p. 179, 'Here is the key to the character and purpose of the beast; it is not merely the exercise of political power – it has the objective of capturing the loyalties of men and diverting them from the worship of God'.

[377] Howard-Brook and Gwyther, *Unveiling Empire: Reading Revelation Then and Now*, p. 215.

[378] Howard-Brook and Gwyther, *Unveiling Empire: Reading Revelation Then and Now*, p. 215: 'John sees war against the holy ones itself as a *demonically liturgical act*' (emphasis mine).

the peoples of the earth (13.7).[379] This authority is acknowledged by the inhabitants of the earth, who continue to worship (προσκυνήσουσιν) the beast; however, the hearers learn that there are those who do not worship – the ones whose names are in the book of life[380] belonging to the Lamb slain from the creation of the world (13.8). John's hearers are to understand the implications of following and worshipping the Lamb. It ensures their ultimate salvation, symbolized by their inclusion in the book of life, even if it puts them in direct confrontation with the beast. The hearers would likely recall the promise of Jesus to the church at Sardis that he would not blot out the names of the overcomers from the book of life (3.5). Now it is made clear that overcoming includes *not* worshipping the beast.[381] Further, their own victory is assured because the Lamb, who has conquered (Rev. 5.5) did so before the beginning of time.[382] The narrative depicts what the hymn of 12.10-12 declares: 'They overcame him by the blood of the Lamb and the word of their testimony'.[383] The believers can refuse to worship the beast because they worship the Lamb in whose victory they already

---

[379] The use of the divine passive is intriguing. Up to this point in Revelation, the divine passive has been used with God as the understood subject. Throughout chapter 13, however, the divine passive is used with the Dragon as the understood subject. While not suggesting that the Dragon is equal with God in authority or power, perhaps John uses the divine passive in chapter 13 to alert his hearers to the fact that Satan is indeed a powerful foe with the ability to *give* power and authority to his agents. Although this authority is temporary (12.12, 14) and not absolute (as is God's authority), it is nonetheless real and potent.

[380] An image likely familiar to the hearers from the Old Testament (Exod. 32.32-33; Ps. 69.27-28; Dan. 7.9-10).

[381] Pattemore, *The People of God in the Apocalypse*, p. 170.

[382] Boring, 'The Theology of Revelation: "The Lord Our God the Almighty Reigns"', pp. 267-68: 'When John refers to what "happened" prior to creation, he only thinks of the Lamb that was slain (13:8) and of the believers' names already written (17:8) in the book of the life, that is God's act in the death of Jesus and the formation of the church was no historical accident but part of God's eternal nature and purpose'. See also, Beale, *Revelation*, pp. 702-703.

[383] Bauckham, *The Theology of the Book of Revelation*, pp. 90-91, points out that the beast's ability to conquer the saints and the saints ability to conquer the beast represents an earthly and heavenly perspective respectively. 'The point is not that beast and the Christians each win some victories; rather, the same event – the martyrdom of Christians – is described both as the beast's victory over them and as their victory over the beast ... The perspective of heaven must break into the earth-bound delusion of the beast's propaganda to enable a different assessment of the same empirical fact: the beast's apparent victory is the martyrs' – and therefore God's – real victory'.

share. The importance of this section of the narrative is revealed in what John records next: Εἴ τις ἔχει οὖς ἀκουσάτω ('If anyone has an ear, let him or her hear') (13.9). This admonition to hear takes the hearers back to the refrain of the prophetic messages: ὁ ἔχων οὖς ἀκουσάτω τί τὸ πνεῦμα λέγει ταῖς ἐκκλησίαις ('Let the one having an ear hear what the Spirit says to the churches') (2.7, 11, 17, 29; 3.6; 13, 22). The use of such similar language in 13.9 would suggest that the hearers are likewise to hear all that has proceeded since the prophetic messages as coming from the Spirit[384] even while the indefinite pronoun opens the call up to *any* who would hear. All who have ears – including the seven churches – are tasked with discerning the difference between true and false worship and to endure, no matter if captivity or death comes their way (13.10).

As if the Dragon and beast are not enough, John sees another beast coming up from the earth (13.11). This beast has two horns like a lamb but speaks like a dragon. The juxtapositioning of these two symbols seems especially frightening as *lamb* and *dragon* are anything but neutral in the Apocalypse. This beast is frightening indeed as he engages in an active campaign of authority and control over the world. First, this beast makes[385] the earth *and* the inhabitants of the earth προσκυνήσουσιν ('worship') the first beast whose wound was healed (13.12). Second, this beast performs σημεῖα μεγάλα ('a great sign') before the people by which he deceives (πλανᾷ) them (13.13-14). The hearers would likely think of the two signs in chapter 12; however, coupled with the deception of the beast, the hearers would see how this beast is like the Dragon, the deceiver of the whole earth (12.9). Further, this beast seeks to dazzle the world by making fire come out of heaven. The hearers would likely perceive this as a parody of the actions of the two witnesses (11.5). Third, the beast makes the people construct an idol to the first beast, and, astonishingly, the second beast gives πνεῦμα ('breath, spirit') to the image so that it can speak (13.15). This language is strikingly similar to the πνεῦμα ζωῆς ('Spirit of life') by which the two witnesses are raised (11.11). In this way, the second beast parodies the Spirit or

[384] So Thomas, *The Apocalypse*, p. 395.

[385] ποιέω (also in vv. 14, 15, 16).

the giving of the Spirit.[386] Fourth, all who do not worship (μὴ προκυνήσωσιν) the image are put to death (13.15). It is at this point that the images of Antipas (2.13), the souls under the altar (6.9-10), the great robed multitude who have washed their robes in the blood of the Lamb (7.14), and the saints who overcome the Dragon by the blood of the Lamb (12.10) converge to reveal the true significance of worship. Worship is about allegiance. The martyrs are just that because of their refusal to worship anyone or anything other than God and the Lamb. This is imperative for the people of God, for 'there is no middle ground' or 'room for compromise'.[387] Finally, this beast makes everyone take a χάραγμα ('mark')[388] on their hand or forehead without which no one can buy or sell (13.16). Whatever else the hearers might associate with this mark, the fact that the 144,000 were *marked* with a seal by God would not be lost upon them. In marking his followers, the actions of this beast parody God's actions,[389] and the community must engage in pneumatic discernment. The marks set humanity at odds as those who bear the beast's mark are now 'rivals' of those who bear God's mark.[390] The ability of the beast to control all aspects of commerce is alarming, but the hearers have learned that any discomfort they will face is only temporary for they will never hunger or thirst when they stand before the throne of God (7.16). This second beast, then, exercises his authority with concrete actions and imposes his will upon the inhabitants of the earth. Not to be missed for John's hearers is that worship is the proof-test for allegiance and an issue of life and death on earth.

---

[386] Smalley, *The Revelation to John*, p. 348; Thomas, *The Apocalypse*, p. 404.

[387] Thomas, *The Apocalypse*, p. 405. So also Bauckham, *The Theology of the Book of Revelation*, pp. 93-94, who says that the 'utterly stark' choice put before John's hearers is to worship the beast or face martyrdom. He further states, 'In the situation John envisages, martyrdom belongs, as it were, to the essential nature of faithful witness. Not every faithful witness will actually be put to death, but all faithful witness requires the endurance and the faithfulness (13:10) that will accept martyrdom if it comes.'

[388] Χάραγμα is always used in Revelation with reference to the followers of the beast (13.16, 17; 14.9, 11; 16.2; 19.20; 20.4). Resseguie, *The Revelation of John*, p. 188, calls it a 'spiritual imprint' that identifies those who 'belong to the counterfeit god'.

[389] Ladd, *A Commentary on the Revelation of John*, p. 185.

[390] Schüssler Fiorenza, *Revelation*, p. 86.

Revelation 14

Revelation 14 stands juxtaposed with the events of Revelation 13. There the inhabitants of the earth are following the Dragon and his beasts; here John sees the Lamb standing (ἑστὸς)[391] on Mount Zion with 144,000 followers. Whatever the hearers might associate historically with Mount Zion, its use here suggests the 'meeting place of the new people of God that now gathers alongside the risen Jesus'.[392] Indeed, Thomas posits that one of the many things that Mount Zion might convey to the hearers is 'the eschatological place of protection and security for God's people (Isa. 24.23; 25.7-10).'[393] That the Lamb stands with 144,000 would no doubt cause the hearers to think of the 144,000 of 7.4-9 who are 'transformed' into the great multitude who *stand* before the Lamb.[394] Here they represent the 'alternative community of the Lamb'.[395] In chapter 13 the inhabitants of the earth bear the mark of the beast on their hands or foreheads; here the followers of the Lamb bear the name of the Lamb and his *Father*[396] upon their foreheads (14.1; see also 7.2-8).[397] The hearers thus discover that the seal *is* the inscribed name of God and the Lamb, just as promised to the overcomers in 3.12. In chapter 13 the inhabitants of the earth worship the beast and his image and sing a hymn of praise to him; here the followers of the Lamb sing a ᾠδὴν καινὴν ('new song') before the throne, the living creatures, and the elders (14.3). The sound of it, John notes, is loud (like rushing water and thunder) yet beautiful, like κιθαρῳδῶν κιθαριζόντων ἐν ταῖς κιθάραις αὐτῶν ('harpists harping on their harps') (14.2). The deafening sound of their song serves to drown out the

---

[391] Pattemore, *The People of God in the Apocalypse*, p. 179, 'The Lamb does nothing here but stand, and it is as though his mere presence is enough to defeat the beasts'.

[392] Richard, *Apocalypse*, p. 118.

[393] Thomas, *The Apocalypse*, p. 418.

[394] Thomas, *The Apocalypse*, p. 419.

[395] Schüssler Fiorenza, *Revelation*, p. 87.

[396] This is the fourth and final use of 'Father' in the Apocalypse. The use of this familial title conveys the intimate relationship between the Jesus, the Son, and God. It also speaks to the 'Father's protective concern for his victorious children'. Smalley, *The Revelation to John*, p. 355.

[397] Richard, *Apocalypse*, p. 118.

'demonic choir' who sing to the beast.[398] The hearers would also likely think of all the worship that has taken place before the throne of God, accompanied by the harps of the elders (5.8). John indicates that they sing a *new song*, but John does not record its lyrics for it is a song that no one can learn except the 144,000 redeemed or purchased (ἠγορασμένοι) from the earth (14.4). The hearers would recall that the Lamb is worshipped in part for purchasing (ἠγόρασας) for God people from every tribe, nation, and tongue (5.9). Such a tie serves to strengthen the intimate connection between the Lamb and those standing with Him. Given that the lyrics of the songs sung to God and the Lamb have to this point been recorded, the absence of *this* song's lyrics is quite unusual. Perhaps this suggests that it is to be identified with the *new song* already sung in 5.8-10,[399] or that John does not hear the words but merely the sound of their singing. Neither option is quite satisfactory given the prominence of hymnic material in the Apocalypse. Perhaps the *learning* and singing of the song is so closely identified with those who refuse to worship the beast and thereby give up their lives (12.10; 13.14) that its veiled lyrics serve as an additional promise of things that await the overcomers. Perhaps this is why John can only describe the *sound* of the song; its lyrics are only unlocked through the experience of martyrdom.[400] The refusal to worship the beast is the churches' primary means of resistance. 'The "reward" for this resistance ... is access to the words of the "new song," which only the 144,000 can learn'.[401] The hearers are presented with two choices: they can participate in the liturgy of the beast or they can participate in the liturgy of heaven. Neutrality is not an option. Koester is correct when he states that 'John did not make such a sharp distinction because the alternatives were obvious to his readers *but because*

---

[398] Howard-Brook and Gwyther, *Unveiling Empire*, p. 218.

[399] So Schüssler Fiorenza, *Revelation*, p. 88: 'But whereas 5:8-10 elaborates the content of the new song, 14:3 focuses on those who can learn it'.

[400] Harris, *The Literary Function of the Hymns in the Apocalypse of John*, p. 163, 'Just like the Lamb is the only one worthy to open the scroll because he was a faithful witness and slain, so too the saints are the only ones able to sing this song because they were faithful to God and followed the Lamb even unto death'.

[401] Howard-Brook and Gwyther, *Unveiling Empire*, p. 217. See also Richard, *Apocalypse*, p. 119: 'Those who resist the beast on earth need to sing the hymn of the martyrs in heaven'.

the alternatives were not obvious.[402] If John's hearers have been tolerating false teachings and false teachers (with a pointed emphasis on idolatry) in their midst as seen in the prophetic messages, they are in danger of collusion with the beast! To participate in the liturgy of heaven, one must be pure,[403] a truth-teller,[404] blameless and, most importantly, be willing to follow the Lamb *wherever* he goes (14.4-5), including to the places of suffering and death, so that they can be *wherever* the Lamb is.

Two other elements to note in this chapter are in the pronouncements of the angels in 14.6-12.[405] First, in 14.6, John sees an angel with the eternal gospel to proclaim to all the inhabitants of the earth. The angel's message is a call to repentance (Φοβήθητε τὸν θεὸν καὶ δότε αὐτῷ δόξαν, 'Fear God and give him glory') in light of pending judgment and an admonition to worship (προσκυνήσατε) the one who made heaven, the earth, the sea, and the springs of water (14.7). The hearers would recall that in the narrative of the two witnesses the remnant who survived the earthquake were fearful and gave glory to God in heaven. Thus, the angel calls the inhabitants of the earth to repentance *before* the coming judgment and encourages them to give worship to the Creator. The churches are likewise tasked with proclaiming the word and calling the inhabitants of the earth to repentance.[406] This reinforces the necessity of witness as part of their worship unto God, for 'conversion rather than destruction' is what God desires for humanity.[407]

---

[402] Koester, *Revelation and the End of All Things*, p. 136 (emphasis mine).

[403] Peters, *The Mandate of the Church in the Apocalypse of John*, p. 68, suggests that the reference to purity, which is often viewed as sexual purity, should rather be understood as a symbol of religious purity; that is, it is 'a symbolic description of the Church kept pure from all defiling relationships with the pagan world system'. See also Howard-Brook and Gwyther, *Unveiling Empire*, pp. 218-19; Gonzáles and Gonzáles, *Revelation*, p. 92.

[404] Minear, 'Far as the Curse is Found', p. 74: 'Just as Genesis traced the world's evil to a lie and to the curses that followed that lie, so John traced victory over that evil to a refusal to lie under threat of death'.

[405] deSilva, 'Honor Discourse and the Rhetorical Strategy of the Apocalypse of John', p. 89, notes, 'The messages of the three angels represents the most extensive, and closest, approximation of direct exhortation after the opening of the visionary experience in Rev. 4.1'.

[406] Ladd, *A Commentary on the Revelation of John*, p. 193.

[407] Koester, *Revelation and the End of All Things*, p. 137.

Second, the third angel specifically addresses the issue of worshipping the beast and his image and taking his mark (14.9-11). It is not without significance that this is the longest of the three proclamations, for the issue of true and false worship is of utmost importance for the hearers.[408] For those who choose to worship the beast, judgment and torment awaits – in the presence of the Lamb and the angels, no less. In addition, the worshippers of the beast will have no rest day or night (14.11); consequently, while the worship of God in heaven goes on day and night (4.8; 7.15), the worshippers of the beast will be unable to rest. The pronouncements of the three angels represent the on-going prophetic task of John and the churches to call the nations to repentance and to the worship of God. Part of their witness involves warning the world of God's coming judgment – a judgment which can be averted if the inhabitants of the earth will repent.[409]

The angelic pronouncements are followed by two additional pronouncements (14.13). The first pronouncement is made by a φωνῆς ἐκ τοῦ οὐρανοῦ ('voice from heaven') and the second is made by τὸ πνεῦμα ('the Spirit'). The voice from heaven instructs John to write Μακάριοι οἱ νεκροὶ οἱ ἐν κυρίῳ ἀποθνῄσκοντες ἀπ᾽ ἄρτι ('Blessed are the dead who die in the Lord from now on'). The placement of this pronouncement on the heels of the message of the third angel as well as in the context of the decrees of the second beast underlines the unwavering assertion throughout the Apocalypse that victory over the forces of evil will most likely come through death.[410] That those who die are *blessed* assures the hearers of Divine favor.[411] This second *blessing* in the Apocalypse sheds light on the first blessing in Rev. 1.3; namely, the hearers now understand fully what *keeping* the words of the prophecy ultimately entails. This blessing is seconded as it were by the ναί ('yes') from

---

[408] deSilva, 'Honor Discourse and the Rhetorical Strategy of the Apocalypse of John', p. 101.

[409] Koester, *Revelation and the End of All Things*, p. 139, 'John is compelled to write because the threat of divine judgment is real, and he is able to write because the hope of averting judgment is also real'.

[410] deSilva, 'Honor Discourse and the Rhetorical Strategy of the Apocalypse of John', p. 104, 'In this passage, the most extreme experience of society's disapproval and censure, namely execution, is pronounced a mark of honor within the community and before the court of God'.

[411] Fee, *Revelation*, p. 198.

the Spirit.[412] The single-word utterance from the Spirit along with the liturgical blessing affirms that losing one's life in witness to the Lamb is an ultimate act of worship. Those who die in the Lord will rest (ἵνα ἀναπαήσονται) from their labors, and their works will accompany them. The contrast between those who die in the Lord and those who choose to worship the beast could not be stronger. Where the latter face eternal torment and no rest (14.11), the former will experience eternal rest (14.13). At the mention of works, the hearers would likely think of the prophetic messages where the Spirit speaks the words of Jesus to the churches concerning their works. It is not insignificant that the crucial task of discernment to ensure that the churches' works are pleasing to Jesus is here connected to the death of the faithful.

Summary of Revelation 12–14

Revelation 12–14 is a pivotal narrative unit in exploring the role of worship in the Apocalypse. Structurally these chapters form an interlude between the second and third judgment cycles and provide a kaleidoscope of images that blur past, present, and future events for the hearers. The vocabulary of worship (προσκυνέω) and activities of worship continue throughout this section yet with a twist. God and the Lamb continue to be worshipped; yet, worship is also offered up to the Dragon and the beast (13.4). Hymns of worship are sung to God and the Lamb (12.10-12; 14.2-3); yet, a hymn of worship is sung to the beast (13.4). Angelic pronouncements encourage the faithful to worship God and warn of eternal consequences for those who worship the beast and receive his mark (14.6-12); yet, a demonic pronouncement makes the whole world worship the image of the beast and kills those who refuse to worship the beast (13.15). The intentional focus on the worship of the Dragon and his beast provides the central thrust of the interlude: to contrast graphically true and false worship for the hearers. The hearers must engage in pneumatic discernment. It is in *their* worship that true worship takes place. It is in *their* prophetic songs that faithfulness to God and the Lamb is rehearsed. It is in *their* worship that they affirm their sole identity as followers of the Lamb. It is in *their* worship that they

---

[412] Richard, *Apocalypse*, p. 124, notes that the Spirit steps in 'to resist the false prophet who acts as the anti-Spirit'.

exist as an alternative community of the Lamb. The urgency of the
prophetic messages by which Jesus speaks to his churches through
the Spirit as they are gathered for worship find further expression in
these chapters. Laid out for the hearers in Revelation 12-14, most
particularly in its two hymns, is the definition of what it means to
be an overcomer. In singing their hymns of worship, the hearers are
filled with anticipation of one day standing with the Lamb and singing a song before the throne that they have earned the right to learn
by not loving their lives so much as to shrink from death (12.11).

In addition, these chapters provide the hearers with further impetus to engage in witness as an important aspect of worship. The
angelic proclamations found in 14.6-12 are targeted at every nation,
tribe, people, and tongue, imploring them to repent and to worship
the God of all creation. So, too, are the people of God to call the
nations to repentance. God is the king of the nations whose desire
is for all nations to engage in true worship. The churches are not
isolated from the world; rather, they are situated in the world to
witness to the Lamb as part of their worship – even in the face of
the beast.

E. Revelation 15–16

Revelation 15–16 contains the final judgment series. Chapter 15 is
another worship scene which also provides the concluding narrative
of the 'signs' begun in chapter 12. Here John sees ἄλλο σημεῖον
ἐν τῷ οὐρανῷ μέγα καὶ θαυμαστόν ('another great and wonderful sign in heaven'). While the first sign in heaven was 'great' (12.1),
John notes that *this* sign is both 'great' and 'wonderful'. The hearers
would not miss that John used θαυμάζω ('marvel, wonder') to express the amazement of the whole earth at the beast (13.3); thus, the
hearers are prepared for something extraordinary. John quickly
identifies the sign as seven angels having the last seven plagues by
which the wrath of God will be completed (ἐτελέσθη) (15.1).[413]
The hearers know that the 'wrath of God' is reserved for those who
worship the beast and take his mark (14.10) and that the second

---

[413] Thomas, *The Apocalypse*, p. 450: 'As in 11.18 and 14.7, God's future actions
are understood as so certain that they are spoken of as already accomplished, with
the divine passive suggesting that it is God himself who completes his wrath
through these last seven plagues'. See also Beale, *The Book of Revelation*, p. 788,
who notes that 'the futuristic use of the aorist places stress on the prophetic certainty of the event'.

harvest (14.17-20) of judgment involves the casting of the grapes into the great winepress of the wrath of God (14.19). Despite the completed action of the verb ἐτελέσθη ('was completed'), the hearers have yet to witness what it will take to complete the wrath of God. While they brace themselves for the actions of the seven angels, another 'dramatic pause' is introduced into the narrative.[414]

John writes that he saw a glassy sea mixed with fire alongside which those who overcame (τοὺς νικῶντας) the beast were standing (ἑστῶτας) with harps (15.2). No doubt several things would converge for the hearers at this point. The glassy sea was last mentioned in the inaugural throne room scene (4.6) albeit without a reference to fire. Nonetheless, the hearers would likely assume that heaven is the setting, as opposed to the sea from which the beast emerged (13.1). This is only strengthened by the appearance of those who overcame the beast, his image, and the number of his name.[415] With the chilling narrative of the beast still fresh in their minds, the hearers *know* what it takes to overcome the beast (12.11; 13.15), as well as the results of such a victory (7.9-17; 14.1-5).[416] Seeing the overcomers in heaven here is thus a climactic point in the narrative for John's hearers who have been repeatedly challenged by the risen Jesus and the Spirit to be overcomers (Revelation 2–3). The point is explicit: the overcomers are those who overcome the Dragon and his beasts by their witness to the Lamb![417] Like the elders and living creatures, the overcomers have harps, yet the notice that the harps were given to them by God seems rather extraordinary.[418] With their harps, they can join in with the elders and living creatures in offering instrumental worship unto God. The over-

---

[414] Trafton, *Reading Revelation*, p. 141.

[415] Resseguie, *The Revelation to John*, p. 205, '[T]he threefold pattern emphasizes their complete victory over the blandishments of the beast'. See also Rotz, *Revelation*, p. 231.

[416] Koester, *Revelation and the End of All Things*, p. 141: 'Repeating the vision of heavenly worship stresses that this is the future that Revelation wants for its readers. *This is where God and the Lamb want people to be*' (emphasis mine).

[417] Richard, *Apocalypse*, p. 126, 'What stands at the center of Revelation is the victory of the martyrs over Satan and the beast'. See also Ladd, *A Commentary on the Revelation of John*, p. 204, 'Although the beast had power to slay them, in reality they have conquered him by remaining true to Jesus; his real purpose was frustrated'.

[418] So Fee, *Revelation*, p. 211, who calls this a 'most remarkable moment in the book'.

comers ᾄδουσιν τὴν ᾠδὴν Μωϋσέως τοῦ δούλου τοῦ θεοῦ καὶ τὴν ᾠδὴν τοῦ ἀρνίου ('sing the song of Moses the servant of God and the song of the Lamb') (15.3). That harps and the explicit reference to singing a new song have only appeared in the 'immediate presence of God' continues to link the overcomers with the 24 elders and the 144,000.[419] Significantly, the song is that of Moses, Israel's great deliverer from Egyptian bondage (after the onslaught of the plagues) who led God's people through the Red Sea, and[420] the song of the Lamb, *the* Deliverer from the bondage of Satan. The combination suggests a cognitive linkage between the deliverance of the Israelites from Pharaoh, which is celebrated in song in Exodus 15, and the deliverance of the saints from the Dragon by means of the blood of the Lamb, which is celebrated in song in 12.11.[421] The hearers might also think of the hymn of praise given to the beast (13.4) which parodied the Exodus story. Although the song in 14.1-5 was not recorded, John does record this song. While Richard suggests that *this* is the song that they are learning in 14.1-5,[422] it is best to see it as another hymn of celebration to God separate from the song in 14.1-5. The hymn of the overcomers is as follows:

Μεγάλα καὶ θαυμαστὰ τὰ ἔργα σου,
κύριε ὁ θεὸς ὁ παντοκράτωρ·
δίκαιαι καὶ ἀληθιναὶ αἱ ὁδοί σου,
ὁ βασιλεὺς τῶν ἐθνῶν·
τίς οὐ μὴ φοβηθῇ, κύριε,
καὶ δοξάσει τὸ ὄνομά σου
ὅτι μόνος ὅσιος,
ὅτι πάντα τὰ ἔθνη ἥξουσιν
καὶ προσκυνήσουσιν ἐνώπιόν σου,
ὅτι τὰ δικαιώματά σου ἐφανερώθησαν

---

[419] Thomas, *The Apocalypse*, p. 452.

[420] Smalley, *The Revelation to John*, p. 386 suggests an epexegetical use of καὶ ('and') so that the song is that of Moses, *even* the song of the Lamb'. Boxall, *The Revelation of St. John*, p. 218, suggests that the genitives used in describing the song as the song *of Moses* and the song *of the Lamb* are subjective genitives'.

[421] So Thomas, *The Apocalypse*, pp. 452-53. See also Fee, *Revelation*, pp. 210-11, 'Pictured here is the ultimate New Exodus, as the martyrs once again stand by the sea, as it were (Exodus 14), anticipating God's judgment against their "Pharaoh"'.

[422] Richard, *Apocalypse*, p. 126. See also W. Fenske, 'Das Lied des Moses, des Knechtes Gottes, und das Lied des Lammes', *ZNW* 90, p. 255.

Great and wonderful are your works,
Lord God the Almighty;
just and true are your ways,
King of the nations.
Who will not fear, Lord,
and glorify your name?
Because you alone are holy,
because all the nations will come
and will worship before you,
because your righteous acts were manifested (15.3b-4).

Thompson identifies this hymn as the most structured hymn in the whole of Revelation, due to its use of a rhetorical question, its address to God in liturgical sentences and its three ὅτι ('because') clauses.[423] This hymn of victory opens with two declaratory statements in synonymous parallelism that celebrates both the justice and nature of God. The hymn draws on OT imagery as well as imagery from the Apocalypse; hence, the two songs (of Moses and of the Lamb) merge into one *new* song. According to Bauckham, 'John writes a new version of the song of Moses in order to provide an interpretation of the deliverance at the Red Sea and its eschatological antitype'.[424] The song draws on the song of Moses in declaring that God's works and ways are great, wondrous, just and true (Exod. 15.11; cf. Deut. 32.4; Ps. 86.8-9; 111.2-8). The hearers would certainly not miss the connection between the great and wondrous sign (15.1) and God's great and wondrous works, which suggests that this song also anticipates the outpouring of the seven bowls of plagues. Situated where it is in the narrative, the song 'serves to place the judgments to follow in the setting of God's holiness and

---

[423] Thompson, *The Book of Revelation*, p. 61.

[424] Bauckham, *The Climax of Prophecy*, p. 298. Bauckham demonstrates how Isaiah 12 draws on the Red Sea experience as well as Psalm 105 in depicting the eschatological salvation of Israel as a new exodus. In Isaiah 12, the words of the songs are new words that provide an eschatological interpretation of the Exodus. Bauckham suggests that John would have been familiar with this Jewish exegetical practice. Additionally, Bauckham demonstrates how the hymn of Revelation 15 is a 'careful interpretation' of Moses' song in Exodus 15. See his thorough discussion of this in pp. 296-307.

justice'.[425] The hymn incorporates names used for God that are both familiar (κύριε ὁ θεὸς ὁ παντοκράτωρ, 'Lord God the Almighty') (Rev. 1.8; 11.17) and new (ὁ Βασιλεὺς τῶν ἐθνῶν, 'the King of the nations') to the hearers. Thus, while it appeared that the Dragon and his beasts would rule the world in Revelation 13, the martyrs' hymn reminds the hearers that the Almighty God is *the* King of the nations. To worship any other being beside God is to engage in false worship.

The hymn's rhetorical question is likely drawn from Jer. 10.7 but its setting here reminds the hearers both of the response of the survivors of the earthquake in 11.13 who were fearful and gave glory to God but also, more significantly, of the song of the followers of the beast (13.4) who ask 'Who is like the beast?' Not only does the sheer length of this song dwarf the hymnic fragment sung to the beast, but it also responds to their question by establishing the 'unique deity of the only true God'.[426] The three ὅτι ('because') clauses offer the reasons why all should fear and glorify God; namely, because God alone is holy, because all the nations will come and worship before God, and because God's righteous judgments have been revealed (15.4). The churches are encouraged to make the song of the overcomers their own song; in this way, they remind themselves in worship that their victory is assured even as they find themselves in the midst of evil. Just as God was faithful to the people of God in the past (as represented in the figure of Moses), so also will God be faithful to those who follow the Lamb, even through the *sea* of martyrdom. Worship links the people of God with the past and the future. Mangina's comment is quite apt: '... the song of the Lamb does not render the song of Moses obsolete, but rather confirms and intensifies it'.[427]

The hymn points to the conversion of the nations to the worship of God. God is the King of the nations,[428] who desires their worship. Koester makes a relevant observation:

According to Revelation, God does not want the nations of the world to be lured into allying themselves with the powers of evil

---

[425] Michaels, *Revelation*, p. 183.

[426] Bauckham, *The Climax of Prophecy*, p. 305.

[427] Mangina, *Revelation*, p. 182.

[428] A title used only here in the Apocalypse.

(13:7-8), but neither does he want the nations to be destroyed. Instead, God's desire is for the conversion of the nations, so that they join in the cosmic chorus of praise that is his will for the world.[429]

Unlike the beast who demands all to worship or else be killed, God allows humanity to choose whom they will worship. In their worship, the churches issue prophetic proclamations of God's will and desire for the world: *all* the nations *will* come and *will* worship before God.[430] The hearers would likely think of Jesus' words in Jn 3.16, which express the love of God for the entire world, or of the declaration that the Lamb purchased for God people from every tribe, tongue, people, and nation (Rev. 5.9). In this hymn is the affirmation that 'salvation and liberation' is not just for the Christian community but for 'all nations which are now oppressed and longing for the experience of God's justice'.[431] The nations thus have an opportunity to respond to the works of God with repentance.[432] It remains to be seen whether they will choose to do so. The final clause – 'for your righteous deeds have been revealed' – looks both backward to God's acts of justice for his people throughout biblical history and forward to the last judgment cycle in which God will act with justice.[433] In light of all of this, it is instructive to note that 'even though the song is sung by the martyrs, they do not sing of themselves or the way in which they have overcome the beast; they are entirely occupied with the sovereignty, justice and glory of

---

[429] Koester, *Revelation and the End of All Things*, p. 142.

[430] Fee, *Revelation*, p. 213, writes that this serves as a reminder to the churches 'that even in the midst of their present difficulties, they themselves, who are part of "all nations," must continue to bear witness to these nations about their king, whom the nations have yet to acknowledge as Lord of all'.

[431] Schüssler Fiorenza, *Revelation*, p. 92.

[432] Osborne, *Revelation*, pp. 567-68. Sweet, *Revelation*, p. 240, sees a reference to the Exodus where God's righteous deed is his deliverance of Israel from Egypt. 'The context requires reference to the exodus deliverance (5.5f., 12.1-11), rather than the plagues which harden men (9.20f., 16.9, 11, 21). This final exodus *is* punitive (11.13, 12.5, 14.20, 19.11ff), but not *simply* punitive' (emphasis his). See also Boxall, *The Revelation of St. John*, p. 220; Prigent, *Commentary on the Apocalypse of St. John*, p. 461.

[433] Boesak, *Comfort and Protest*, p. 109.

God'.[434] The intended effect of both the Lamb's sacrifice and the witness of the saints through martyrdom is to lead the world to the acknowledgment and worship of God.[435]

Before the final plagues are unveiled, the worship scene ends very much like the worship scene in Rev. 11.15-19 with John seeing the opening of the heavenly temple,[436] here called ὁ ναὸς τῆς σκηνῆς τοῦ μαρτυρίου ('the temple of the tabernacle of witness') (15.5). While it is hard to know what the hearers might have understood by this description, they would likely connect it with the Ark of the Covenant (11.19) which housed the tablets of the Testimony (Exod. 34.29). That it is the temple of the tabernacle of *witness* might also lead the hearers to think of Jesus, the faithful witness, or that they are called to witness to the nations.[437] Whatever the case might be, the imagery signifies that whatever comes out of the temple is to be linked with God and the Lamb. Emerging from within the temple are the seven angels with the seven plagues (15.5-6). The hearers know that these angels constitute the great and wondrous sign in heaven with which the chapter began. John describes their apparel: they are dressed in clean white linen and have golden sashes, an image familiar to the hearers from Jesus' own attire (1.13). By this, the angels 'share in the work of God in Christ'.[438] The angels receive golden bowls full of the wrath of God, who lives forever and ever. Finally, John records that the temple is filled with the smoke from the glory of God and his power. The imagery of smoke combined with the glory of God might cause the hearers to think of the presence of God that rested over the tabernacle (Exod. 40.34-35) or the smoke that filled the temple in Isaiah's vision (Isa. 6.3-4). In the Apocalypse, however, the hearers have only to recall where the smoke of the incense was mingled with the prayers of the saints (in golden bowls) going up before God (8.4; also 5.8). Such an intratextual connection suggests that the bowls of wrath are a response

---

[434] Ladd, *A Commentary on the Revelation of John*, p. 206.

[435] Bauckham, *The Climax of Prophecy*, pp. 306-307.

[436] Murphy, *Fallen is Babylon*, p. 334 sees this not as a second opening of the Temple but a 'recapitulation of the opening in 11:19'.

[437] Smalley, *The Revelation to John*, p. 390; Thomas, *The Apocalypse*, pp. 460-61.

[438] Smalley, *The Revelation to John*, p. 390.

to the prayers of God's people for justice (also 6.10; 8.3-5).[439] That response is symbolized in a theophanic manifestation of God's consuming presence that bars anyone from entering into the temple until God has finished. It is thus through the lens of this worship scene that the final judgment series is to be understood. As Thomas keenly notes, '… God's acts of judgment are not random acts, but are indeed righteous acts designed to encourage true worship even amongst those who rebelliously worship the dragon, the beast, and the image of the beast'.[440]

Revelation 16

Revelation 16 contains the narrative of the seven bowls of the wrath of God first introduced in 15.1. As with the seal and trumpet cycles, the bowl judgments are numbered. The bowl judgments unleash events strikingly similar to the trumpet judgments (and the plagues on Egypt) yet with a greater sense of finality. Aside from revealing the contents of the bowls, this chapter continues to address the theme of worship. The chapter opens with a μεγάλης φωνῆς ('great voice') from the temple commanding the angels to pour the seven bowls of God's wrath upon the earth. Although the great voice is unidentified, the hearers would likely surmise that it is the voice of God since no one is able to enter the temple (15.5).[441] At the pouring out of the first bowl, 'bad' and 'evil' sores break out upon τοὺς ἀνθρώπους τοὺς ἔχοντας τὸ χάραγμα τοῦ θηρίου καὶ τοὺς προσκυνοῦντας τῇ εἰκόνι αὐτοῦ ('the people having the mark of the beast and the ones worshipping his image') (16.2). It is significant that the first bowl of God's wrath is targeted at those who have identified with the beast by taking his mark and worshipping his image.[442] While God's wrath against them is unleashed, unlike the Dragon and beasts, who kill those who refuse to

---

[439] So Osborne, *Revelation*, p. 570. See also Blount, *Revelation*, p. 292; Smalley, *The Revelation to John*, p. 391; Boxall, *The Revelation of St. John*, p. 222.

[440] Thomas, *The Apocalypse*, p. 460.

[441] Ladd, *A Commentary on the Revelation of John*, p. 210, identifies the voice as God since, according to 15.8, 'all others had been excluded from the temple until the seven plagues were ended'. Also Beasley-Murray, *Revelation*, p. 241; Smalley, *The Revelation to John*, pp. 399-400; Thomas, *The Apocalypse*, pp. 465-66.

[442] Resseguie, *The Revelation of John*, p. 201: 'The outer corruption of their flesh parallels their inner corruption'.

worship them, God inflicts terrible suffering upon those who worship the beast. That they are not killed hints at the fact that repentance is still possible. The pouring out of the second bowl results in the death of the sea and all within it (16.2-3). Although the beast emerged from the sea (13.1), the total destruction of the sea (as it turns to blood) and its inhabitants is shocking and heightens the finality of this judgment. At the pouring of the third bowl, the rivers and fountains of waters, like the sea, become blood (16.4). It is at this point that the narrative sequence is interrupted as John hears the angel of the waters speak:

Δίκαιος εἶ, ὁ ὢν καὶ ὁ ἦν, ὁ ὅσιος,
ὅτι ταῦτα ἔκρινας,
ὅτι αἷμα ἁγίων καὶ προφητῶν ἐξέχεαν
καὶ αἷμα αὐτοῖς δέδωκας πιεῖν,
ἄξιοί εἰσιν

You are just, the One who is and who was, the Holy One,
because you have judged these things,
because the blood of the saints and prophets they shed
and you have given them blood to drink,
for they are worthy (16.5b-6).

Before the hearers can even process the words of the angel, the altar issues an antiphonal response:

Ναὶ κύριε ὁ θεὸς ὁ παντοκράτωρ,
ἀληθιναὶ καὶ δίκαιαι αἱ κρίσεις σου

Yes, Lord God, the Almighty,
true and just are your judgments (16.7b).

The hearers might recall that following the proclamation of the third angel in Rev. 14.9-12, two voices speak: a voice from heaven and the Spirit. The Spirit confirms the words of the voice from heaven with ναί ('yes') before pronouncing a blessing on those who die in the Lord (14.13). Here, the proclamation of the angel, which most likely by this point in the Apocalypse would be experienced by the hearers as a hymn,[443] is a declaration about God. Even

---

[443] Smalley, *The Revelation to John*, p. 402, identifies vv. 5-7 as 'hymnic interludes'.

though the pouring out of the third bowl has resulted in a thorough pollution of the waters, the angel of the waters proclaims that God is just and holy. The hearers would recall that in the previous hymn, God's ways were declared δίκαιαι ('just') (15.3) and now here, for the first time, God *is* the 'Just One'. It is first and foremost the justice of God that the angel lauds. Second, God is the 'One who is and who was' – a description familiar to the hearers (11.17) and one that continues to provide continuity throughout the narrative. The same God who sends greetings of grace and peace to the churches (1.4), the same God who sits on the throne of heaven (4.8) is the God who is just in his being and actions.[444] The third clause – 'and who is to come' – is missing yet here the angel supplies a third element in the substantive ὁ ὅσιος ('the Holy One').[445] This is the second time this particular word for 'holy' has occurred (see 15.4). That ὅσιος is found in two hymns extolling the justice of God indicates that God's holiness is directly connected to His judgment.[446]

The hymn contains two ὅτι ('because') clauses that are linked to God's justice and holiness. First, because God has judged, God is righteous (ὅτι as causal).[447] Second, God will vindicate the death of the saints and prophets by giving their persecutors blood to drink for they are worthy. The second clause makes it very clear that God's justice is being poured out because the blood of the saints and prophets was poured out. Although in 11.18, saints and prophets were paired together among the group to whom God would give rewards, the hearers would likely think again of the spilled blood of Antipas, the souls under the altar, the two witnesses, and certainly the overcomers before the throne.[448] The reference to blood continues to reinforce the idea that following the Lamb is

---

[444] Thomas, *The Apocalypse*, p. 470, 'If the hearers are tempted to misunderstand these wrathful activities of God as too severe, they are immediately reassured that they come from the hand of a righteous God whose ways are "true and righteous" (15.3)'.

[445] Jörns, *Das hymnische Evangelium*, p. 134.

[446] Blount, *Revelation*, p. 297.

[447] Aune, *Revelation 6–16*, p. 856.

[448] Blount, *Revelation*, p. 298: 'He is speaking not about the saints and prophets of old but about the very witnesses to the lordship of God and the Lamb who have been the center of his attention throughout the narrative'.

costly.[449] The blood which has contaminated the sea and all the waters in the pouring out of the second and third bowls becomes the deadly drink for the persecutors of God's people. The final clause – 'for they are worthy' – is laden with irony. The hearers know that God and the Lamb are worthy (4.11; 5.9, 12), yet they would also recall that Jesus declared the saints in Sardis to be worthy because they had not soiled their garments (3.4). The persecutors of God's people are worthy or, better, *deserving* of God's judgment because of their actions against God's people (see also 6.9-11).[450] The hymn announces divine justice against those who refuse to acknowledge the lordship of God and the Lamb. Not to be forgotten is the proclamation of the angel in chapter 14 in which the inhabitants of the earth are forewarned of the coming judgment and admonished to repent. The visual of the bowls of God's wrath becomes the impetus for the on-going prophetic witness of God's people in calling all people to serve the one true God and the Lamb before they find themselves as recipients of God's judgment.

The second voice John hears is the altar. The altar has played a significant role in the Apocalypse as the place from which the martyrs cry for justice (6.9-11), and upon which the prayers of the saints are placed (8.3). Here the altar, which has sheltered the martyrs and heard the prayers of God's people, comes to life in John's vision and sings forth its own hymn:[451] '*Yes*, Lord God, the Almighty One! True and just are your judgments'. Although the hearers would scarcely be surprised that the altar itself speaks[452] given all the

---

[449] Thomas, *The Apocalypse*, p. 472.

[450] Boxall, *The Revelation of St. John*, p. 228, argues the phrase 'they are worthy' is a statement 'of the worthiness of the oppressed' rather than a statement about the oppressors. He argues this based on the fact that in Revelation, 'worthy' is always used positively in connection with God (4.11), the Lamb (5.9, 12), or the saints (3.4). He adds, 'Because they are judged worthy, like the Lamb that they followed even to death, their bloody deaths have now been vindicated in the heavenly hall of judgment'. The flow of the hymn here does not seem to support Boxall's argument. The natural antecedent in the phrase 'they are worthy' would be those mentioned in the previous line – the oppressors. They (the oppressors of God's people) are given blood to drink precisely because they have shed the blood of God's people. So Ladd, *A Commentary on the Revelation of John*, p. 211, 'The judgment of those who have martyred the saints is suited to the evil they have done'.

[451] Thomas, *The Apocalypse*, p. 473, identifies these two hymns as 'testimonial' hymns.

[452] So Peters, *The Mandate of the Church in the Apocalypse of John*, pp. 71-72.

extraordinary things they have heard to this point, it is more likely that John hears someone speak, perhaps the angel from the altar (14.18), the martyrs as a whole,[453] or the voice of one representative martyr.[454] This imagery of the altar reinforces the importance of prayer as an act of worship. The prayers of God's people for justice and for the coming of God's kingdom do not go unheard in the heavens; rather, the prayers move the One who sits on the throne.[455] By its use of ναὶ ('yes') as a word of affirmation, the antiphonal response of the altar both confirms the truth of the hymn of the angel as well as echoes the song of the overcomers that God's ways are just and true (15.3).[456] The repetition of the titles for God first seen in Rev. 1.8 continues to assign all that is happening to God on the throne.

At the pouring out of the fourth bowl, the sun is allowed to burn people with fire (16.8). The response of those being burned is in stark contrast to the response of the angel and the altar: καὶ ἐβλασφήμησαν τὸ ὄνομα τοῦ θεοῦ τοῦ ἔχοντος τὴν ἐξουσίαν ἐπὶ τὰς πληγὰς ταύτας καὶ οὐ μετενόησαν δοῦναι αὐτῷ δόξαν ('and they blasphemed the name of God, the one having authority over these plagues, and they did not repent to give him glory') (16.9). That the people blasphemed the name of God would remind the hearers both of the blasphemy of the ones calling themselves Jews but who are declared by Jesus to be a synagogue of Satan (2.9) and of the beast from the sea who blasphemes God's name (13.6). In blaspheming God's name, the people show their allegiance to Satan; thus, the hearers are not surprised that they did not repent or give glory to God. Reminiscent of Rev. 6.17 is that the people *know* that what is happening is from God. Instead of declaring the justness of God in concert with the overcomers (15.3), the angel of the waters (16.5-6) and the altar (16.7), they curse

---

[453] So Pattemore, *The People of God in the Apocalypse*, p. 100; Beale, *The Book of Revelation*, p. 820; Murphy, *Fallen is Babylon*, p. 339.

[454] Aune, *Revelation 6–16*, p. 888, argues that τοῦ θυσιαστηρίου is a partitive genitive, 'someone from the altar'.

[455] Prigent, *Commentary on the Apocalypse of St. John*, p. 467.

[456] Smalley, *The Revelation to John*, p. 404.

God.[457] This continues to provide urgency to Jesus' calls for repentance in the prophetic messages. Refusal to do so reveals one's allegiance and brings about the wrath of God and the Lamb.

The fifth bowl is poured out ἐπὶ τὸν θρόνον τοῦ θηρίου ('upon the throne of the beast') resulting in his kingdom becoming dark and people gnawing their tongues in pain (16.10). The hearers would recall that the Dragon gave his throne, identified in 2.13, to the beast (13.2). Now the One on the throne pours out judgment upon Satan's throne, plunging his kingdom into darkness. His followers do not bow to the One on the throne; instead ἐβλασφήμησαν τὸν θεὸν τοῦ οὐρανοῦ ἐκ τῶν πόνων καὶ ἐκ τῶν ἑλκῶν αὐτῶν καὶ οὐ μετενόησαν ἐκ τῶν ἔργων αὐτῶν ('they blasphemed the God of heaven because of their pain and because of their sores and they did not repent from their works') (16.11). As in the previous scene, the followers of the beast know that God – the God of heaven – is at work against them, yet they continue to blaspheme and refuse to repent of their works.

The sixth bowl is poured out on the great Euphrates River which dries up in preparation for the kings from the east (16.12). John sees three evil spirits like frogs come out of the mouth of the Dragon, the beast, and the second beast (here called the 'false prophet' for the first time). While the beast's kingdom may be plunged into darkness, satanic activity continues as these demonic spirits perform signs which are designed to gather the kings of the whole world for a war on the great day of God Almighty (16.13-14).[458]

While the hearers brace for the final bowl, they hear instead the words of Jesus: Ἰδοὺ ἔρχομαι ὡς κλέπτης. μακάριος ὁ γρηγορῶν καὶ τηρῶν τὰ ἱμάτια αὐτοῦ, ἵνα μὴ γυμνὸς περιπατῇ καὶ βλέπωσιν τὴν ἀσχημοσύνην αὐτοῦ ('Behold I am coming like a thief. Blessed is the one watching and keeping his or her garments, in order to not walk around naked exposing his or her shame') (16.15). This interruption in the description of Satan's

---

[457] Beasley-Murray, *Revelation*, p. 243, 'The mark of the beast on their bodies has penetrated their souls, instilling in them the hostility towards God and his holiness which is characteristic of the beast himself'.

[458] Aside from Jesus' statement that he will war with the sword of his mouth against those in Pergamum who do not repent, the language of war to this point in the Apocalypse has been associated with Satan (11.7; 12.17; 13.7). See Klassen, 'Vengeance in the Apocalypse of John', p. 306.

battle plan, which continues in the next verse, is significant for Jesus has not *spoken* since the prophetic messages to the churches.[459] Jesus' opening words, in fact, are familiar from the prophetic messages, where Jesus indicates that he will come like a thief if they do not keep watch (3.3). Thus, while Satan and his horde are busy preparing to wage war, Jesus declares he is coming.[460] Jesus pronounces a blessing on all who are watching and keeping their garments on so that they will not walk around naked and ashamed. This blessing picks up on the opening blessing of the prologue (1.3). The blessing echoes language from Jesus' message to the Sardis church to keep watch (3.4) and from his message to the Laodicean church to buy garments from him so that the shame of their nakedness is removed (3.18). Jesus' words here call the churches to spiritual alertness and discernment in light of the events around them so that they do not experience the 'fate of the godless'.[461] Foremost in their minds must be the coming of Jesus. Jesus' admonition is urgent, for the churches themselves have 'agents' of the beasts in their midst (2.14, 20)![462] As with the prophetic messages, this present word of Jesus is experienced by the churches in their worship through the activity of the Spirit.

As the last bowl is poured out, a voice out of the temple from the throne speaks: Γέγονεν ('It is done') (16.17). With the utterance of this verb, a sense of finality settles over the narrative. Johannine hearers might recall something similar (albeit a different verb) in Jesus' cry from the cross (Jn 19.30), and given the Apocalypse's understanding of the implications of the Lamb's work on the cross, the hearers would not be wrong in connecting the judgments of the bowls – the overcoming of evil – with the cross.[463] A number of events take place which point to the finality of God's wrath: the theophanic elements appear here for the last time, coupled with a great earthquake that splits the great city into three parts; God

---

[459] Sweet, *Revelation*, p. 249: 'The Christ of the letters breaks in here in case the churches should miss it'.

[460] Boxall, *The Revelation of St. John*, p. 234: 'A state of readiness, of active perseverance and faithful witness, is what continues to be required'.

[461] Beasley-Murray, *Revelation*, p. 245.

[462] Smalley, *The Revelation to John*, p. 411.

[463] Rotz, *Revelation*, p. 243.

remembers Babylon the great and gives her the cup of his wrath to drink; all the islands flee and the mountains are not found; and, last-ly, great hail falls from heaven upon humanity (17.18-21). John rec-ords the response of the inhabitants of the earth to this final bowl: καὶ ἐβλασφήμησαν οἱ ἄνθρωποι τὸν θεὸν ἐκ τῆς πληγῆς τῆς χαλάζης, ὅτι μεγάλη ἐστὶν ἡ πληγὴ αὐτῆς σφόδρα ('and the people blasphemed God because of the plague of hail, because so great is the plague') (16.21). For the third time John records the blasphemy of humanity against God. Their proclivity to blasphemy reveals the depth of their spiritual commitment to the Dragon and the beasts. The inhabitants of the earth know that the plagues are from God (as in 6.17; 16.9, 11), thus their blasphemy is willful and indicative of their obdurate nature. This chapter continues to un-derscore the idea that one's response to the actions of God reveals one's allegiance. The followers of the Lamb respond with worship and an acknowledgement of the justice and holiness of God; the followers of the Dragon respond, like the beast, with blasphemous words against God.

Summary of Revelation 15–16

While the hearers think that Revelation 15 is going to narrate the final judgment cycle, they are instead treated to another worship scene. The great and marvelous sign *is* the portrayal of the over-comers who have gained victory over the beast through the blood of the Lamb and the word of their testimony. This scene, with its background in Exodus 15, dwarfs the worship scene of Revelation 13.4 which likewise parodies Exodus 15. God and the Lamb are extolled in a great hymn of praise by the overcomers. In addition to extolling God as the Lord God Almighty and King of the nations, the hymn anticipates both the further activity of God (the bowls of wrath) and the future activity of the nations who will gather and worship God because of his righteous actions. In the unfolding of Revelation 16, in which the bowls of judgment are poured out, God's just and righteous judgments are affirmed in the antiphonal hymns sung by the angel of the waters and the altar (16.5-7). The three hymns of Revelation 15–16 affirm the hearers in their unwa-vering worship of God and the Lamb in the on-going face of suf-fering. The demonic battle plans chronicled in the description of the sixth bowl suggest an intensification of evil. The hearers must discern their surroundings and continue in their worship of God and the Lamb. As with all the hymns to this point, these three hymns continue to inform their theological understanding of God and God's ways in the world. The hearers thus worship in anticipation of what is to come, knowing that God is at work in the world. This stands in stark contrast to the response of the inhabitants of the world to the bowl judgments. They continue to blaspheme God, refuse to repent, and refuse to bring God glory. The judgments on the followers of the Dragon indicate how essential it is for the churches to heed Jesus' call for repentance.

The reappearance of the altar in 16.7 is a reminder to the hearers of the importance of prayer as a liturgical activity. Since the altar is connected to the souls under the altar and their plea for justice, the 'voice' of the altar serves to alert the hearers that their prayers are being answered in God's righteous judgments.

The final element that pertains to worship is the fact that Jesus speaks to the hearers (16.15). Jesus' words, with their close association to his words spoken in Revelation 2–3, continue to reveal the intimate connection between Jesus and his churches. Jesus indeed is in their midst speaking to them, revealing to them the things to come, and reminding them of his soon coming. As in the earlier messages, this message is to be experienced as a word delivered by the Spirit who speaks the words of Jesus to the worshipping communities. As in the earlier prophetic messages, the hearers are exhorted to watchfulness and spiritual discernment in light of the escalation of events around them. Prophetic words are a vital activity of worship. It is not insignificant that Jesus' words come on the heels of the description relating the activities of the Dragon and his beasts nor that the second beast is called the false prophet (16.13). Prophetic words must be discerned. This provides further impetus for the hearers to disassociate with the false *prophetess* 'Jezebel' (2.20). Her judgment is intimately linked with those who follow after the beast. The church must engage in prophetic witness to the nations and call them to repentance. God's desire is that the nations be converted, not destroyed. The church must share this desire and spend itself in behalf of the world, for Jesus *is* coming.

IV. ἐν πνεύματι – 'In the Wilderness: Babylon' (17.1–21.8)

The third ἐν πνεύματι ('in the Spirit') segment moves John from heaven to the desert. From this new setting, John and his hearers experience the judgment on Babylon, the great harlot (Revelation 17–18), the great celebration in heaven that ensues (19.1-10), the appearance of the rider on the white horse (19.11-16), the thousand year reign of Christ and the defeat of Satan (20.1-10), the great white throne judgment (20.11-15), and the new heaven and earth (21.1-8). As in 1.9 and 4.1, John is said to be ἐν πνεύματι. Since at no point in the narrative is John said to be *out of* the Spirit, this notification provides continuity in the narrative by emphasizing the role of the Spirit in all that John is seeing. Likewise, the churches receive and discern John's vision in the Spirit as they are gathered together for worship.

A. Revelation 17–18

Several elements emerge in Revelation 17–18 that are of relevance for this study. First, the great prostitute, also identified as the great city, Babylon in 17.5,[464] is closely affiliated with false worship. When John is taken ἐν πνεύματι ('in the Spirit') to see the judgment of the great harlot, she is in the desert[465] riding the beast from the sea (13.1-8). Her association with the beast, and thus the Dragon, is

---

[464] While 'Babylon' is typically viewed as a code word for Rome, the narrative seems to resist such a definitive identification. In Revelation 11, the *great city* is the place where Jesus was crucified and where the two witnesses were put to death (vv. 8-9). In Revelation 16 it is the city split into three parts as a result of the pouring out of the seventh bowl (v. 19). Even though the great city is here called Babylon, a dogmatic identification does not seem to be John's point. Barr, *Tales of the End*, p. 109: 'But we should not get trapped in the false question of whether the great city is Rome or Jerusalem; in fact it is crucial to John's purpose that the image elide from one to the other'. As in the narrative of the two witnesses, any place that sets itself up in opposition to God is the great city, is Babylon. For a powerful critique of South Africa's former oppressive regime as Babylon, see Boesak, *Comfort and Protest* (especially ch. 6).

[465] It is striking that the harlot is in the desert – the same environment as the woman clothed with the sun in Revelation 12. Trafton, *Reading Revelation*, p. 155, suggests that this desert is distinct from the desert where the woman of chapter 12 is located because John eliminates the definite article in 17.3 (*a* desert). One wonders if John's hearers would make so nuanced a distinction, so Barr, *Tales of the End*, p. 133, who maintains that the harlot is a foil to the woman clothed with the sun.

clear. The hearers know that it is *this beast's* image that the world is forced to worship; thus, the great prostitute aligns herself with the worship of the beast. She also shares a striking similarity to 'Jezebel' (2.20-23) in that both women lure their followers into sexual immorality.[466] The great harlot holds a golden cup full of detestable things and the uncleanness of her adulteries (17.4). It is this cup which holds the wine on which the inhabitants of the earth have made themselves drunk (17.2). Perhaps the hearers would see her cup of filth as a parody and mockery of the churches' cup of the Eucharist.[467] The recollection that 'Jezebel' was given time to repent but refused would likely cause the hearers to see that her judgment is linked with the judgment on Babylon now at hand. Such a connection would underscore the need for discernment within the churches to recognize their own surroundings *and* their own identity. The harlot is marked upon her forehead with a label that names her as the mother of all prostitutes and of the abominations of the earth (17.5). The martyrs are marked on their foreheads with the name of God and the Lamb (14.1). Babylon is drunk on the blood of the saints and the blood of the witnesses of Jesus (17.6). Since the hearers know that those who refuse to worship the beast are killed (13.15), the implication is that it is *their* blood in her cup. In this way, Babylon is intimately connected with their deaths. Her drunkenness reveals her unquenchable blood-lust as well as her complete approval of their deaths at the hands of the beast. It is for her participation in the death of the saints that she is ultimately destroyed, as will be revealed in 18.24. God has given Babylon time to repent – the calls for repentance have rung out throughout the narrative – yet she, like 'Jezebel' and the inhabitants of the earth, has refused.

The second thing of relevance is John's reaction to Babylon: Καὶ ἐθαύμασα ἰδὼν αὐτὴν θαῦμα μέγα ('And after seeing her I marveled a great marvel') (17.6). The hearers would likely be shocked to discover John's response of wonderment. The verb θαυμάζω was

___

[466] That the great harlot is called ἡ μήτηρ τῶν πορνῶν ('the mother of all prostitutes') suggests that Jezebel, because of her activities, should be viewed as her daughter.

[467] So D. Campbell, 'Antithetical Feminine-Urban Imagery and a Tale of Two Women-Cities in Book of Revelation', *Tyndale Bulletin* 55.1 (2004), p. 100. Rotz, *Revelation*, p. 251, sees it as a 'tragic contrast to "the prayers of the saints" that fill the heavenly "golden bowls" (5:8)'.

used in 13.3 to express the wonderment of the whole world when the wounded head of the beast is healed. This sense of awe and wonder leads the world to worship the Dragon and the beast (13.4). Could it be that John is so awe-struck by Babylon that he is tempted to worship her? Despite her atrocities, which John catalogues in his description of her, he nevertheless is overwhelmed in her presence. The angel's question (Διὰ τί ἐθαύμασας, 'Why do you marvel?') is both a rebuke to John and a warning to the hearers. 'If John, who is "in the Spirit" at the time, could be so tempted, could anyone be immune from such seduction'?[468] John's response to Babylon reveals the deceptive and subtle nature of evil that has the power to capture both the great (the kings of the earth) and the small (the inhabitants of the world) (17.2). The hearers must discern evil for what it is so that they are not seduced into false worship.

The third element of significance is the way in which Babylon's destruction is heralded in Revelation 18. The description of Babylon's fall is presented as a funeral oration[469] in which Babylon's many sins – oppression, arrogance, excess – are catalogued. Given the heavy concentration of hymnic language throughout the Apocalypse, it is entirely possible that the hearers would *hear* all of chapter 18 as hymnic. At the very least, there are three tightly structured laments offered over Babylon that are embedded in the heavenly announcements of judgment against her. The laments give voice to the sorrow over Babylon's destruction as expressed by the kings of the earth, the merchants, and the seafarers (18.9-19). Each lament begins in identical fashion (Οὐαὶ, οὐαί, ἡ πόλις ἡ μεγάλη, 'Woe, woe the great city'), identifies Babylon either directly or indirectly by appealing to prior descriptions provided in the text, and ends with a statement that Babylon's destruction happens μιᾷ ὥρᾳ ('in one hour') (18.10, 16-17, 19). This careful structure suggests that the laments function almost like a chorus, repeating Babylon's doom. If these are hymnic laments, perhaps parodies of biblical lamentation,[470] they represent false worship being offered to Babylon even while Babylon is being destroyed. The hearers, however, must not

---

[468] Thomas, *The Apocalypse*, p. 502.

[469] So Campbell, 'Antithetical Feminine-Urban Imagery', p. 92.

[470] Beasley-Murray, *Revelation*, p. 262.

share the perspective of the mourners, for they have been called to come out of Babylon (18.4). They are not to be economically or religiously entangled with her.[471] Discernment is called for in order that the churches not be enticed by the seductive trappings of evil. Babylon is *less* a physical location, although it could be, and *more* a spiritual reality: choosing to *live* in Babylon means participating in her sins and receiving her plagues!

The fourth element relates to the role of music. After the last lament, John hears a call for heaven along with the saints, apostles, and prophets to rejoice (and *not* lament!) over Babylon and her destruction (18.20). This call leads to John witnessing her symbolic destruction as a mighty angel throws a millstone into the sea and announce a series of things never (οὐ μή) to be found in Babylon again (18.21-23). Among the five things never again to be found is the music of harpists, musicians, flute players, and trumpeters (18.22). Music has played a prominent role in the Apocalypse: the heavens resound with the hymns of various singers, the heavenly elders and martyrs have harps, and the trumpet has sounded in the second judgment series. With the exception of the trumpet blasts, music (instrumental and vocal) is connected to the worship of God and the Lamb. Music is a central activity of worship both in heaven and, presumably, in John's churches. The hearers also have learned that there is competing music. However reticent he might have been to do so, John has also recorded the *music* of false worship – the song sung to the beast (13.4) and (possibly) the laments sung to Babylon (18.10, 16-17, 19). Babylon is clearly connected to the Dragon and his beasts; it is the false worship given to them that more than any other factor clearly distinguishes the followers of God and the Lamb from the followers of the Dragon. The cessation of Babylon's music attests to the surety of God's judgment on false worship and false worshippers.[472]

B. Revelation 19.1-10

Revelation 19.1-10 is the final extended heavenly worship scene in the Apocalypse. It is the longest and most complex of the worship scenes and contains the most hymnic material; thus it functions as a

---

[471] Bauckham, *The Climax of Prophecy*, pp. 376-78

[472] Wall, *Revelation*, p. 218, 'The stilling of the creative arts tells of God's absence'.

climax to all the heavenly worship scenes. The dirge and laments of
Revelation 18 give way (Μετὰ ταῦτα) to the joyous celebration of
Revelation 19.[473] If the sound of music is no longer to be found in
Babylon (18.22a), heaven resounds with it!

John hears as a great voice ὄχλου πολλοῦ ἐν τῷ οὐρανῷ ('a
great crowd in heaven') (19.1). The hearers would likely connect
this great multitude to the great multitude in Revelation 7 since they
are described in identical terms. The great multitude, like a choir,
begins the heavenly celebration called for by the angel in 18.20[474]
with a hymn of praise:

Ἀλληλουϊά·
ἡ σωτηρία καὶ ἡ δόξα καὶ ἡ δύναμις τοῦ θεοῦ ἡμῶν,
ὅτι ἀληθιναὶ καὶ δίκαιαι αἱ κρίσεις αὐτοῦ·
ὅτι ἔκρινεν τὴν πόρνην τὴν μεγάλην
ἥτις ἔφθειρεν τὴν γῆν ἐν τῇ πορνείᾳ αὐτῆς,
καὶ ἐξεδίκησεν τὸ αἷμα τῶν δούλων αὐτοῦ
ἐκ χειρὸς αὐτῆς

Hallelujah!
Salvation and glory and power to our God,
for true and just are his judgments;
for he judged the great prostitute
who corrupted the earth with her fornication,
and he has avenged the blood of his servants
from her hand (19.1-2).

This hymn of victory[475] introduces for the first time the exclamation
Ἀλληλουϊά ('Hallelujah').[476] This word evokes the great Hallel
psalms of the Old Testament (Psalms 113–118) and is used
throughout the Psalms as an expression of praise.[477] Its appearance
here in Revelation suggests an unbroken link in the language of
worship from God's people both past and present. Its usage

---

[473] Bauckham, *The Climax of Prophecy*, p. 340 argues that 19.1-8 is needed to complete the depiction of the fall of Babylon.

[474] Beasley-Murray, *Revelation*, p. 270; Ruiz, 'The Politics of Praise', p. 382.

[475] Thompson, *The Book of Revelation*, p. 62.

[476] This is the first occurrence of 'Alleluia' in Christian literature. D.E. Aune, *Revelation 17–22* (WBC 52c; Nashville: Thomas Nelson, 1988), p. 1024.

[477] Psalms 106.1; 135.1, 3, 21; 146.1, 10; 147.1, 20; 148.1, 14; 149.1, 9; 150.1, 6.

denotes a 'sharp contrast in tone and mood' from Revelation 18.[478] That this acclamation of praise is placed here alerts the hearers to the extraordinary significance of Babylon's destruction. If 'praise YHWH' is the response of heaven then it behooves the hearers to discern the spiritual implications of Babylon's (symbolic) destruction. Although the narrative presents Babylon's demise as a fact that is celebrated by the great multitude, it is still a *future* event for John's hearers. The heavenly liturgy beckons them to experience the destruction of Babylon proleptically and to discern it pneumatically. It is the power of liturgy that enables the worshippers to celebrate the certainty of her demise in the present.[479] Such celebration reminds them of their true identity as followers of the Lamb, as partakers in the heavenly liturgy even *now*, and as those who have ears to hear what the Spirit is saying to the churches.

The ascriptions to God of salvation, glory, and power are familiar to the hearers from previous worship scenes. Here *the* salvation, glory and power of God are lauded because God's judgments are true and just. This third occurrence of salvation (see 7.10; 12.10) conveys finality, 'focusing upon salvation in its most comprehensive, eschatological sense'.[480] Glory is ascribed to God and the Lamb throughout the narrative (4.11; 5.12, 13; 7.12). Indeed, the narrative instructs that giving glory to God is the proper response to God (11.13; 14.7; 15.4) which makes any refusal to do so (as in 16.9) all the more striking. The third ascription, power, is likewise associated with God and the Lamb (4.11; 5.12; 7.12; 11.17; 12.10), but also with the Dragon and his beasts (Revelation 13), the kings of the earth (17.13), and Babylon (18.3). That Babylon is no more conveys the transitory and fleeting nature of their power in comparison to God's eternal power. The declaration of God's judgments as

---

[478] Thomas, *The Apocalypse*, p. 553.

[479] Filho, 'The Apocalypse of John as a Visionary Experience', p. 233, sees Rev. 19.1-8 as the point where present and future meet. The use of liturgical language invites the hearers to keep the prospect of Babylon's judgment in their memory. 'The Babylon of those days had not yet fallen, but the perspective of memory presented through liturgy would help to establish the theological certainty that it would fall ... It is precisely the liturgical dimension of 19.1-8 that make it possible to speak of these eschatological events as if they had already happened ...'

[480] Thomas, *The Apocalypse*, p. 553.

true and just echoes the earlier proclamation of the altar (16.7). The second explanatory ὅτι ('for') points to God's action *against* Babylon: She is judged for corrupting or ruining the *earth* with her harlotry and *for* the blood of the saints who are avenged for their death by her hand. The hearers would certainly recognize the verb ἐξεδίκησεν ('he avenged') from its earlier occurrence in 6.10; the appeal of the souls under the altar is *finally* answered. They suffered under the hand of Babylon; Babylon is destroyed by the hand of God. Can the themes of vengeance and retribution be lyrics for worship to be sung by the people of God? Indeed, for it is God who takes vengeance and his ways are just, as has been consistently presented throughout the hymns of the Apocalypse. Such a motif also must spur the prophetic witness of the churches to the *Babylon* around them. The judgment on Babylon is only for those who choose to remain in her; those who choose to repent and become followers of the Lamb will not share in her fate. The cry of the angel in 18.4 – 'Come out of her my people' – is also to be the churches' cry to the world around them.

This opening hymn is immediately followed by a second short hymnic burst:

Ἁλληλουϊά·
καὶ ὁ καπνὸς αὐτῆς ἀναβαίνει εἰς τοὺς αἰῶνας τῶν αἰώνων

Hallelujah!
And the smoke from her rises up forever and ever (19.3).

This second hymn functions as an antiphonal response to the first hymn – a pattern seen throughout the worship scenes. The repetition of Ἁλληλουϊά ('Hallelujah') continues to reinforce the extraordinary impact of the destruction of Babylon from heaven's perspective. The song declares that her smoke ascends forever and ever, thus affirming the words of the angel in 14.11. The imagery of smoke also serves as a graphic contrast to the smoke of the incense – the prayers of the saints – which go up before God (5.8; 8.4). That Babylon's smoke rises forever suggests that the prayers of

God's people are now answered. The eternity formula affirms the decisive and total victory of God over Babylon.[481]

Following this hymn, the 24 elders and the four living creatures ἔπεσαν καὶ προσεκύνησαν τῷ θεῷ τῷ καθημένῳ ἐπὶ τῷ θρόνῳ λέγοντες, 'Αμὴν 'Αλληλουϊά ('fell and worshipped God, the one sitting on the throne, saying, 'Amen Hallelujah') (19.4). It is not without significance that the hearers are once again reminded that God is the one sitting on the throne or that the elders and living creatures are giving their worship to God. More than merely recapturing earlier imagery, this serves to underscore the supremacy of God whose decisive victory over evil took place in the death and resurrection of the Lamb.[482] It also reinforces, particularly after the depictions of false worship in Revelation 13–18, that God alone is to be worshipped. Although the elders heard the song of the redeemed in 14.1-4, they, along with the living creatures, have been silent since the song of the elders in 11.15-18. With their final liturgical ἀμὴν ('amen') the elders and living creatures give their approval to the hymns of worship being sung[483] and add their own 'Αλληλουϊά ('Hallelujah') in praise of God. By falling down and worshipping God, the elders and living creatures continue to model prostration as a fitting liturgical response (4.9-10; 5.14; 7.11; 11.16). The liturgical actions of the elders and living creatures bracket the narratives of Revelation 6–18, framing all the events taking place within them in worship. The 'Amen, Hallelujah' in 19.4 functions as a benediction for *all* that has taken place in the Apocalypse. The hearers, who have likely looked to the elders and living creatures as models for their own worship, are invited to join them in exclaiming 'Αλληλουϊά.[484]

The exclamation of the elders and living creatures is followed by a voice from the throne who issues a call to worship:

---

[481] Wall, *Revelation*, p. 221, in noting the irony between the smoke of Babylon's demise and the incense of heavenly worship in 8.3-4 writes, 'Such is the dynamic of worship and praise. The reality of God's reign, which centers all Christian devotion, forms a dialectic between God's judgment of evil and the triumph of good through Christ.'

[482] Wall, *Revelation*, p. 221.

[483] Harris, *The Literary Function of the Hymns in the Apocalypse of John*, p. 195.

[484] Thomas, *The Apocalypse*, p. 559.

Αἰνεῖτε τῷ θεῷ ἡμῶν
πάντες οἱ δοῦλοι αὐτοῦ
[καί] οἱ φοβούμενοι αὐτόν,
οἱ μικροὶ καὶ οἱ μεγάλοι

Praise our God
all his servants
and those fearing him,
both small and great (19.5).

The call to worship is an exhortation in hymnic style which flows immediately from the 'dual benediction' of the elders and creatures.[485] While the voice is unidentified, 'the phrase "from the throne" at the very least indicates the divine authorization of the speaker'.[486] The voice calls for *praise* to be given to God. Despite its lone appearance here, the verb αἰνέω ('praise') is often used in Scripture to connote joyful praise that finds expression in doxologies, hymns or prayers.[487] The exhortation to 'praise our God' extends beyond the heavens; that is, *all* of God's servants and those who fear Him are to join in the anthems of praise in celebration of God's judgment against evil. 'Servants of God' has been a term used of the people of God (1.1; 11.18), and especially the martyrs (7.3; 19.2). The phrase 'those who fear God' picks up language from the angelic proclamation to all the world in 14.7, suggesting that indeed some have heeded the angel's words (and the prophetic witness of the church) and joined with the people of God.[488] The final descriptor – both small and great – is a comprehensive term reminiscent of Rev. 11.18 ('God will give rewards to the small and the great'). All who make up the people of God are invited to worship and praise God. Such an admonition – calling *every* person to worship God – would likely function as a prophetic challenge to John's hearers.[489]

After the exhortation to worship, John hears the voice of a great multitude sounding like φωνὴν ὑδάτων πολλῶν καὶ ὡς φωνὴν

---

[485] So Thompson, *The Book of Revelation*, p. 62.

[486] Aune, *Revelation 17–22*, p. 1027.

[487] H. Schlier, 'αἰνέω, αἶνος', *TDNT*, I, pp. 177-78.

[488] Thomas, *The Apocalypse*, pp. 559-60; Schüssler Fiorenza, *Revelation*, p. 102.

[489] Ruiz, 'The Politics of Praise', p. 376.

βροντῶν ἰσχυρῶν ('the sound of many waters and like the sound of strong thunders') (19.6). The dual imagery of rushing waters and ear-splitting thunder conveys the loudness of the final heavenly anthem that bursts forth:

Ἀλληλουϊά,
ὅτι ἐβασίλευσεν κύριος
ὁ θεὸς [ἡμῶν] ὁ παντοκράτωρ.
χαίρωμεν καὶ ἀγαλλιῶμεν
καὶ δώσωμεν τὴν δόξαν αὐτῷ,
ὅτι ἦλθεν ὁ γάμος τοῦ ἀρνίου
καὶ ἡ γυνὴ αὐτοῦ ἡτοίμασεν ἑαυτὴν
καὶ ἐδόθη αὐτῇ ἵνα περιβάληται
βύσσινον λαμπρὸν καθαρόν·
τὸ γὰρ βύσσινον τὰ δικαιώματα τῶν ἁγίων ἐστίν

Hallelujah!
For the Lord our God the Almighty reigns.
Let us rejoice and exult
and give glory to him,
for the wedding of the Lamb has come
and his bride has prepared herself
and she was given fine linen, bright and clean, to clothe herself
for the fine linen is the righteous deeds of the saints (19.6-9).

In response to the call for praise, John, for the fourth time, hears Ἀλληλουϊά ('Hallelujah'). It is as if no other word captures the essence of worship for what God has done for His people.[490] The Hallelujah resounds because God reigns – the Lord God Almighty reigns! This is the sixth appearance of the title 'Lord God Almighty' (1.8; 4.8; 11.17; 15.3; 16.7). The declaration that God reigns is reminiscent of Rev. 11.15 where God and Christ reign forever and ever. In between these two declarations about the reign of God, the hearers have traversed through the harrowing narratives of the Dragon, beasts, and Babylon. On the other side of those stories – and especially the destruction of Babylon – this announcement of the reign of the Almighty God is imbued with a fuller understanding of what the reign of God truly means. By means of three hortatory subjunctive verbs, the hearers are invited to rejoice, exult, and

---

[490] Osborne, *Revelation*, p. 666; Mangina, *Revelation*, pp. 217-18.

give glory to God. The first verb has been used to this point in Rev. 11.10 as the world rejoiced at the death of the witnesses.[491] Now the hearers rejoice and exult in God's activity! The third verb has appeared in contexts indicating that those who give glory to God are aligned with God (4.9; 11.13; 14.7). The verbs are not simply casting a backward glance or limiting the enthusiastic celebration to the destruction of Babylon, for by means of the ὅτι ('for'), the hearers are given another reason to rejoice, exult, and give glory to God; namely, the wedding of the Lamb has come and his bride has prepared herself!

Nothing in the Apocalypse prepares the hearers for the 'marvelously mixed metaphor' of the wedding between the Lamb and his bride.[492] The contrast with the great prostitute could not be more apparent for the hearers. The great harlot and the bride are clearly distinguished by their alliances: the former with the Dragon; the latter with the Lamb.[493] The bride has prepared *herself* for this event. In light of all that has come before in the Apocalypse, the hearers would likely see themselves as the bride, the beloved of the Lamb (1.5). Their preparation is bound up in their worship of and identity with God and the Lamb. Refusal to worship the beast, for which they will likely give their lives, will result in eternal unity with the Lamb. The bride is adorned in fine linen that is further described as bright and clean (19.8). While fine linen is one of the wares of Babylon (18.12), the wedding garment of the bride is the *finest* of the garments given to the saints in the Apocalypse.[494] The final line of the hymn discloses the symbolism of the linen – the righteous acts of the saints. Of Babylon, it was noted that God remembered her ἀδικήματα ('unrighteousness') (18.5) and for such she is destroyed; here, it is the δικαιώματα ('righteous deeds') of God's people that unites them with the Lamb. It is by her righteous acts, that the bride

---

[491] The verb is found throughout the Fourth Gospel (Jn 3.29; 4.36; 8.56; 11.15; 14.28; 16.22; 20.20).

[492] Trafton, *Reading Revelation*, p. 174.

[493] Gonzáles and Gonzáles, *Revelation*, p. 126.

[494] Harris, *The Literary Function of the Hymns in the Apocalypse of John*, p. 196, sees the use of the aorist passive ἐδόθη as asserting that God is 'behind the acts of martyrdom, in some way controlling them'; however the narrative suggests that the saints become martyrs because of the actions of the beast and Babylon.

has prepared *herself.* To this point in the Apocalypse, the Greek verb ἡτοίμασεν ('prepared') has occurred in a number of contexts which assume the 'direct activity and intervention of God' (8.6; 9.7, 15; 12.6; 16.12). These prior contexts suggest that the preparation is a 'co-operative, if not reciprocal activity between the bride of the Lamb and God'.[495] Salvation is a reciprocal activity – cooperation between the human and the divine. God is righteous (16.5), God's ways are righteous (15.3), and God works righteously on behalf of His people (15.4). Because of the work of the Lamb (1.5-6; 5.9-10), the saints are righteous and are to act righteously on behalf of God. The actions of the churches 'reflect the God who has given them salvation'.[496] By means of the symbolism of the wedding, the churches are given a glimpse into what awaits the faithful followers of the Lamb; that is, the imagery presents for the hearers the eschatological reward for fidelity to God and the Lamb.[497] In worship the churches sing of their Beloved, the Bridegroom, who not only walks in their midst but also is preparing for a glorious wedding for them.

This final hymn is followed by the fourth blessing in the Apocalypse which John is instructed to write: Μακάριοι οἱ εἰς τὸ δεῖπνον τοῦ γάμου τοῦ ἀρνίου κεκλημένοι ('Blessed are the ones hving been called to the wedding supper of the Lamb') (19.9). The blessing is bestowed upon those who have been called to the marriage supper of the Lamb. Those who have been called are all those who are faithful followers of the Lamb (17.14). The use of the perfect passive participle indicates that the call, the invitation to the

---

[495] Thomas, *The Apocalypse*, p. 564; Sweet, *Revelation*, p. 279; Beasley-Murray, *The Book of Revelation*, p. 271; Prigent, *Commentary on the Apocalypse of St. John*, p. 526, 'There is no doubt about the author's intention to underline expressly the active responsibility of Christians in this preparation'.

[496] Thomas, *The Apocalypse*, pp. 566-67. Ruiz, 'The Politics of Praise', p. 384, suggests that John's hearers were to participate in the 'choruses of heavenly praise' … 'not simply by singing alone, not through cultic activity, but by their righteous conduct. This identification of the bride's fine linen as the righteous deeds of the saints is a crucial statement about how God's servants in the seven churches of Asia were to carry out the exhortation to accompany the heavenly chorus.'

[497] F. Macchia, 'The Covenant of the Lamb's Bride: A Subversive Paradigm', *The Living Pulpit* (July-Sept 2005), p. 15.

supper, is still open to them.[498] God will reward those who are faithful! That for which the bride has prepared herself for *will* come to pass. This imagery of a supper, like the similar imagery in the prophetic messages (2.8, 17; 3.20), could have eucharistic overtones for the hearers; that is, the wedding supper represents the culmination of the Eucharist meal. The beatitude challenges the hearers to discern 'their condition and their conduct in the light of the worldview that 19:1-8 celebrates'.[499]

The one speaking to John joins to the beatitude the following statement: Οὗτοι οἱ λόγοι ἀληθινοὶ τοῦ θεοῦ εἰσιν ('These are the true words of God') (19.9b). If these words apply to the announcement of the wedding banquet, then they provide absolute certainty that the banquet, a yet future event, will come. John recounts his response to these words: καὶ ἔπεσα ἔμπροσθεν τῶν ποδῶν αὐτοῦ προσκυνῆσαι αὐτῷ ('and I fell before his feet to worship him'). For this response, John is immediately rebuked by the speaker: Ὅρα μή ('do not do it') (19.10). As in Revelation 10, John moves from narrator to participant; albeit, here John's participation is misguided. The hearers would recall how John falls before the risen Jesus (1.17), and the elders and living creatures fall before God and the Lamb – all without rebuke. That John *is* rebuked here gives clear indication as to the inappropriateness of his actions. Perhaps John assumed the speaker to be divine because of his words.[500] If so, John is clearly wrong. In fact, the speaker identifies himself as a fellow servant (σύνδουλός) of John and of all who hold to the testimony of Jesus. The speaker thus connects himself with John and with the churches, and he offers correction: τῷ θεῷ προσκύνησον ('worship God'). John's attempt to worship the messenger is a warning to the churches that the worship of *anything* or *anyone* other than God and the Lamb constitutes idolatry and is false worship.[501] The speaker continues: ἡ γὰρ μαρτυρία Ἰησοῦ ἐστιν

---

[498] Thomas, *The Apocalypse*, p. 568.

[499] Ruiz, 'The Politics of Praise', p. 387.

[500] Thomas, *The Apocalypse*, pp. 570-71, suggests that the speaker might be one of the souls under the altar since the language of 'fellow servants' occurs here and in 6.11. If so, the speaker is an heir to the promises given to the overcomers (Revelation 2–3) and perhaps is viewed in John's mind as worthy of worship, 'for he would be thought to share extensively in Jesus' identity'.

[501] Ruiz, 'The Politics of Praise', p. 388. See also Thompson, 'Worship in the Book of Revelation', p. 51.

τὸ πνεῦμα τῆς προφητείας ('for the testimony of Jesus is the S/spirit of prophecy'). The question arises as to whether Ἰησοῦ is a subjective or objective genitive. Is it Jesus' testimony or the testimony about Jesus that is the S/spirit of prophecy? Perhaps such a distinction is unnecessary as it creates too much of a chasm between what Jesus says and what Jesus' followers say about him, for in the Apocalypse the followers of the Lamb bear witness to Jesus, the Faithful Witness.[502] The testimony of Jesus is also linked to the S/spirit of prophecy. The hearers would likely associate τὸ πνεῦμα ('the spirit') with the Holy Spirit given all the ways that the Spirit has functioned in the Apocalypse. The Spirit is before the throne of God (1.4) and is the eyes of the Lamb (5.6). The Spirit is closely linked with Jesus in the prophetic messages as the Spirit speaks the words of Jesus to the churches. The churches are inspired by the Spirit to be prophetic witnesses to Jesus, who himself bears witness to God.[503] In this final heavenly worship scene, then, the prophetic task of the church, to give Spirit-inspired witness to Jesus, is concomitant to the central imperative of Revelation: 'Worship God!'

C. Revelation 19.11–21.8

Revelation 19.11–21.8 consists of a final series of seven un-numbered events which John sees (εἶδον; 19.11-16, 17-18, 19-21; 20.1-3, 4-10, 11-15; 21.1–22.6a). The opening scene, the return of Jesus as depicted in the rider on the white horse (19.11-16), serves as the catalyst for the events which follow. Each successive event 'portrays a distinct and critical aspect of God's coming victory in Christ'.[504] These events 'wrap up' the dual story lines of Revelation as the hearers learn of the fate of Satan, the beasts, and their followers, and the destiny of the people of God.

The coming of Jesus spells the end for the beast and the false prophet. The beast gathers an army to war against the rider on the white horse (19.19). The hearers would recall the battle plans of the Dragon, the beast and the false prophet described in the pouring out of the sixth bowl (16.13-14, 16) as well as the words of Jesus – 'Behold I come like a thief' – that occur in the midst of that

---

[502] Murphy, *Fallen is Babylon*, p. 385; Thomas, *The Apocalypse*, p. 572.

[503] See Keener, *Revelation*, p. 452; Thomas, *The Apocalypse*, pp. 572-73.

[504] Wall, *Revelation*, p. 227.

description (16.15). Here in 19.11-16, Jesus does indeed come – as a mighty warrior who, with righteousness, will judge and make war![505] While the hearers brace for a physical war, none is to be had as the beast and false prophet are simply captured and thrown into the lake of fire (19.20). Their followers, the kings of the earth (19.19) are likewise destroyed, not by weapons of steel but by the sword of judgment coming out of the mouth of Jesus, and the birds gorge on their flesh (19.21). After the narrative of the thousand year reign (20.1-6), Satan, who has been removed from the *earth* and bound in the *Abyss* for the duration of the thousand years,[506] is released[507] to again gather an army of followers to go to war against God's people (20.8-9a).[508] When fire from heaven devours Satan's army, Satan is thrown into the lake of fire to join the beast and the false prophet. The aorist passive ἐβλήθη ('he was thrown') points to God's final action against Satan. It forms an inclusio with the future passive τελεσθῇ ('be completed') in 20.7, reminding the hearers that God is in control, even of Satan. In the lake of fire βασανισθήσονται ἡμέρας καὶ νυκτὸς εἰς τοὺς αἰῶνας τῶν αἰώνων ('they will be tormented day and night forever and ever') (20.10). The hearers would not miss that as worship goes on day and night forever (4.8; 5.13), so will the torment of Satan, the beast, and the false prophet.[509]

Juxtaposed with the demise of evil is the depiction of what happens to the overcomers. Those who worship the Lamb on earth and are killed by the beast because of their testimony and because of the word of God come to life and reign with Christ a thousand years (20.4-6),[510] a time concurrent with the binding of the Dragon.

---

[505] Resseguie, *The Revelation of John*, p. 237.

[506] Mangina, *Revelation*, p. 225, John's four-fold description of the Dragon forms an *inclusio* with 12.9. See also Michaels, *Revelation*, p. 221, who shows that Revelation 12 and 20 form the 'frame' of the Dragon's career.

[507] The use of the divine future passive λυθήσεται ('he will be released') points to God's activity. The hearers know from 20.3 that it is necessary (δεῖ) for Satan to be released for a short time.

[508] Rotz, *Revelation*, p. 286: 'Satan's objectives do not change during his incarceration'.

[509] J.P.M. Sweet, *Revelation*, p. 292.

[510] John records the time-span of a thousand years five times in the space of verses 1-6. In this way, the reign of Christ (and the martyrs) dwarfs any other span of time in the Apocalypse. Wall, *Revelation*, p. 236, sees that the thousand

The hearers would know that John is on Patmos for the same reason that the martyrs are killed. John states that these who will come to life and reign are the ones who did not worship the beast or his image and who did not receive his mark on their foreheads or hands. The hearers would likely think of the overcomers celebrated in 12.10 as well as the overcomers in 15.1-4 singing the song of Moses and the Lamb. It is these for whom the second death has no authority (20.6). Jesus holds the keys of death (1.18), thus his followers will not be hurt by the second death (2.11). Such words of encouragement would affirm the hearers in their resolve to remain faithful in the worship of God and the Lamb on earth even if it leads to death, for 'the reward for would-be-martyrs is a place in the millennial reign'.[511] It is in this context that the hearers experience the fifth blessing of the Apocalypse: μακάριος καὶ ἅγιος ὁ ἔχων μέρος ἐν τῇ ἀναστάσει τῇ πρώτῃ ('Blessed and holy are the ones having part in the first resurrection') (20.6). The pronouncing of a liturgical blessing upon the martyrs – those who had already given their lives, and those who will yet give their lives – not only indicates divine approval of their refusal to worship any being but God but also grounds their worship in hope. The One who was dead and now lives (Rev. 1.18) will raise to life those who die[512] for him. The addition of ἅγιος ('holy') to the beatitude anticipates the on-going worship activities for the people of God in the millennium, for they will be ἱερεῖς τοῦ θεοῦ καὶ τοῦ Χριστοῦ ('priests of God and of Christ') (20.6). The hearers already know this to be a crucial role for the people of God made possible by the work of the Lamb (Rev. 1.6; 5.10). Once again there is a convergence between the present and the future; that is, the hearers are to see their present identification as priests – those who worship and minister

---

years is an idiom that John uses (similarly to 2 Pet. 3.8) to express the faithfulness of God. Bauckham, *The Theology of the Book of Revelation*, p. 107, argues that the 'theological point' of the millennium narrative is 'solely to demonstrate the triumph of the martyrs'.

[511] Boxall, *The Revelation of Saint John*, p. 282; see also Richard, *Apocalypse*, pp. 151-52.

[512] John states that he saw the souls of those having been beheaded (πεπελεκισμένων) for their testimony of Jesus. What is unclear is whether or not the hearers would understand this as the fate of all the martyrs. Rotz, *Revelation*, p. 284, suggests that the term is used symbolically for the death of all the martyrs or all persecution in general.

before God while on earth – in anticipation of their role as priests who will worship and minister in the very *presence* of God *and* the Lamb.[513] John twice notes (20.4, 6) that they will share (as *priests*)[514] in the Lamb's reign (5.10; 11.15) and reign *with* him.

The end of Satan's role in the story (20.7-10) segues into the judgment before the One seated on a great white throne (20.11-15). The hearers would likely link this great white throne and its occupant to the inaugural throne room scene where God sits upon the throne (Revelation 4). That all the dead are *standing*[515] before the throne implies a resurrection of some sort even though John offers no explanation. The dead *arise* from the sea and from death and Hades. Perhaps the hearers would think of Jesus' statement that he holds the keys of death and Hades (1.18). Perhaps, too, they would recognize the inevitable conclusion that *all* – great or small, righteous or unrighteous, follower of the Lamb or follower of the beast – will stand before the throne of God.[516] Of primary concern is the basis of judgment: record books,[517] particularly the book of life already familiar to the hearers (3.5; 13.8; 17.8). Those whose names are not in the book of life experience the second death; that is, they are thrown into the lake of fire[518] (20.11-15). Earlier narratives have already explicitly identified these whose names are not in the book of life, for they are the ones who worshiped the beast (13.8) and were in awe of Babylon (17.8). It is here, then, that the fate of the followers of the Dragon is finally revealed. Although John does not explicitly narrate here that those whose names were *in* the book of life experience union with the Lamb, the hearers have already been

---

[513] Thomas, *The Apocalypse*, pp. 606-607.

[514] Michaels, *Revelation*, p. 223: 'Nothing in the text suggests that *they* are given the right to judge others. These martyrs are *priests of God and of Christ* (v. 6)'.

[515] Ladd, *A Commentary on the Revelation of John*, p. 273; Smalley, *The Revelation to John*, p. 517.

[516] Thomas, *The Apocalypse*, p. 615; Boxall, *The Revelation of Saint John*, p. 290.

[517] Wall, *Revelation*, pp. 240-41, writes of the opening of the books: 'This act does not represent God's smothering omniscience so that every person's every deed has been recorded by God to be broadcast at some later time. Rather the proper meaning of this image is to note with confidence that God's record is accurate and fair and God's judgment is "faithful and true".'

[518] This follows death and Hades being thrown into the lake of fire; thus, the hearers witness the *death* of death. Such an extraordinary event would be of great encouragement to John's hearers (see also 21.4). Smalley, *The Revelation to John*, p. 519; Thomas, *The Apocalypse*, p. 617; Michaels, *Revelation*, p. 232.

assured of this (7.9-17; 14.1-5; 15.2-3; 20.1-6). The contrast between the destinies of the followers of the Lamb and the followers of the Dragon reminds the hearers that what they do[519] in this life and who or what they worship and give allegiance to has eternal consequences. Those who identify themselves through their deeds and their worship with the Dragon and his beasts will ultimately experience their destiny.[520]

In 21.1-8, John sees two remarkable things. First, John sees οὐρανὸν καινὸν καὶ γῆν καινήν ('a new heaven and new earth'). John narrates the reason for this in a remarkably simple and straight-forward way: ὁ γὰρ πρῶτος οὐρανὸς καὶ ἡ πρώτη γῆ ἀπῆλθαν καὶ ἡ θάλασσα οὐκ ἔστιν ἔτι ('for the first heaven and the first earth passed away and the sea is no longer') (21.1). This extraordinary event in the vision is left for the hearers simply to note as a new and amazing future reality, for John moves on: 'and I saw the holy city New Jerusalem descending out of heaven from God, having been prepared as a bride beautifully dressed for her husband') (21.2). Two previous referents would likely come to mind for the hearers. First, the explicit mention of New Jerusalem recalls Rev. 3.12 where Jesus promises to write upon the overcomers the name of New Jerusalem. Second, the mention of the bride recalls the joyous announcements of the wedding (19.7) and the wedding *supper* of the Lamb (19.9). The reality of those anticipated events find expression here in 21.2. Perhaps the hearers would be reminded of John the Baptist's identification of Jesus as the νυμφίος ('bridegroom') in Jn 3.28-29.[521] This association would provide further encouragement to the hearers to identify themselves as the

---

[519] The emphasis that each one is judged by his or her ἔργα ('works') would certainly remind the hearers of Jesus' repeated claim in the prophetic messages: Οἶδά σου τὰ ἔργα ('I know your works') (2.2, 19; 3.1, 8, 15). See also 9.20; 14.13; 16.11; 18.6.

[520] Thomas, *The Apocalypse*, p. 618. Sweet, *Revelation*, p. 293 suggests that it is better 'to see here not so much the "who's who" of judgment as its criterion, which in the last resort is not "works" but the Lamb's *book*: not to be found written there is to have sided finally with the beast'.

[521] Webster, *Ingesting Jesus: Eating and Drinking in the Gospel of John*, p. 39.

νύμφη ('bride'). This is the climax – the destiny of the overcomers, the faithful followers of the Lamb.[522]

While seeing all of this, John also hears a voice from the throne[523] declaring, Ἰδοὺ ἡ σκηνὴ τοῦ θεοῦ μετὰ τῶν ἀνθρώπων, καὶ σκηνώσει μετ᾽ αὐτῶν ('Behold the tabernacle of God is with humanity, and he will tabernacle with them') (21.3). This harkens back to Rev. 7.15 as well as draws on Jesus, the Logos, who took on flesh and ἐσκήνωσεν ('tabernacled') with humanity on earth (Jn 1.14). To this point in the Apocalypse, *heaven* has been the dwelling place of God, yet now John sees New Jerusalem coming *down* from (a *new*) heaven. All of this speaks to immediacy; that is, God will *live* with humanity![524] Bauckham argues that New Jerusalem functions as a multivalent symbol for people, place, and presence.[525] New Jerusalem symbolizes the *people* of God.[526] As *place* it is where God dwells with humanity (21.3), yet it is not a location on any map for 'it is God's dwelling place *in the saints* rather than their dwelling place on earth'.[527] The ultimate *new* reality, however, will be life permeated with the immediate *presence* of God. No longer will any barriers exist between God and God's people; rather, a mutual indwelling will exist between them (21.3). God's people will dwell fully in God and worship.[528] God, with tenderness and compassion, will wipe away every tear for death, mourning, and crying will be no more (21.4).[529] That God speaks here (21.5-8) indicates that God's people will have unmediated access to God, allowing them to hear

---

[522] R. Raber, 'Revelation 21:1-8', *Interpretation* 40.03 (2001), p. 296.

[523] The voice is unidentified but the notice that it comes forth from the throne indicates that the voice carries God's authority. Murphy, *Fallen is Babylon*, p. 410.

[524] Boring, *Revelation*, p. 215, 'For John, God is not finally one "item" in the new Jerusalem; God is himself the eschatological reality who embraces all things'.

[525] Bauckham, *The Theology of the Book of Revelation*, pp. 136-43.

[526] On this, see especially R.H. Gundry, 'The New Jerusalem: People as Place, Not Place for People', *NovT* 29 (July 1987), pp. 254-64. Richard, *Apocalypse*, p. 161: 'In Revelation Jerusalem is a myth, a symbol for the people of God or the community … The symbol of Jerusalem as a city expresses community, people, humankind organized'.

[527] Gundry, 'The New Jerusalem', p. 256 (emphasis mine).

[528] Murphy, *Fallen is Babylon*, p. 430.

[529] Raber, 'Revelation 21:1-8', p. 300: 'God of the reiterated selfhood in verse 3, who personally wipes away "every tear …," in a kind of once-and-for-all expungement that eliminates the root causes of such symptoms of lamentation'.

God's voice.[530] Within New Jerusalem there is a transformation of human existence as the hearers see the fulfillment of God's declaration: Ἰδοὺ καινὰ ποιῶ πάντα ('Behold I make all things new') (21.5).[531] All things – everything in creation – will one day be made anew by God's own spoken word! The hearers can be assured, for God, who is the Alpha and Omega (1.8), the Beginning and the End, declares it so: Γέγοναν ('It is done') (21.6).

God will give water without cost to the thirsty – those who seek after God (21.6). The hearers already know that the great multitude in heaven will never hunger or thirst again because the Lamb will lead them to streams of living water (7.16-17). Johannine hearers would also likely think of Jesus' offer of living water to any and all who would receive it (Jn 4.14; 7.37-38). The water which God offers is salvific.[532] In contrast to the *lake* of fire given to those who follow the beast, God's desire is to give the water of salvation to *any* who thirst for God.[533] God does not desire any to perish (Jn 3.16); he longs for the nations to be converted.[534] Those who overcome (ὁ νικῶν) will inherit New Jerusalem and become a υἱός ('son') of God (21.7). Throughout the Johannine literature, the language of 'son' is only used for Jesus in expressing his relationship with God the Father; therefore, the overcomers are to be in relationship to God in a way not unlike Jesus' own relationship to God in terms of its depth and intimacy.[535] This promise of *sonship* is the apex of *all* the promises to the overcomers, yet the promise is followed by a warning that there are those who will by their actions in this life be excluded from the people of God. Their deeds, catalogued in 21.8, demonstrate that their names are not in the book of life and that their destiny is the lake of fire, the second death. 'The call to faithful witness remains as necessary as ever for the churches, even as they

---

[530] Boxall, *The Revelation of Saint John*, p. 295.

[531] See Waddell, 'Revelation and the (New) Creation', pp. 30-50.

[532] Webster, *Ingesting Jesus*, p. 55.

[533] F.J. Murphy, *Apocalypticism in the Bible and its World* (Grand Rapids: Baker Academic, 2012), p. 124.

[534] Smalley, *The Revelation to John*, p. 541, 'The "spring of living water" … stands for the salvific presence of God through faith in the redeeming Lamb, and the life which results for the saints from eternal fellowship with them. This is available for all, not just for the martyrs …'

[535] Thomas, *The Apocalypse*, p. 630.

hear in their liturgical assemblies of what God assuredly has in
store. It still remains possible to have one's name blotted out of the
Lamb's scroll of life'.[536]

Summary of Revelation 17.1–21.8

Revelation 17.1–21.8 constitutes the third ἐν πνεύματι ('in the
Spirit') section of the Apocalypse which opens with the vision of
the great harlot, Babylon, and closes with the descent of the bride
of the Lamb, New Jerusalem. In the middle of this section John
presents the final worship scene of the Apocalypse that celebrates
the complete destruction of Babylon and anticipates the marriage of
the Lamb (19.1-10). The heavenly worship scene in Revelation 4–5
and the final worship scene in 19.1-10 stand as bookends, encasing
all the narratives contained within them. Like Revelation 4–5, this
worship scene is full of hymnic material. The first two hymns celebrate God's complete destruction of Babylon as witnessed in Revelation 18. The repetition of 'hallelujah' in these hymns evidences the
crescendo of heaven's jubilation as if no other word is adequate to
capture it. Only after having traversed the narratives of Revelation
12–18 can the hearers fully appreciate why heaven responds in this
unprecedented way. The final hymns encourage more praise of God
as the wedding of the Lamb – the final cultic celebration – is announced. The wedding supper, which accompanies the wedding,
would likely cause the hearers to think of their own cultic celebration of worship, the Eucharist. Their participation in it as a worshipping community on earth foreshadows their participation in the
wedding supper of heaven where they will be forever united with
the Lamb.

The elders and living creatures reappear in this final worship
scene as participants in the heavenly liturgy. Whereas the elders and
living creatures have played a more central role in earlier scenes,
their appearance here is nevertheless important. The elders and living creatures fall and worship the One on the throne in response to
the antiphonal hymns of the great multitude. The hearers know this
about the elders and living creatures, yet John continues to repeat it.
The sheer repetition of their action impresses upon the hearers the
appropriateness of kinesthetic worship before God. Additionally,

---

[536] Boxall, *The Revelation of Saint John*, p. 297.

they offer words of worshipful acclamation in the 'amen' and 'halle-lujah'. Exclamatory words of praise must be part of the worship vocabulary of the hearers. Such words are to be offered to God and in response to God's actions.

The final element in this worship scene is a prohibition against false worship. John's attempt to worship the one speaking to him earns him a sound rebuke. The command ('Worship God!') func-tions as the definitive word to the worshipping communities re-minding them that only God and the Lamb are to be worshipped. It is in their worship of God in the face of Babylon and the beast that they will prepare themselves for their union with the Lamb.

On the heels of the worship scene, a magnificent vision of Jesus as the rider on the white horse is presented (19.11-16). It is this event that ushers in final judgment on evil and final vindication on the righteous. Satan, the beast, and the false prophet are thrown into the lake of fire, but so are their followers (20.11-15). Those who refused to worship the beast or take his mark are raised to life to reign with Christ, free from the second death (20.1-6). In these narratives the hearers are confronted with the consequences of true and false worship. The followers of the beast and the followers of the Lamb are identified by their worship. The worship of the Drag-on and his beasts leads to eternal death; the worship of God and the Lamb leads to eternal life. The angelic command to worship God (19.10) is a call to *all* people. The hearers have been shown the future, both for themselves and for those who engage in false wor-ship. As part of their on-going worship, they must witness to the world around them who stand in danger of sharing in the fate of Satan by calling them to God who offers water to all who thirst and New Jerusalem to all who will identify with the Lamb.

V. ἐν πνεύματι – 'On a Mountain: New Jerusalem' (21.9–22.5)

With 21.9, the final ἐν πνεύματι ('in the Spirit') section begins. This marker continues to provide structural continuity in the narra-tive. On a deeper level, however, it continues to reinforce the close connection between the Spirit and John's vision, the Spirit and prophecy, and the Spirit and the community.[537] The final ἐν πνεύματι section begins just like the previous ἐν πνεύματι section; that is, both sections open with one of the seven angels from the bowl judgments inviting John to see something. While this repetition would likely cause the readers to pay close attention, they will quickly discover the stark contrast in what John sees, for John does not see a harlot but a bride, the wife of the Lamb.[538] John is carried away ἐν πνεύματι to a great and high, yet unnamed,[539] mountain from which he sees the Holy City, Jerusalem, descending from God (21.10). The mountain serves as the third venue, following the heavenly throne room (4.1-2) and the desert (17.3), to which John has been taken in the Spirit. Although John earlier narrated that the mountains could not be found after the great earthquake following the pouring out of the seventh bowl of plague (16.20), nevertheless it is to a mountain that John is taken. From the vantage point of the high mountain, John has an unhindered view of the descending New Jerusalem. In size and splendor, New Jerusalem dwarfs any earthly city, especially Babylon.[540] A number of elements about New Jerusalem are relevant to this study.

First, in narrating the descent of New Jerusalem, John repeats information already familiar to the hearers from 21.1-2. This would likely give the hearers pause; that is, the fact that the Spirit takes John to see something he has already seen suggests that John (and the hearers) need to *see* it again from a clearer or, perhaps, more removed vantage point. The mountain affords John the opportunity both to watch the descent of the city and to examine its features. The hearers would recall from 21.1-2 that the city was described as a bride having been adorned for her husband – recapturing the imagery used for the people of God from 19.7-8. Here, John understands that the same image that he *now* sees is not just the bride but also the *wife* of the Lamb. A wife is a step beyond a bride; that is, the imagery of wife speaks of full union and intimacy with the

---

[537] Murphy, *Fallen is Babylon*, p. 417.

[538] Mounce, *Revelation*, p. 377; Trafton, *Reading Revelation*, p. 204.

[539] Mounce, *The Book of Revelation*, p. 378, points out that the mountain is neither a symbol nor a literal mountain but 'the mountain "existed" in John's vision of eternal realities' and is 'an appropriate vantage point from which to view the descent of the eternal order'.

[540] Resseguie, *The Revelation of John*, p. 20.

Lamb.[541] The wife of the Lamb, descending from God's abode, is so magnificent that any vestiges of attraction to the great harlot, Babylon, are erased. The city is Revelation's final vision and ultimate destiny for the people of God – the 'eschatological future towards which they may live'.[542] The city *is* the people of God;[543] that is, John is afforded a glimpse of the people of God fully united with the Lamb. Although it yet awaits them, it represents the fulfillment and goal of the churches' worship – union with the Lamb – where the *wife* will have unhindered and immediate access to her husband, the Lamb. The figure of Jesus, the Lamb, is prominent throughout the description of the holy city, thereby reinforcing the imagery of marriage to and intimacy with his wife. The metaphor of marriage brings to fulfillment the theme of companionship with the Lamb seen in such places as Rev. 14.1-5 and 19.11-16. New Jerusalem is the glorious fulfillment of the churches' expectation when gathered for worship. In their worship, they encounter the living Jesus via the Spirit; through their worship, the Spirit prepares them for the coming day when they will fully live in God and God will dwell in them (21.3).

Second, the city that John sees descending from heaven shines with τὴν δόξαν τοῦ θεοῦ ('the glory of God') (21.11). The noun δόξα ('glory') has occurred throughout the Apocalypse as an attribute given to God and the Lamb in the worship scenes; however, after its appearance in 21.3 the hearers would likely connect this glory with God's dwelling amongst humanity.[544] Further, Johannine hearers might connect both 21.3 and the glory of God here in 21.11 with the description of Jesus, the Logos, whose glory is that of the only begotten of the Father (Jn 1.14). Thus, the glory represents the presence of God, and that the city, the wife of the Lamb, shines with it suggests that the people of God are fully enveloped in the presence of God and the Lamb, again creating a picture of immediacy and full union with the Lamb.

---

[541] Mounce, *Revelation*, p. 377, 'As bride the church is pure and lovely, and as wife she enjoys the intimacy of the Lamb'. See also Smalley, *The Revelation to John*, p. 545.

[542] Bauckham, *The Theology of the Book of Revelation*, p. 130.

[543] Pattemore, *The People of God in the Apocalypse*, pp. 199-200.

[544] Smalley, *The Revelation to John*, p. 547.

Third, John describes the city as having a great wall with 12 gates inscribed with the names of the 12 tribes of Israel (21.12) and 12 foundations bearing the names of the 12 apostles of the Lamb (21.14). The city is measured by the angel speaking with John and found to be a perfect cube (12,000 stadia in each direction) with a wall that is 144 cubits thick (21.15-17). Perhaps a number of things would converge for the hearers. First, the architectural language of walls, gates, and foundations would remind them of Jesus' promise to the Philadelphian overcomers to make them pillars in the temple of God (3.12). Second, that the architectural elements are inscribed with *names* continues to call to mind the Philadelphian message that the overcomers would have inscribed upon them the *name* of God, the *name* of the New Jerusalem, and the *name* of Jesus (3.12). The hearers learn that the servants of God indeed will have the *name* of God on their foreheads (22.4). Third, the measurements of the city and the wall make use of the same numbers found in the sealing of the 144,000 (12,000 from each tribe of Israel) (7.1-8). Fourth, the hearers would recall the measuring of the temple and its worshippers in 11.1-2. Both the sealing of the 144,000 and the measuring of the temple and its worshippers were symbolic of divine protection and safety for the people of God. All of this suggests that the people of God are incorporated *fully* both into the city and into God. The contention that the 12 tribes and 12 apostles add up to 24, the number of the elders present in the throne room where the glory of God resides and in which worship takes place (Revelation 4–5) provides further impetus for seeing the city itself as the culmination of worship.[545]

Fourth, John indicates that he did not see a ναὸν ('temple') in the city (21.22). Such an announcement would likely be surprising to the hearers given the prominent role the heavenly temple has played (11.19; 14.15, 17; 15.5-8). More surprising is the reason for this: ὁ γὰρ κύριος ὁ θεὸς ὁ παντοκράτωρ ναὸς αὐτῆς ἐστιν καὶ τὸ ἀρνίον ('for the Lord God Almighty and the Lamb is its temple') (21.22). The coupling of God and the Lamb that has been so characteristic throughout the Apocalypse has its climax here: God and the Lamb *is* the temple! If the hearers had any thoughts

---

[545] See Beale, *The Book of Revelation*, p. 1069; Smalley, *The Revelation to John*, p. 549.

that the dwelling of God among humanity (21.3) would be *in* a temple such an idea is here put to rest.[546] This announcement expands the earlier image of the great multitude who, having come through the great tribulation, are depicted as worshipping God ἐν τῷ ναῷ αὐτοῦ ('in his temple') (7.14-15). Pattemore speaks of this 'interpenetration of God and his people': 'On the one hand God indwells his people (the city), and on the other hand the people/city are in the temple (God)'.[547] The churches have the mediated presence of the living Jesus who walks among them and speaks to them through the Holy Spirit. It is to God and the Lamb that they give worship as the gathered community. New Jerusalem symbolizes a new reality when they will fully be with their Lord and their Lord with them. New Jerusalem – the people of God among whom God and the Lamb dwell – is *sacred*.[548]

Fifth, John indicates that the kings of the earth will bring τὴν δόξαν αὐτῶν ('their glory') into the city (21.24) and that τὴν δόξαν καὶ τὴν τιμὴν τῶν ἐθνῶν ('the glory and honor of the nations') will be brought into the city (21.26). Perhaps the hearers would be surprised to learn that the kings of the earth and the nations are *in* New Jerusalem since the terms have had negative associations (with the exception of the positive use of kings and kingdom in 1.5-6)[549] throughout the narrative; that is, the nations and kings of the earth have aligned themselves with the beast. Here, however, a most positive picture is presented. The hearers would recall the prophetic lyrics of the song of Moses and the Lamb announcing that the nations will come and worship before God (15.4); indeed, now they see its

---

[546] Pattemore, *The People of God in the Apocalypse*, p. 200 notes that in saying the city has no temple but God and the Lamb is its temple, John's audience is forced to 'rethink their image of the city'. Guntry, 'The New Jerusalem', p. 262, argues that in light of Rev. 22.21, Rev. 3.12 (pillars 'in the temple of my God') should be read as a genitive of apposition (pillars 'in the temple that is my God').

[547] Pattemore, *The People of God in the Apocalypse*, p. 200-201; Trafton, *Reading Revelation*, p. 209.

[548] Beasley-Murray, *Revelation*, p. 327; Boxall, *The Revelation of Saint John*, p. 308.

[549] Herms, *Universal Traditions in the Book of Revelation*, p. 206. He argues further (pp. 211-13) that the present text forms an *inclusio* with 1.5. Both Rev 1.5 and 21.24 (positive statements about kings) stand outside the scenes of judgment in which the 'kings of the earth' are opposed to God.

fulfillment.[550] The prophetic witness of the church is to lead to the conversion of the nations as seen in 11.13. That the kings and the nations are coming into New Jerusalem would likely encourage the hearers that their witness, even unto death, is not without effect; that is, not all kings and nations follow the Dragon and the beasts, nor are all the kings consorts of Babylon. There will be kings and nations who bring their *glory* and *honor* into the city; in other words, they will join in with the worshippers (thereby becoming worshippers themselves) in ascribing glory and honor to God and the Lamb (4.11; 5.11, 13; 7.12).[551] The notification in v. 27 with its emphatic declaration of those exempt from the city (καὶ οὐ μὴ εἰσέλθῃ εἰς αὐτὴν πᾶν κοινὸν καὶ [ὁ] ποιῶν βδέλυγμα καὶ ψεῦδος εἰ μὴ οἱ γεγραμμένοι ἐν τῷ βιβλίῳ τῆς ζωῆς τοῦ ἀρνίου, 'and no profane things will ever enter into it nor anyone practing abomination and falsehood, but only those whose names have been written in the Lamb's book of life') gives indication that the kings and nations present are indeed part of the people of God for only those whose names are inscribed in the Lamb's book of life can be a part of the city. The book of life has served as a dominant image throughout the Apocalypse. The hearers would recall the following: Jesus promises not to blot out the names of the overcomers in Sardis from the book of life (3.5), the inhabitants of the earth whose names have not been written in the book of life will be astonished at the beast (17.8), and at the white throne judgment anyone whose name was not written in the book of life will be thrown into the lake of fire, the second death (20.15). Here, the hearers would not miss that βδέλυγμα ('abomination') was used in describing Babylon as the mother of all impurities (17.5) nor that the *place* of all those who are impure or are liars is in the lake of fire (21.8). Implicit in this is that all who worship the beast are those whose names are not in the book of life and who are cast into the lake of fire. The

---

[550] Bauckham, *The Climax of Prophecy*, p. 241; Pattemore, *The People of God in the Apocalypse*, p. 202; Michaels, *Revelation*, p. 245.

[551] Bauckham, *The Climax of Prophecy*, pp. 315-16: 'The nations no longer claim glory and honour independently for themselves, in idolatrous rejection of the divine rule, but acknowledge that they come from and should be given back *in worship* to God, to whom all glory and honour belong' (italics mine).

hearers are thus reminded once again that they still live in the present world of Revelation 2–3 even while New Jerusalem beckons.[552]

Sixth, John sees the river of the water of life[553] flowing ἐκ τοῦ
θρόνου τοῦ θεοῦ καὶ τοῦ ἀρνίου ('from the throne of God and
the Lamb') (22.1). Along each side of the river stands the tree of life
which bears fruit every month and whose leaves are for the healing
of the nations (22.2). The imagery speaks to provision; namely, the
people of God will have access to both the water of life and the tree
of life. Perhaps the hearers would think of the biblical garden of
Eden (Gen 2.8-14), or, in light of the Apocalypse itself, they would
likely recall Jesus' promise to the Ephesian overcomers to eat from
the tree of life in the paradise of God (2.7) as well as God's invitation to the thirsty to drink without cost from the spring of the water
of life (21.6). Maybe the imagery of food and drink would remind
them of Jesus' words to the Laodicean church ('If anyone hears my
voice and opens the door, I will come in and eat with him, and he
with me'. – 3.20). Johannine hearers would likely think of Jesus'
words in John 6 about eating his flesh and drinking his blood, both
of which are given for the life of the world (vv. 41-58). If this is imagery of the Eucharist, then it behooves the hearers to *see* that what
is anticipated in their present experience of the Eucharist as part of
their worship will be fully realized in their eating of the tree of life
and drinking of the water of life in the full presence of God. Mangina connects this with the proclamation of the church: 'What the
church finally has to offer the nations is God's promise of life and
communion. That life and that communion are present in the
church's supper, an anticipation of the great supper of the Lamb on
the last day'.[554]

---

[552] Sweet, *Revelation*, p. 310, 'the perspective is that of the letters, in which
commerce with the heavenly Jerusalem as with the harlot Babylon is a present
possibility'. See also Smalley, *The Revelation to John*, p. 560, 'The vision of Paradise
at the end has implications for everyday life in the present'.

[553] See Mangina, *Revelation*, p. 246, who suggests that the river is the Holy
Spirit. He writes, 'Revelation's own concern is less with establishing inner-
trinitarian relations than with affirming the Spirit's central role in the ecology of
the new age; and here he certainly is a joint gift of the Father and the Son. Together, they irrigate the city with the one who is himself "the Lord and giver of
life".'

[554] Mangina, *Revelation*, p. 248.

Seventh, the vision of New Jerusalem closes by noting that the people of God will worship (λατρεύσουσιν) God and the Lamb[555] (22.3), see (ὄψονται) God and the Lamb (22.4), and reign (βασιλ-εύσουσιν) forever and ever (22.5). The use of λατρεύω ('worship') takes the hearers back to Rev. 7.15 where the ones who have come through the great tribulation are before the throne and worship (λατρεύουσιν) day and night. With them, the elder says, God dwells. Because God dwells within them, the people of God will *see* their God. Seeing God is the goal of worship! It is experiencing fully God's presence.[556] The people of God are known by God and marked as God's own with God's name upon their forehead (see also 3.12; 7.2-3; 14.1; contrast 13.16-17). Finally, as God and the Lamb reign forever (Rev 11.15; 19.6), so now will the people of God (22.5). The people of God will share in the activity of God; indeed, they will sit with Jesus on his throne (3.21).[557]

Summary of Revelation 21.9–22.5

Revelation 21.9–22.5 is the final ἐν πνεύματι ('in the Spirit') section of John's vision. Here John is shown the descent of the holy city, New Jerusalem. In describing the city, John provides a collage of images that unveil for the hearers a state of immediacy between the people of God and their God. The city itself, as seen in its architecture, dimensions, and designation as the dwelling place of God, signifies the culmination of worship where the people of God will dwell with God and the Lamb. Worship will not be confined to a temple for God and the Lamb *is* the temple! Every activity is thereby sacred. Ruiz reflects on this redefinition of worship for John's hearers: '...worship serves as a way of describing *every* activity, both cultic and otherwise, by which the ekklesia expresses its exclusive and uncompromising commitment to God and the Lamb'.[558] This vision complements the prophetic messages to the churches in that the promises to the overcomers find fulfillment here thus creating a synergistic relationship between the earthly churches and New Jerusalem. The vision of the holy city calls the churches to continue in their worship of God and the Lamb even

---

[555] The singular αὐτῷ continues to maintain the unity of God and the Lamb.

[556] Rotz, *Revelation*, p. 306.

[557] Thomas, *The Apocalypse*, p. 665.

[558] Ruiz, 'The Politics of Praise: A Reading of Revelation 19:1-10', p. 375.

while evil runs rampant. It is by means of worship that Satan and his beasts are defeated; it is by means of worship that the End comes and invades the present.[559] Worship as experienced in the churches is a foretaste of the intimate and immediate state of worship they will one day experience in full. New Jerusalem, as people and as a place filled with the presence of God, is the destiny of all those who will worship and bring glory unto God and the Lamb.

VI. Epilogue (22.6-21)

The epilogue to Revelation is contained in 22.6-21. The epilogue bears similarities to the prologue,[560] yet 'the intervening visions have cast the opening of the book in a new light'.[561] Although the epilogue functions structurally as a cue alerting the hearers that John's writing is coming to an end, the hearers' experience of the text has no doubt altered their initial perceptions. The epilogue's rehearsal of key elements in the Apocalypse is expressed through liturgical language that reinforces the liturgical framework of John's writing as well as the liturgical setting of John's churches in which it is read and experienced.

The epilogue begins with the words of an unnamed speaker: Οὗτοι οἱ λόγοι πιστοὶ καὶ ἀληθινοί, καὶ ὁ κύριος ὁ θεὸς τῶν πνευμάτων τῶν προφητῶν ἀπέστειλεν τὸν ἄγγελον αὐτοῦ δεῖξαι τοῖς δούλοις αὐτοῦ ἃ δεῖ γενέσθαι ἐν τάχει ('These words are faithful and true, and the Lord, the God of the spirits of the prophets, has sent his angel to show to his servants what is necessary to take place quickly') (22.6). Although these words are very similar to the opening of the Apocalypse, their presence here reinforces for the hearers that *all* the words John has heard are faithful and true. The repeated emphasis on this in the final phases of the

---

[559] Barr, *Tales of the End*, p. 148.

[560] Parallels between the prologue and epilogue are as follows: the revelation 'to show to his servants what is necessary to take place quickly' (1.1 = 22.6); the beatitude (1.3 = 22.7, 9); the identification of the work as prophecy (1.3 = 22.7, 10, 18, 19); John's name (1.1, 4 = 22.8); John hearing and seeing these things (1.2 = 22.8); 'the time is near' (1.3 = 22.10); the use of 'testimony' (1.1-2 = 22.16); 'I am the Alpha and Omega' (1.8 = 22.13); the Spirit (1.4 = 22.16, 20); the Parousia (1.3, 7 = 22.7, 12, 20); the keeping of the words of the prophecy (1.3 = 22.7).

[561] Trafton, *Reading Revelation*, p. 218.

vision (19.9; 21.5; 22.6) is likely intentional. John's hearers must pay careful attention to the *words* of the prophecy (1.3). Further, the speaker reviews the chain of dissemination as well as the necessity of revealing to God's servants the things about to take place. This would be familiar to the hearers from Rev. 1.1-2, yet here at the end it suggests that John faithfully fulfilled his task. The hearers now *know* the things that must take place soon. These things have been revealed ἐν πνεύματι ('in the Spirit') to John (1.10; 4.2; 17.3; 21.10) and experienced *through* the Spirit in the worshipping communities. The Spirit who facilitated John's visions will aid the communities in discerning them. The Spirit thus plays a vital role in both prophecy and worship.

These words are followed by words that can only be attributed to Jesus. Perhaps since no change in speaker is noted, the hearers would likely understand that Jesus is the un-named speaker in v. 6 as well.[562] In fact, the hearers would likely be struck by how much Jesus *speaks* in the epilogue. Jesus states: ἰδοὺ ἔρχομαι ταχύ. μακάριος ὁ τηρῶν τοὺς λόγους τῆς προφητείας τοῦ βιβλίου τούτου ('Behold I am coming quickly. Blessed is the one keeping the words of the prophecy of this book') (22.7). At this point, the hearers would be reminded of the prophetic announcement of Jesus' coming in Rev. 1.7, the repeated statements of his coming in the prophetic messages (2.5, 16, 25; 3.3, 11), the warning of his coming in 16.15, and the portrayal of his coming in 19.11-16. Jesus' words here announce to the hearers that of *all* the things that will be taking place, his soon coming must be in the forefront of their worship gatherings. The prophetic messages have revealed to them how distracted they have become. The seductive call of Babylon has infiltrated their ranks, competing with the voice of the Spirit who speaks the words of the risen Jesus. They have been summoned to repent, to worship in the face of the beast, and to be faithful followers of the Lamb. To hear *Jesus* declare his return bolsters the churches in their worship and witness and provides the motivation for their faithful endurance because they know that New Jerusalem – perfect union with the Lamb – is the goal of their identity as worshippers. Jesus also pronounces a blessing upon those who keep the

---

[562] Smalley, *The Revelation to John*, p. 567. The connective καὶ ('and') linking vv. 6 and 7 also facilitates this understanding.

words of the prophecy. This, the sixth liturgical blessing found in the Apocalypse (see 1.3; 14.13; 16.15; 19.9; 20.6), creates an inclusio with 1.3 with its emphasis on *keeping* the words of the prophecy, thus affirming the prophetic nature of all that the hearers have seen, heard, and experienced between these blessings. The blessing serves as words of encouragement for the hearers to persevere for the hearers now know what is required of them to *keep* faithfully the words of the prophecy.[563] That *Jesus* pronounces a blessing on them in close connection with his return provides additional impetus for the churches to heed Jesus' words to them in the prophetic messages as well as the entirety of the Apocalypse.[564]

In 22.8, John reminds his hearers that he is the one hearing and seeing these things. The appearance of John's name in the prologue and epilogue of the prophecy provide a witness to its authenticity. The present tense of the participles (ἀκούων, βλέπων, 'hearing, seeing') speaks to the 'immediacy' of the visions.[565] The next words John pens are quite unexpected for he relates that when he heard and saw, he fell to worship (προσκυνῆσαι) before the feet of the angel who was showing these things to him (22.9). This second occurrence of John's attempt to worship a heavenly messenger is followed by the same rebuke Ὅρα μή ('do not do it'). In 19.10, the speaker identified himself as a fellow-servant with John and all those holding to the testimony of Jesus; here, the angel identifies himself as a fellow-servant with John, with the other prophets, and with the ones keeping the words of this book. As in 19.10, the messenger here 'disclaims' his status as 'the giver of prophetic revelation' and reasserts his rank as 'a creaturely instrument' through whom John receives the revelation.[566] The angel likewise issues the same command as was given in 19.10: τῷ θεῷ προσκύνησον ('worship God'). Why would John record his inappropriate behavior a second time?[567] Is he simply overwhelmed with all that he has

---

[563] Beasley-Murray, *Revelation*, pp. 335-36; Thompson, *The Book of Revelation*, p. 55.

[564] Rotz, *Revelation*, p. 311.

[565] Smalley, *The Revelation to John*, p. 568.

[566] Bauckham, *The Climax of Prophecy*, p. 134.

[567] Bauckham, *The Climax of Prophecy*, p. 133: 'A literary artist as skilful as John will not have duplicated this incident other than by careful design'.

seen and heard? Bauckham suggests that John repeats the motif in order to ensure that the churches understand that the divine authority behind John's prophecy is Jesus.[568] The hearers are reminded for a final time that worship is only to be directed towards God and the Lamb. With this final injunction, the hearers are also reminded of the worship offered to the Dragon and the beasts and even John's temptation to worship the prostitute, Babylon; yet, they also know of the fate of the Dragon, the beasts, Babylon, and those who worship them. Worship is the crucial test of allegiance for John and for his churches. No one or nothing else is to be worshipped. To do so is to be an idolater,[569] and the hearers know that such activity will exempt them from participation in New Jerusalem (21.8; 22.15). Perhaps the hearers would be discomforted and disturbed by John's third temptation to engage in false worship; perhaps false worship is more of an enticement than they realize.[570] The call to worship God is thereby a call to communal self-discernment.[571] Obedience – keeping the words of the prophecy – is required *now* for John's hearers, ὁ καιρὸς γὰρ ἐγγύς ἐστιν ('for the time is near') (22.10). John's prophecy, unlike Daniel's prophecy (Dan. 12.9) is not to be sealed or hidden for a later time; the soon return of Jesus compels the churches to worship God and the Lamb and witness to the world of his coming in salvation and judgment.

The hearers would certainly be struck by the fact that twice more Jesus declares he is coming soon (22.12, 20). Coupled with v. 7, these declarations infuse the epilogue with urgency and thereby inculcate the hearers to persevere in the present. In 22.12-13 Jesus indicates that at his coming he will give rewards to everyone based on their works. The hearers would recall that at the white throne judgment people were judged according to their works (20.11-15). Further, as evidenced in the prophetic messages, works are important to Jesus – he *knows* the works of each church. The return of Jesus

---

[568] Bauckham, *The Climax of Prophecy*, p. 135, writes, '[W]hen it comes to distinguishing the giver of revelation from the instrument of revelation it is clear that for John Jesus belongs with God as giver, while the angel belongs with John as instrument'.

[569] Smalley, *The Revelation to John*, p. 569.

[570] Contra Wall, *Revelation*, p. 264, who maintains that John would not have fallen prey to such idolatrous practice since he stood 'so firmly in the apostolic tradition'.

[571] Rotz, *Revelation*, p. 311.

brings rewards for both the faithful and the faithless – rewards based upon their works in the present. Jesus' authority to give rewards is based on his identity as God, for Jesus declares himself to be τὸ Ἄλφα καὶ τὸ Ὦ, ὁ πρῶτος καὶ ὁ ἔσχατος, ἡ ἀρχὴ καὶ τὸ τέλος ('the Alpha and the Omega, the First and the Last, the Beginning and the End') (22.13). The hearers would recall the title 'Alpha and Omega' used of God in Rev. 1.8 and 21.6 (along with 'Beginning and the End'). Extraordinarily, Jesus here declares himself to be who God is.[572] The additional title – 'First and the Last' – was used by Jesus to identify himself to John (1.17) and to the church at Smyrna (2.8). Together the three pairs of terms describe *fully* Jesus' sovereignty, power, and authority. Not only do these ascriptions affirm the churches in their worship of Jesus by providing additional liturgical language, they also affirm the full deity of Jesus as God. It is *this* Jesus, who walks in the midst of the churches and holds them in his hand, who will return; it is through their worship that the churches will keep their robes washed (22.14) as they await Jesus' return. Through the vision, the hearers know that the return of Jesus sets into motion unalterable events both for the faithful and the faithless. Jesus is coming! The repetition concretizes the *reality* of his return. The hearers must not delay in heeding the words of Jesus spoken in the prophetic messages; they must ready themselves for Jesus' return.

Jesus[573] offers the final benedictory blessing of the Apocalypse: Μακάριοι οἱ πλύνοντες τὰς στολὰς αὐτῶν, ἵνα ἔσται ἡ ἐξουσία αὐτῶν ἐπὶ τὸ ξύλον τῆς ζωῆς καὶ τοῖς πυλῶσιν εἰσέλθωσιν εἰς τὴν πόλιν. ἔξω οἱ κύνες καὶ οἱ φάρμακοι καὶ οἱ πόρνοι καὶ οἱ φονεῖς καὶ οἱ εἰδωλολάτραι καὶ πᾶς φιλῶν καὶ ποιῶν ψεῦδος ('Blessed are the ones washing their robes, so that they may have the right to the tree of life and may enter into the city through the gates. Outside are the dogs and sorcerers and fornicators and murderers and idolaters and everyone loving and practicing falsehood') (22.14-15). That the hearers have a choice is indicated by the fact that those who *are washing* their robes will enter the city while those who have refused to worship God will remain outside the city. The idea of washing would likely cause the hearers

---

[572] Skaggs and Benham, *Revelation*, p. 233.

[573] Smalley, *The Revelation to John*, p. 573, suggests that this is John, rather than Jesus, speaking yet nothing in the narrative indicates a change in speakers.

to think of the great multitude in Revelation 7 who came through
the great tribulation and washed their robes in the blood of the
Lamb. There the language of washing, used in the aorist tense, is
associated with the cleansing (whitening) blood of the Lamb's sacrifice as well as the martyrdom of the saints; here, the language of
washing addresses the present and on-going spiritual activity that is
required of the churches as they await the return of Jesus.[574] In light
of the prophetic messages and the ensuing visions, 'washing their
robes' could be a metaphor for worship; that is, through their acts
of worship they keep themselves spiritually clean. It is through their
worship that they 'come out of Babylon' and serve God alone.
Their works will determine their right to all that Jesus has promised.
This elevates the critical importance of the prophetic messages that
Jesus speaks to the churches, for he knows their works, and they
know the outcomes for both the faithful, who will have access to
the tree of life and New Jerusalem, and the faithless, those excluded
from the city.

In v. 16 Jesus himself[575] confirms that what John has written is
for the churches.[576] He then identifies himself with two more descriptive phrases: ἐγώ εἰμι ἡ ῥίζα καὶ τὸ γένος Δαυίδ, ὁ
ἀστὴρ ὁ λαμπρὸς ὁ πρωϊνός. ('I am the Root and Offspring of
David, the bright morning star'). The hearers would recognize Jesus' use of the 'I AM' as well as recall that Jesus identifies himself in
relation to David in 3.7 and that the Lamb is identified as the root
of David in 5.5. The connection to David point to Jesus as the
promised Messiah and King; the 'I AM' identifies Jesus as God.
Thomas notes, '… Jesus is indeed the Alpha and Omega, the First
and the Last, the Beginning and the End for he is both the origin of
Davidic kingship and its culmination! He is that for which it comes
and that to which it leads!'[577] The addition of 'the bright morning
star,' taken from Num. 24.17, adds to the portrait of Jesus as Messiah. The hearers would recall that the overcomers at Thyatira are

---

[574] Skaggs and Benham, *Revelation*, p. 233; Rotz, *Revelation*, p. 314.

[575] This is the first place in the Apocalypse where Jesus identifies himself by
name. Thomas, *The Apocalypse*, p. 681.

[576] Mounce, *Revelation*, p. 394, '[The] revelation is not a private affair but for
the entire church'.

[577] Thomas, *The Apocalypse*, p. 682.

promised the Morning Star (2.28) – a participation 'in the messianic status of Christ himself'.[578] That this very Jewish language is in the context of the things having been written for the *churches* confirms that the people of God are all those – from Jacob, to David, to John and the hearers – who walk faithfully with God.

In response to the announced return of Jesus is the three-fold call for Jesus' return (22.17 (twice), 20b) that must stand at the heart of the churches' worship. Jesus says that the Spirit and the bride say: Ἔρχου ('Come') (22.17). In the prophetic messages, the words of Jesus and the words of the Spirit were co-terminus; here, the Spirit speaks in unity with the churches. This speaks to the presence of the Spirit within the churches. The Spirit, who mediates the words of Jesus to the churches, also shares in the experience of the church as well as the eschatological longing of the church for the return of Jesus. The church is to see herself *now* as the bride – the one longing for her husband. She must align herself with the Spirit and heed the Spirit's call for repentance in the prophetic messages. She cannot continue to be arrayed in soiled garments (3.4). The prayer of the church and of the Spirit within her midst is for the return of Jesus. Taken as such, this first use of ἔρχου ('come') is addressed to Jesus in response to the declarations of his coming and Jesus is giving voice to their call.[579] In light of the next two statements which follow, however, it is also possible to see an additional layer to the call of the Spirit and the bride. The narrative has depicted the outcomes for the followers of the Lamb and the followers of the Dragon. While the church certainly longs for and cries out for Jesus to return, she also calls out prophetically and in concert with the Spirit to the nations to worship God. Jesus *is* coming soon, and the reality of that fact calls for humanity to respond to the witness of the church. Thus, Jesus, here, acknowledges the call of the Spirit and the Bride to the *world* to come to Jesus.[580] This is then linked to

---

[578] Smalley, *The Revelation to John*, p. 577. Bauckham, *The Climax of Prophecy*, pp. 318-26, sees two prophetic texts from Isaiah (11.10; 60.3) standing in the background. Both texts envision the nations coming to God. By applying these texts to Jesus, as John does here, Jesus is portrayed as 'the one to whom the nations come for salvation' (p. 325).

[579] So Beasley-Murray, *Revelation*, p. 343-44.

[580] Ladd, *A Commentary on the Revelation of John*, pp. 294-95; Mounce, *The Book of Revelation*, p. 395; Osborne, *Revelation*, p. 793; Thompson, *Revelation*, p. 188; Skaggs and Benham, *Revelation*, p. 235; Murphy, *Fallen is Babylon*, p. 439; Thomas,

the next statement as those who hear also join in the invitation being proclaimed by the Spirit and the Bride. Throughout Revelation,
those who hear are those who obey and follow the Lamb knowing
full well it will likely lead them to death. The prophetic witness of
the church is intended to draw all to Jesus. Those who hear and
choose to respond now join in inviting others to come. The third
invitation continues this missional focus; that is, the thirsty and all
who wish to take the free gift of living water are invited to come.
The water of life is a part of the new creation of the future (21.6);
the invitation to partake in that new creation is extended to any and
all who will receive it in the present.[581] The church's witness in the
world is to extend Jesus' invitation of living water to the nations
and invite them to *come*.

The epilogue contains an integrity formula warning of adding or
taking away from its words and the ensuing consequences of those
who would (22.18-19).[582] These words are spoken by Jesus since
there is no indication of a change of speaker. Jesus' warning is directed at those who *hear* the words of the prophecy. Jesus emphasizes that John's work is a *prophecy* (stated twice in vv. 18-19); thus,
the *entire* book is a prophecy that is to be read, heard, and kept.
Those who add to the words will have the plagues described in the
prophecy *added* to them. Significantly, however, the judgment for
taking away words has eternal consequences; namely, denied access
to the tree of life and denied entrance into the holy city. Such ominous words are likely directed toward the churches – and perhaps
especially the false prophets and teachers such as 'Balaam' and 'Jezebel' – rather than outsiders, for it is the faithful who will have the
right to eat from the tree and enter the city (22.14).[583] These

---

The Apocalypse, pp. 682-84; Rotz, *Revelation*, p. 316; Blount, *Revelation*, p. 412, who
suggests that the grammatical difficulty of the second person singular imperative
can be solved if the nations or unbelievers are viewed as a single entity.

[581] Trafton, *Reading Revelation*, p. 220. However, see Wall, *Revelation*, pp. 267-
68, who argues that the invitation is for 'those readers who are in need of God's
sanctifying grace. It is for the rededication of believers rather than for the conversion of the lost'.

[582] For a thorough discussion of integrity formulas in antiquity see Aune, *Revelation 17–22*, p. 1208-13.

[583] Aune, *Revelation 17–22*, p. 1232, suggests that the integrity formula and ac-
companying curses point to the 'prophetic conflict' within the churches.

warnings serve to heighten the calls for repentance in the prophetic messages. Those who *hear* the words have an obligation to *keep* the words – *all* the words – of the prophecy.

The prophecy closes with a final call and response (22.20). Jesus, the faithful witness (1.5; 3.14) *witnesses* to *all* that John has written. His final words are familiar to the hearers: Ναί, ἔρχομαι ταχύ ('Yes, I am coming quickly') (22.20). This third declaration of his coming, affirmed with the emphatic intensive particle, reinforces for the churches that 'the revelation of Jesus Christ which John and his hearers experience is oriented by this extraordinary promise' of Jesus' coming.[584] Here, at the end of the Apocalypse, this announcement of Jesus' coming likely refers to his 'final, decisive eschatological coming',[585] yet it is possible that the hearers would also reflect on Jesus' admonitions to *come* to them in the prophetic messages.[586] The particle ναί appears in liturgical and antiphonal contexts in the Apocalypse (1.7; 14.13; 16.7), suggesting a similar usage here.[587] John, the one who bore witness to the word of God and the witness of Jesus (1.2), offers an antiphonal response in the form of a liturgical invocation: Ἀμήν, ἔρχου κύριε Ἰησοῦ ('Amen, come Lord Jesus'). The ἀμήν ('amen') is used in the prologue at the conclusion of the doxological confession (1.6) and at the conclusion of the prophetic announcement of Jesus' return (1.7).[588] Jesus identifies himself as the Ἀμήν ('Amen') to the church at Laodicea (3.14). The ἀμήν occurs in response to the worship of God and the Lamb (5.14; 7.12 [2x]; 19.4). Its usage here reflects such a worship context; that is, the ἀμύη is an exclamation of worship, uttered not by the heavenly elders but, now, by John (and the churches). The ἀμύη is followed with an eschatological prayer of longing for the return of his Lord, Jesus.[589] Despite present circumstances, both of John on Patmos and the churches under Roman political domination, the

---

[584] Thomas, *The Apocalypse*, p. 686.

[585] Aune, *Revelation 17–22*, p. 1234.

[586] Smalley, *The Revelation to John*, p. 585; Richard, *Apocalypse*, p. 45.

[587] Smalley, *The Revelation to John*, p. 585.

[588] Wall, *Revelation*, p. 269, sees the 'amen' as concluding the announcement of Jesus' coming rather than introducing the antiphonal response of John.

[589] Along with 22.21, this is the only occurrence of 'Lord Jesus'.

hearers are to persevere in light of Jesus' return.[590] Their intoning of the liturgical ἀμήν acknowledges the truthfulness of Jesus' promise to return. The hearers know through their experience of the Apocalypse what the return of Jesus means both for them and for the world around them. Thus, to cry out for their Lord's return is also to participate in self-examination and discernment. Smalley writes, 'John's hearers are being urged not only to listen carefully to the gospel in Revelation but also to be aware of what is involved in praying that God may come in Christ to save people through his judgment'.[591] The coupling of self-examination with prayer for the return of Jesus could suggest a Eucharistic setting.[592] Barr goes so far as to suggest that the whole story of Revelation functions 'as an explanation of what happens in the Eucharist: Jesus comes, evil is overthrown, the new Jerusalem descends out of heaven'.[593] Such an idea does not seem out of the realm of possibility in the Apocalypse given the Eucharistic allusions found throughout. With John, the churches' response to the 'revelation of Jesus Christ' is worship – worship that culminates in anticipatory prayer for the return of Jesus, the Lord. The use of the vocative κύριε addresses Jesus in his role as the exalted Lord of the churches. The 'one like a son of man' who appeared to John on Patmos and who walks in the midst of his churches is indeed *the* Lord.

The Apocalypse comes to a close with a brief benediction: Ἡ χάρις τοῦ κυρίου Ἰησοῦ μετὰ πάντων ('The grace of the Lord Jesus be with all') (22.21). On the one hand, the appearance of the benediction reflects its epistolary nature;[594] on the other hand, the benediction serves as a conclusion to the entire worship setting of the Apocalypse, likely reflecting the benediction spoken as the conclusion to the worship services in the seven churches. The benediction upon *all* is communal,[595] an open-ended offer of grace that is not limited to just the seven churches but to all who would hear and

---

[590] Thompson, *Revelation*, p. 189.

[591] Smalley, *The Revelation to John*, p. 585.

[592] Smalley, *The Revelation to John*, p. 585, 'There seems ... every reason to suppose that Revelation ... was designed to be read aloud (1.3) on the Lord's Day (1.10) in a setting which was both liturgical and eucharistic'.

[593] Barr, *Tales of the End*, p. 144.

[594] Thompson, *The Book of Revelation*, p. 55.

[595] Thompson, *The Book of Revelation*, p. 56.

respond to the Lamb.[596] Grace, used only here and in 1.4, serves to envelop between its appearances all the words, sights, sounds, and revelations of the prophecy. Perhaps, even in these final words, the hearers would recognize echoes of the Fourth Gospel where Jesus is said to be both *full* of grace (Jn 1.14) and the *bestower* of abundant grace to believers (Jn 1.16). It is this grace – saving, keeping grace from the One who is Savior and Lord – that is freely made available to all.[597] The benediction, then, is not a perfunctory ending to John's letter but a profound theological statement of hope for all who would worship God and the Lamb.[598]

Summary of Revelation 22.6-21

The epilogue brings the Apocalypse to a conclusion and reminds the hearers of its epistolary framework. As such it rehearses key themes begun in the prologue and developed throughout the visions. The epilogue brings the hearers back to the narrative present; that is, John is on Patmos and they are in Asia Minor. All that has taken place between the prologue and epilogue is experienced both by John and the hearers as prophetic words given by the Spirit for the churches. As John experiences the visions in worship (*in the Spirit* [on the Lord's Day]), so also do the communities experience the words of the prophecy in worship. It is *in* worship that the Spirit breaks in upon the worshipping community with prophetic words and visions given by Jesus. The admonition to worship God alone suggests that the propensity to false worship is stronger than one might think. True worship keeps God and the Lamb as its proper and singular object for all else is idolatry. At the heart of the churches worship must be the cry for the return of Jesus – an event which ushers in un-alterable events for both the faithful and the faithless. Thus, the Spirit and the Bride call out for all to join in the worship of God and the Lamb even as the Bride calls out in longing for the return of the Bridegroom. The hearers now know that the return of Jesus is not escapism; rather, they must be willing to give

---

[596] Blount, *Revelation*, p. 417. Mangina, *Revelation*, p. 254, 'Just as there is no qualification for drinking the living water, other than the fact of being thirsty, so there is no potential hearer who is not embraced in this "all"'.

[597] Wall, *Revelation*, p. 270, offers a sobering thought on the 'darker side of grace' found in God's judgments.

[598] Beasley-Murray, *Revelation*, p. 350, 'As in revelation, so in history: grace shall have the last word!'

their lives, to worship in the face of the beast, and to witness in the midst of hostility. The benediction, like the opening greeting of 1.4-5, reminds the hearers of the communal nature of the Apocalypse.[599] The final word of the Apocalypse is *grace*, the saving grace of the grace-filled Lamb made available to all who will worship God.

---

[599] Smalley, *The Revelation to John*, p. 586.

5

TOWARD A PENTECOSTAL THEOLOGY OF WORSHIP IN LIGHT OF THE APOCALYPSE

I. Introduction

The final piece of this study is to attempt to make a contribution to the Pentecostal tradition[1] by offering some overtures toward a Pen-

---

[1] I am using the term 'Pentecostal' in a broad sense, fully cognizant of the diversity of Pentecostalism both in its North American context as well as its global context. While my comments about Pentecostalism in this chapter are directed at my own North American context, I believe that worship is a consistent feature of global Pentecostalism; therefore, the Apocalypse offers insights applicable for global Pentecostal worship. For a recent study on worship in Asia, see W. Ma, 'Pentecostal Worship in Asia: Its Theological Implications and Contributions', *AJPS* 10.1 (2007), pp. 136-52. Ma notes four characteristics of Asian Pentecostal worship: 1) intensity and liveliness of Pentecostal worship, which she suggests comes from a sense of expectation of an encounter with God; 2) participatory worship where the Spirit enables all to minister; 3) spontaneity in worship, evidenced in tongues speech, dreams, visions, or impressions that are seen as God speaking to the congregation; and 4) experience of the transcendental – a 'tangible encounter' which affects the whole being (pp. 141-50). Ma states that worship is an avenue for 'corporate theologization' (p. 151). For a recent study on worship in Ghana, see J. Quayesi-Amakye, 'God in Ghanaian Pentecostal Songs', *JPT* 22 (2013), pp. 131-51, where he describes the 'Pentecostal psalmists' who are known for 'locally composed songs' given by the Spirit which are 'received spontaneously during revival and prayer meetings, worship services, and church conventions' and which are 'received through times of personal devotions and life experiences of the psalmist' (pp. 131-32). He demonstrates that the overarching theme of Pentecostal songs in Ghana is the being of God (God as Creator, parent, friend, lover, king of the universe, and source of productivity). He also shows how their songs use the same categories to speak of Jesus. 'They have no problem worshipping Jesus as God, though with their traditional supernatural understanding they conceive God the father as the supreme being whose son Jesus also deserves the

tecostal theology of worship in light of the Apocalypse. Although many Christian traditions would argue for the importance of worship, for the Pentecostal community worship is its central feature. However, worship is not simply a type of song or style of music; worship is an event – a supernatural encounter with God. Increasingly, Pentecostal scholars are writing about the worship practices found in Pentecostalism. In describing Pentecostal worship, Keith Warrington observes, 'Two pertinent words when referring to Pentecostal spirituality are "expectancy" and "encounter". Pentecostals expect to encounter God. It undergirds much of their worship and theology and may even be identified as another way of defining worship.'[2] Daniel Albrecht maintains that the term 'worship' is understood amongst Pentecostals in three primary ways: 1) 'as a way of Christian life'; 2) 'as the *entire* liturgy, the whole of the Pentecostal service'; and 3) 'as a *specific* portion, or *rite* within the overall liturgy'.[3] Worship, for Pentecostals, is a *felt* experience. This experiential element is not merely external show; rather, Pentecostal exuberance and manifestations bubble up from an inner and profoundly intimate experience of the Spirit. The Spirit 'facilitates' the worship encounter between the Divine and the human; indeed, true worship takes place in *Spirit* and Truth (Jn 4.24).[4] At the core of Pentecostal worship and spirituality is the knowledge that the worshipper is engaging in a personal encounter with the Holy Spirit.[5]

Albrecht adopts the language of 'ritual' in defining Pentecostal worship. Rituals are 'those acts, actions, dramas and performances

---

worship they ascribe to him' (p. 144). See also O.U. Kalu 'Holy Praiseco: Negotiating Sacred and Popular Music and Dance in African Pentecostalism' *Pneuma* 32 (2010), pp. 116-40 for an insightful look into ways that Pentecostal music and dance have emerged in the general African culture (political, business, entertainment) and how Pentecostals have reappropriated indigenous and secular music in the church for Godly use. The author points to the potential dangers of this convergence for Pentecostalism both within and outside the church.

[2] K. Warrington, *Pentecostal Theology*, p. 219.

[3] D.E. Albrecht, 'An Anatomy of Worship: A Pentecostal Analysis', in W. Ma and R. Menzies (eds.), *The Spirit and Spirituality: Essays in Honour of Russell P. Spittler* (JPTSup 24; London, T&T Clark, 2004), p. 71.

[4] Warrington, *Pentecostal Theology*, p. 220. J.C. Thomas, 'The Spirit in the Fourth Gospel', *The Spirit of the New Testament* (Blandford Forum: Deo Publishing, 2005), p. 161, suggests that in the Fourth Gospel 'Truth' is a 'subtle reference to Jesus' based on the associations between truth and Jesus in Jn 1.14, 16, 17; 3.21 and the explicit claim of Jesus in 14.6.

[5] Albrecht, 'An Anatomy of Worship', p. 74.

that a community creates, continues, recognizes and sanctions as ways of behaving that express appropriate attitudes, sensibilities, values, and beliefs within a given situation'.[6] According to Albrecht, the corporate worship service functions as a ritual for Pentecostals, complete with attending liturgical rites.[7] The sanctuary or facility which houses the worshipping community functions as a ritual place, 'a "micro-world" in which to experience their God'.[8] The ritual enactments experienced in the Pentecostal worship service create a sense of community among the worshippers as well as codify their beliefs.[9]

Although worship is central to Pentecostalism, studies on Pentecostal worship are largely descriptive[10] with a full-scale Pentecostal *theology* of worship yet to emerge. The purpose of this chapter is to offer a contribution to this emerging discipline by encouraging Pentecostals to look to the Apocalypse as a rich source for both their worship as well as for their understanding of worship. While many Pentecostals would regard tradition as *anti*-liturgical, Pentecostalism, like all traditions, has its own liturgy and is thereby liturgical.[11] In

---

[6] Albrecht, *Rites in the Spirit*, p. 22.

[7] Albrecht, *Rites in the Spirit*, p. 22: 'The Pentecostal service lies at the heart of the Pentecostal/Charismatic (Pent/Char) spirituality and with its attending rites and practices constitutes the most central ritual of Pentecostalism'. See his Appendix B (pp. 254-59) for a listing of what he identifies as 'liturgical rites, foundational rites, and microrites'.

[8] Albrecht, *Rites in the Spirit*, p. 127.

[9] Albrecht, *Rites in the Spirit*, p. 205, 'Pentecostals experience and enact their beliefs in the liturgy ... the ritual teaches what it means to live and behave as Christians in a faith community'.

[10] For monograph-length studies, see especially Albrecht's *Rites in the Spirit*; also J.H.S. Steven, *Worship in the Spirit: Charismatic Worship in the Church of England* (Carlisle, Cumbria and Waynesboro, Georgia: Paternoster Press, 2002). See also Cartledge, *Testimony in the Spirit*, pp. 29-54.

[11] J.K.A. Smith, *Desiring the Kingdom: Worship, Worldview, and Cultural Formation* (Grand Rapids: Baker Academic, 2009), p. 152, is helpful on this: 'All Christian worship – whether Anglican or Anabaptist, Pentecostal or Presbyterian – is liturgical in the sense that it is governed by norms, draws on a tradition, includes bodily rituals or routines, and involves formative practices'. Although Smith's book is not focused per se on Pentecostal worship, he encourages Pentecostals (and all traditions) to reassess their understanding of worship. In particular, see ch. 5 (pp. 155-214) where he guides the reader through an assessment of worship practices (from the gathering to the benediction) and exegetes their significance. The theological importance that he assigns to these practices can be of immense benefit to Pentecostals.

recognizing this, Pentecostals can tap into a deep and nourishing root of the Church even while contributing their own liturgical structures and practices. The Apocalypse is a liturgical narrative;[12] as such, it can make a substantial contribution to a Pentecostal theology of worship. In the remainder of this chapter, I will sketch what I believe to be the central message of the Apocalypse pertaining to worship and offer overtures toward the construction of a Pentecostal theology of worship.

II. What the Apocalypse Reveals about Worship

First, this study has demonstrated that Revelation is at its heart a narrative about worship.[13] On a structural level, worship is woven into the very fabric of the narrative through the use of the ἐν πνεύματι ('in the Spirit') statements that divide the phases of the vision (1.10; 4.2; 17.3; 21.10). The vocabulary of worship is found in words such as λατρεύω ('worship, service', 7.15; 22.3) and forms of προσκυνέω ('worship', 4.10; 5.14; 7.11; 9.20; 11.1, 16; 13.4 (2x), 8, 12, 15; 14.11; 16.2; 19.4, 10, 20; 20.4; 22.8). Traditional liturgical forms – doxology (1.5b-6), blessings (1.3; 14.13; 16.15; 19.9; 20.6; 22.7, 14), benediction (22.21) – combine with liturgical imagery, such as incense, altar, and temple. Throughout the narrative are liturgical acclamations such as Ἀμήν ('amen', 1.6, 7; 3.14; 5.14; 7.12 (2x); 22.20) and Ἀλληλουϊά ('Hallelujah', 19.1, 3, 4, 6), liturgical hymns (4.8, 11; 5.9-10, 12, 13; 7.10, 12, 15-17; 11.15-18; 12.10-12; 15.3-4; 16.5-6; 19.1-2, 3, 5; 6-8), and the liturgical practice of prostration (1.17; 4.10; 5.14; 7.11; 19.4, 10; 22.8). The claim that John received the vision 'in the Spirit on the Lord's Day' (1.10) reflects both the practice of worship and the acknowledgment of liturgical time. The appearance of doxology, blessing, and benediction suggest formal elements within a service of worship with which the hearers would likely be familiar. Scenes of heavenly worship are

---

[12] P. Vassiliasdis, 'Apocalypse and Liturgy', *St. Vladimir's Theological Quarterly* 41.2-3 (1997), p. 103 states that 'the Apocalypse is, or at least should be, the key to discovering the real meaning of Christian liturgy and its relation to history'.

[13] Boxall, *Revelation: Vision and Insight*, p. 150, 'The whole Apocalypse cries out to be understood, and to be read, liturgically'.

embedded in the narrative (4-5; 7.9-17; 11.15-19; 12.10-12; 14.1-5; 15.1-8; 19.1-8). They are directly tied to the stories around them and aid the hearers in interpreting and discerning them – always from heaven's perspective. Such juxtapositioning creates a sense of ebb and flow throughout the story and demonstrates that whatever the people of God face while on earth, true reality is what is taking place in heaven. The worship scenes thus create an alternate reality that is the *true* reality for the people of God. This alternate reality is differentiated from the earthly reality of false worship that is given to the Dragon, the beasts, and to Babylon in Revelation 13–18. In the Apocalypse, it is worship which reveals one's allegiance. If the whole world is worshipping the Dragon and the beast, the people of God must worship God and the Lamb. Revelation presents worship as 'the definitive act of Christian resistance' to any and all that are opposed to God.[14] This initial observation about the embedded nature of worship in the structure of the Apocalypse is instructive for Pentecostals who have often been conditioned to see the Apocalypse as a road-map for end-time events. This has not always been the case, for as chapter 3 of this study demonstrated, early Pentecostals were profoundly affected by the worship found in the Apocalypse. In their encounters with the Holy Spirit, they *experienced* the Apocalypse in ways not unlike John. Their testimonies, songs, and poems bear witness to the importance of the Apocalypse. To *hear* the Apocalypse as a liturgical text allows Pentecostals to rediscover and retrieve it as a resource for worship.

Second, the Apocalypse asserts that true worship takes place ἐν πνεύματι ('in the Spirit'). The statement about John being *in the Spirit* (Rev. 1.10) serves as more than a structural marker within the narrative. It is a profound statement both about worship and the central role of the Holy Spirit. Worship is an engagement with and participation in the Spirit of God. *Spirit*ed worship turns ordinary places like Patmos or the seven churches into sacred spaces and ordinary time into eschatological time.[15] John receives his vision on

---

[14] Saunders, 'Revelation and Resistance', p. 118.

[15] C. Bridges Johns, 'The Light That Streams from the End: Worship Within the Coming Christendom', *The Living Pulpit* 12.3 (2003), p. 14. See also Albrecht, *Rites in the Spirit*, p. 127, who observes that when Pentecostals come together for worship, the space for worship becomes a 'ritual place' or 'micro-world' in which to experience God.

the Lord's Day – the churches' day of worship; thus, he stands in solidarity and *in the Spirit* with the seven churches in worshipping God even while in apparent exile on Patmos. John is *in the Spirit* because worship takes place *in the Spirit*. Worship is not confined to a designated time or place; rather, true worship takes place whenever and wherever one is communing with God *in the Spirit*. It is in this state of deep communion that the worshipper and the worshipping community are open to prophetic impartations from the Spirit. It is *in the Spirit* that John is granted a vision of the risen Jesus (1.9-18), subsequently to be shown the things that are necessary to take place quickly (1.1). In the prophetic messages, it is *in the Spirit* that the churches hear the voice of Jesus who is in their midst (Revelation 2–3). It is *in the Spirit* that the transcendent God is made immanent[16] and the churches find themselves in the realm of heaven where they see, hear, and experience its liturgy (e.g. Revelation 4–5). It is *in the Spirit* that the churches ascertain their true identity as New Jerusalem, the wife of the Lamb (21.2, 9), despite the fact that they currently find themselves in Babylon, the consort of the Dragon (Revelation 17–18). Worship *in the Spirit* creates a context for pneumatic discernment – a crucial assignment for the people of God. Further, it is *in the Spirit* that the community both calls for Jesus to return and calls for the nations to come to Jesus (22.17). In this, the Spirit and the Bride, like the Spirit and Jesus in Revelation 2–3, speak in concert, which continues to attest to the importance of the churches hearing what the Spirit has to say.[17]

The Apocalypse's insistence that worship takes place in and through the Spirit is conducive for Pentecostals. Pentecostals define themselves as people of the Spirit,[18] and they understand their

---

[16] Bauckham, *The Theology of the Book of Revelation*, p. 46, helpfully notes that God as transcendent does not mean that God is distant from God's people; rather, 'The transcendent God, precisely because he is not one finite being among others, is able to be incomparably present to all, closer to them than they are to themselves'. He sees this as particularly evident in Rev. 21.3 where 'the God whose transcendence is so emphasized can in the new creation make his home with human beings'.

[17] Only in Rev. 14.13b does the Spirit speak independently.

[18] Land, *Pentecostal Spirituality*, p. 169, writes that to be filled with the Spirit 'is to be decisively determined by and oriented to the things of the Spirit, to what the Spirit is saying and doing'.

worship to be in and led by the Spirit.[19] Jerome Boone states that the 'single most important goal of any Pentecostal worship service is a *personal encounter with the Spirit of God*'.[20] Delton Alford writes that Pentecostals strive for 'a spirit of reverence and love wherein the Holy Spirit itself may lead and direct the congregation into meaningful, purposeful worship of God'. He continues, 'At all times prime importance must be placed on an awareness of and sensitivity to the moving of the Holy Spirit in the midst of the congregation. Herein lies the significance and strength of the contemporary Pentecostal worship service.'[21] Early Pentecostals, as documented in chapter 3 of this study, were fully cognizant of and reliant upon the Spirit within their midst. Their reception of visions and songs and poems *in the Spirit* came during times of worship.[22] Pentecostals view worship as an experiential encounter; thus, they value *experiences* in worship.[23] Though often criticized for their emphasis on experience (and sometimes rightly so), Pentecostals can find in the Apocalypse confirmation that true worship *is* experiential, involving the whole person – body, mind and spirit – in encounter with God *in the Spirit*. In the Apocalypse, the experience of worship is that

---

[19] Warrington, *Pentecostal Theology*, p. 220; Steven, *Worship in the Spirit*, p. 183, notes that a feature of Charismatic worship is the affirmation of the Spirit's role 'as the enabler of the human vocation to worship'.

[20] R.J. Boone, 'Community and Worship: The Key Components of Pentecostal Christian Formation', *JPT* 8 (1996), p. 138 (emphasis added).

[21] D. Alford, *Music in the Pentecostal Church* (Cleveland: Pathway Press, 1967), pp. 60-61.

[22] In a lengthy testimony in the *AF* 1.11 (October-January, 1908), p. 3, Antoinette Moomean recounts her experience of Spirit baptism in which the Lord showed her the cross. She then relates the following: 'One morning the Spirit dealt with me, singing through me –
Must Jesus bear the cross alone,
And all the world go free:
No, there's a cross for every one,
And there is one for me.
The last line He just seemed to burn into my soul by repeating it over and over again. *Sometimes the Spirit would sing a line and then sob out a line.* Although I wept and was in anguish of soul, it was all in the Spirit' (emphasis mine). Her testimony speaks to the sense amongst Pentecostals that worship afforded a deep connection to the Spirit and that they were giving voice to the words and longings of the Spirit.

[23] Martin, 'Longing for God', p. 75: 'Genuine encounter with God results in dramatic experience'.

which will *mark* the hearers as followers of the Lamb, as theologically formed worshippers who understand that through their worship they participate in the sights, sounds, and activities of the heavenly realm. *Spirit*ed worship is also sensory; John sees the Lamb, hears the trumpets, smells the incense, tastes the scroll, and touches the measuring rod. The hearers are invited to the same sensory experience as they worship *in the Spirit*. In the same way, Pentecostals can find in the Apocalypse an invitation to a *Spirit*ed sensory experience of worship – an experience of worship as 'ritual play' whereby the Spirit takes them into the throne room to worship before God and the Lamb.[24]

Third, worship creates a context for the prophetic voice of the Spirit. The Apocalypse is a prophecy (1.3; 22.7, 10, 18, 19) given to John, a prophetic figure (10.11; 22.9), for churches in which prophets apparently function (10.7; 19.10; 22.9). The calls to pneumatic discernment in the narrative (Revelation 2–3; 13.18; 14.12) suggest that discernment is an essential activity in relation to prophecy. Further, Jesus' solemn warning for adding or taking away from the words of the prophecy (22.18-19) confirms the necessity of prophecy, or at the very least this particular prophecy, for the churches.[25] That the Apocalypse is also a liturgical narrative suggests an integral connection between worship and prophecy. Because the Apocalypse is meant to be read and heard when the churches gather for worship, worship becomes the context for the giving and receiving of prophetic revelation; because worship is intimately linked to the Spirit, prophetic words and visions are a means by which the Spirit communicates to the churches.[26] It is not the *words* of this prophecy that the churches are called on to discern (hence the curse formula of 22.18-19); rather, by means of the prophecy they are called to

---

[24] For the idea of worship as ritual play, see S. Chan, *Pentecostal Theology and the Christian Spiritual Tradition* (JPTSup 21; Sheffield: Sheffield Academic Press, 2000), pp. 116-19; also P. Althouse and M. Wilkinson, 'Playing in the Father's Love: The Eschatological Implications of Charismatic Ritual and the Kingdom of God in Catch the Fire World', *Arc* 39 (2011), pp. 93-116.

[25] Thomas, *The Apocalypse*, p. 686: 'The seriousness with which the resurrected Jesus treats the words of this prophecy is indicated in part by the fact that four times reference is made to what is written in this book within the span of two verses. There could be no mistaking that one's response to the words of the prophecy of this book are [*sic*] of eternal consequence ...'

[26] R. Jeske, 'Spirit and community in the Johannine Apocalypse', p. 463.

discern their *own condition* (Revelation 2–3) as well as the *culture* around them. By means of the words of this prophecy, the Spirit aids the churches in properly discerning the insidious workings of the Dragon and beasts (Revelation 12–13),[27] so that in their worship the churches can sing the song of Rev. 12.10-12. By means of the words of this prophecy, the Spirit aids the churches in properly discerning their true identity as the Bride of the Lamb, so that in their worship they can sing the songs of Rev. 19.6-8. The words of the prophecy are to be received *in the Spirit* because John receives them *in the Spirit*. The climactic statement – 'the testimony of Jesus is the S/spirit of prophecy' (19.10; also 12.17) – fuses together prophetic proclamation and worship.

Pentecostals believe that the Spirit can speak to the worshipping community through a variety of means.[28] Pentecostals view prophecy as having its origin in the Spirit of God based especially on Acts 2.17-18 and 1 Corinthians 12 and 14. As documented in chapter 3, upon receiving the baptism in the Holy Spirit, Pentecostals would often speak out prophetic words given to them by the Spirit. The transcribing of these messages from the Spirit in some of the early issues of the *Latter Rain Evangel* demonstrates their conviction that the Spirit was speaking to the churches. Writing it down thereby allowed all who read the *Latter Rain Evangel* to hear the words of the Spirit.[29] Perhaps contemporary Pentecostals should reflect on the role of the prophetic in their churches in light of the close connection between the Spirit and prophecy evidenced in the Apocalypse and confirmed amongst early Pentecostals to ensure that in those moments when the Spirit speaks, the words of the Spirit are given their full due.[30] While not denying that there is a human component

---

[27] See also Rev. 2.24 where Jesus reveals that 'Jezebel' teaches 'the deep things of Satan'.

[28] Pentecostals would understand that the Spirit speaks to the church through preaching, tongues and interpretation, prophetic words, and testimonies.

[29] See the *Latter Rain Evangel* in chapter 3 of this study.

[30] Perhaps local Pentecostal churches could consider writing down what the Spirit speaks in their midst as a way to give serious attention to the voice of the Spirit. This is not to create another canon but it is to acknowledge that if Pentecostals affirm that the Spirit speaks a present word to the community, then we should truly listen and respond to that word. Too often in Pentecostal circles, the response to a prophetic word from the Lord is a handclap or hurried 'Amen' before moving on to the next part of the worship service. Pentecostals celebrate the fact that the Spirit speaks to the corporate body, yet few, if any, remember

in prophecy that can lead to misuse and abuse and thereby must be discerned by the community, Pentecostals might re-imagine the giving and receiving of prophetic words and visions (as well as discerning them) as integral to their corporate worship experience.[31]

Fourth, the Apocalypse demonstrates that worship is the central purpose for *all* of creation, whether in heaven or on earth. It is not insignificant that the first thing John sees and hears in heaven is worship rendered to God and the Lamb (Revelation 4–5). The songs of worship begun by the elders and living creatures crescendo as the angels and then all of creation add their voices to produce a symphony of praise to God and the Lamb. This scene anticipates the eschatological goal for all creation to worship God and the Lamb.[32] As the vision progresses, John is shown scene after scene of heavenly worship where God and the Lamb continue to be lauded for their character and their works. In many of the worship scenes, John also sees the overcomers – those who, while on earth, gave their lives for the Lamb – worshipping around the throne in heaven (7.9-17; 14.1-5; 15.1-8). That those who refuse to worship the beast on earth are put to death (Revelation 13) but then found to be alive and around the throne reinforces for the hearers the primacy of worship both while on earth *and* continuing in heaven. That the overcomers are in the presence of God and fully engaged in worship bolsters the hearers in their own practice of worship in the midst of potential suffering.[33] The worship of heaven is thereby paradigmatic and pedagogical, for worship is the primary purpose of the people of God and forms a crucial component of the witness

---

what the Spirit actually said because we often do not give time for reflecting on or responding to the Spirit's message. Finding ways to retain the message of the Spirit, such as writing it down, could assist Pentecostals in their desire to be people led by the Spirit.

[31] See Cartledge, *Testimony in the Spirit*, p. 48, where he discusses the prophetic words given in the Hockley Pentecostal Church. While he cites them as evidence of the theocentric and Christocentric theology of Pentecostalism, they function within that community as an important part of their worship.

[32] Bauckham, *The Theology of the Book of Revelation*, p. 33.

[33] This is helpful for Pentecostals in developing a much-needed theology of suffering. See Warrington, *Pentecostal Theology*, pp. 303-308.

of the church in the world.[34] Additionally, the Apocalypse portrays for the hearers the goal of worship: to be New Jerusalem, to be intimately united with God and the Lamb in a state of unhindered worship and adoration. John's hearers are invited to enter into an alternate reality – an escape from their present situation. Likewise, Pentecostal worship offers an escape to the worshipper into 'ultimate reality'.[35] The testimony of the early Pentecostals – that they suddenly found themselves transported to the throne of God or saw the table spread for the marriage supper of the Lamb – affirms what the Apocalypse has portrayed; namely, that in worship, the boundary between the present and the future is breached. The Spirit transports the worshippers back and forth between heaven and earth. The Apocalypse's revelation of worship in its various expressions as the featured activity of heaven and, thereby a crucial task of the church, invites Pentecostals to evaluate both their definition of 'worship' and its role within their communities.

Simon Chan calls Pentecostals to the discerning task of examining what they are practicing in worship. He identifies two 'models' of worship in the contemporary Pentecostal church: the charismatic model and the evangelical model:

> The charismatic model is usually organized around the singing of praises, as seen in the way the contemporary worship service is called: 'prayer and praise' or 'praise and worship'. When worship is largely reduced to a string of praise ditties the aim of worship subtly shifts from encountering God … to mood creation and possibly psychological manipulation … In the evangelical model, worship is reduced to preaching. Singing is only a preparation to hear the sermon … Reductionistic worship simply practices a

---

[34] Thompson, 'Worship in the Book of Revelation', p. 47: '[T]he question of our worship is a fundamental and ultimate question. For John, worship of God is the purpose of human life'.

[35] R. Jaichandran and B.D. Madhav, 'Pentecostal Spirituality in a Postmodern World', *AJPS* 6.1 (2003), p. 59. Althouse and Wilkinson, 'Playing in the Father's Love', p. 96, see that the significance of understanding worship as ritual play is that it allows participants to 'imagine a different world'.

reductionistic theology even when the church's theology may be theoretically sound.[36]

The Apocalypse refuses 'reductionistic worship' by offering a robust theology of worship by which Pentecostals might measure and develop their own theology of worship – a theology of experience and encounter that places authentic *Spirit*ed worship of God at its heart. Further, Pentecostals should view worship as a formational[37] and catechetical rite. Cheryl Bridges Johns calls the Pentecostal church to see itself as 'the primary agent of conscientization'. As such, the community helps the believer to 'understand reality in a new way and to see himself or herself as actors in history of both the church and the world'. The liturgical elements common to Pentecostals, which 'serve to initiate and instruct believers', are the means by which this new reality is constructed and maintained.[38] She urges Pentecostals to envision worship as formation: as worshippers participate in the 'rituals of Pentecostal worship, they are incorporated, enculturated, and apprenticed. They are also transformed inasmuch as the liturgies are alive with the power of the Holy Spirit. The church retains its prophetic identity, maintaining an ongoing dialectic between itself and the socio-political environment in which it exists.'[39] The Apocalypse is for the churches who by their worship and witness are to be agents of conscientization among the inhabitants of the earth. As the churches participate in and appropriate for themselves the worship of heaven, they *are* incorporated, enculturated, and apprenticed.[40] Not only are the worshippers incorporated into communion with God but also into communion with fellow worshippers, both in their own pew and

---

[36] Chan, *Pentecostal Theology*, pp. 36-37. Chan follows this with the suggestion that the way forward for Pentecostals is to consider a eucharistic model of worship as a way to ensure 'sound, holistic worship' (p. 29).

[37] Contra Smith, *Desiring the Kingdom*, p. 150 who argues that 'The point of worship is not formation; rather, formation is an overflow effect of our encounter with the Redeemer in praise and prayer, adoration and communion'.

[38] Johns, *Pentecostal Formation*, p. 125. The specific liturgical rituals that she lists are water baptism, communion, footwashing, testimony, healing rituals, Spirit baptism, and songs and dances (pp. 125-29). Also Boone, 'Community and Worship: The Key Components of Pentecostal Christian Formation', pp. 129-42.

[39] Johns, *Pentecostal Formation*, pp. 129-30.

[40] Miller and Yamamori, *Global Pentecostalism: The New Face of Christian Social Engagement*, p. 134, note that collective worship reinforces shared values.

with those around the world.[41] Worship serves as an apprenticeship for that day when worshippers from every tribe and tongue will stand around the throne and worship God and the Lamb. The lure of Babylon fades; the magnificence of New Jerusalem beckons; and, it takes place in worship.

Fifth, the Apocalypse demonstrates that God alone is to be worshipped. This is so because of who God is.[42] God is holy (4.8), and the Creator of *all* things that are (4.11; 10.6) and all things that will *be* – the new heaven and earth (21.1, 5). God as holy and Creator identifies the 'most elemental forms of perception of God' and requires a response of worship.[43] To offer worship to anyone or anything else constitutes idolatry – a practice that is anathema in the Apocalypse (9.20; 13.4, 8; 21.8; 22.15; also 19.10; 22.9). God is the One who was, and is, and is to come (1.4, 8; 4.8; also 11.17; 16.5 [who was and is]), the Almighty (1.8; 4.8; 11.17; 15.3; 16.7; 19.6, 15; 21.22), the Alpha and Omega (1.8; 21.6) who sits on the throne (Revelation 4; 5; 6.16; 7.10; 19.4; 20.11; 21.5) and lives forever (4.9; 10.6; 15.7). God is Father (1.6; 2.27), Sovereign Lord (6.10), and Judge (15.3; 16.5, 7; 18.20; 19.2; 20.11-15) who from the throne, reigns over all (11.17; 19.6). It is this God who reigns supreme and whose will and plan is unveiled; it is this God who will inaugurate a new heaven and earth where God will dwell with humanity (21.3) and they will see God's face and bear God's name upon their foreheads (22.4). For who God is and for all that God has done, is doing, and will do, God is worthy of worship; thus, worship must be oriented *theo*logically.

With that said, the Apocalypse also reveals that the center of redemption history is found in the person and work of Jesus Christ.[44] Like God, Jesus is given various titles in the Apocalypse. The dominant designation is Lamb (Revelation 5; 6.1, 3, 5, 7, 16; 7.9, 14, 17;

---

[41] J. Alvarado, 'Worship in the Spirit: Perspectives on Liturgical Theology and Praxis', *JPT* 21 (2012), p. 140-41, writes of the 'spiritual connectedness' that takes place in worship. 'It is through worship that humanity is connected most significantly in communion with the divine, and it is through the Spirit that all worshippers are connected with each other to the glory of God'.

[42] Bauckham, *The Theology of the Book of Revelation*, p. 32, aptly notes that 'true knowledge of who God is is inseparable from worship of God'.

[43] Bauckham, *The Theology of the Book of Revelation*, p. 33.

[44] Boxall, *Revelation: Vision and Insight*, p. 152.

12.11; 14.1, 4, 10; 15.3; 17.14; 19.7; 21.22; 22.3) which symbolizes Jesus' supreme role as Redeemer. Jesus is also the Faithful Witness, Firstborn from the dead, and the Ruler of the kings of the earth (1.5). To John and to the seven churches, Jesus identifies himself as the First and the Last, the Living One, and the One who holds the keys to Death and Hades (1.17-18; also 2.8; 3.14; 22.13). Further, Jesus is 'one like a son of man' (1.13-16; 14.14), the Son of God (2.18), the Amen (3.14), Shepherd (7.17), Christ (1.1-2; 11.15; 12.10; 20.4, 6), King of kings and Lord of lords (17.14; 19.16), Faithful and True (19.11), and Word of God (19.13). Jesus is the Root and Off-spring of David (22.16), the Morning Star (22.16; also 2.28) and Lord (22.20-21). It is this Jesus who is coming soon (1.7; 16.15; 22.7, 12, 20; also Revelation 2–3). In Revelation 4, the worship af-forded to God is extended to the Lamb in Revelation 5. The pro-found implications of that chapter's final hymn being addressed to 'the one who sits on the throne *and* to the Lamb' (5.13) can scarcely be overstated! Jesus is worshipped as the one who brings about God's salvation through his death and resurrection. The worship of God includes the worship of Jesus, not as two separate objects of worship but as one; thus, the worship of God *and* Jesus re-defines monotheistic worship.[45] Evidentiary of this is that throughout the Apocalypse, Jesus acts and speaks as God acts and speaks; in fact, the hearers can scarcely distinguish John's divine referents,[46] which is surely the point. God and the Lamb *is* Alpha and Omega, the Be-ginning and the End (1.8; 22.13);[47] God and the Lamb *is* the temple within New Jerusalem (21.22). Worship and worshippers must be oriented *theo*logically and *christo*logically and not to the exclusion of one or the other. The worship of God and the Lamb would not be complete without giving consideration to the worship of the Spirit.

---

[45] Thompson, 'Worship in the Book of Revelation', pp. 50-51: 'Worship of Christ was not a development in early Christianity that occurred at the expense of monotheism, but precisely within an *unrelenting monotheistic framework*' (emphasis mine).

[46] E.g. Rev. 11.15 (use of the singular verb βασιλεύσει even though God and Christ are mentioned together); 22.3-4 uses singular forms of αὐτος when the antecedent is God and the Lamb. Bauckham, *The Theology of the Book of Revelation*, p. 60 says that John is 'prepared to defy grammar for the sake of theology'.

[47] Bauckham, *The Theology of the Book of Revelation*, p. 58, states that the titles Je-sus shares with God 'indicate that he shared the eternal being of God from be-fore creation'.

While this is not made explicit in the Apocalypse, the very fact that the Spirit is depicted in relation to God (as the seven-fold Spirit before the throne of God, 1.4; 4.5) and to the Lamb (the seven eyes as the seven-fold Spirit sent out into the world, 5.6) clearly links the Spirit with God and Jesus, both of whom receive worship. As already noted, the Spirit is the enabler of worship; true worship takes place *in the Spirit*. It does not seem to be a stretch to suggest that the worship of God and the Lamb *includes* the worship of the Spirit.[48] This implies a more expansive understanding of the divinity of the Holy Spirit than is generally attributed to the Apocalypse.[49]

Land states, that for Pentecostals, 'God is the last thing ... Therefore Pentecostals should focus their attention and theological efforts on an understanding of God as the eschatological Trinitarian presence and not on speculative end-time sequences'.[50] Pentecostal worship is about encounter with God. The Apocalypse provides Pentecostals with a cadre of ascriptions for God and Jesus in combination with a rich liturgy that extols the character and works of God that can inform all aspects of Pentecostal worship. Pentecostal worship should be God-centered rather than centered on the worshipper. James K.A. Smith states, 'Worship is not *for me* ... worship is about and for God'.[51] Worship is about God's story; the Apocalypse depicts God's story, especially as revealed in Jesus the Lamb. Pentecostals should ensure that their worship proclaims the narrative of God and God's works in the past, the present, and the future.

Sixth, the Apocalypse differentiates between legitimate and illegitimate worship. This is a theme which permeates the Apocalypse. Fundamental to the Apocalypse is that God alone is to be worshipped. The twice-repeated injunction – 'Worship God' (19.10; 22.9) – reverberates as the heart of the Apocalypse. John's proclivity

---

[48] See Thomas, *The Apocalypse*, pp. 226-30.

[49] Bauckham, *The Theology of the Book of Revelation*, pp. 23-25 underscores that from Rev. 1.4-5 on, John depicts the divine in 'threefold' terms. John, states Bauckham, is concerned 'to include Jesus, as well as the Spirit, in Jewish monotheistic faith in God' (p. 24). He further expands on the role of the Spirit in the Apocalypse in ch. 5 (pp. 109-25). See also Waddell, *The Spirit of the Book of Revelation*.

[50] Land, *Pentecostal Spirituality*, p. 197.

[51] Smith, *Desiring the Kingdom*, p. 150.

to worship a being other than God (19.10; 22.9; also 17.6b) gives indication to the hearers of just how subtle false worship can be. The first hints of the subtleness of false worship come in the prophetic messages when the hearers are confronted with the realization that false worship has infiltrated their sacred spaces. 'Balaam' (2.14) and 'Jezebel' (2.20) are false teachers/prophets intentionally seeking to lure the churches into idolatrous practices. After the events associated with the sixth trumpet, John records that the inhabitants of the earth did not stop *worshipping* demons and idols (9.20). The full exegesis of illegitimate worship comes in Revelation 12–13. In these chapters, the hearers discover their adversaries, the Dragon, and his beasts. This evil trinity launches a full-scale campaign aimed at turning all of humanity from the worship of God by demanding worship of the beast. The inhabitants of the earth – those whose names are *not* in the book of life (13.8) – willingly give their worship and sing, 'Who is like the beast?' (13.4). Those who refuse to worship the beast – those whose names *are* in the Lamb's book of life – are killed (13.15). In Babylon the harlot, the hearers are confronted with another entity demanding their worship (Revelation 17). The sight of her is so wondrous that John's amazement at her teeters on worship – even while knowing that she is drunk on the blood of the saints (17.6-7). This again points to the subtle nature of false worship. Worship becomes a pledge of allegiance; that is, the followers of the Lamb and the followers of the beast are identified by their worship. True and false worship also leads people to specific eternal destinies; namely, to followers of the beast enter into the lake of fire (Rev. 20.11-15) while the followers of the Lamb enter into and are New Jerusalem (Revelation 21–22). The fate of the followers of the beast is not pre-determined, for the proclamations of the three angels in Revelation 14 go out to *everyone*: The first angel pleads, 'Fear God and give him glory ... Worship him ...' (14.7). The second angel prophesies the destruction of Babylon (14.8). The third angel announces the judgment that waits *if* any worship the beast (14.9-11). *Who* to worship becomes a conscious choice on the part of the worshipper. The recalcitrant who continues to refuse to worship God (as shown again in 16.9, 11, 21) will participate in the same fate as the Dragon and the beasts. The thread of what constitutes true and false worship woven throughout the Apocalypse is not just to show what happens to the followers of the beast. The Apocalypse is written for the churches. It is the people of God who must diligently guard against the subtle (and not so subtle) pressure to render worship to anyone or anything other than God and the Lamb. The images John employs – a Dragon, beasts, a harlot – are designed for maximum impact on the hearers. Bauckham writes, 'False worship, such as John portrays in the worship of the beast, is false precisely because its object is not the transcendent mystery, but only the mystification of something finite'.[52] This is why the churches are first taken up into heaven, along with John, to fall before the God of all creation and the Lamb, their Redeemer. They hear and participate in the thunderous worship repeatedly afforded to God and the Lamb. To them is shown the outcome of their perseverance and their refusal to worship the beast. It is in the context of dying due to a refusal to worship the beast that the hearers realize the true *blessedness* of 'those who die in the Lord' (Rev. 14.13), for it is the martyrs – those who refuse to worship the beast – who are alive in heaven, singing the song of Moses and the Lamb (Rev. 15.1-4). It is by engaging in the liturgy of heaven that John's hearers are to counter the false liturgies around them.

For Pentecostals, the temptation towards false worship might seem to be irrelevant; after all, Pentecostals seek above all an authentic and experiential encounter with God. Pentecostals, however, should constantly discern whether or not they are unwittingly engaging in false worship. It can come in the guise of elevating Pentecostal pastors or leaders onto platforms from which the glory reserved for God is ascribed to them. It can happen in worship where style is worshipped more than God. It can happen when edifices are built 'to the glory of God' but then the community has no resources or desire to engage the world outside its doors. The rising popularity of Pentecostalism and its growing acceptance in the mainstream of American culture likely offers the most subtle temptation. While the Apocalypse called John's hearers to resist the trappings of Babylon, it calls Pentecostals to resist the trappings of current culture. Smith discusses the impact of culture and maintains that cultural practices be viewed as 'secular liturgies': 'We need to recognize that these practices are not neutral or benign, but rather intentionally

---

[52] Bauckham, *The Theology of Revelation*, p. 45.

loaded to form us into certain kinds of people – to unwittingly make us disciples of rival kings and patriotic citizens of rival kingdoms'.[53] Such liturgies wear away at Pentecostal self-identity by demanding that Pentecostals accommodate themselves to the trends of contemporary culture. Early Pentecostals recognized that the move of the Spirit that they were experiencing put them at odds with their culture. Seymour wrote, 'O beloved, our reigning time has not come yet. We are to be with the Babe from the manger to the throne. Our reigning time will come when Jesus comes in great power from the throne. Until then we are to be beaten, to be spit upon, and mocked. We are to be like His son'.[54] Perhaps contemporary North American Pentecostalism has drifted away from its early self-understanding. If so, then the message of the Apocalypse is uncomfortable and even unwelcomed, for the Apocalypse calls for the followers of the Lamb to refuse to engage in false worship and to self-identify as overcomers – those willing to lose their lives for the sake of the Lamb. As noted earlier by Albrecht, Pentecostals often define worship as a way of Christian life. The Apocalypse takes this a step further so that even death is viewed as an act of worship. This is not to be morbid but rather to stretch the gaze of the hearers from the world around them to the world awaiting them. Pentecostals might engage in critical self-reflection to ensure that they are not participating in anything that can be labeled as false worship. They might also reflect on ways in which their liturgy can engage the imagination of the worshippers so that the culture of New Jerusalem so fills their hearts and minds that the contemporary culture of Babylon loses all allure. The call of the Spirit to come out of Babylon (18.4) is as urgent for contemporary Pentecostals as it was for John's hearers. Ever before the hearts and minds of Pentecostal worshippers must be the mantra of the Apocalypse: 'Worship God!'

Seventh, the Apocalypse describes numerous liturgical activities which are expressions of worship.

A. *Hymns.* The most recognizable expressions of worship in the Apocalypse are the hymns which resound throughout the

---

[53] Smith, *Desiring the Kingdom*, pp. 90-91.
[54] Seymour, *AF* 1.10 (September, 1907), p. 2.

narrative.[55] The hymns heard in heaven are exclusively focused on the person and work of God and the Lamb. As such, the hymns reflect the tenor throughout the Apocalypse that worship is fiercely monotheistic, with the understanding that God and the Lamb (and the Spirit) are viewed in unity; that is, the worship of God includes the worship of Jesus (and the worship of the Spirit). The hymns are profoundly theological and thereby become melodic vehicles for catechesis.[56] It is largely through the music of the Apocalypse that the hearers are formed in their understanding of God as discussed above. The hymns of heaven are the hymns of the churches; that is, one can scarcely imagine John's churches not singing these songs as part of their worship. It does not matter whether John composed these songs or adapted them from the churches' worship known to him; what matters is that in John's claim to hear these sung in heaven, the hymns have divine sanction and approval. The hearers are thereby encouraged to agree with and, indeed, adopt the 'premises' established in the hymns.[57] To sing them or to pattern songs on them is thus of utmost importance. The hymns of heaven demonstrate that the hymns of the church must be, above all, theological expressions of praise directed to God. This feature of the hymns of the Apocalypse should encourage Pentecostals, who love to sing and who often define worship wholly in terms of songs and singing,[58] to evaluate both the content and function of their own hymnody. Warrington points out that music in Pentecostal worship is often 'very personal in terms of endearment and communication between the singer and God' and that the lyrics 'have increasingly taken the form of more directional expressions to God than doctrinal reflections on his character'.[59] The hymns of the Apocalypse, with their clear exultation of God and God's character, can serve as a helpful corrective to this tendency within contemporary Pentecostal churches. The hymns of the Apocalypse, for example, neither

---

[55] Rev. 4.8, 11; 5.9-10, 12, 13; 7.10, 12, 15-17; 11.15-18; 12.10-12; 15.3-4; 16.5-6; 19.1-2, 3, 5; 6-8; also 13.4.

[56] R. Webber, *Ancient-Future Worship: Proclaiming and Enacting God's Narrative* (Grand Rapids: Baker Books, 2008), p. 168: 'Music is the vehicle that communicates worship in the language of the people'.

[57] Harris, *The Literary Function of the Hymns in the Apocalypse*, p. 284.

[58] Albrecht, *Rites in the Spirit*, pp. 155-56.

[59] Warrington, *Pentecostal Theology*, p. 224.

make use of first person pronouns nor offer the worshippers' perspective or desires; rather, the hymns form the hearers into *theo*logical singers.[60] If Pentecostals sing their theology, then a robust *theo*logy should ring out loud and clear from their music.

The hymns of the Apocalypse also assist the hearers in reinterpreting present reality. Many of the hymns are embedded in the midst of narratives depicting trouble and danger for the people of God; nevertheless, the songs never devolve into dirges acutely focused on pain and suffering. Instead, the hymns locate the present in the Apocalypse's theme of the coming of God's kingdom (7.10-12; 11.15-18; 12.10-12; 19.1-8). The suffering inherent in the reality of martyrdom is not denied or ignored (7.15-17; 16.6) but assuaged with the assurance that God will wipe away every tear and the Lamb will shepherd those who have come through the great tribulation (7.13-17). It is the martyrs – those who have imitated their Lord in death and thereby become overcomers, like their Lord – who can sing 'Great and marvelous are your deeds, Lord God Almighty. Just and true are your ways, King of the ages' (15.3). The hymns reorient reality and remind the hearers that worship in song interprets all earthly existence from heaven's perspective. This, too, is instructive for Pentecostals. Pentecostal music should not consist of lyrics that teach the congregants to deny or divorce themselves from the reality of life; rather, in singing should be the recognition that the present is fused with the future so that 'the problems of life are revisited in light of the end of all things. The power of the end is made available in the present to the degree that the present does not have

---

[60] Smith, *Desiring the Kingdom*, p. 150, notes that 'the grammar of our worship' is often centered on the worshipper rather than on God. 'For instance, consider the number of worship choruses that make "I" (the worshiper) the subject of the sentence rather than God. Thus, unwittingly, we actually end up singing about ourselves – *our* devotion, *our* worship, *our* surrender – rather than about God.' See also Chan, *Pentecostal Theology*, p. 118, who laments that Pentecostal worship 'is often hampered by a preoccupation with individualistic concerns' which is 're-flected in the overwhelming number of charismatic songs which focus on the big 'I'. Songs which focus on the worshipper or on his/her desires and longings are not inappropriate (see the Psalms); however, an over-abundance of such songs leads to an imbalanced theology. Often contemporary praise and worship songs used in many Pentecostal churches do not mention God or Jesus directly but instead use vague pronouns. My point is not to advocate for the removal of such songs but to invite Pentecostals to examine their repertoire of music to ensure that it is theologically focused.

the final word.'[61] The hymns of the Apocalypse become the churches' language of resistance; they provide the means by which the worshipper can overcome the Dragon and his beast and sing the songs of the Lamb even in the face of death (12.10-12). Songs become a 'way to sound out suffering in the community whereby the Holy Spirit redeems the suffering by transforming the sufferers and their circumstances.'[62]

The hymns of the Apocalypse are prophetic – declaring what is and what will be. By this, the hearers are encouraged to be steadfast and to endure for despite the seeming unending reach of the Dragon and the beasts, the kingdom of our Lord and of his Christ has come (11.15), rewards will be given to the people of God (11.18), the accuser has been cast down (12.10), the smoke of Babylon goes up for ever and ever (19.3) and the wedding of the Lamb is to come (19.7). The hymns thus inform and sustain the worshippers on their journey through perilous times and events knowing that New Jerusalem – the final goal of worship – is just ahead.[63] At the heart of the prophetic nature of the hymns is the Spirit, for it is *in the Spirit* that John and the churches hear the hymns. Pentecostals might consider whether or not songs in their own body of music serve this prophetic task or whether there are other ways to engage the prophetic through music. To this end, as early Pentecostals discovered, singing in the Spirit can be a means for the Spirit to sing a prophetic word in the midst of the worshipping community.[64] As noted in chapter 3 of this study, many of the songs found in the pages of early Pentecostal periodicals included the notation that they were given to the individual by the Spirit (either in tongues

---

[61] Johns, 'The Light That Streams from the End', p. 15.

[62] Daniels, '"Gotta Moan Sometime"', p. 28.

[63] Land, *Pentecostal Spirituality*, p. 113, notes that the oral-narrative liturgy of early Pentecostalism was a 'rehearsal of and for the kingdom of God'. He states that Pentecostals 'rehearsed for the coming of the Lord, the final event of the historical drama; and the songs, testimonies and so on were a means of grace used to sanctify, encourage, mobilize and direct them on their journey'.

[64] Dove, 'Hymnody and Liturgy in the Azusa Street Revival, 1906-1908', p. 248-49 states, 'Of the more than 130 references to hymns or singing reported in the *Apostolic Faith* newspaper, at least eighty-four are of people singing in the Spirit…' Dove calls singing in the Spirit 'the quintessential expression of the free liturgy of Azusa Street' as it 'appeared to be unplanned and untraceable to human origins'.

[and subsequently translated] or in the vernacular of the worshipper). As many of these songs treated the theme of the return of Jesus, they served as prophetic songs for the worshipping communities.[65] In many contemporary Pentecostal churches, this ritual of singing in the Spirit is seldom given space within the liturgy, yet perhaps a renewed understanding of it as a means for the Spirit to speak a prophetic word will lead to a retrieval of this Spirit-led liturgical activity.[66] Such a practice can become another way for Pentecostal churches to hear what the Spirit is saying in their midst.

B. *Musical instruments.* Musical instruments – trumpets and harps – are found throughout the Apocalypse. Seven angels each sound a trumpet by which six judgments are released on the earth (Rev. 8.6-9.19), and the seventh trumpet announces a heavenly worship scene (11.15-19). Harps appear exclusively in the worship scenes (5.8; 15.2; also 14.3).[67] In Rev. 5.8, the living creatures and the elders each have a harp, which suggests that they use the harps to accompany the songs sung to the Lamb (5.9-10, 12, 13). In Rev. 15.2, those who had been victorious over the beast have harps given to them by God, by which they likewise accompany their singing (15.3-4). Although admittedly not occupying a large space on the narrative stage, the presence of musical instruments in the context of the worship scenes suggests their suitability in worship. While it can be argued that John never explicitly states that the harps are being strummed, one cannot imagine any other reason for holding a harp except for playing. This seems to be confirmed by the proximity of the mentioning of harps to the hymns sung by the worshippers

---

[65] Even if uninterpreted, singing in the Spirit is a way for the individual or corporate body to sing in concert with the Spirit of God. Pentecostals find basis for such a practice in 1 Cor. 14.15.

[66] See Miller and Yamamori, *Global Pentecostalism*, pp. 146-47, for their observations of speaking and singing in tongues as they studied global Pentecostalism. Although the authors are not Pentecostal and they label themselves (perhaps tongue-in-cheek) as 'two jaded sociologists', they note that speaking and/or singing in tongues in the context of worship 'seems altogether natural – that is, after one has observed the phenomenon a few dozen times'. They conclude: 'Pentecostals obviously place the phenomenon within a theological framework of the Holy Spirit speaking through them ...' (p. 147). See C.M. Johansson, 'Singing in the Spirit', *Paraclete* 24.2 (1990), pp. 20-23.

[67] In Rev. 14.3, John sees the Lamb standing on Mt. Zion with the 144,000, and he says that the sound he heard from heaven was like that of 'harpists harping their harps'.

(5.8; 15.2). Plausibility for this assumption can be found in the explicit sounding of the seventh trumpet which yields, and perhaps even accompanies, the hymns of Revelation 11. All of this suggests that musical instruments are appropriate vehicles for the expression of worship. John's hearers would likely think of the musical instruments listed in the Psalms and even of King David, the harpist, as well as any musical instruments used in their own worship contexts. Musical instruments point to the presence of musicians. In the Apocalypse, the living creatures and elders as well as the overcomers seem to be singers and musicians. While the verbal worship found in the hymns is that which is most noted in the Apocalypse, the creation of instrumental worship is often overlooked. In the Apocalypse, worship is a performance (in its most positive sense) before God and the Lamb.[68] For contemporary Pentecostals, congregational singing is almost always accompanied by instruments.[69] The harp of the Apocalypse is replaced by the guitar (acoustic, electric, and/or bass), and to it are often added keyboards and drums, as well as any number of brass and woodwind instruments.[70] Undoubtedly the instruments found in the Apocalypse contribute to the *loudness* of the book in much the same way that Pentecostal worship services are usually loud; however, the performance of worship should always be to and for God and the Lamb. Just as instruments serve to express creative worship to God in the Apocalypse, Pentecostal musicians should maintain this singular focus and see the valuable contribution they add to the creation and expression of

---

[68] Jaichandran and Madhav, 'Pentecostal Spirituality in a Postmodern World', p. 57, write about worship as performance 'that attends closely to God. God is the audience and the congregation is to perform the drama of praise'.

[69] D. Daniels, '"Gotta Moan Sometime": A Sonic Exploration of Earwitnesses to Early Pentecostal Sound in North America', *Pneuma* 30 (2008), p. 17, explains how important music and music-making was to the Azusa Revival but also how debates arose over musical instruments. 'Sacred instruments included the piano and organ; homemade instruments included washboards, bones, jugs, and kazoos; and "worldly" or "the devil's" instruments included the violin (fiddle), banjo, guitar, and drums'. He also documents how guitars, drums, and brass instruments made their way into the Pentecostal soundscape (pp. 20-22).

[70] Albrecht, *Rites in the Spirit*, pp. 143-47, identifies music in the Pentecostal church as an 'auditory icon' that 'embraces the Pentecostal worshipers in an analogous fashion to the manner in which icons visually surround the Eastern Orthodox faithful in their sanctuaries'. He further identifies musical instruments (along with sound, lighting equipment, etc.) as 'ritual objects'.

worship within the worshipping community. Early Pentecostals testified to receiving the gift of suddenly being able to play an instrument for which they had no prior training, and they were adamant that this gift came from the Holy Spirit. They testified that it was the Holy Spirit playing through them. Pentecostal musicians in tune with the Spirit should likewise see themselves as musicians who play *in the Spirit*. The creative and spontaneous flow of music that connects the musician to God in a worship experience that is deep and unexplainable is the Spirit playing through them. Pentecostals might seek intentional ways both to foster this sense of playing *in the Spirit* and to encourage the community to hear what the Spirit is saying through instrumental worship.

C. *Kinesthetic movement.* The Apocalypse depicts kinesthetic movement as an appropriate liturgical response to God. Throughout the narrative, John witnesses various characters prostrating or falling down before the throne of God. The first example of this comes in Rev. 4.10 where, in response to the worship given to God by the living creatures, the 24 elders fall down before the throne of God and worship. In Rev. 5.14, the elders fall down and worship before God and the Lamb when the living creatures pronounce the Ἀμήν ('amen'). When John sees the great multitude singing before the throne and before the Lamb, he also sees all the angels, the elders, and the living creatures falling down[71] before the throne and worshipping (7.11). Finally, in 19.4 the elders and living creatures fall down and worship God on the throne. The repetition of this liturgical act by the elders and living creatures confirms that prostration is, at least for the Apocalypse, the most appropriate response to the presence of God. While John witnesses these worshipful responses of the elders and living creatures, such a response is not new to John, for John himself falls down before the risen Christ (1.17). Given the liturgical cast of the Apocalypse, John's response of prostration is also a response of worship, as he finds himself in the overwhelming presence of Jesus. Prostration demonstrates that the worshipper recognizes the presence of the Divine. Such recognition demands a response not only of mind but of body. If the elders and living creatures who dwell continuously in the presence of

---

[71] The Greek uses the third plural ἔπεσαν ('they fell') which suggests that the angels, elders, and living creatures are the subject.

God respond to God in such a way, how much more so should the hearers respond to the presence of God in their midst with an act of bodily worship. In the Apocalypse, it is this singular act of kinesthetic worship (not the clapping, raising hands, dancing, and so forth of the Psalter) that gives full expression to the experience of being overwhelmed by God.[72] The early Pentecostals looked to the Apocalypse as verification for their experiences of being 'slain in the Spirit',[73] and contemporary Pentecostals most often experience 'being under the power of the Spirit' during times of prayer. In the Apocalypse, however, the ritual act of prostration takes place in and as worship. This suggests that *Spirit*ed worship is embodied worship. Pentecostals expect to encounter God in their Spirit-led worship, but perhaps they have stopped short of seeking an encounter which overwhelms both mind and body; the Apocalypse presents prostration as an appropriate worshipful response to that encounter.[74] Smith states that Pentecostalism is an 'embodied spirituality' because Pentecostals use their whole bodies to worship.[75] Lying prostrate, he further suggests, is 'embodied humiliation'.[76] I would suggest that this falls short of capturing the full significance this

---

[72] The rebuke that John receives when he attempts to prostrate himself before the heavenly messengers reinforces that prostration is an act of worship reserved for God alone.

[73] Land, *Pentecostal Spirituality*, p. 113, notes that the early Pentecostals 'had a total "body life" of worship. The whole body responded and each person presented his or her body in receptivity and yieldedness to the Lord.'

[74] This is not to replace kinesthetic movements such as hand-clapping, hand-raising, or dancing before the Lord. All of these are very important in Pentecostal worship. Through clapping and dancing, Pentecostals engage in exuberant worship; through hand-raising, Pentecostals express surrender and give allegiance to God. My point is to suggest that prostration should be viewed as an appropriate total-body response of worship to the overwhelming presence of God experienced in worship.

[75] J.K.A. Smith, 'Teaching a Calvinist to Dance', *Christianity Today* 52.5 (2008), p. 44. Albrecht, *Rites in the Spirit*, p. 247, states that 'Pentecostals seek to worship their God with their whole being. They have intuitively presented their bodies, their physicality, as instruments of worship. They seek to move with the Spirit, but not as incorporeal selves'. See also Miller and Yamamori, *Global Pentecostalism*, p. 138 who identify worship as a 'full-bodied expression'. They go on to say that Pentecostalism 'encourages people to merge mind and body into a unified expression that honors emotional and physical expressions as integral elements of worship' (p. 142).

[76] Smith, 'Teaching a Calvinist to Dance', p. 44.

liturgical activity plays in the Apocalypse and can play in the *Spirit*ed worship of Pentecostalism. Falling prostrate, like being slain in the Spirit, is an embodied response of being so overwhelmed by the very presence of God that standing is no longer possible.

D. *Prayers.* In the Apocalypse, prayer is a liturgical activity of the people of God. In Rev. 5.8 and 8.3-4, the prayers of the saints are portrayed as incense offered up in golden bowls to God on the golden altar before the throne. The significance of the prayers of the saints is in their location – the throne room of God. The prayers of the saints are offered to God and the Lamb as part of the ongoing worship in heaven (5.8-10). In the unsealing of the fifth seal, John hears the prayer of lament from the souls under the altar who call on God to judge the inhabitants of the earth and avenge their blood (6.9-10). The answer to this prayer for justice begins to unfold with the seven trumpets (8.3-5). The message for the hearers is clear: prayer matters; that is, God hears and responds to the prayers of the people of God. Prayer constitutes a liturgical act that is pleasing to God – like the fragrance of incense.[77] Although the references to prayer are brief, they are nonetheless important as reminders that, as Mangina notes, 'the commerce between heaven and earth moves both ways'.[78] The churches offer up prayers with confidence, knowing that their prayers reach the throne of God. The subsequent events of the Apocalypse suggest that prayer moves the hand of God. Prayer is not a silent affair in the Apocalypse for the souls under the altar *cry out* to God (6.10). The verb κράζω ('I cry out') carries the sense of crying out or even shouting, and suggests a visceral and loud lament. The people of God likewise must continue to cry out to God, for God will vindicate them in the end when Christ returns (19.11-16). Self-preservation does not seem to be an appropriate prayer in the world of the Apocalypse; rather, a prayer for boldness in the face of the beast would seem more in keeping with its tenor. 'Prayer', states Steve Land, 'is the primary theological'

---

[77] Thomas, *The Apocalypse*, p. 230, 'The prayers of the saints are not simply a ritual to be rendered in a perfunctory way, but are reflected in the activity around the throne of God himself. If the prayers of the saints on earth enable them to participate in heavenly worship, surely the same would be true of other forms of worship.'

[78] Mangina, *Revelation*, p. 119.

and 'most significant activity' of Pentecostals.[79] Pentecostals expect God to answer their prayers.[80] It is this sense of expectancy borne out of an encounter with God through worship that galvanizes prayer as central to Pentecostal spirituality – God is present and God will respond.[81] Prayers, therefore, are not superfluous or added at the end of worship; prayers are a vital act of worship.

Pentecostals should find encouragement to offer prayers of lament and cries for justice like those sounded forth by the souls under the altar.[82] Prayers often collapse into self-centered wish lists that reflect personal wants and needs, yet in the Apocalypse, the cries of lament reflect the realities of an oppressed people – a people for whom God is their only source of help. Cheryl Bridges Johns urges the Pentecostal community to learn the language of lament and engage in it. 'In doing so, Pentecostals do not escape from reality. Rather, they take hold of reality and bring it to the One who reveals to them victory.'[83] In addition, the Apocalypse reminds Pentecostals to continue to pray, like their predecessors did, for Jesus to return. Such a prayer reminds the community that this world is not their home, that though they reside in Babylon, Babylon does not reside in them. The prayer for Jesus to return is not to be prayed lightly or flippantly but fervently and with the knowledge of what his return entails. For Pentecostals, the foundational prayer which defines them as people of the future should be the same as

---

[79] Land, *Pentecostal Spirituality*, p. 166.

[80] Warrington, *Pentecostal Spirituality*, p. 216. Boone, 'Community and Worship', p. 140, identifies prayer as 'a rite performed with the expectation of results'.

[81] P. Neumann, 'Spirituality' in Adam Stewart (ed.), *Handbook of Pentecostal Christianity* (DeKalb: Northern Illinois University Press, 2012), p. 198.

[82] Daniels, '"Gotta Moan Sometime"', pp. 17-18, describes early Pentecostal prayer meetings in which 'whispers, cries, moanings, groanings, wailing, weeping, shrieks, and hollers' could all be heard. 'It was a setting in which a wide range of sounds was permitted rather than policed'.

[83] C. Bridges Johns, 'The Adolescence of Pentecostalism: In Search of a Legitimate Sectarian Identity', *Pneuma* 17.1 (Spring 1995), p. 15. See also S.A. Ellington, 'The Costly Loss of Testimony', *JPT* 16 (2000), pp. 48-59 who argues that 'the result of the removal of lament from the prayer language of the church has often been the de-legitimization of suffering and the silencing of questioning and protest' (p. 54). He encourages Pentecostals to look to the Psalter for the interdependent relationship between testimony and lament. He suggests that if the Pentecostal church silences lament it will lose its testimony both in the community and in the world (p. 59).

that voiced by John, 'Come, Lord Jesus' (Rev. 22.20).[84] Prayers for healing, a staple in early Pentecostalism, need not be neglected in the contemporary Pentecostal church, for it is in New Jerusalem that, among other things, pain will cease (Rev. 21.4), and the leaves of the tree of life will be for the healing of the nations (Rev. 22.2).[85] Pentecostals might reflect on how their understanding of Jesus as healer[86] is enacted in their worship as well as what it might look like to pray *now* for the healing of the nations.

E. *Words of worship.* Specific liturgical words, Ἀμήν ('amen', 1.6, 7; 3.14; 5.14; 7.12 (2x); 22.20) and Ἀλληλουϊά ('hallelujah', 19.1, 3, 4, 6), are found in the Apocalypse. The 'amen', or 'so be it', expresses 'affirmation and solidarity'[87] while the 'hallelujah' serves as the supreme exclamatory response to the destruction of Babylon. The frequency with which 'amen' occurs in the worship scenes suggests that it functions as a word of worship; the reserving of 'hallelujah' for the final worship scene and its four-fold use suggests that it is a very special exclamatory word of worship – a word reserved for expressing unbridled jubilation at the work of God. Although these words of worship do not dot every page of John's vision, their presence suggests their importance for John's hearers. Most likely, these were words of worship used in their own worship gatherings. Pentecostals also make use of these words, which Albrecht terms 'sacred expletives', when they gather for worship.[88] In most Pentecostal circles, the 'amen' is sounded in response to the sermon or to testimonies given to show that the community gives affirmation to what is being expressed. 'Hallelujah' is more commonly heard in worship but also in response to points made in a sermon or testimony.[89] These words, and others like them ('Thank you, Jesus', 'Glory', 'Bless God'), can lose their impact for Pentecostals when

---

[84] Smith, *Desiring the Kingdom*, p. 158.

[85] See also Rev. 3.18 where Jesus counsels the Laodicean church to buy from him salve to put on their eyes so that they can see – an image that suggests healing.

[86] For an excellent treatment of Jesus as healer in Revelation, see McQueen, *Toward a Pentecostal Eschatology*, pp. 248-57.

[87] Rotz, *Revelation*, p. 49.

[88] Albrecht, 'An Anatomy of Worship', p. 78.

[89] Ma, 'Pentecostal Worship in Asia', p. 141, remarks that in Asian Pentecostal churches, verbal responses, such as amen or Hallelujah, are expected.

used casually or flippantly or as responses that have nothing to do with the worship of God. The Apocalypse reveals that these words belong to the worship of God. To utter the 'amen' in worship is to affirm the extraordinary encounter with God found in *Spirit*ed worship; to lift up the 'hallelujah' is to enthusiastically 'Praise God!' for God's extraordinary works. Pentecostals might reflect on the need to preserve a *holy vernacular* – sacred words reserved for sacred worship.

F. *Silence.* The Apocalypse is often described as a *loud* book. John hears loud voices raised in worship, loud trumpet blasts announcing judgment, angels issuing proclamations in loud voices, and so forth. Yet tucked in the midst of the loudness and as John sees the Lamb open the seventh seal, a 30-minute period of silence blankets the throne room (8.1). This silence allows for a dramatic pause in the narrative, yet it does not appear that all activity is suspended until the period of silence is over; rather, most scholars conclude that the time of silence is to allow for the prayers of the saints to be heard (8.4), with the seven trumpets serving as a response to those prayers. This certainly provides assurance for the hearers that God indeed hears and responds to their prayers. This period of silence suggests that worshippers should take time to be silent before the Lord and *listen* for God's response. Silence is thereby not passive but active as the worshipper engages God non-verbally and from deep within their spirit.[90] As such, silence is a much needed element of worship that is missing from Pentecostal worship services. One of the pitfalls Ma identifies of lively and loud worship is that the loudness may mean that Pentecostals have 'lost their ability for meditation and reflective spiritual disciple' which contributes to a 'shallow spirituality'.[91] Seeing silence as an important element of worship could lead Pentecostals in developing a deeper spirituality. David Daniels writes about the prayer meetings of the early Pentecostals: 'Prayer meetings were one of the few places within early Pentecostalism in which the shunning of silence rarely occurred.

---

[90] Warrington, *Pentecostal Theology*, p. 221: 'Pentecostals have rarely exploited the benefits of silence and meditation as means of responding to God in a corporate gathering; to do so will provide another means of engaging with God'.

[91] Ma, 'Pentecostal Worship in Asia', p. 142.

Silence, even stretches of silence, was welcomed.[92] It is often in the silence –
the holy hush that suddenly envelops the worshipping community –
that God does extraordinary things. Pentecostals might consider
ways both to allow for silence as well as to discern what the Spirit is
saying and doing in those moments.

G. *Repentance*. In five of the seven prophetic messages to the
churches, Jesus calls the churches to corporate repentance as he
reveals things that are displeasing to him in their worship (2.5, 16,
22; 3.3, 19). Repentance is thus a crucial worship activity for the
churches. The repeated refrain – 'Let the one having ears hear what
the Spirit says to the churches' (2.7, 11, 17, 29; 3.6, 13, 22) – is more
than a literary device; for, with each successive use, the hearers are
confronted with the reality of the Spirit in their midst to reveal what
Jesus *knows* about the churches. Repentance is an act of worship
whereby the whole community responds to the discipline of the
Lord (3.19). Throughout the Apocalypse, repentance is connected
with worship. Through her teaching 'Jezebel' seeks to lure the saints
into idolatry (2.20). That she *refuses* to repent even though she has
been given time to do so (2.21-22) attests to the role of the Spirit in
bringing conviction (Jn 16.8) but also reveals the voluntary nature
of repentance. Over and over the inhabitants of the earth *refuse* to
repent and continue to *worship* idols and the beast (9.20-21; 16.9,
11). Those who refuse to repent share in the fate of the Dragon and
the beasts. The churches can ill afford to ignore the calls to repentance. Repentance, in many Pentecostal circles, is a private and indi-
vidualized act. The Apocalypse advocates for the appropriateness of
corporate confession and repentance as an integral part of worship.
One way forward might be for Pentecostals to look to their predecessors for a retrieval of footwashing (John 13) as a way for the
community to engage in a liturgical act of confession and repentance.[93]

H. *The Eucharist*. The Apocalypse also appears to contain allusions to the Eucharist. In the prophetic messages, Jesus speaks of
eating from the tree of life (2.7), partaking of the hidden manna

---

[92] Daniels, '"Gotta Moan Sometime"', p. 18.

[93] The early Pentecostals often practiced footwashing with the celebration of
the Eucharist. On this see Green, *Toward a Pentecostal Theology of the Lord's Supper*,
pp. 82-181. On footwashing, see J.C. Thomas, *Footwashing in John 13 and the Johannine Community* (JSNTS 61; Sheffield: JSOT, 1991).

(2.17), and eating with those who will open the door (3.20). At the end of the narrative, the hearers are told about the marriage supper of the Lamb (19.9), the imagery of the river of the water of life, and the tree of life which grows on each side of the river (22.1-2).[94] These images of eating and drinking suggest that partaking in the Eucharist may well have been a regular part of their corporate worship. Further, it is possible that one of the settings for the reading and hearing of the Apocalypse could have been a Eucharistic worship service. Barr's suggestion that the Apocalypse enacts the Eucharist[95] points not only to the evocative power of the narrative but also to the pedagogical significance of this rite of worship for the people of God. The prospect of conjoining the Apocalypse with the Eucharist could lead Pentecostals into a deepened appreciation of both. Reading and hearing the Apocalypse (or portions of it) while partaking of the Lord's Supper reminds Pentecostals that they are an eschatological community oriented 'to the future and the beyond'.[96] The Lord's Supper simultaneously beckons the worshippers to remember the slaughtered Lamb and to anticipate the marriage supper of the Lamb.[97] Green argues that the Lord's Supper should be at the core of Pentecostal worship and calls for a revisioning of Pentecostal worship around the Supper. He images the Eucharist-event as 'the hearth around which all the other liturgical furniture is arranged'. In the celebration of the Supper, 'the Spirit reminds worshippers that the whole of created life centers in the story of Jesus Christ, who has brought, shall bring, and is bringing all reality into communion with God'.[98] In ways unlike any other New Testament writing, the Apocalypse reveals this vision of reality. It is *this* Jesus, the one who is remembered, celebrated, anticipated, and worshipped in the Eucharist, who is unveiled in the Apocalypse as the

---

[94] The cup of abomination in the hand of Babylon (17.4) likely appears as a parody to the cup of the Eucharist.

[95] Barr, *Tales of the End*, p. 144. See also Boxall, *Revelation: Vision and Insight*, pp. 150-55 who argues for a eucharistic appropriation of the Apocalypse.

[96] Chan, *Pentecostal Theology*, p. 109.

[97] Green, *Toward a Pentecostal Theology of the Lord's Supper*, pp. 254-62 discusses the Lord's Supper as *anamnesis*. In the Supper, the worshippers remember Jesus as he *was* (as a historical figure), as he *is* ('the once-dead, now-risen-and-enthroned one'), and as he *shall be* (the coming one).

[98] Green, *Toward a Pentecostal Theology of the Lord's Supper*, pp. 316-17.

Risen Lord, the Lamb, the King of kings, the Alpha and Omega, and the one who is coming soon.

Finally, the Apocalypse conceives of witness as worship. Vocabulary related to the idea of witness or testimony is plenteous in the Apocalypse.[99] Jesus is the Faithful Witness (1.5) to whom John's writing gives witness (1.2), for whom Antipas (Jesus' faithful witness) gives his life (2.13), and by whom the saints, through their testimony, overcome the Devil (12.11). The two witnesses prophesy for 1260 days, and while the content of their testimony is not revealed and their lives are taken by the beast at the completion of their testimony (11.7), their vindication by God serves to validate the importance of their witness (11.11-12). What the churches read and hear in the Apocalypse is what they are called to proclaim to the world around them through their witness. The churches' witness is not separate from their worship. In their witness, the churches look outward to the inhabitants of the earth and, like John, submit to the prophetic task announced by the angel, 'You must prophesy again ...' (10.11). Like the two witnesses, the churches give their testimony without fear of the beast because they have already overcome the Devil through the Lamb and through their testimony (12.10-12). Losing their lives because of their testimony (11.7; 13.15) is their final act of worship while on earth; however, they will continue their witness to the Lamb through their worship before the throne of God in heaven (11.9-17; 14.1-5; 15.1-8). The optimistic view of the Apocalypse that the nations and kings of the earth will be in New Jerusalem indicates that witness is an act of worship in which the heart of the community is in tune with the heart of God (Jn 3.16). God *makes known* (εὐηγγέλισεν) his salvific purposes to the prophets (10.7), so that God's people will, in turn, make those purposes known to the world. Prophetic witness is further modeled for the churches in the proclamation of angels who *preach* (κηρύσσοντα) of one who is worthy to open the scroll (5.2),[100] and who *proclaim* (εὐαγγελίσαι) to the inhabitants of the

---

[99] μαρτυρέω appears in Rev. 1.2; 22.16; μαρτυρία is used in 1.2, 9; 6.9; 11.7; 12.11, 17; 19.10 (2x); 20.4; μαρτύριον is used in 15.5; μάρτυς is used in 1.5; 2.13; 3.14, and 11.3.

[100] Thomas, *The Apocalypse*, p. 220, suggests that the verb κηρύσσοντα 'could well convey the idea that this angel's activity is not simply an invitation to anyone who might be worthy to open the scroll, but, owing to the theological signifi-

earth the eternal gospel and call the nations to worship God.[101] The churches give witness to a God who offers water without cost (21.6), and they call to the world to come and receive this free gift (22.17). They give witness to Jesus' soon return (1.7; 16.15; 22.7, 12, 20) and to their own anticipation of the wedding of the Lamb (19.7-8; 21.2). The Spirit is linked to witness: John gives his witness through the Spirit; the Spirit is described as the eyes of the Lamb 'sent out into all the earth' (5.6); and the witness of Jesus *is* the S/spirit of prophecy (19.10). According to John's Gospel, both the Spirit and the people of God testify about Jesus (Jn 15.26-27). Pentecostals maintain that the Spirit is the 'empowering resource' for mission.[102] To claim to be people of the Spirit means Pentecostals should certainly follow the Spirit in testifying to the world. Land states that to refuse to disciple is to 'hate, or worse, to be indifferent'.[103] This is not the attitude that the Apocalypse portrays for the people of God; rather, God's people are to follow their Lord in giving their lives in witness in hopes that the world will repent and give glory to God (Rev. 11.13).[104] All of this is gathered up in worship – in *Spirit*ed worship where the community longs for the whole world to encounter God; in *prophetic* worship where through their songs, their prayers, and their proclamation, the community declares what is and what will be as revealed by the Spirit; and in *embodied* worship where the community is not afraid to prostrate themselves before

---

cance of the term, carries with it implicit proclamation; a proclamation suggesting that there is indeed one who is worthy to open the scroll'.

[101] Smalley, *The Revelation to John*, p. 361.

[102] Warrington, *Pentecostal Theology*, p. 249. Seymour, *AF* 1.5 (1907), p. 2, writes: 'The Holy Spirit has not time to magnify anything but the Blood of our Lord Jesus Christ. Standing between the living and the dead, we need to so bear the dying body of our Lord, that people will only see Christ in us, and never get a chance to see self. We are simply a voice shouting, 'Behold the Lamb of God!' When we commence shouting something else, then Christ will die in us ...'

[103] Land, *Pentecostal Spirituality*, p. 207.

[104] Warrington, *Pentecostal Theology*, p. 249, states that the 'emphasis on heaven, hell and the belief in the eternal punishment awaiting unbelievers has been of major importance in stimulating Pentecostals to evangelism, the concept of the Pentecostal being a "watchman" (Isa. 21.11; Ezek. 3.17; 33.7), entrusted with the destiny of humanity, being a sobering reminder of the responsibility to share the Gospel with others'. Perhaps contemporary Pentecostals need a counter-balance to this approach by also presenting what the Apocalypse sets forth concerning the glorious hope for the followers of the Lamb.

the Lamb, or, if required, before the world as an ultimate act of worship (11.8).

To recognize witness *as* worship[105] rather than distinct from it is to suggest a more holistic and integrative understanding of both witness *and* worship than is currently found in many Pentecostal circles. Witness as worship calls for a conscious evaluation of daily activities to ensure that all of life is lived as worship before God and in behalf of the world. Witness as worship might lead Pentecostals to renewed prophetic critique or even activism against the evil structures of Babylon by standing in solidarity with the oppressed even while continuing to call both oppressed and oppressor to God. 'Acts of justice and peace are … acts of the Holy Spirit'.[106] Pentecostals can gain from the Apocalypse the courage needed to be the prophetic counter-witness to the dominant culture in which they exist. Like early Pentecostals, contemporary Pentecostals might consider the revival of the testimony as an important liturgical activity. Testimonies give witness both to the people of God *and* to the inhabitants of the world of the 'power and reality of God in the lives of the members of the community of faith'.[107] Often in testimony, the witness to the community is about witness to a hostile world not unlike that depicted in the Apocalypse. Hearing such testimony can strengthen the community in their resolve to witness even in the face of the Dragon. Testimonies carry 'a sense of participation in the future' and become a way to express 'the dissonance of living in the kingdom of God while waiting on the full reign of God'.[108] *Spirit*ed worship *is* witness; *Spirit*ed witness *is* worship.

III. Summary

In this chapter I have sketched out what I believe to be the central message of the Apocalypse as pertaining to worship and have made

---

[105] Contra Peters, *The Mandate of the Church in the Apocalypse*, pp. 73-75, who argues that worship serves the larger mandate of witness.

[106] Johns, *Pentecostal Formation*, p. 99, maintains that the church must call for justice and freedom without becoming 'submerged within historical struggles. The church remains a critique, a prophetic witness to both the oppressors and the oppressed.'

[107] Ellington, 'The Costly Loss of Testimony', p. 48.

[108] Johns, *Pentecostal Formation*, p. 132.

overtures toward the construction of a Pentecostal theology of worship. First, the Apocalypse is a narrative about worship. Liturgical language, forms, and imagery abound in the narrative, as do worship scenes which are embedded into the narratives. The worship scenes direct the hearers to the worship of God and the Lamb. Conversely, the Apocalypse depicts the false worship offered to the Dragon, the beasts, and to Babylon. Worship becomes a test of allegiance. This liturgical thrust is helpful for Pentecostals who have been conditioned to read the Apocalypse for its end-time scenario. An understanding of the Apocalypse as a liturgical text might allow Pentecostals to rediscover its depth and richness.

Second, the Apocalypse demonstrates the true worship takes place ἐν πνεύματι ('in the Spirit'). John's statement of being *in the Spirit* reflects his understanding that worship is generated *in the Spirit*. John worships on Patmos in solidarity and *in the Spirit* with his hearers, the seven churches of Asia. It is *in the Spirit* that visions and dreams, prophetic words, and the songs of heaven are received in the worshipping communities. It is *in the Spirit* that the worshippers understand their identity as the Bride of the Lamb and their destiny as New Jerusalem. Worship thus creates the context for pneumatic discernment. Pentecostals can find in the Apocalypse affirmation for their understanding of experiential worship that is directed by the Spirit.

Third, worship makes room for the prophetic voice of the Spirit. The Apocalypse is a prophetic text. The close connection between the prophetic and the liturgical elements indicates that worship is the proper context for the giving and receiving of prophetic words and/or visions. The prophecy is mediated by the Spirit, and it is the Spirit who assists the community in the important task of discerning the prophecy. Pentecostals might evaluate their liturgy to ensure that the Spirit is given space to speak prophetically to the worshipping community.

Fourth, the Apocalypse demonstrates that worship is the central purpose for *all* of creation, whether in heaven or on earth. The worship scenes document that worship is rendered night and day by the residents of heaven, including the overcomers – those who lose their lives on earth for their refusal to worship the beast. That they are alive and worshipping around the throne of God affirms the primacy of worship for the hearers even in the midst of potential suffering. Worship is formational; it orients the worshipper to the reign of God. Pentecostals might evaluate their practices of worship and reimagine their liturgical rites as catechesis.

Fifth, the Apocalypse insists that God alone is to be worshipped. In this, the Apocalypse is fiercely monotheistic, yet as the hearers discover, John's monotheism is redefined to include Jesus and the Spirit; thus, the worship of God includes the worship of Jesus and the Spirit. The Apocalypse provides Pentecostals with a cadre of ascriptions for the triune God in combination with a rich liturgy that extols the character and works of God that can inform Pentecostal worship.

Sixth, the Apocalypse differentiates between legitimate and illegitimate worship. As early as the seven prophetic messages, the subtlety of false worship is exposed in 'Balaam' and 'Jezebel' as the hearers discover that false worship has infiltrated their sacred spaces. Revelation 12–13 provides a full treatise on false worship whereby the Dragon, the two beasts, and their attack on all of humanity are exposed. It is in these chapters that the hearers understand how worship serves to distinguish the followers of the Lamb from the followers of the beast. The followers of the Lamb are those who refuse to worship the beast and thereby forfeit their earthly lives; the followers of the beast are those who worship the beast and thereby forfeit their eternal lives. The Apocalypse also portrays the temptation to worship Babylon – the culture in which the churches find themselves. Pentecostals could heed the Apocalypse's solemn warning to 'Come out of Babylon' and to engage in critical self-reflection as to whether or not they unwittingly participate in false worship. Allegiance to the Lamb demands all of one's life and possibly one's death; Pentecostals can stand over and against the culture of Babylon and worship, both in life and in death, as overcomers.

Seventh, the Apocalypse describes numerous liturgical activities. A). The hymns are directed to God and the Lamb and extol their character and works. The hymns of heaven become the hymns of the hearers; singing them tunes both their ears and their hearts to the realm of heaven. The hymns interpret the narratives into which they are embedded and become the churches' language of resistance to the Dragon, the beasts, and to Babylon. The hymns are prophetic – declaring what is and what is to come. Pentecostals might look to the hymnody of the Apocalypse as a template for evaluating its own body of music and composing new hymns. B). The brief references to musical instruments in the Apocalypse (harps and trumpets) points to the presence of musicians as well as legitimates the performance of instrumental worship. Pentecostal musicians could find in the Apocalypse affirmation for their musical offering of worship and should reflect on what it means to play *in the Spirit*. C). Kinesthetic movement is an expression of worship in the Apocalypse. John sees the heavenly residents fall down before the throne of God in worship; John himself falls down before the risen Jesus. Prostration is perhaps the most fitting response to the overwhelming presence of God; however, to prostrate oneself before anyone or anything else, as John attempts to do (19.10; 22.9) is idolatry. Pentecostals, for whom kinesthetic movement is a hallmark, might look to the Apocalypse's preference for prostration as a sanctioned response to an encounter with God that completely overwhelms both mind and body. D). Prayers are a liturgical activity of the people of God. The location of the prayers of the saints – symbolized as incense in the throne of God – provides assurance that prayers do indeed come before God. The visceral lament of the souls under the altar suggests that cries for justice are acceptable prayers before God – and prayers which God answers. Pentecostals can find encouragement to present their petitions and their laments before the God of heaven and expect God to answer. Space within Pentecostal liturgy should be given for corporate prayers – prayers of lament, prayers for boldness, and prayers for the return of Jesus. E). Words of exclamatory worship – 'Amen' and 'Hallelujah' – are used in the Apocalypse as worshipful exclamations that should only be used in the worship of God and the Lamb. Pentecostals, who use these and other 'sacred expletives', might consider the need to preserve a sacred vernacular – sacred words used in the worship of a holy God. F). The Apocalypse contains a brief yet poignant period of silence in which the prayers of the saints rise up before God on the throne. This period of silence suggests that worshippers should take time to be silent before the Lord and *listen* for God's response to their prayers. Pentecostals might consider active silence as an essential liturgical activity and look for ways to incorporate active listening to God as part of their worship. G). The Apocalypse appears to contain allusions to the Eucharist, suggesting that the churches partook of the Eucharist as part of their corporate life of worship. The suggestion that the Apocalypse was read as part of a eucharistic celebration is impossible to prove with certainty, yet the images of eating and drinking, of the tree of life, hidden manna, and the river of life, point to this possibility. The joining together of the Apocalypse with the celebration of the Eucharist holds great promise for Pentecostals as another way to remind them that they are an eschatological people.

Finally, the Apocalypse conceives of witness as worship. The vocabulary of witness/testimony abounds in the Apocalypse, and the central narrative of the two witnesses indicates that God's people are called to witness to the world even if that witness is not received. The witness of the church is not to be separated or compartmentalized from their worship; rather, through witness, the people of God give worship unto God and the Lamb. For Pentecostals, this integrative understanding should encourage them to conceive of worship as a prophetic counter-witness to the dominant culture around them through their songs, prayers, proclamation, and testimonies.

CONCLUSION

I. Contributions of this Study

This study makes several contributions to the scholarship on worship in the Apocalypse as well to the emerging development of a Pentecostal theology of worship.

First, this study provides the most comprehensive overview to date of the most recent scholarship on the theme of worship in the Apocalypse. This survey reveals a growing interest into the topic yet a monograph-length treatment of worship in the Apocalypse has yet to be produced. The survey also reveals that Pentecostal scholars have yet to contribute to this area of research. This study responds to both of these concerns.

Second, this study presents a Pentecostal reading strategy informed by the most up to date developments within Pentecostal hermeneutics and other recent developments in hermeneutics, namely *Wirkungsgeschichte* and the use of narrative.

Third, this study provides the most comprehensive survey of the use of *Wirkungsgeschichte* by Pentecostals.

Fourth, it offers the first effective history of how the worship in the Apocalypse impacted the worship of early Pentecostals as recorded in the early Pentecostal periodical literature (1906–1916). Periodicals from both the Wesleyan-Holiness and Finished Work streams of the tradition were read with the discovery that despite theological differences that emerge, the spirituality of the early Pentecostals remained remarkably consistent. This is significant given that the research of both Kimberly Alexander and Larry McQueen reveals that in the early Pentecostal literature there are marked theological differences between the two streams pertaining to healing and eschatology respectively.[1]

Fifth, this study offers the first effective history of early Pentecostal North American periodical literature on an entire biblical book.

Sixth, it presents the most extensive narrative approach to the theme of worship in the Apocalypse from a Pentecostal perspective. As such, the role of the Spirit and worship are explicitly connected to the structure of the Apocalypse in the four ἐν πνεύματι ('in the Spirit') phrases. I offer a fresh hearing of the prophetic messages of Revelation 2–3 as glimpses into the worship practices of the churches. My study of Revelation 4–22 demonstrates that the Apocalypse is first and foremost a liturgical narrative concerned with the proper worship of God and the Lamb over and against the false worship of the beast.

Finally, drawing on the insights gained from early Pentecostal literature and my reading of the Apocalypse, this study is the first to offer overtures towards the construction of a Pentecostal theology of worship based on the Apocalypse. The central features pertaining to worship are put into conversation with Pentecostal spirituality as a way to encourage contemporary Pentecostals to re-discover the Apocalypse as a liturgical text that has much to contribute to Pentecostal worship.

II. Suggestions for Further Research

In light of the contributions of this study, several suggestions for further research present themselves.

First, my reading of the first ten years of early Pentecostal periodical literature reveals that the spirituality of the early Pentecostals from both streams of the tradition was highly influenced by the worship found in the Apocalypse so that their spirituality transcended the doctrinal differences that developed. It would be interesting to see if this trend is found in other early Pentecostal periodicals not examined for this study due either to their falling just

---

[1] Alexander, *Pentecostal Healing: Models in theology and Practice*; L. McQueen, *Toward a Pentecostal Eschatology*. My findings, however, are consistent with C. Green, *Towards a Pentecostal Theology of the Lord's Supper*, who likewise discerns no major differences in the two traditions concerning the Eucharist.

outside the selected time frame (such as *The Pentecostal Holiness Advocate* which began in 1917) or being outside North America (such as Boddy's *The Confidence* published in England).

Second, does this trend continue in the literature beyond the early period especially given the mounting pressure exerted by Dispensationalism upon Pentecostals to understand the Apocalypse in conjunction with Daniel's prophecy as a treatise on end-time events?

Third, aside from worship, what other aspects of the Apocalypse would lend themselves to an exploration via *Wirkungsgeschichte?*

Fourth, what other biblical books might be explored through *Wirkungsgeschichte?*

Fifth, in light of what the Apocalypse conveys about worship, Pentecostal biblical scholars would be wise to consider exploring the theme of worship in other biblical books as well as developing whole biblical theologies of worship. Such inquiries would offer substantial contributions to biblical studies as well as to Pentecostal theology.

Sixth, while some helpful work by Pentecostal scholars is being done on the Apocalypse, clearly more intense engagement with it would be a fruitful area of study.

Seventh, the integration of the Apocalypse with Pentecostal praxis suggests that other biblical books could be used for such an approach.

BIBLIOGRAPHY

Early Pentecostal Periodicals

The Apostolic Faith (Azusa Street Mission, Los Angeles, CA)
The Bridegroom's Messenger (The Pentecostal Mission, Atlanta, GA)
The Christian Evangel (Assemblies of God, Plainfield, IN; Findley, OH)
The Church of God Evangel (Church of God, Cleveland, TN)
The Latter Rain Evangel (Stone Church, Chicago, IL)
The Pentecost (J. Roswell Flower, Indianapolis, IN)
Weekly Evangel (Assemblies of God, St. Louis, MO; Springfield, MO)
Word and Witness (E.N. Bell, Malvern, AR; Findley, OH; St. Louis, MO)

Other Works Cited

Achtemeier, P., 'Revelation 5:1-14', *Interpretation* 40.3 (2001), pp. 285-86.
Albrecht, D.E., *Rites in the Spirit: A Ritual Approach to Pentecostal/Charismatic Spirituality* (JPTSup 17; Sheffield: Sheffield Academic Press, 1999).
——'An Anatomy of Worship: A Pentecostal Analysis', in W. Ma and R. Menzies (eds.), *The Spirit and Spirituality: Essays in Honour of Russell P. Spittler* (JPTSup 24; London, T&T Clark, 2004), pp. 70-82.
Alexander, K.E., *Pentecostal Healing: Models in Theology and Practice* (JPTSup 29; Blandford Forum: Deo Publishing, 2006).
Alford, D., *Music in the Pentecostal Church* (Cleveland: Pathway Press, 1967).
Althouse P., and M. Wilkinson, 'Playing in the Father's Love: The Eschatological Implications of Charismatic Ritual and the Kingdom of God in Catch the Fire World', *Arc* 39 (2011), pp. 93-116.
Alvarado, J. 'Worship in the Spirit: Perspectives on Liturgical Theology and Praxis', *JPT* 21 (2012), pp. 135-151.
Anderson, A., *An Introduction to Pentecostalism* (Cambridge: Cambridge University Press, 2004).
Anderson, A., and W.J. Hollenweger (eds.), *Pentecostals After a Century: Global Perspectives on a Movement in Transition* (JPTSup 15; Sheffield: Sheffield Academic Press, 1999).
Andersen, F.I., '2 (Slavonic) Apocalypse of Enoch', in J.H. Charlesworth (ed.), *The Old Testament Pseudepigrapha* (Garden City: Doubleday & Co., 1983), pp. 103-40.

Anderson, R., *Vision of the Disinherited: The Making of American Pentecostalism* (Peabody: Hendrickson Publishers, 1979).

Archer, K.J., *A Pentecostal Hermeneutic: Spirit, Scripture and Community* (JPTSup 28; London: T&T Clark International, 2005; Cleveland: CPT Press, 2009).

Archer, M.L., 'The Worship Scenes in the Apocalypse, Effective History, and Early Pentecostal Periodical Literature', *JPT* 21 (2012), pp. 87-112.

——'Pentecostals and the Apocalypse: A Survey of Recent Pentecostal Biblical Scholarship on the Apocalypse', *JPT* (forthcoming).

Arrington, F.L. *Christian Doctrine: A Pentecostal Perspective,* I (Cleveland: Pathway Press, 1992).

Aune, D.E., *Revelation 1–5* (WBC 52A; Nashville: Word, Inc., 1997).

——*Revelation 6–16* (WBC 52B; Nashville: Thomas Nelson Publishers, 1998).

——*Revelation 17–22* (WBC 52C; Nashville: Thomas Nelson Publishers, 1998).

——'The Influence of Roman Imperial Court Ceremonial on the Apocalypse of John' in D. Aune (ed.), *Apocalypticism, Prophecy and Magic in Early Christianity* (Tübingen: Mohr Siebeck, 2006), pp. 99-119.

Barkun, M., 'Divided Apocalypse: thinking about the end in contemporary America', *Soundings* 66.3 (Fall 1983), pp. 257-80.

Barr, D.L., *Tales of the End* (Salem: Polebridge Press, 1998).

Bauckham, R.J., 'The Role of the Spirit in the Apocalypse', *The Evangelical Quarterly* 52.2 (April-June 1980), pp. 66-83.

——'The Worship of Jesus in Apocalyptic Christianity,' *NTS* 27 (1981), pp. 322-41.

——'Jesus, Worship of', in D.N. Freedman (ed.), *ABD,* III (Garden City: Doubleday, 1992), pp. 812-19.

——*Climax of Prophecy: Studies in the Book of Revelation* (Edinburgh: T&T Clark, 1993).

——*The Theology of the Book of Revelation* (Cambridge: Cambridge University Press, 1993).

Beale, G.K., *John's Use of the Old Testament in Revelation* (JSNTSup 166; Sheffield: Sheffield Academic Press, 1998).

——*The Book of Revelation* (NIGTC; Grand Rapids: Eerdmans, 1999).

——'The Purpose of Symbolism in the book of Revelation', *Calvin Theological Journal* 41(2006), pp. 53-66.

Beasley-Murray, G.R., *Revelation* (Grand Rapids: Eerdmans, 1981).

Biguzzi, G., 'A Figurative and Narrative Language Grammar of Revelation', *NovT* 45.4 (2003), pp. 382-402.

Blount, B.K., *Can I Get a Witness? Reading Revelation Through African American Culture*: (Louisville: Westminster/John Knox Press, 2005).

——*Revelation: A Commentary* (Louisville: Westminster John Knox Press, 2009).

Boesak, A., *Comfort and Protest: The Apocalypse from a South African Perspective* (Philadelphia: Westminster Press, 1987).

Boone, R.J., 'Community and Worship: The Key Components of Pentecostal Christian Formation', *JPT* 8 (1996), pp. 129-42.

Boring, M.E., *Revelation* (Louisville: John Knox Press, 1988).

——'The Theology of Revelation: "The Lord Our God the Almighty Reigns"', *Interpretation* 40.3 (2001), pp. 263-64.

Bovon, F., 'John's Self-presentation in Revelation 1:9-10', *CBQ* 62.4 (Oct 2000), pp. 693-700.

Boxall, I., *The Revelation of St. John* (BNTC; London: Continuum, 2006).

Briggs, R., *Jewish Temple Imagery in the Book of Revelation* (New York: Peter Lang; 1999).

Büchsel, F., 'βαστάζω', in G. Kittel (ed.), *TDNT*, I (Grand Rapids: Eerdmans, 1964), p. 596.

Caird, G.B., *The Revelation of St. John the Divine* (New York: Harper & Row, 1966).

Campbell, D., 'Antithetical Feminine-Urban Imagery and a Tale of Two Women-Cities in the Book of Revelation', *Tyndale Bulletin* 55.1 (2004), pp. 81-108.

Cartledge, M.J., *Testimony in the Spirit: Rescripting Ordinary Pentecostal Theology* (EPPET; Farnham, UK: Ashgate Publishing Limited, 2010).

——'Text-Community-Spirit: The Challenges Posed by Pentecostal Theological Method to Evangelical Theology', in K.L. Spawn and A.T. Wright (eds.), *Spirit & Scripture: Examining a Pneumatic Hermeneutic* (London: T&T Clark, 2012).

Carey, G., *Elusive Apocalypse* (Macon, GA: Mercer University Press, 1999).

Chan, S., *Pentecostal Theology and the Christian Spiritual Tradition* (JPTSup 21; Sheffield: Sheffield Academic Press, 2000).

Charles, R.H., *A Critical and Exegetical Commentary on the Revelation of St. John,* I (Edinburgh: T&T Clark, 1920).

Collins, A. Yarbro, *Crisis and Catharsis: The Power of the Apocalypse* (Philadelphia: Westminster, 1984).

Conn, C., *Like a Mighty Army* (Cleveland: Pathway Press, 1977).

Cox, H., *Fire From Heaven: The Rise of Pentecostal Spirituality and the Reshaping of Religion in the Twenty-First Century* (Reading: Addison-Wesley, 1995).

Cross, T.L., 'The Divine-Human Encounter: Towards a Pentecostal Theology of Experience', *Pneuma* 31 (2009), pp. 3-34.

Cullmann, O., *Early Christian Worship* (London: SCM, 1953).

Daniels, D., '"Everyone Bids You Welcome" A Multicultural Approach to North American Pentecostalism', in M. Dempster, B. Klaus, D. Petersen (eds.), *The Globalization of Pentecostalism: A Religion Made to Travel* (Oxford, Regnum Books International, 1999), pp. 222-52.

——'"Gotta Moan Sometime": A Sonic Exploration of Earwitnesses to Early Pentecostal Sound in North America', *Pneuma* 30 (2008), pp. 5-32.

Davies, A., 'What Does it Mean to Read the Bible as a Pentecostal?', *JPT* 18 (2009), pp. 216-29.

Dayton, D.W., *Theological Roots of Pentecostalism* (Peabody: Hendrickson Publishers, 1987).

Deichgräber, R., 'Die hymnischen Stücke in der Apokalypse', in *Gotteshymnus und Christushymnus in der frühen Christenheit* (Göttingen: Vanderhoeck & Ruprecht, 1967), pp. 44-59.

deSilva, D.A., 'Honor Discourse and Rhetorical Strategy of the Apocalypse of John', *JSNT* 71 (1998), pp. 79-110.

——*Seeing Things John's Way: The Rhetoric of the Book of Revelation* (Louisville: Westminster John Knox Press, 2009).

De Smidt, J.C., 'Hermeneutical Perspectives on the Spirit in the Book of Revelation', *JPT* 14 (1999), pp. 27-47.

——'A Meta-Theology of Ο ΘΕΟΣ in Revelations [*sic*] 1:1-2', *Neot* 38.2 (2004), pp. 183-208.

——'The First μακαρισμός in Revelation 1:3', *Acta Patristica et Byzantina* 15 (2004), pp. 91-118.

Dove, S., 'Hymnody and Liturgy in the Azusa Street Revival, 1906–1908', *Pneuma* 31 (2009), pp. 242-63.

Duff, P., *Who Rides the Beast? Prophetic Rivalry and the Rhetoric of Crisis in the Churches of the Apocalypse*, (New York: Oxford University Press, 2001).

Dunn, J.D.G., *Unity and Diversity in the New Testament* (London: SCM Press, 1977).

Du Rand, J., '"Now the Salvation of Our God Has Come …" A Narrative Perspective on the Hymns in Revelation 12–15', *Neot* 27.2 (1993), pp. 313-30.

Ellington, S.A., 'Pentecostalism and the Authority of Scripture', *JPT* 9 (1996), pp. 16-38.

——'The Costly Loss of Testimony', *JPT* 16 (2000), pp. 48-59.

——'Locating Pentecostals at the Hermeneutical Round Table', *JPT* 22.2 (2013), pp. 206-25.

Ellul, J., *Apocalypse: The Book of Revelation* (trans. G.W. Schreiner; New York: The Seabury Press, 1977).

Emmerson, R.K., 'Introduction: The Apocalypse in medieval culture', in R.K. Emmerson and B. McGinn (eds.), *Apocalypse in the Middle Ages* (Ithaca: Cornell University Press, 1992), pp. 293-332.

Enroth, A.M., 'The Hearing Formula in the Book of Revelation', *NTS* 36 (1990), pp. 598-608.

Faupel, D.W., *The Everlasting Gospel: The Significance of Eschatology in the Development of Pentecostal Thought* (JPTSup 10; Sheffield: Sheffield Academic Press, 1996; Blandford Forum: Deo Publishing, 2009).

Fee, G.D., *Revelation* (NCCS; Eugene: Cascade Books, 2011).

Fenske, W., '"Das Lied des Mose, des Knechtes Gottes, und das Lied des Lammes" (Apokalypse des Johannes 15,3f): Der Text und seine Bedeutung für die Johannes-Apokalypse', *BZNW* 90, pp. 250-64.

Filho, J.A., 'The Apocalypse of John as a Visionary Experience: Notes on the Book's Structure', *JSNT* 25.2 (2002), pp. 213-34.

Fiorenza, E. Schüssler, 'Redemption as Liberation: Apoc 1:5f and 5:9f', *CBQ* 36.2 (1974), pp. 220-32.

——*Revelation: Vision of a Just World* (Minneapolis: Fortress Press, 1991).

Friesen, S.J., *Imperial Cults and the Apocalypse of John: Reading Revelation in the Ruins* (Oxford, U.K.: Oxford University Press, 2001).

Gause, R.H., *Revelation: God's Stamp of Sovereignty on History* (Cleveland: Pathway Press, 1983).

Gloer, W.H., 'Worship God! Liturgical Elements in the Apocalypse', *Review and Expositor* 98 (2001), pp. 35-57.

Goff, J.R., Jr, 'Parham, Charles Fox', in S.M. Burgess and E.M. van der Maas (eds.), *NIDPCM* (Grand Rapids: Zondervan, 2002), pp. 955-57.

Goldingay, J., *Models for Interpretation of Scripture* (Grand Rapids: Eerdmans, 1985).

Gonzáles, C., and J. Gonzáles, *Revelation* (Louisville: Westminster John Knox Press, 1997).

Gorman, M., *Reading Revelation Responsibly* (Eugene: Cascade Books, 2011).

Green, C.E.W., *Toward a Pentecostal Theology of the Lord's Supper: Foretasting the Kingdom* (Cleveland: CPT Press, 2012).

Green, J.B., 'The (Re-)Turn to Narrative', in J.B. Green and Michael Pasquarello III (eds.), *Narrative Reading, Narrative Preaching* (Grand Rapids: Baker Academic, 2003), pp. 11-36.

Gundry, R.H., 'The New Jerusalem: People as Place, Not Place for People', *Novum Testamentum* 29 (July 1987), pp. 254-264.

Guthrie, D., 'The Lamb in the Structure of the Book of Revelation', *Biblical and Historical Essays from London Bible College* (London: the London Bible College, 1981), pp. 64-71.

Harris, M., The *Literary Function of the Hymns in the Apocalypse of John* (Ann Arbor: UMI Dissertation Service, 1989).

Hauck, F., 'μολύνω, μολυσμός' in G. Kittel (ed.), *TDNT*, IV (Grand Rapids: Eerdmans, 1967), pp. 736-37.

Hemer, C., *The Letters to the Seven Churches of Asia in their Local Settings* (JSNTS 11; Sheffield: JSOT Press, 1986).

Herms, R., *An Apocalypse for the Church and for the World: The Narrative Function of Universal Language in the Book of Revelation* (BZNW 143; Berlin; New York: Walter deGruyter, 2006).

——'Invoking the Spirit and Narrative Intent in John's Apocalypse', in K.L. Spawn and A.T. Wright (eds.), *Spirit & Scripture: Examining a Pneumatic Hermeneutic* (London: T&T Clark, 2012), pp. 99-114.

Hollenweger, W.J., *The Pentecostals* (Peabody: Hendrickson, 1972).

——'After Twenty Years Research on Pentecostalism', *International Review of Mission* 75 (January, 1986), pp. 3-12.

——'Pentecostals and the Charismatic Movement,' in C. Jones, G. Wainwright & E. Yarnold, SJ (eds.), *The Study of Spirituality* (London: SPCK, 1986), pp. 549-54.

——'The Black Roots of Pentecostalism' in A. Anderson and W.J. Hollenweger (eds.), *Pentecostals after a Century: Global Perspectives on a Movement in Transition* (JPTSup 15; Sheffield: Sheffield Academic Press, 1999), pp. 33-44.

Homcy, S.L., '"To Him Who Overcomes": A Fresh Look at What "Victory" Means for the Believer According to the Book of Revelation', *JETS* 38.2 (June 1995), pp. 193-201.

Horn, S.N., 'Hallelujah, the Lord our God, the Almighty Reigns: The Theology of the Hymns of Revelation', in G.L. Stevens (ed.), *Essays on Revelation: Appropriating Yesterday's Apocalypse in Today's World* (Eugene: Pickwick Publications, 2010), pp. 41-54.

Howard-Brook, H. and A. Gwyther, 'The Empire of the World Has Become the Empire of Our Lord and of His Messiah: Liturgy and Worship in Revelation', *Unveiling Empire: Reading Revelation Then & Now* (Maryknoll: Orbis Books, 1999), pp. 197-221.

Hurtado, L.W., 'Revelation 4–5 in the Light of Jewish Apocalyptic Analogies', *JSNT* 25 (1985), pp. 105-24.

Jaichandran, R., and B. D. Madhav, 'Pentecostal Spirituality in a Postmodern World', *AJPS* 6.1 (2003), pp. 39-61.

Jauhiainen, M., 'ΑΠΟΚΑΛΥΨΙΣ ΙΗΣΟΥ ΧΡΙΣΤΟΥ (Rev. 1:1): The Climax of John's Prophecy', *Tyndale Bulletin* 54.1 (2003), pp. 99-117.

Jeske, R.L., 'Spirit and Community in the Johannine Apocalypse,' *NTS* 31 (1985), pp. 452-66.

Johansson, C.M., 'Singing in the Spirit', *Paraclete* 24.2 (1990), pp. 20-23.

Johns, C. Bridges, *Pentecostal Formation: A Pedagogy among the Oppressed* (JPTSup 2; Sheffield; Sheffield Academic Press, 1993).

——'The Adolescence of Pentecostalism: In Search of a Legitimate Sectarian Identity', *Pneuma* 17.1 (Spring 1995), pp. 3-17.

——'The Light That Streams from the End: Worship Within the Coming Christendom', *The Living Pulpit* 12.3 (2003), pp. 14-15.

342 '*I Was in the Spirit on the Lord's Day*'

Jörns, K.-P., *Das hymnische Evangelium* (Gütersloh: Gütersloher Verlagshaus Gerd Mohn, 1971).

Kalu, O.U., 'Holy Praiseco: Negotiating Sacred and Popular Music and Dance in African Pentecostalism', *Pneuma* 32 (2010), pp. 116-140.

Kee, H.C., 'Testaments of the Twelve Patriarchs', in J.H. Charlesworth (ed.), *The Old Testament Pseudepigrapha* (Garden City: Doubleday & Co., 1983), pp. 788-90.

Keener, C.S., *Revelation* (NIV Application Commentary; Grand Rapids: Zondervan, 2000).

Kelly, B.H., 'Revelation 7:9-17', *Interpretation* 40.03 (2001), pp. 288-95.

Kittel, G., 'ἀκούω', in G. Kittel (ed.), *TDNT*, I (Grand Rapids: Eerdmans), pp. 219-20.

Klassen, W., 'Vengeance in the Apocalypse of John', *CBQ* 28.3 (1966), pp. 300-311.

Koester, C.K., *Revelation and the End of All Things* (Grand Rapids: Eerdmans, 2001).

Kovacs, J., and C. Rowland, *Revelation* (Blackwell Bible Commentaries; Oxford: Blackwell Publishing Ltd, 2004).

Kraft, H., *Die Offenbarung Des Johannes* (Tübingen: Mohr, 1974).

Kraybill, J.N., *Apocalypse and Allegiance: Worship, Politics and Devotion in the Book of Revelation* (Grand Rapids: Brazos Press, 2010).

Krodel, G.A., *Revelation* (ACNT; Minneapolis: Augsburg Press, 1989).

Ladd, G.E., *A Commentary on the Revelation of John* (Grand Rapids: Eerdmans, 1972).

Land, S.J., *Pentecostal Spirituality: A Passion for the Kingdom* (JPTSup 1; Sheffield: Sheffield Academic Press, 1993).

Landrus, H., 'Hearing 3 John 2 in the Voices of History', *JPT* 11.1 (2002), pp. 70-88.

Laws, S., *In the Light of the Lamb: Imagery, Parody, and Theology in the Apocalypse of John* (Wilmington: Michael Glazier, 1988).

Louw-Nida, *Greek-English Lexicon of the New Testament*, I (New York: United Bible Societies, 1989), pp. 478-79.

Luz, U., *Matthew in History: Interpretation, Influence, and Effects* (Minneapolis: Fortress Press, 1994).

——'A Response to Emerson B. Powery', *JPT* 14 (1999), pp. 19-26.

Ma, W., 'Pentecostal Worship in Asia: Its Theological Implications and Contributions', *AJPS* 10.1 (2007), pp. 136-52.

Macchia, F.D., 'The Struggle for Global Witness: Shifting Paradigms in Pentecostal Theology', in M. Dempster, B. Klaus, D. Petersen (eds.), *The Globalization of Pentecostalism: A Religion Made to Travel* (Oxford: Regnum Books International, 1999).

——'Theology, Pentecostal', in S.M. Burgess and E.M. van der Maas (eds.), *NIDPCM* (Grand Rapids: Zondervan, 2002), pp. 1120-41.

——'The Covenant of the Lamb's Bride: A Subversive Paradigm', *The Living Pulpit* (July-Sept 2005), pp. 14-15.

Mangina, J.L., *Revelation* (BTCB; Grand Rapids: Brazos Press, 2010).

Martin, L.R., *The Unheard Voice of God: A Pentecostal Hearing of the Book of Judges* (JPTSup 32; Blandford Forum: Deo Publishing, 2008).

——'Longing for God: Psalm 63 and Pentecostal Spirituality', *JPT* 22 (2013), pp. 54-76.

Mathewson, D., 'Verbal Aspect in the Apocalypse of John: An Analysis of Revelation 5', *NovT* 50 (2008), pp. 58-77.

Mayo, P.L., *Those Who Call Themselves Jews: The Church and Judaism in the Apocalypse of John* (PTMS 60; Eugene: Pickwick Publications, 2006).

McQueen, L.R., *Joel and the Spirit: The Cry of a Prophetic Hermeneutic* (JPTSup 8; Sheffield: Sheffield Academic Press, 1995; Cleveland: CPT Press, 2009).

——*Toward a Pentecostal Eschatology: Discerning the Way Forward* (JPTSup 39; Blandford Forum: Deo Publishing, 2012).

Michaelis, W., 'κράτος, κρατέω, κραταιός, κραταιόω, κοσμοκράτωρ, παντοκράτωρ', in G. Kittel (ed.), *TDNT*, III (Grand Rapids: Eerdmans, 1965), pp. 905-15.

Michaels, J.R., *Revelation* (IVPNTC; Downers Grove: IVP, 1997).

Miller, D.E., and T. Yamamori, *Global Pentecostalism: The New Face of Christian Social Engagement* (Berkeley and Los Angeles: University of California Press, 2007).

Mills, R., 'Musical Prayers: Reflections on the African Roots of Pentecostal Music', *JPT* 12 (1998), pp. 109-26.

Minear, P.S., 'Ontology and Ecclesiology in the Apocalypse', *NTS* 13 (1966), pp. 89-105.

——'Far as the Curse is Found: The Point of Revelation 12:15-16', *NovT* 33.1 (1991), pp. 71-77.

Moore, R.D., 'Canon and Charisma in Deuteronomy', *JPT* 1 (1993), pp. 75-92.

Morton, R., 'Glory to God and to the Lamb: John's Use of Jewish and Hellenistic/Roman Themes in Formatting his Theology in Revelation 4–5', *JSNT* 83 (2001), pp. 89-109.

——*One Upon the Throne and the Lamb: A Tradition Historical/Theological Analysis of Revelation 4–5* (New York: Peter Lang, 2007).

Moule, C., *An Idiom Book of New Testament Greek* (Cambridge: Cambridge University Press, 1953).

Mounce, R.H., *The Book of Revelation* (Grand Rapids: Eerdmans, 1977).

Mowry, L., 'Revelation 4–5 and Early Christian Liturgical Usage', *JBL* 71.2 (June 1952), pp. 75-84.

Murphy, F.J., *Fallen is Babylon* (Harrisburg: Trinity Press International, 1998).

——*Apocalypticism in the Bible and its World* (Grand Rapids: Baker Academic, 2012).

Neumann, P., 'Spirituality', in Adam Stewart (ed.), *Handbook of Pentecostal Christianity* (DeKalb: Northern Illinois University Press, 2012), pp. 195-201.

Newton, J., 'Reading Revelation Romantically', *JPT* 18 (2009), pp. 194-215.

O'Rourke, J.J., 'The Hymns of the Apocalypse', *CBQ* 30 (1968), pp. 399-409.

Osborne, G. R., *Revelation* (BECNT; Grand Rapids, MI: Baker Books, 2002).

Pattemore, S., *The People of God in the Apocalypse: Discourse, Structure and Exegesis* (SNTSMS 128; Cambridge: Cambridge University Press, 2004).

Paul, I., *The Value of Paul Ricoeur's Hermeneutic of Metaphor in Interpreting the Symbolism of Revelation Chapters 12 and 13* (Unpublished PhD study, Nottingham Trent University, 1998).

——'Ebbing and Flowing: Scholarly Developments in Study of the Book of Revelation', *The Expository Times* 119.11 (2008), pp. 523-31.

Paulien, J., 'The Lion/Lamb King: Reading the Apocalypse from Popular Culture', in D.L. Barr (ed.), *Reading the Book of Revelation: A Resource for Students* (Atlanta: Society for Biblical Literature, 2003), pp. 151-62.

Perkins, P., 'Crisis in Jerusalem? Narrative Criticism in New Testament Studies', *Theological Studies* 50 (1989), pp. 296-313.

Peters, O.K., *The Mandate of the Church in the Apocalypse of John* (New York: Peter Lang, 2004).

Pinnock, C.H., *The Scripture Principle* (San Francisco: Harper & Row, Publishers, 1984).

——'The Work of the Holy Spirit in Hermeneutics', *JPT* 2 (1993), pp. 3-23.

——'The Work of the Spirit in the Interpretation of Holy Scripture from the Perspective of a Charismatic Biblical Theologian', *JPT* 18 (2009), pp. 157-71.

Piper, O., 'The Apocalypse of John and the Liturgy of the Ancient Church' *Church History* 20.1 (1951), pp. 10-22.

Powell, M.A., *What is Narrative Criticism?* (Minneapolis: Fortress Press, 1990).

——'Narrative Criticism', in J.B. Green (ed.), *Hearing the New Testament: Strategies for Interpretation* (Grand Rapids: Eerdmans; Carlisle, UK: The Paternoster Press, 1995), pp. 240-41.

Powery, E.B., 'Ulrich Luz's *Matthew in History*: A Contribution to Pentecostal Hermeneutics?' *JPT* 14 (1999), pp. 3-17.

Prigent, P., *Commentary on the Apocalypse of St. John* (trans. W. Pradels; Tübingen: Mohr Siebeck, 2001).

Quayesi-Amakye, J., 'God in Ghanaian Pentecostal Songs', *JPT* 22 (2013), pp. 131-51.

Raber, R., 'Revelation 21:1-8', *Interpretation* 40.03 (2001), pp. 296-301.

Resseguie, J.L., *Narrative Criticism of the New Testament: An Introduction* (Grand Rapids: Baker Academic, 2005).

——*The Revelation of John: A Narrative Commentary* (Grand Rapids: Baker Academic, 2009).

Richard, P., *The Apocalypse: A People's Commentary on the Book of Revelation* (Maryknoll: Orbis Books, 2005).

Robeck, C.M., Jr, 'Seymour, William Joseph', in S.M. Burgess and E.M. van der Maat (eds), *NIDPCM* (Grand Rapids: Zondervan, 2002), pp. 1053-57.

——*The Azusa Street Mission and Revival: The Birth of the Global Pentecostal Movement* (Nashville: Thomas Nelson, Inc., 2006).

Rotz, C., *Revelation: A Commentary in the Wesleyan Tradition* (Kansas City: Beacon Hill Press, 2012).

Rowland, C., *Revelation* (London: Epworth Press, 1993).

Ruiz, J.-P., *Ezekiel in the Apocalypse: The Transformation of Prophetic Language in Revelation 16,17–19,10* (European University Studies 23, 376; Frankfurt am Main: Peter Lang, 1989).

——'Betwixt and Between on the Lord's Day: Liturgy and the Apocalypse', *SBLSP* 31 (1992), pp. 654-72.

——'Revelation 4:8-11; 5:9-14: Hymns of the Heavenly Liturgy', *SBLSP* 34 (1995), pp. 216-19.

——'The Politics of Praise: A Reading of Revelation 19:1-10', *SBLSP* 36 (1997), pp. 374-93.

Saunders, S., 'Revelation and Resistance: Narrative and Worship in John's Apocalypse' in J.B. Green and M. Pasquarello III (eds.), *Narrative Reading, Narrative Preaching* (Grand Rapids: Baker Academic, 2003), pp. 119-22.

Schimanowski, G., *Die himmlische Liturgie in der Apokalypse des Johannes: Die frühjüdischen Traditionen in Offenbarung 4–5 unter Einschluss der Hekhalotliteratur* (Tübingen: Mohr Siebeck, 2002).

Schlier, H., 'αἰνέω, αἶνος', in G. Kittel (ed.), *TDNT*, I (Grand Rapids: Eerdmans, 1964), pp. 177-78.

——'ἀρνέομαι', in G. Kittel (ed.), *TDNT*, I (Grand Rapids: Eerdmans, 1964), pp. 469-71.

Schrenk, G., 'ἄδικος, ἀδικία, ἀδικεω, ἀδίκημα', in G. Kittel (ed.), *TDNT*, I (Grand Rapids: Eerdmans, 1964), pp. 149-63.

Skaggs, R. and P. Benham, *Revelation* (Pentecostal Commentary Series; Blandford Forum: Deo, 2009).

Skaggs, R. and T. Doyle, 'Violence in the Apocalypse of John', *CBR* 5.2 (2007), pp. 220-34.

——'Lion/Lamb in Revelation', *CBR* 7.3 (2009), pp. 362-75.

Smalley, S.S., *The Revelation to John* (Downers Grove: IVP, 2005).

Smith, J.K.A., 'Teaching a Calvinist to Dance', *Christianity Today* 52.5 (2008), pp. 42-45.

——*Desiring the Kingdom: Worship, Worldview, and Cultural Formation* (Grand Rapids: Baker Academic, 2009).

Spatafora, A., *From the Temple of God to God as the Temple: A Biblical Theological Study of the Temple in the Book of Revelation* (Rome: Gregorian University Press, 1997).

Stefanovic, R., 'The Meaning and Significance of the ἐπὶ τὴν δεξιάν for the Location of the Sealed Scroll (Revelation 5:1) and Understanding the Scene of Revelation 5', *Biblical Research* 46 (2001), pp. 42-54.

Sternberg, M., *The Poetics of Biblical Narrative* (Bloomington: Indiana University Press, 1985).

Steven, J.H.S., *Worship in the Spirit: Charismatic Worship in the Church of England* (Carlisle, Cumbria and Waynesboro, Georgia: Paternoster Press, 2002).

Stevens, G.L., 'A Vision in the Night: Setting the Interpretive Stage for John's Apocalypse', in G.L. Stevens (ed.), *Essays on Revelation: Appropriating Yesterday's Apocalypse in Today's World* (Eugene: Pickwick Publications, 2010), pp. 1-15.

——'One Like a Son of Man: Contemplating Christology in Rev 1:9-20' in G.L. Stevens (ed.), *Essays on Revelation: Appropriating Yesterday's Apocalypse in Today's World* (Eugene: Pickwick Publications, 2010), pp. 16-40.

Sweet, J.P.M., *Revelation* (Philadelphia: The Westminster Press, 1979).

Synan, H.V., *The Holiness-Pentecostal Movement in the United States* (Grand Rapids: Eerdmans, 1971).

——'Cashwell, Gaston Barnabas' in S.M. Burgess, G.B. McGee, and P.H. Alexander (eds.) *DPCM* (Grand Rapids: Zondervan, 1998), pp. 109-10.

Szittya, P., 'Doomesday bokes: The Apocalypse in medieval English literary culture', in R.K. Emmerson and B. McGinn (eds.), *Apocalypse in the Middle Ages* (Ithaca: Cornell University Press, 1992), pp. 374-97.

Tanner, C., 'Climbing the Lampstand-Witness-Trees: Revelation's Use of Zechariah 4 in Light of Speech Act Theory', *JPT* 20 (2011), pp. 81-92.

Thomas, J.C. *Footwashing in John 13 and the Johannine Community* (JSNTS 61; Sheffield: JSOT Press, 1991).

——'Women, Pentecostals and the Bible: An Experiment in Pentecostal Hermeneutics', *JPT* 5 (1994), pp. 41-56.

——'Pentecostal Theology in the Twenty-First Century', *Pneuma* 20.1 (1998), pp. 3-19 (now in J.C. Thomas, *The Spirit of the New Testament* [Blandford Forum: Deo Publishing, 2005], pp. 3-22).

——'Healing in the Atonement: A Johannine Perspective', in *The Spirit of the New Testament* (Blandford Forum: Deo Publishing, 2005), pp. 175-89.

——'The Spirit in the Fourth Gospel: Narrative Explorations', *The Spirit of the New Testament* (Blandford Forum: Deo Publishing, 2005), pp. 157-174.

——*The Spirit of the New Testament* (Leiden-Blandford Forum: Deo Publishing, 2005).

——'Pneumatic Discernment: The Image of the Beast and His Number', in S. Land, R. Moore, J.C. Thomas (eds.), *Passover, Pentecost and Parousia: Studies in Celebration Of the Life and Ministry of R. Hollis Gause* (JPTSup 35; Blandford Forum: Deo Publishing, 2010), pp. 106-24.

——'The Mystery of the Great Whore: Pneumatic Discernment in Revelation 17', in P. Althouse and R. Waddell (eds.), *Perspectives in Pentecostal Eschatologies: World Without End* (Eugene: Pickwick Publications, 2010), pp. 111-38.

——*The Apocalypse: A Literary and Theological Commentary* (Cleveland: CPT Press, 2012).

——'"What the Spirit is Saying to the Church" – The Testimony of a Pentecostal in New Testament Studies', in K.L. Spawn and A.T. Wright (eds.), *Spirit & Scripture: Examining a Pneumatic Hermeneutic* (London: Continuum, 2012), pp. 115-29.

Thomas, J.C. and K.E. Alexander, '"And the Signs Are Following": Mark 16.9-20 – A Journey into Pentecostal Hermeneutics', *JPT* 11.2 (2003), pp. 147-70.

Thomas, R.L., 'John's Apocalyptic Outline', *Bibliotheca Sacra* 123.492 (Oct-Dec 1966), pp. 334-41.

Thompson, L.L., *The Book of Revelation: Apocalypse and Empire* (New York & Oxford: Oxford University Press, 1990).

Thompson, M.M., 'Worship in the Book of Revelation', *Ex Auditu* 8 (1992), pp. 45-54.

Trafton, J.L., *Reading Revelation: A Literary and Theological Commentary* (Macon: Smyth & Helwys, Inc., 2005).

Vander Stichele, C., 'Apocalypse, art and abjection: images of the great whore', in G. Aichele (ed.), *Culture, Entertainment and the Bible* (Sheffield: Sheffield Press, 2000), pp. 124-38.

Vassiliasdis, P., 'Apocalypse and Liturgy', *St. Vladimir's Theological Quarterly* 41.2-3 (1997), pp. 95-112.

Vondey, W., 'The Making of a Black Liturgy: Pentecostal Worship and Spirituality from American Slave Narratives to American Cityscapes', *Black Theology: An International Journal* 10.2 (2012), 147-68.

Waddell, R., *The Spirit of the Book of Revelation* (JPTSup 30; Blandford Forum: Deo Publishing, 2006).

——'Revelation and the (New) Creation: A Prolegomenon on the Apocalypse, Science, and Creation', in A. Yong (ed.), *The Spirit Renews the Face of the Earth: Pentecostal Forays in Science and Theology of Creation* (Eugene: Pickwick Publications, 2009), pp. 30-50.

——'What time is it? Half-past three: How to calculate eschatological time', *JEPTA* 31.2 (2011), pp. 141-52.

Wall, R.W., *Revelation* (NIBC; NTS 18; Peabody: Hendrickson, 1991).

——'A Response to Thomas/Alexander, 'And the Signs are Following' (Mark 16.9-20)', *JPT* 11.2 (2003), pp. 171-83.

Wallace, D., *Greek Grammar Beyond the Basics* (Grand Rapids: Zondervan, 1996).

Warrington, K., *Pentecostal Theology: A Theology of Encounter* (London: T&T Clark, 2008).

Webber, R., *Ancient-Future Worship: Proclaiming and Enacting God's Narrative* (Grand Rapids: Baker Books, 2008).

Webster, J., *Ingesting Jesus: Eating and Drinking in the Gospel of John* (Atlanta: Society of Biblical Literature, 2003).

Wilson, E., 'They Crossed the Red Sea, Didn't They? Critical History and Pentecostal Beginnings' in M. Dempster, B. Klaus, D. Petersen (eds.), *The Globalization of Pentecostalism: A Religion Made to Travel* (Oxford: Regnum Books International, 1999), pp. 85-115.

M. Wilson, 'Revelation 19.10 and Contemporary Interpretation', in M. Wilson (ed.), *Spirit and Renewal: Essays in Honor of J. Rodman Williams* (JPTSup 5; Sheffield: Sheffield Academic Press, 1994), pp. 191-202.

—— *The Victor Sayings in the Book of Revelation* (Eugene: Wipf & Stock Publishers, 2007).

Yong, A. *Spirit-Word-Community: Theological Hermeneutics in Trinitarian Perspective* (Eugene: Wipf & Stock, 2002).

Index of Biblical and Other Ancient References

OTHER ANCIENT REFERENCES

Pseudepigrapha

Early Jewish and Christian

Classical References

Name Index

www.ingramcontent.com/pod-product-compliance
Lightning Source LLC
Chambersburg PA
CBHW060038100426
42742CB00014B/2632